PRINCIPLES OF HUMAN COMMUNICATION

Fifth Edition

Robert E. Smith
Purdue University

With exercises by
R. E. Smith and Suzanne Collins

With Appendix: A Library Resource Strategy
for Communication by
Scott Mandernack

KENDALL/HUNT PUBLISHING COMPANY
4050 Westmark Drive   Dubuque, Iowa 52002

Photograph by
 Bob Coyle, Dubuque, IA
 Nancy Ann Dawe, Decatur, GA

Quick Reference Contents

Contents

Study Materials and Exercise Contents

Preface

Unlike other works such as novels, plays, and film, textbooks are always in the process of being revised. The effectiveness of a textbook depends on how well it reflects the tradition of a field and the latest ideas and information. Its effectiveness also depends on how well it adapts to its ever changing audience of students.

This Fifth Edition is another step in the evolution of *Principles of Human Communication*. The text retains its broad focus on the field of communication and introduces students to several significant areas of communication: communication theory, interpersonal communication, small group communication, and public speaking. Major revisions have been made in the area of small group communication. The public speaking section follows the same format as the fourth edition, but the material also has been revised.

As with the Fourth Edition, the text and workbook materials have been combined into one volume. Each chapter in the text is followed by study questions, exercises, response sheets, and assignment sheets pertinent to the unit. This arrangement eliminates the need for teachers and students to shift back and forth between the separate books.

Audience

This book is written for the beginning college student who may have only a vague knowledge of communication, a person, for example, who may think of communication as limited to public speaking or who may think that common sense is all we need to know about communication. The book has four goals:

1. To introduce the reader to communication and communication studies,
2. To provide an understanding of the process of communication in various contexts (interpersonal, small group, public speaking),
3. To supply practical knowledge useful in improving communication skills in interpersonal, small group, and public speaking contexts,
4. To provide a solid foundation in communication for those wishing to go beyond the basic course in formal or individual study.

Organization

The book is divided into four main sections. The first is an introduction to communication.

Chapter One confronts a common question asked by many students in a communication class, "Why should I study communication?" The answer is that communication and communication study is an inevitable part of our existence and its study informs and improves our lives.

Chapter Two defines and discusses the process of communication. The chapter provides an overview of the field of communication to introduce students to the breadth of communication study and to create an awareness of the universality of communication.

Chapter Three looks at the combination of elements that create each of us as communicators: culture, language, and nonverbal communication.

Chapter Four discusses the ethics of communication. Having introduced the idea of communication and choices in the earlier chapters, we discuss the nature of those choices in this chapter. Guidelines are given for ethical communication.

The second major division of the book is interpersonal communication.

Chapter Five addresses interpersonal communication. The chapter deals with the nature of interpersonal communication and the skills needed in three major areas of interpersonal communication: conversation, comforting, and conflict resolution.

The third major division of the book is small group communication.

Chapter Six introduces students to the basic concepts of small groups. Topics include group purposes, types of groups, group tasks, group relationships, and balancing group tensions.

Chapter Seven looks at the pragmatics of working in groups. It contrasts ineffective methods of problem solving with the rational model of problem solving. Group leadership and members' roles are detailed.

Chapter Eight discusses difficult situations that may arise in groups. Its two main topics are how to manage conflict in small groups and how to deal with difficult group members.

Chapter Nine is a chapter devoted to the pragmatics of creating and giving a small presentation. The chapter traces the process chronologically. It also contains advice on how to handle communication apprehension.

Chapter Ten introduces a popular application of small groups that students may well encounter in the workplace: self-directed work teams. The chapter shows how a typical academic small group assignment shares many characteristics with SDWT.

Chapter Eleven links contemporary technology with small group work as it discusses computer-mediated small groups. The chapter shows how both proximate and distanced small groups may use computer-mediation to enhance their group work.

The last major division of the text is public speaking. The two types of speaking addressed in this section are informational speaking and persuasive speaking.

Chapter Twelve looks at basic factors inherent in most speaking situations. Of particular interest is its discussion of creativity as it pertains to speaking. Other important topics in the chapter are analyzing the speaking situation, finding and narrowing topics, and patterns of organization.

Chapter Thirteen builds on the preceding chapter and discusses further organization of a presentation such as how to create introductions, transitions, and conclusions. As practice is an important part of creating a speech, the chapter discusses effective techniques for rehearsal.

Chapter Fourteen deals specifically with informational presentations. The chapter details several ways in which topics may be approached as well as the principles and skills necessary for good informational speaking.

Chapter Fifteen addresses performance concerns, how speakers can coordinate the elements of a speech to good effect. Notes, visual aids, the speaking voice, and physical communication are discussed, as is communication apprehension.

Chapter Sixteen deals with persuasive presentations. It provides a definition and discussion of persuasion as well as the ethics of persuasion. It also details the process of decision making.

Chapter Seventeen provides the procedures for composing a persuasive speech. It discusses audience analysis, styles of persuasive speaking, persuasive thesis statements, and organization. The chapter includes the important areas of evidence and speaker credibility.

Chapter Eighteen deals with the arguments and lines of reasoning speakers might use in persuasive speaking. Deductive reasoning, inductive reasoning, and fallacious reasoning are discussed with examples provided of each.

Special Features

Beyond the basics in communication, the book offers several features which may be of special interest. It begins with a topic which should be of major interest to students, themselves, then moves into ever widening patterns of communication. Its discussion of culture as a factor in communication provides students with a basis for understanding the communication patterns of others as well as their own.

The overall view of the text is not so much on the products of communication as it is on the process of communication. The public speaking section is notable for not approaching public speaking from the standpoint of "giving a speech." Instead, it emphasizes creating presentations that link ideas, composition, and performance.

Other features include a section on voice, which is missing from many textbooks. Each chapter is followed immediately by study questions that reinforce chapter concepts and provide review material for exams. Two brand-new chapters address recent innovations in small groups: self-directed work teams and computer-mediated groups.

The text-workbook format combines factual material with exercise material into one package. The arrangement of materials is easy to follow and provides concepts and reinforcement of those concepts.

Acknowledgments

When working on a project such as this textbook, it is gratifying to have available friends and colleagues upon whom one can call for assistance and expertise. I have numerous people to thank for their help with this volume:

→ The Department of Communication at Purdue for its support
→ The Assistant Directors, past and present, of the basic course whose initiative and industry have lightened my load considerably: Derek Arnold, Craig Booth, Jacquelyn Buckrop, Suzanne Collins, Paula M. E. Mendenhall, Lisa Goodnight, Ron Sandwina, Juli Phillips, and Sarah Bonewits
→ Special thanks to Suzanne Collins for her work on the study materials
→ My colleagues for their contributions of time and expertise: Brant Burleson, Chris Nelson, Robert Ogles, Linda Putnam, William Rawlins, Cynthia Stohl, Glen Sparks, Leon Trachtman, Joanne Holman, Marifran Mattson
→ Omar Swartz for his work on the persuasion and reasoning chapter
→ Scott Mandernack for his preparation of the material on research in communication
→ The Department of Communication office staff: Diana Cable, Carolyn Parrish, and Bonnie Parker
→ Finally, Pauletta Smith, my wife, for her support throughout.

What Happens When We Do Not Communicate?

In 1895, Rudyard Kipling published *The Jungle Book*. It is the story of Mowgli, an Indian boy who is abandoned by his family and rescued by a pack of wolves. He grows up without human contact as the wolf pack and other animals educate him. He becomes a strong individual who possesses remarkable knowledge from his association with the animals.

In 1912, Edgar Rice Burroughs created another classic figure. The first in a long series of books, *Tarzan, the Ape Man* introduces another character reared apart from human contact. After the death of his parents on the shores of Africa, Tarzan is found by great apes, one of which adopts him. Living in close contact with nature, he learns the languages of the animals, develops strength and wisdom, and becomes a formidable person who proves his mettle in a number of encounters with fierce beasts and predatory humans.

These characters span two worlds. They develop human speech and thought, and at the same time, they have the senses and knowledge of the animals. This education in the wild produces a person with capabilities far beyond those of us who are raised within the confines of civilization.

This idea holds great fascination for us. It was the philosophical ideal of Jean Jacques Rousseau who saw the "Noble Savage" as the height of human development. Mowgli and *The Jungle Book* have become classics of children's literature. Beyond Burroughs' numerous Tarzan novels, Tarzan has been the subject of over 50 movies in English besides foreign language versions, both authorized and unauthorized, as well as comic books and comic strips.

With the dramatic lives of Mowgli and Tarzan, we might wonder what it would be like to grow up in their circumstances. As with other engaging ideas encountered in books and films, real life cannot measure up. We have a few examples of children who have actually grown up in the wild with little or no human contact. Rather than being wise and capable as Mowgli or Tarzan, the people were, unfortunately, stunted by the experience rather than enhanced by it.

The Wild Boy of Aveyron tells of one of the first recorded cases. In 1800, a boy, thought to be about 12, was captured digging in a garden. He was undersized and undernourished. He had no animal protectors or teachers. He possessed no language and only made noises. Attempts to adapt him to human society met with limited success. The boy learned only the rudiments of language, never adapted, and died at an early age.

Cases of feral—wild—children attract our curiosity, evoke our pity, and even motivate us to examine how we define humanity (Shattuck). The stories still make it clear that if we are to develop to our fullest, we need the company of others. Through others, we learn language, patterns of behavior, and how to build relationships that sustain us. In short, in the company of others, we learn how to communicate and to use our communicative skills for good or ill.

What happens if we do not communicate?

We do not become super-humans like Mowgli and Tarzan. Rather, we never become truly human.

Feral Child Bibliography

Burroughs, Edgar Rice. *Tarzan of the Apes*. New York: Ballantine Books, 1975.

———. *The Return of Tarzan*. New York: Ballantine Books, 1975.

Candland, Douglas Keith. *Feral Children and Clever Animals: Reflections on Human Nature,* 1993.

Holtsmark, Erling B. *Tarzan and Tradition: Classical Myth in Popular Literature*. Westport, CO: Greenwood Press, 1981.

———. *Edgar Rice Burroughs*. Boston: Twayne Publishers, 1986.

Kipling, Rudyard. *The Jungle Book*. New York: Doubleday and Company, 1948.

Maclean, Charles. *The Wolf Children*. New York: Hill and Wang, 1977.

Shattuck, Roger. *The Forbidden Experiment: The Story of the Wild Boy of Aveyron*. New York: Farrar Straus Giroux, 1980.

The Study of Communication

KEY CONCEPTS

Communication as a Human Activity
The Importance of Communication Study

It is one of the best known stories from the ancient world, a story of conflict, strategy, and a famous message.

In 490 BC, the fate of Athens and the other free city-states of Greece hung in the balance. Seeking to extend the Persian empire, a large army of Persians landed on the plain of Marathon about twenty-five miles from Athens. Facing them was an outnumbered force of Athenians. Defeat looked inevitable.

The Athenian general, however, struck a bold plan. Instead of concentrating his forces at the center, he concentrated them in the flanks. Then, instead of waiting in a defensive position, he charged.

The Persians were routed. Herodotus, the Greek historian, reports that the Persians lost 6,200 men to the Athenians' 192 (6, 117).

As soon as it was clear that Athens was saved, the general sent a message as swiftly as he could. He selected a runner, Phidippides, to carry the news to Athens. Phidippides set off at his best pace, eager to let the Athenians know the outcome of the battle.

He ran the long distance from Marathon to Athens, reached the city, shouted the notable words, "Victory! We conquer!" then collapsed and died from exhaustion.

The story remarks on numerous ideas: the bravery of the Greeks, their dedication to preserving their freedom, the bold stroke that may wrench victory from impending doom, and the importance of communication.

The ability to respond to a story such as the one above speaks to the multiplicity of talents we have as human beings to link ourselves to others. The original story was carried word of mouth, yet somehow it has been preserved into other forms so that it is available to us today. The story has had an existence in oral form, writing, printing, film, and video. Even though it happened over twenty-four hundred years ago, we are still able to recall it. That our communicative abilities allow us to move between time periods is itself something of a marvel.

Beyond the transmission of the story, we discover that communication begets more communication. We not only receive the story, but we respond to it. We may recount the tale to someone else. We may muse on the story to decide its application to our situations. Based on this story, the Olympic committee created the modern long distance race, the marathon, in 1896 (Benyo 6). Hearing one story, we may feel motivated to tell a story of our own, a phenomenon known as the "Canterbury Effect." We might add, in a poetic note to history, that the first Olympic marathon was won by a Greek, Spiridon Louys (Guttman 19). We may subject the story to a variety of critiques and analyses. One historian notes, for example, that "Herodotus' account is far from being above criticism" (Hart 91).

Interestingly enough, analyses of the above story show that, while it is widely accepted, major portions of it are probably false. Indeed, the Athenians defeated the Persians at Marathon in 490 BC. No runner, however, breathlessly staggered into Athens, proclaimed victory, and collapsed. Once again, what appear to be the facts are not as entertaining as their embellishment.

Herodotus tells of Phidippides, a courier, but his role was to run to Sparta, not to Athens. He ran before the battle, not after, and his mission was to secure reinforcements (6, 105–106). The Spartans delayed because they were engaged in a religious festival. When they eventually arrived, as one historian puts it, "They inspected the field, complimented the Athenians, and went home" (Evans 97).

The study of communication is an inevitable part of life.

Knowing the second version, however, makes the story more fascinating. How and why was the story preserved in the first place? Why do we have two versions of the story? Have we, perhaps, lost other versions? How did the original events become embroidered? Why is the first version more dramatic than the second? What different ideas and values does each version carry? How do we judge that the second version is closer to the truth than the first?

Communication as Human Activity

These questions point to one of our most human characteristics. Not only do we possess communicative abilities that are magnitudes beyond those of other creatures, we are the only creatures who can communicate about communication itself. We possess not only the ability to send and receive messages but also the ability to create, analyze, and change our own patterns of communication.

The process of communicating, analyzing communication, and changing our patterns of communication is the heart of this textbook. In short, it is a study of communication with the goal of providing both knowledge about communication and improving communication skills.

The study of communication is an inevitable part of life. That people are able to read this page, decipher the symbols on the page, and to comment on the ideas is testimony to our abilities to learn language, to process symbols, and to respond to others. Training in communication is a mixture of informal and formal study. We do not, for example, go to class to learn how to speak our first language. We learn from a process of imitation, trial and error. To learn to read, however, we typically attend school.

The life process is shaped by communication. Through communication we create and sustain all our endeavors.

This book and the class it accompanies are a more formal way of approaching the study of communication. Instead of learning through imitation, learning takes places through an examination of the nature of communication as a human endeavor and analyses of communication in a variety of settings: interpersonal, small groups, and public speaking. Coupled with the exercises in communication, the course will provide us with a combination of knowledge and practice.

The Importance of Communication Study

Communication study is important because *communication is a decidedly human activity.* Through communication we create and sustain all our endeavors. Like art, play, aggression, and relationships, communication is woven into our very beings. Because it is a part of being human, communication demands our attention.

Communication study is important because *it is a fascinating study of human activity*. To look at communication is to look at ourselves. The life process is shaped by communication. How we see ourselves and others, how we perform at work, and how we relate to our families are all shaped by the ways in which we communicate. Through communication study we become aware of our behavior and the behavior of others and begin to see why we act as we do. Why, for example, is it common in the United States for us to stand one-and-a-half to two feet apart when we converse? Why do we feel threatened when someone moves closer than that? How are we persuaded to move from one opinion to another? How do we structure our organizations? If we ever wonder why we behave as we do, communication study can supply some of the answers to our questions.

Communication study is important because *it provides us with insights and skills* necessary to understand and solve the problems we face in our lives. To live is to confront problems, and inherent in the solution of those problems is the use of communication.

Some of the problems we face are simple. Daily we decide how to greet people, make requests, or respond to a conversational opener. Other problems are more complex. How do we resolve a conflict within our families or at work? How do we persuade people to accept our view? How do we function effectively within an organization? How do we respond to someone who is distraught over personal problems? How do we function effectively in a small group?

These kinds of situations are ones that we will face whether or not we study communication. Having studied communication, we will be better able to respond.

In our highly technological world, the temptation is to think that problems will be solved by better technology. We will communicate better when we have better computer networks. We will all speed down the information superhighway into ultimate knowledge.

The technological is certainly part of human endeavors, but technology is not the only part. No matter how much technology we deal with, we ultimately deal with people. As one has astutely observed, "Today there are no problems with strictly technological solutions" (Ringel). Any significant effort will have implications for humans.

An engineer may have excellent training in materials, mathematics, and methods, but as one engineering professor succinctly put the matter, "If you can't talk to your clients, you won't be a good engineer" (Satterly).

In the 1960s, three counties in the San Francisco area initiated what was to have been a state of the art transportation system, the Bay Area Rapid Transit system, commonly known as BART. It involved the best and newest computer technology, the best and newest trains and tracks, and it hired a staff of ex-

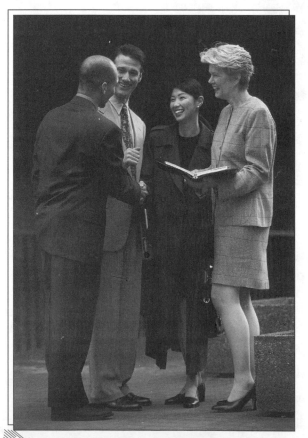

\\\ No matter how much technology we deal with, we ultimately deal with people.

perts in engineering, transportation, computer science, and other relevant fields.

From the beginning, however, the project was hampered by numerous problems. When it finally opened, it was "many years after it was originally scheduled, at a cost well in excess of its original estimates, and in a context of genuine and widespread dissatisfaction. . . ." (Anderson, et al. 256).

A study of the system discovered interesting data. The problems were due to several factors, one of the most important being the communication environment. Examined as individuals, those involved in the project were doing their

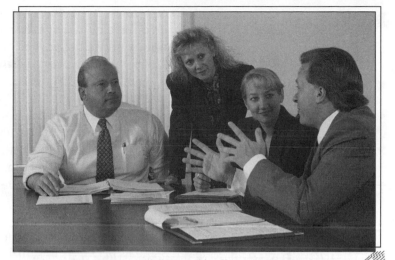

We must use "people skills" to work effectively with others.

jobs in good faith. The failure was not in the technology, but in the relationships between people.

One problem was external in that BART had difficulty persuading its clientele to support the system (Anderson, et al. 341–43). Another problem, and perhaps the most important, was the manner in which the system was organized. Work was contracted to outside organizations in a way that placed BART employees in a secondary role in directing the work. Selection of the board of directors cast the board in the role of interest group advocates instead of a deliberative body. The organizational and administrative structure was such that people were forced into roles "almost predestined to create conflict and dysfunctional communication" (Trachtman).

Further, the system was set up to encourage "narrow specialization of roles" (Anderson, et al. 352) which meant that the various elements of the project could not or did not communicate well with each other. As long as the computer programers saw their programs running well, they saw no problem. That the trains were stopping a hundred yards before loading platforms was somebody else's concern. As long as the rolling stock kept rolling, engineering was fine no matter the financial difficulties. The lack of communication created a lack of cooperation which undercut the success of the venture. The problem with BART lay not so much in its technology, as in its failure to create and foster an environment of productive communication.

Another common mistake is to think that communication is simple. "All you need is common sense," some claim. The problem with this view is that common sense grows out of knowledge and experience.

How should one behave in a typical interpersonal situation, say a job interview? Any number of interviewing books will provide guidelines: one should dress appropriately, be on time, create answers to typical questions, learn about the company, provide positive nonverbal responses, and prepare questions to ask the interviewer. These behaviors make sense in the interview situation and become part of the "common sense" of interviewing.

Yet when one passes a placement center and reads the remarks of the interviewers, their complaints mirror the above advice. Potential employees do not dress properly, they show up late, they know nothing of the company, the questions they ask are shortsighted and self-centered. Somehow, these

We do not simply *know* how to respond; we must *learn* how to respond.

interviewees missed the "common sense" of interviewing. We do not simply *know* how to respond; we must *learn* how to respond. When something strikes us as "common sense," it does not necessarily mean the idea is trivial. What we may be observing is a process in which "common sense makes clear that which I think I already know" (Yoder).

Finally, the study of communication is important because *it is one of the few areas of learning that is transferable from one situation to another, from job to job, and from relationship to relationship.* Graduating college seniors face the challenge of securing a first job, but that is only the beginning. Fifteen years ago, a study concluded that "today's workers will change jobs five times before they are forty and that they will change careers three times before they retire" ("Involvement in Learning . . ." 43.) Years later, the pattern continues. A more recent study concludes that "on the average, a student leaving college today can be expected to have three, four, or five careers and ten, eleven, or twelve jobs during a work life that will last 40/50 years" (Birch 40). Job-related skills learned for one career may have little meaning in a subsequent career.

Within all the change, however, certain skills and attributes will always be needed. Among these skills are critical thinking, mathematics, language skills, and "people skills." Whatever professions we pursue, whatever situations we find ourselves in, we will need some abilities in these areas. The study of communication supplies us with an education in three of the areas. We must use critical thinking skills to appropriately interpret communication situations. We must use language skills to create, send, and interpret messages. We must use "people skills" to work effectively with others.

> The study of communication commends itself to us because communication is integral to our natures and to our lives.

Communication is not only something we use, but it is something that makes us, even as we use it. We not only respond to relationships with communication, we build the very relationships by the patterns with which we communicate. The study of communication commends itself to us because communication is integral to our natures and to our lives. To study communication is to study ourselves, and this is the fundamental basis of education.

Discussion Questions ⬗

1. What instances of informal communication training can you think of?

2. What instances of formal communication training can you think of?

3. Why is communication an integral part of our humanity?

4. What kind of situations have you observed that would have been improved by better communication?

5. How might technological innovations such as the telephone, television, and e-mail affect our communication?

6. Why would skills such as mathematics, critical thinking, language, and communication be important in our lives?

Sources and References 〽️

Anderson, Robert M., Robert Perucci, Dan E. Schendel, and Leon E. Trachtman. *Divided Loyalties: Whistle-Blowing at BART*. West Lafayette, Indiana: Purdue University Office of Publications, 1980.

Benyo, Richard. *Masters of the Marathon*. New York: Atheneum, 1983.

Birch, David L. "The Coming Demise of the Single-Career Career." *Journal of Career Planning and Employment*. Winter (1990).

Evans, J. A. S. *Herodotus*. Boston: Twayne Publishers-G. K. Hall and Company, 1982.

Guttman, Allen. *The Olympics: A History of the Modern Games*. Urbana: University of Illinois Press, 1992.

Hart. John. *Herodotus and Greek History*. London: Croom Helm Ltd., 1982.

Herodotus. *The History of Herodotus*. Trans. David Green. Chicago: The University of Chicago Press, 1987.

"Involvement in Learning: Realizing the Potential of American Higher Education." *Chronicle of Higher Education* 24 October 1984. 43.

Ringel, Robert L. Commencement Address. University of Missouri, Columbia, Missouri. 10 December 1988.

Satterly, Gilbert. Professor of Civil Engineering, Purdue University. Conversation with the author.

Trachtman, Leon E. Note to the author. 29 April 1994.

Yoder, Don. Central States Communication Association Convention. Oklahoma City, Oklahoma. 7 April 1994.

_____ ⤜ Study Questions ⤛ _____

The Study of Communication

1. Describe the Canterbury Effect.

   _____

   _____

2. Animals have been shown to be able to communicate. List at least two things related to communication which distinguish human communication from animal communication.

   1. _____

   2. _____

3. Why is a formal study of human communication important?

   _____

   _____

Preface To Supplemental Materials

The material following each chapter supplements the ideas and concepts of the text. Whereas the emphasis in the text is on presenting the theory and underlying principles of communication, the supplementary material provides an application for those ideas. Through completing the exercises and speaking assignments explained in them students will develop their communication skills.

The full **course schedule** provides an overview of what will be covered in the course. You can read ahead if necessary to adapt course demands to your own time blocks.

Each assignment begins with a clearly defined **purpose.** It explains the skills that will be mastered when the assignment is completed. Assignments are arranged for progressive skill building. With each assignment you build upon previously learned material by adding new speaking skills.

Basic requirements listing minimum criteria for successful completion of the assignment are listed next. These make it easy for you to clearly understand what is expected. You can check off each requirement as it is met to ensure success on the assignment.

Sometimes the most difficult part of speech writing is selecting a speech topic. **Suggested topics** for speaking assignments are listed to serve as a springboard for your own creative thinking. Success is further ensured because you choose a topic of personal interest.

Worksheets are included to serve as a centralized record for brainstorming and topic development. They include a skeleton speech outline to fill in which aids in organization and speech development.

Grading criteria specify what an instructor will be looking for when evaluating the finished product. These criteria make the evaluation process less subjective and more objective for all parties.

Two important aspects of a speech class are learning speaking techniques by watching speeches delivered by classmates and offering constructive observations about them. **Student evaluation sheets** encourage students to focus on construction techniques as well as delivery skills. Feedback should be positive, specific and practical. Student evaluation sheets provide feedback which supplements the instructor's evaluation.

Each unit has **exercises** designed to illustrate concepts from the text readings. They are a hands-on way to learn theoretical concepts.

Sample exam questions enable you to spot-check your comprehension of the textbook material. Answers are provided for self-assessment.

Library Research in Communication provides you with basic procedures to identify and locate information and resources across a broad spectrum of fields to aid in speech development.

While course policies, grading scales and the development of the sixteen week course schedule are specific to the needs of the basic communication course at Purdue University, they can easily be adapted for use in any university's one semester course. They have proven workable when used by the 5,000 students who annually take this class, and are thus included for consideration.

Assignments and Grading

There are six major graded assignments in this course: a small group presentation, a written analysis of the small group process, three speeches, and one examination. Due to the nature of this course, a great deal of learning takes place during in-class exercises. They constitute a lab for this course. Therefore, in addition to the major assignments, students will be graded on attendance and class participation.

Assignments are weighted for computing the final class grade. Each completed assignment is evaluated and assigned a letter grade by the instructor, which is then converted to a point value by the student. Uncompleted assignments will receive an F/00.00.

The following chart should be filled out to maintain an unofficial record of class grades.

Directions for Maintaining a Class Grade Record

1. After each assignment record the appropriate letter grade in the blank under column 1.
2. Using the scale for "individual assignment point value," record the appropriate point value in column 2.
3. Multiply the number entered in column 2 by the number in column 3, and enter the total in column 4, or see the tables on page 13 for the appropriate number.
4. At the completion of the semester add the figures in column 4 and enter the sum in blank 5.
5. Using the scale for "course letter grade," convert the course final point total to the course final letter grade, and enter it in blank 6.

The student, not the instructor, is responsible for the accuracy of the calculations entered in the chart and any decisions made as a result of those calculations.

Falsification of Information

This course works on the assumption that students are acting in good faith when they interact with university staff and submit materials. Should that, however, not be the case, falsification of information constitutes grounds for failure of the assignment, failure of the course, and disciplinary action by the university. Falsification of information would include such actions as citing sources that do not exist, forging absence excuses, or misrepresenting yourself or your situation.

Plagiarism

Plagiarism is the unauthorized or inappropriate use of the words or ideas of others. Plagiarism occurs when written or spoken material is borrowed, in whole or in part, and passed off as original by another writer or speaker. Plagiarism includes, but is not limited to, presenting someone else's speech, paper, or outline as original. It also includes not documenting the source of word-for-word or PARAPHRASED material in speeches or papers.

The following examples illustrate possible plagiarism situations for this class: using someone else's outline for a speech; working with a friend on a topic and both using the same outline or giving the same speech; failing to cite during a speech or paper the source of information, ideas, or statements taken from material found during research.

It is course policy to pursue plagiarism cases vigorously, to fail the plagiarist on the assignment in question, to fail the plagiarist in the course as a whole, and to report cases to the dean of students for possible further action.

	Individual Assignment Point Value Scale		Course Letter Grade Scale		
A+	=	4.25	3.51 to 4.25	=	A
A	=	4.00	2.51 to 3.50	=	B
A–	=	3.75	1.51 to 2.50	=	C
B+	=	3.25	.51 to 1.50	=	D
B	=	3.00	.50 and below	=	F
B–	=	2.75			
C+	=	2.25			
C	=	2.00			
C–	=	1.75			
D+	=	1.25			
D	=	1.00			
D–	=	.75			
F	=	.00			

Assignment	Letter Grade	Point Value	Weighting	Final Value
			(From Left scale above)	
	1.	2.	3.	4.
Exam	_____	= _____	× .20	= _____
Sm. Gp. Project	_____	= _____	× .10	= _____
Sm. Gp. Analysis	_____	= _____	× .10	= _____
Speech 1	_____	= _____	× .12	= _____
Speech 2	_____	=	× .18	= _____
Speech 3	_____	= _____	× .23	= _____
Attendance/Part.	_____	= _____	× .07	= _____

Course Final Point Total   5. _____

Course Final Letter Grade   _____

(from Right scale above)   6. _____

Calculations for Exam

.20 × A+ (4.25) = .85
.20 × A (4.00) = .80
.20 × A− (3.75) = .75
.20 × B+ (3.25) = .65
.20 × B (3.00) = .60
.20 × B− (2.75) = .55
.20 × C+ (2.25) = .45
.20 × C (2.00) = .40
.20 × C− (1.75) = .35
.20 × D+ (1.25) = .25
.20 × D (1.00) = .20
.20 × D− (.75) = .15
.20 × F (.00) = .00

Calculations for Small Group

.10 × A+ (4.25) = .43
.10 × A (4.00) = .40
.10 × A− (3.75) = .38
.10 × B+ (3.25) = .33
.10 × B (3.00) = .30
.10 × B− (2.75) = .28
.10 × C+ (2.25) = .23
.10 × C (2.00) = .20
.10 × C− (1.75) = .18
.10 × D+ (1.25) = .13
.10 × D (1.00) = .10
.10 × D− (.75) = .08
.10 × F (.00) = .00

Calculations for Presentation I

.12 × A+ (4.25) = .51
.12 × A (4.00) = .48
.12 × A− (3.75) = .45
.12 × B+ (3.25) = .39
.12 × B (3.00) = .36
.12 × B− (2.75) = .33
.12 × C+ (2.25) = .27
.12 × C (2.00) = .24
.12 × C− (1.75) = .21
.12 × D+ (1.25) = .15
.12 × D (1.00) = .12
.12 × D− (.75) = .09
.12 × F (.00) = .00

Calculations for Presentation II

.18 × A+ (4.25) = .77
.18 × A (4.00) = .72
.18 × A− (3.75) = .68
.18 × B+ (3.25) = .59
.18 × B (3.00) = .54
.18 × B− (2.75) = .50
.18 × C+ (2.25) = .41
.18 × C (2.00) = .36
.18 × C− (1.75) = .32
.18 × D+ (1.25) = .23
.18 × D (1.00) = .18
.18 × D− (.75) = .14
.18 × F (.00) = .00

Calculations for Presentation III

.23 × A+ (4.25) = .98
.23 × A (4.00) = .92
.23 × A− (3.75) = .86
.23 × B+ (3.25) = .75
.23 × B (3.00) = .69
.23 × B− (2.75) = .63
.23 × C+ (2.25) = .52
.23 × C (2.00) = .46
.23 × C− (1.75) = .40
.23 × D+ (1.25) = .29
.23 × D (1.00) = .23
.23 × D− (.75) = .17
.23 × F (.00) = .00

Calculations for Attendance

.07 × A+ (4.25) = .30
.07 × A (4.00) = .28
.07 × A− (3.75) = .26
.07 × B+ (3.25) = .23
.07 × B (3.00) = .21
.07 × B− (2.75) = .19
.07 × C+ (2.25) = .16
.07 × C (2.00) = .14
.07 × C− (1.75) = .12
.07 × D+ (1.25) = .09
.07 × D (1.00) = .07
.07 × D− (.75) = .05
.07 × F (.00) = .00

Course Schedule

Following is a schedule of activities and assignments for the semester. Note that the readings listed are TO HAVE BEEN COMPLETED by the day noted, and are NOT assignments given that day for completion by the next class.

Day	Text Assignment	Activities
Day 1	The Study of Communication (Chapter One)	orientation
Day 2	Field of Communication (Chapter Two)	lecture/discussion
Day 3	You as a Communicator (Chapter Three) The Ethics of Communication (Chapter Four)	lecture/discussion
Day 4		culture inventory
Day 5		culture inventory
Day 6	Interpersonal Communication (Chapter Five)	lecture/discussion
Day 7		interpersonal exercises
Day 8	Small Group Assignments Nature of Small Groups (Chapter Six, Chapter Seven)	explain small group assignment
Day 9	Working in Small Groups: Roles and Leadership (Chapter Eight, Chapter Nine)	lecture/discussion
Day 10	Working in Small Groups: Problem Solving Procedures (Chapter Ten, Chapter Eleven)	lecture/discussion
Day 11		small group exercises
Day 12		small group workshop
Day 13		small group workshop
Day 14		GROUP 1 PRESENTATION
Day 15		GROUP 2 PRESENTATION
Day 16		GROUP 3 PRESENTATION
Day 17		GROUP 4 PRESENTATION
Day 18		GROUP 5 PRESENTATION
Day 19	Intro to Public Speaking	assign first speech
Day 20	Beginning Public Speaking (Chapter Twelve)	lecture/discussion
Day 21	Selecting a Topic/Thesis Statements	
Day 22	Developing your Speech (Chapter Thirteen)	lecture/discussion
Day 23	Informational Speaking (Chapter Fourteen, Chapter Fifteen)	

Day 24		INFORMATIVE PRESENTATION I
Day 25		INFORMATIVE PRESENTATION I
Day 26		INFORMATIVE PRESENTATION I
Day 27		INFORMATIVE PRESENTATION I
Day 28		INFORMATIVE PRESENTATION I
Day 29		INFORMATIVE PRESENTATION I
Day 30	Improvement Review Day	
Day 31		INFORMATIVE PRESENTATION II
Day 32		INFORMATIVE PRESENTATION II
Day 33		INFORMATIVE PRESENTATION II
Day 34		INFORMATIVE PRESENTATION II
Day 35		INFORMATIVE PRESENTATION II
Day 36		INFORMATIVE PRESENTATION II
Day 37	Why We Believe (Chapter Sixteen)	lecture/discussion
Day 38	Developing Presentational Speeches (Chapter Seventeen)	lecture/discussion
Day 39	Evidence and Credibility; Persuasion and Reasoning (Chapter Eighteen)	lecture/discussion
Day 40		PRESENTATIONAL SPEECH
Day 41		PRESENTATIONAL SPEECH
Day 42		PRESENTATIONAL SPEECH
Day 43		PRESENTATIONAL SPEECH
Day 44		PRESENTATIONAL SPEECH
Day 45		PRESENTATIONAL SPEECH
Day 46	EXAM	

The "I Am" Speech

As one of your first speaking assignments, you may be asked to present a short speech about yourself. The speech will be, very loosely, a three part speech. This is an informal presentation to introduce yourself to the class and to introduce you to the speaking situation.

In the speech, you should discuss topics such as the following:

Your Past	where born
	brothers and sisters
	early childhood
	pets
	interesting places you have lived, etc.
Your Present	favorite subjects
	activities
	hobbies
	sports, etc.
Your Future	plan of study
	plans after graduation

Your instructor may give you added suggestions.

Adapted from: Corey, James W. "The 'I Am' Speech." *The Speech Communication Teacher* II, iv (Summer 1988): p. 1. Used by permission of National Communication Association.

s we have pointed out, communication permeates and shapes our lives. To pursue the study of communication, we need to know what communication is and how communication influences our learning and our practice. Let us begin by offering a definition of communication.

Defining Communication

Defining communication is not an easy task since it is a complex blend of numerous entities. We will incorporate major areas of the concept by defining it as: *Communication is the process of sending, receiving, and interpreting messages through which we relate to each other and to our larger world as well.*

Process

The first important concept in this definition is "process." By process, we mean that communication is not a single act but a series of interconnected acts moving through time. This means, first of all, that communication is *ongoing*. It begins when two or more parties (senders and receivers) come into contact with each other and continues until the parties break contact. The parties may be two people, a group of people, a large audience and a speaker, or even individuals communicating with themselves via "intrapersonal communication."

> **Because it exists in time, communication is *irreversible*. Once the process begins, it cannot go back to its beginnings and start all over.**

Because it exists in time, communication is *irreversible*. Once the process begins, it cannot go back to its beginnings and start all over. A common experience is that we, from time to time, say things we wish we had not said. Much as we would like to recall the message, to counteract its negative effect, we cannot. We can try to reframe the message, but we cannot "erase the tape."

Since communication is ongoing and irreversible, it is also an activity in which the elements are *interdependent*. Each part of an interchange influences what follows. Each portion builds on what went before it.

Communication is more like a game than it is like a play in which the lines are all known in advance. In tennis, for example, player A serves the ball to player B. Player B attempts to return the serve. Where and how B hits the ball will be determined by where and how A served and what kind of player B is. Player A's volley will respond to B's return of the serve, and they will continue reacting to each other until one of them fails to return the ball over the net.

In communication, one person makes a statement, sends a greeting, answers the phone, or calls a meeting to order. Others respond to that initiation. That response calls forth another response and that response, yet another. What each party contributes to the interchange adds to the situation and at the same time changes it. The final result and shape of the interchange is not known until the very end.

Senders and receivers are necessary for communication to occur. How many senders and receivers are seen or implied in this situation? (Dawe)

Messages

What passes between the parties in communication are *messages*. Messages are signals sent with the intent of creating understanding in the receiver. While the concept of messages is familiar to us, we need to realize the wide variety of messages that exist.

On a personal level, we send verbal and non-verbal messages through our voices and our bodies. We send written transmissions through a wide variety of communication channels: letters, faxes, newspapers, magazines, advertising brochures, etc. We send aural messages through telephones, radios, and various types of musical devices. We reach one person through conversation; we reach

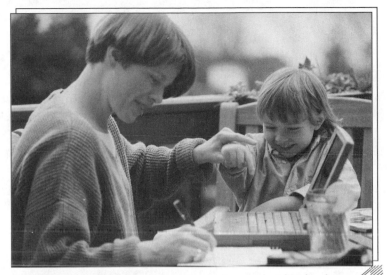

As children, our parents communicate to us what kinds of behavior are acceptable or not acceptable.

millions through mass communication. Some even communicate through the use of drums, flags, fireworks, mirror flashes, waggling airplane wings, and firing shots across the bow.

Interpretation

Interpretation is the act of bringing to understanding. Whatever messages we receive, we try to make sense of them. As long as sender and receiver use the same language and operate in familiar settings, responses are easy to make. When the context of communication begins to include the unfamiliar, then interpretation is more difficult and, in some cases, impossible.

One would think that people speaking English could readily understand each other. Americans, for example, have general agreements on the meanings of words such as "napkin," "dear," and "lavatory." The first is something we put in our laps when we eat; the second is someone or something toward which we feel affection; the third is a sink. Should one be travelling in the British Isles, however, one might discover to one's embarrassment that those terms in British English are interpreted as "diaper," "expensive," and "commode."

As meaning is not automatic and as interpretation is necessary in communication, *misunderstanding is always a possibility in communication.* Both sender and receiver may be thoroughly convinced that they have done all that is necessary for effective communication yet discover later that the messages are still garbled and confusion exists.

> As meaning is not automatic and as interpretation is necessary in communication, *misunderstanding is always a possibility in communication.*

Relationships

Communication is a linking of selves in some ways, be those ways serious or superficial. The quality and type of our relationships are highly dependent on the quality and type of our communication.

Saying "good morning" to someone and having that person respond with "good morning" seems simple enough. When we think, though, of the number of "good mornings" that occur in a university housing unit, a family, or a huge industrial complex such as IBM or General Motors, the number becomes staggering. When we move from simple greetings to all the social communication, conflicts, group discussion, and decision making that occurs in a family, much less a corporation, we have a mind boggling amount of communication to consider. All of the communication contributes to the nature of that unit.

Communication also shapes our relationship to our larger world, be it local or international. As children, our parents communicate to us what kinds of behavior are acceptable or not acceptable, including how our communication should be patterned. Friends and institutions such as schools, clubs, athletic teams, and religious organizations further shape our consciousness and foster patterns of interaction.

When we move beyond the personal, we rely on mass media. Our perceptions and judgments of events are often dependent on how newspapers, radio, and television communicate an event. The naive conception of these media is that they simply report the facts of a case. Upon closer inspection, we discover that the stories communicate a viewpoint, one of the many possible viewpoints available to observers.

A school closes in a town. The local newspaper and television station cover the story. As they cannot report every aspect of the event, reporters pick and choose which elements they wish to feature. They put their information into a format appropriate for print or broadcast and the composition process involves another set of choices.

One approach to the story would be to show how the school building is aging, how it needs repairs. The superintendent is quoted about the need to save money and to provide educational opportunities for students. Pictures are shown of the new, more modern building that the children will attend next year. The report portrays the school closing as an improvement in educational quality for all concerned.

Another approach would be to show teachers boxing up materials, hugging children goodbye for the last time, and sadly leaving the old building. Parents are quoted on how much they dislike the fact that their children can no longer walk to school but will be bussed far from home. Long time residents of the neighborhood talk about how the school has added to the neighborhood. Pictures of the new school emphasize how large, cold, and impersonal it seems. The second version of the story shows the school closing to be destructive to relationships and educational quality.

Which story is the truth? Neither one and both. All the elements, both good and bad, are part of the story. The selection and organization of those elements into a message will convey a viewpoint. Dependent as we are on others for information, the viewpoint communicated will shape our perceptions and hence the way we react to the world.

The communicative process of sending, receiving, and interpreting involves us at all levels, from the intimacy of our private lives to the world view of our political lives. Messages do not simply come to us. They are shaped by their senders, and we, in turn, shape them through our perceptions.

Areas of Communication Study

As an essential part of human activities, communication invites study, study which provides us with insights into ourselves as human beings.

> The communicative process of sending, receiving, and interpreting involves us at all levels.

The following are not an exhaustive listing of areas of communication study, but they provide a survey of some of the different ways in which we may approach the study of communication.

Public Communication

Perhaps the best known area of communication is *public communication* or *public speaking*. This communication is marked by an individual addressing an audience which may number from several to thousands. Examples of public speaking include political speakers and speakers at service organizations, convocations, lectures, religious services, and dedication ceremonies.

Public speaking was a topic of high importance to the Greeks twenty-four hundred years ago, and the people who wrote then are still studied today for what they can tell us about the process of communication. Plato and Aristotle were the most important of these people, but they were only two of a number of people talking about talk and how we influence each other through communication. One of their main concerns was how cases should be argued in courts of law. Aristotle provided us with a classic description of *rhetoric* when he labelled it as "the faculty of discovering in any given case the available means of persuasion" (*Rhetoric* 1355b). Another way of phrasing this idea is to say that rhetoric is "finding all the available means of persuasion in a given situation." The study of communication and rhetoric has extended in an unbroken line from that time to this.

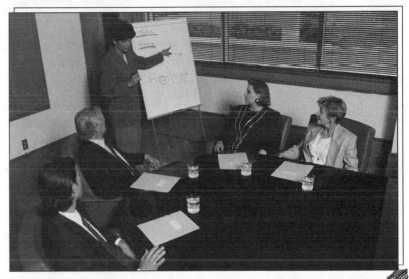

Most professions, be they technical or artistic, will demand that we make presentations to audiences.

Public speaking is an integral part of our lives. Most professions, be they technical or artistic, will demand that we make presentations to audiences. Architects show plans to clients. Agronomists tell farmers of developments in seeds. Financial officers diagnose their company's fiscal health. The study of public communication puts us in front of audiences, develops confidence, and makes us aware of the importance of organizing our thoughts well for effective communication.

Scholars in rhetoric and public communication look, naturally enough, at public discourse. These may be examined from an historical context in which one studies the forces that produced the speech, or they may be studied from other viewpoints such as style, type, or philosophy. In looking at speeches and speaking, rhetoricians look at the processes by which we accommodate ourselves to our changing political and intellectual environments. Rhetorical scholars are interested in what one calls "adjusting ideas to people and people to ideas" (Bryant 413). This view of rhetoric allows us to examine such diverse areas as presidential rhetoric, ceremonial rhetoric, and social movements.

Interpersonal Communication

When we deal with people individually or in small groups, we engage in what is generally designated *interpersonal communication*. Interpersonal communication could include such situations as talking with a friend, going through a job interview, arguing with a roommate, negotiating with sales personnel, and comforting a friend or family member. Interpersonal communication is often labelled *dyadic* (from the Greek word for "two") communication since much of it is between two people. Three people communicating would, naturally enough, be *triadic* communication.

Numerically, the next step in interpersonal communication is small group communication. Small groups may form for a number of purposes. Some, such as social groups, exist for the sake of the relationships within the group, while other small groups exist primarily for the accomplishment of tasks. Sales meetings, quality circles, board meetings, study groups, bridge foursomes and even tailgate parties would qualify as small groups.

When we deal with people individually or in small groups, we engage in what is generally designated interpersonal communication.

Interpersonal communication research examines how we respond to each other in various settings and under varying conditions. Studies might detail the kind of communication that goes on between friends, between married couples, between superiors and subordinates, and between parents and children. Studies might also look at how we communicate through the way we use our bodies or the way in which we learn how to take turns in conversations. Those interested in small groups might study the life cycles of groups as they form, function, and then disband. Others examine the patterns of communication within groups or how groups contribute to a larger whole such as a business or organization, an approach closely linked to organizational communication.

> Interpersonal communication research examines how we respond to each other in various settings and under varying conditions.

Organizational Communication

Organizational communication centers on the process of sending, receiving, and interpreting messages within and between organizations. As W. Charles Redding has observed, organizations consist of interdependent, goal-oriented activities of people who work together within a system or rules, norms, and routines. People band together in organizations to accomplish their purposes: businesses make money and service organizations relieve problems. Goals, however, are not always singular or explicit. To achieve their objectives, organizational members perform a variety of tasks that are linked to the activities of other members. The size of organizations may range from small, such as a neighborhood day-care center, to a multinational corporation.

Another important aspect about organizations is that they are formed and maintained through communication. In effect, an organization has a life of its own. The activity of organizing continues even when particular individuals leave or retire from a company. Large corporations such as Ford, Exxon, RCA, and Beatrice have employed thousands of people and experienced many changes in their operations, but these businesses typically survive despite the inflow and outflow of people. Hence, organizations are dynamic activities rather than static collections of people.

Studies in organizational communication focus on many elements of the organizing process. Areas of study include modes and channels of communication, interaction between superior and subordinates, and formal and informal relationships among organizational members. Other researchers look at the use of communication to socialize new members, to make decisions, to resolve conflicts, and to shape the environment and climate of organizations. Other areas of study include who uses written communication and who uses face-to-face communication and for what type of messages? Researchers also study the influence of computer interaction on the communication patterns of an organization.

Organizations require constant adjustments of people, resources, and goals. Thus, mediation and conflict management are a large part of the study of organizational communication. Communication in organizations also establishes a sense of "culture" through sharing stories of organizational events, using particular language patterns such as military or technical jargon, and telling tales of company history. This culture may reflect an atmosphere or climate which casts an organization as "a big happy family," "a dull sweatshop," or even "a strange zoo." Communication is also an integral part of the process organizations go through as they shape and adapt to their external environments.

Mass Communication

Another major area of communication and communication study is *mass communication*. Two major considerations determine whether or not communication is considered mass communication. The first, and most obvious, is that mass communication involves large numbers of people. Instead of a personal audience or a small group, or even a large audience for a public speech, mass communication reaches far more people and its audiences are dispersed, rather than collected in one place. While hundreds or even thousands of people may come together for a public speech, thousands more can watch a newscast without leaving their homes.

The second major characteristic of mass communication is that it is mediated communication. Something comes between the sender and the final receiver of the message. Rather than the firsthand directness of interpersonal communication, mass communication distances senders and receivers. The "something" that comes between sender and receiver is both mechanical and human. Mass communication is dependent on both senders and receivers possessing the appropriate technology such as cameras, tape, film, editing equipment, and receiving equipment (radios, television sets, networked computers, etc.). Mass communication also imposes the shaping consciousness of a third party between the event and the receiver.

> Organizations require constant adjustments of people, resources, and goals. Thus, mediation and conflict management are a large part of the study of organizational communication.

We can see the mediation process in mass communication by following a typical story. A reporter attends a meeting to report the University's board of trustees' decision on an important issue such as raising tuition. The television tape of the meeting is edited, the reporter writes the commentary, and the board's decision is recounted in a minute or so of the evening news. People watching the program receive the news of the meeting but do it through a television set rather than obtaining the information directly from the reporter. Further, the account of the meeting has been shaped by the perceptions of the reporter and the format of television news. This is not to say that the reported story is untrue, but that, rather, the story will necessarily reflect one viewpoint of the many available.

A great deal of discussion has been generated in the study of mass communication on the influence of the medium on its audience and on society. Numerous studies have been done, for example, on the effects of television violence on people who watch such programming. Other researchers examine how people use mass communication and what needs it satisfies in people's lives. Others look at how messages are shaped by the media. Some study the effect of mass media on society. Studies, for example, have indicated that the more people watch television, the more they think they are likely to be the victim of a crime (Ogles and Sparks "Question Specificity . . ." and "Television Violence . . .").

Public Affairs and Issue Management

Coming into prominence is another area of communication studies, *public affairs and issue management.* The field is allied to public relations but is much larger than the techniques of running campaigns and writing press releases. Issue management is an outgrowth of the traditional study of rhetoric.

Public affairs and issue management investigates how organizations affect and are, in turn, affected by aspects of the communicative environment. Some of these aspects include government regulatory agencies, politicians, consumers, competitors, and other organizations. The area studies how organizations seek to adjust to the demands of their publics and how they seek to adjust the public's views of the organizations. Organizations may be for-profit or not-for-profit and in corporate, political, and private contexts.

An oil tanker runs aground in Alaska and dumps thousands of gallons of crude oil into the ocean, polluting the ocean, destroying wildlife, and fouling the beaches. The oil company responds to the situation as do the municipal, state, and federal governments and environmental groups. Issue management would examine the ways in which each of these groups defines the situation and how each group argues for and counterargues to convince the public of the rightness of its stance.

While much of the work in public affairs and issue management is in reaction to crises of various kinds, not all is reactive. One aspect of issue management involves planning ahead to help shape public opinions in the direction desired by the organization. A hospital, for example, might foresee a need for a routine raise in revenue because of projected increases in salaries, maintenance costs, supplies, and equipment. Prior to raising fees, the hospital would make a strong effort to explain its situation to the community via press releases, seminars, speeches, and newsletters. The communication could stress the high quality of the hospital's care, its dedication to maintaining high standards, and the

Public affairs and issue management investigates how organizations affect and are, in turn, affected by aspects of the communicative environment.

rising cost of providing quality health care. If the campaign were successful, the public would be more accepting of the increased charges than if the charges were put into effect with no explanation.

Conclusion

Communication is a wide ranging field that permeates our lives and creates relationships. Communication is the sending, receiving, and interpreting of messages. The study of communication includes a number of areas: public communication and rhetoric, interpersonal communication, organizational communication, mass communication, and issue management, among others. Research and study in communication investigate the patterns of communication in our personal and professional lives and encompasses a wide spectrum of behavior from business to art. Understanding communication allows us to know ourselves better and to understand better how we function as individuals and as a society.

Discussion Questions ////

1. How do you see communication influencing your view of the world?

2. When is communication a process and when is communication a product?

3. What examples can you think of that illustrate sending and receiving in communication?

4. What kinds of communication would you classify as public communication or public speaking?

5. What does it mean when it is said that the function of rhetoric is to "adjust ideas to people and people to ideas"?

6. What types of communication would be classified as interpersonal?

7. What examples of organizational communication can you see functioning in a university?

8. Do you think that mass communication shapes the ideas of society or does it simply reflect the ideas of society?

9. How would rhetoric function as a part of issue management?

Sources and References ⁄⁄⁄

Aristotle. *The Rhetoric and Poetics of Aristotle.* Trans. W. Rhys Roberts and Ingram Bywater. New York: The Modern Library, 1954.

Bauman, Richard. *Verbal Art as Performance.* Rowley, Massachusetts: Newbury House Publishers, 1977.

Berlo, David. *The Process of Communication: An Introduction to Theory and Practice.* New York: Holt, Rinehart and Winston, Inc., 1960.

Bryant, Donald. "Rhetoric: Its Function and Scope." *The Quarterly Journal of Speech* 29 (1953): 401–24.

Dominick, Joseph R. *The Dynamics of Mass Communication.* 4th ed. New York: McGraw-Hill, 1993.

Littlejohn, Stephen W. *Theories of Human Communication.* 5th ed. Belmont, California: Wadsworth Publishing Company, 1997.

McLuhan, Marshall. *Understanding Media: The Extensions of Man.* New York: McGraw-Hill Book Company, 1964.

Ogles, Robert M. and Glen G. Sparks. "Question Specificity and Perceived Probability of Criminal Victimization." *Mass Comm Review* 20 (1993): 51–61.

———. "Television Violence and Perceptions of Crime: The Cultivation Effect." *Mass Comm Review* 16 (1989): 2–11.

Putnam, Linda L. and George Cheney. "Organizational Communication: Historical Development and Future Directions." *Foundations of Organizational Communication.* Eds. Steven R. Corman, Stephen P. Banks, Charles R. Bantz, and Michael E. Mayer. New York: Longman Publishers, 1990: 44–61.

Redding, W. Charles. *Communicating Within the Organization.* New York: Industrial Communication Council, Inc., 1972.

Ruben, Brent D. *Communication and Human Behavior.* 2nd ed. New York: Macmillan Publishers, 1988.

Scheckner, Richard. *Essays on Performance Theory 1970–1976.* New York: Drama Books Specialists (publishers), 1977.

Tompkins, Philip K. *Communication as Action: An Introduction to Rhetoric and Communication.* Belmont, California: Wadsworth Publishing Company, 1982.

⧸⧸⧸ Study Questions ⧸⧸⧸

The Field of Communication

1. How does the text define communication?

   _____

   _____

2. How does dyadic communication differ from small group communication?

   _____

   _____

3. What would a communication researcher in interpersonal communication study?

   _____

   _____

4. What are areas of interest for research in organizational communication?

   _____

   _____

5. What two characteristics separate mass communication from other forms of communication?

   A. _____

   B. _____

6. What is public affairs and issue management?

   _____

   _____

   _____

7. Develop your personal definition of communication.

   _____

   _____

   _____

Photo Analysis

Turn to page 20.
Turn to page 20.
    Analyze the picture on that page on the basis of the following questions.

1.   What types of communication are being demonstrated in this picture?

2.   How many senders and receivers are being implied in the situation?

3.   How might the presence of the various audiences affect what the interviewers say and do? How might they affect what the interviewee says and does?

4.   How does the television reporting of the interview affect the message received by the viewing audience?

The Nature of Communication

3

KEY CONCEPTS

Culture
Language
  Symbol System
  Arbitrarily Chosen Symbol System
  Shared Meanings
  Meanings and Communication
Nonverbal Communication
  Types of Nonverbal Communication
    Communicating with the Body
      Facial Expressions
      Posture and Gestures
      Clothing
      Artifacts
    Communicating with Space
      Distance and Communication
      Touch and Communication
    Communicating with Time
    Paralinguistics
  Is Nonverbal Communication Nature or Culture?
Implications for Communication
  Communication Model
  Encoding
  Channel
  Feedback

e are not born independent of history. First, we come into the world with a set of commands buried in our DNA, genes, and chromosomes that determine a number of factors about us. As a result of those commands, we are male or female, tall or short, light skinned or dark skinned, athletic or klutzy, and possibly even extrovert or introvert, and a great deal more.

> Through communication, we are taught the nature of the world, and through communication we, in turn, give shape to our worlds.

Beyond being a unique assemblage of biological components, we are, at any point in our lives, the result of forces that have shaped us. The amount and type of food we eat determines how healthy we are. Our families, friends, and society influence what we become psychologically. Similarly, our communication is shaped by a variety of influences.

Communication, by its very nature, implies connection with other human beings. Through communication, we are taught the nature of the world, and through communication we, in turn, give shape to our worlds. To understand how we go about creating the process of communication, several important aspects need to be understood.

Culture

In realizing the influence our social world has on us, one of the first things we need to recognize is the importance of culture. We all develop and function within a culture or even within various cultures. A culture is *a set of assumptions held by a large number of people about how things should be done, what values are prized, and how people should behave.* These assumptions are not focused on isolated incidents but cover the full range of our lives from birth to death. The cycle of human life is almost unvaryingly uniform and in reaction to it, we have developed a broad range of activities which move from birth to death, from how we treat newborn babies to how we dispose of corpses.

Culture is something we pick up as we live and grow. The learning process is both conscious and unconscious with much of it so subtle that we seem to absorb our cultural norms rather than learn them. When we look at others, we can often readily identify and describe important aspects of their cultures.

For example, let us note how some societies react to the passages we make through the stages of life. The Kota people of the Congo mark the transition from adolescence to adulthood by having boys paint their faces blue. The "masks of blue . . . signify the phantom of their childhood" (*Circle* 66). To prepare for marriage, young Balinese women have their teeth filed. The tooth filing is to reduce the intensity of the six human passions: lust, anger, greed, stupidity, intoxication, and jealousy (*Circle* 132). In the final transition, the passing from life to death, people also exhibit a range of customs. In Papua New Guinea, the

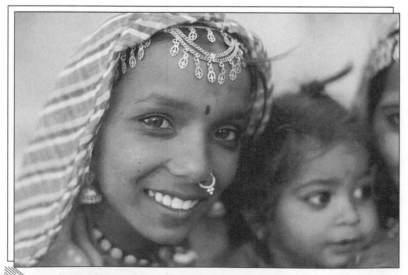
We all develop and function within a culture or even within various cultures.

Kuku-kuku honor the dead by a ceremony in which they "mummify their deceased relatives by smoking them over a fire" (*Circle* 217).

When we turn the cultural microscope upon ourselves, however, things often go out of focus. To view our own cultural practices is difficult for several reasons. For one, our society is a complex one. Not only do we function within local and regional cultures, but we possess a national culture as well. The United States, for example, is a constitutional democracy. We change governments by voting people into and out of office rather than by staging armed coups. We look to written documents for the final word on legal matters. We place a high premium on individual rights. To us, these practices appear to be the norm, but even a cursory review of international news shows that in many societies these principles are not the norms but aberrations.

Besides participating in a national culture, we also participate in local cultures and subcultures. Even in a small town one can find a mixture of cultures as people divide along social lines, religious lines, professional lines, and economic lines.

The major obstacle to perceiving our culture is ourselves. Consider what is an important rite of passage for many people. On a designated spring night, those in late adolescence dress in a style of clothing radically different from their regular dress. Families will even undergo financial hardship to provide the appropriate costume for their offspring. The participants are paired off male-female. The couples eat a sumptuous meal together but not in their residences. After the meal, they go to a site selected beforehand. Between the meal and the site, they may change costumes. Their transportation should be in the most impressive vehicle available, preferably an expensive rented one. The chosen site is a large room, decorated beforehand, in a public building. At the site, loud music is played, and they spend the majority of their time engaging in two forms of dance: they either clench together or independent of each other, improvise free style body movements.

After a number of hours of this activity, the large gathering breaks up. Smaller groups assemble at residences or less formal settings than the original dancing site. They again change costumes. In place of their formal attire, they put on play clothes and play games and continue dancing. They are not allowed to sleep for the remainder of the night. In the morning, they are fed breakfast and they return to their residences. The event signals their anticipated freedom from their homes. Through a mock marriage which lasts only the one night and the breaking of curfews, a last reminder of childhood, they indicate their readiness to participate in the adult realm.

A strange ritual from an exotic land? Only if you perceive your home town and high school to be exotic and the annual senior prom to be strange.

Children at an early age presume that their family's way of doing things is the only correct way to behave (Swensen 28). As they grow up, they begin to see that other families behave in ways different from their own. They eat differently. They provide discipline and approval in different ways. They talk to each other differently. One of the tasks of maturation is to make sense of these kinds of differences.

As adults, we may make the same kind of mistake but on a larger scale. We presume that what we consider, consciously and unconsciously, to be norms are norms for everyone. Everything we do seems so natural that we feel that whatever differences exist between people are only superficial differ-

> Even in a small town one can find a mixture of cultures as people divide along social lines, religious lines, professional lines, and economic lines.

ences (Hall, *Hidden Dimension* 183). As long as we stay within our own set of values and assumptions, we will experience little conflict or discord with our presumptions. When we contact other cultures, we start to discover conflicts and differences.

One of the interesting areas where we see our cultural preferences at work is in the world of sports. A sport or game, by its definition, is an activity engaged in for its own sake and has no import beyond itself. Yet, we load onto games a great deal of emotional weight and involve ourselves deeply with them. We fail to see how anyone could not appreciate a sport so interesting as the one we like to watch. Basketball, for example, is a sport that has traditionally commanded a great deal of attention in the Midwest. The madness of the state high school basketball tournament in Indiana is described as "Hoosier Hysteria." The Big Ten Conference produces leading teams. People discuss the outcomes of games as if they were confrontations between global superpowers instead of school athletic teams. Why such value on ten people exhausting themselves trying to put an air-filled spheroid through a metal hoop?

The value placed on basketball—or any other sport, for that matter—is a matter of culture. One reason that basketball became such an integral part of midwestern society is that it fit into the patterns of midwestern agriculture. Players, isolated on farms, could still, by themselves, hone their skills. All they had to do was hang a basket on the side of the barn or a utility pole. Before consolidation, schools were small. Because basketball is an inexpensive sport (as compared to football) and requires few players, even the smallest school could field a team. The basketball season came after fall harvest and before spring planting. With free time in the winter, families could attend games, and because it fit easily with societal conditions, the sport became an integral part of the culture.

In an interesting reverse twist, basketball has become a popular urban sport for a different set of reasons. Again, cultural conditions come into play. Cities are crowded and space is at a premium. A sport that can be played by a large number of people in a small area fits well into the societal conditions. Twenty people can play two half-court games in about the same area that a maximum of four people can play tennis. Other regions developed sports based on similar combinations of economics, convenience, and practicality. Northern states, for obvious reasons, play ice hockey more than southern states.

The same ready assumptions we make about the import of popular games in our area carries over into our feelings about other aspects of our lives. We grow accustomed to certain foods and new diets strike us as strange. Someone raised on meat and potatoes finds it difficult to see how anybody could enjoy eating bean sprouts, tofu, and brown rice. Conversely, a person raised on this diet may find it difficult to understand how anybody could eat so much grease, fat, and starch.

In the same way that we grow accustomed to ways of eating and playing, we grow accustomed to ways of communicating. We learn the norms of our societies. We learn how to function within the framework of complicated rules by being part of a culture. We learn how we are to address our parents, our siblings, our elders, co-workers, superiors, and so on. We learn how to behave in a variety of situations such as games, meetings, religious services, funerals, weddings, classes, dates, and family gatherings.

A person growing up on the south side of Chicago in an almost totally African-American urban setting will see the world differently and communicate differently than someone growing up on a farm in predominantly white southern Indiana. In between the two, an upper class African-American living in Indianapolis will have a different set of perceptions and ways of behaving and communicating.

The main point about culture is that our lives and our communication grow out of an entire set of values, beliefs, and behavior we have learned. To recognize this fact is not to make a value judgment about any system over another or to denigrate any beliefs we hold. We may still hold and defend our beliefs. To communicate clearly about those beliefs, or any other topic, we must be as aware as possible of our own culture and how it has shaped us, and we must be aware of the culture and assumptions of the people with whom we communicate.

Language: Our Linguistic Heritage

Within our cultures, we communicate in a number of different ways. Basic to almost all our communication is the use of language.

As we have noted, we "grow into" our culture by observing and imitating those around us. We "grow into" language in much the same way, acquiring language skills by imitation, trial and error. Contact with other language users is a necessity for learning how to speak.

In the manner of animals, human beings are born with the ability to make sounds and make them in reaction to their circumstances. Cries indicate discomfort; coos indicate comfort, etc. Then we move beyond sounds as a reaction to the present situation. As perceptive powers and muscular control develop, human beings then make a leap of truly momentous proportions. We assign sounds to an object, we name something and become able to consider that object whether it is present or not.

Language Is a Symbol System

The leap to naming moves us into a realm of sophisticated thought. Human beings can be characterized in many ways, but one way is to use the label applied to the species by a twentieth century philosopher, Kenneth Burke. Burke's description of humans is that we are "the symbol using animal" (Burke 3).

A symbol is something that stands for something else by association or connotation. Symbols may be physical in nature. Be they of countries, organizations, or events, flags are typically symbolic. Religious emblems such as the cross, the Star of David, the Crescent, and the wheel all have meanings beyond their physical characteristics. Schools have mascots. Jewelry serves symbolic purposes when people wear wedding rings, class rings, or lapel pins.

Beyond the physical, symbols take other forms. In language, sounds constitute the primary form of the symbols. Language begins with the association of sounds with objects or concepts. Combinations of sounds come to stand for the object or idea to be discussed. Instead of referring directly to a flower or a body of water or combustion, we can say "rose," "ocean," or "fire" and be sure that most English speakers will understand us even if no rose, ocean, or fire can be seen.

From the association of sounds with objects and ideas, the next step is to link the object or ideas to a marking system, the alphabet. Marks come to stand for sounds which stand, in turn, for the objects of discussion. Writing emerges

> Within our cultures, we communicate in a number of different ways. Basic to almost all our communication is the use of language.

and changes the shape of communication. The invention of the alphabet makes possible the creation of messages that can exist outside the direct presence of their creators. No longer does a message have to be passed orally from one person to the next. The message can be set down and left for others to discover.

Language Is an Arbitrarily Chosen Symbol System

The sounds and markings of words pass into our culture. As they are used by a large number of people, they seem to take on a life of their own. We do not usually make up our own language as we grow up. We appropriate the language of those around us. Thus, the learning process seems to be one of discovering tools that already exist.

That sense of discovery may mask one of the chief characteristics of language, that it is an *arbitrary* symbol system. By "arbitrary," we mean that no direct correspondence exists between a word and the sounds or letters that make it up. This is not an easy concept to grasp at first since, as one linguist points out, "It is generally difficult to make a complete divorce between objective reality and our linguistic symbols of reference to it" (Sapir 9). Still, should enough language users decide that a certain combination of sounds signified a given object, that would be the object's name. As Shakespeare reminds us, "A rose by any other name would smell as sweet," but we should note that with another name, the flower would no longer be a rose.

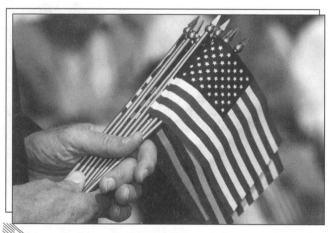
A symbol is something that stands for something else by association or connotation.

The attribution of meaning becomes abundantly clear when one sets out to learn a second language. One may, for example, describe the relationship with a male sibling by calling that person "brother," "bruder," "hermano," "brat," or "otoko no kyodai." The relationship remains the same but the words, the combinations of sound specifying the person, change from English to German to Russian to Spanish to Japanese.

Communication Depends on Shared Meanings

The arbitrariness of language points to the true source of the meanings of words. Language does not give meaning to its users so much as its users give meaning to it. The meanings of words reside not in the words themselves, but in the people who use the words.

> Language does not give meaning to its users so much as its users give meaning to it.

One way of understanding the process of meaning in words is to put the process into a three point scheme as did C. K. Ogden and I. A. Richards, two noted linguists (8–13). At one point, we place the symbol, the word or words that must be interpreted. At the top of the triangle, we place the perceiver who receives and interprets the message. At the third point, we place the referent, what the perceiver assumes the word to mean (Figure 3.1).

The meaning of the word, the referent, will be dependent on the perceptions of the user or interpreter. For a readily recognized word, like "dog," the relationship would look like this (Figure 3.2).

Even with a word like "dog," though, the referents will differ among perceivers. Some will see a miniature poodle, others a pit bull, others Lassie. For a

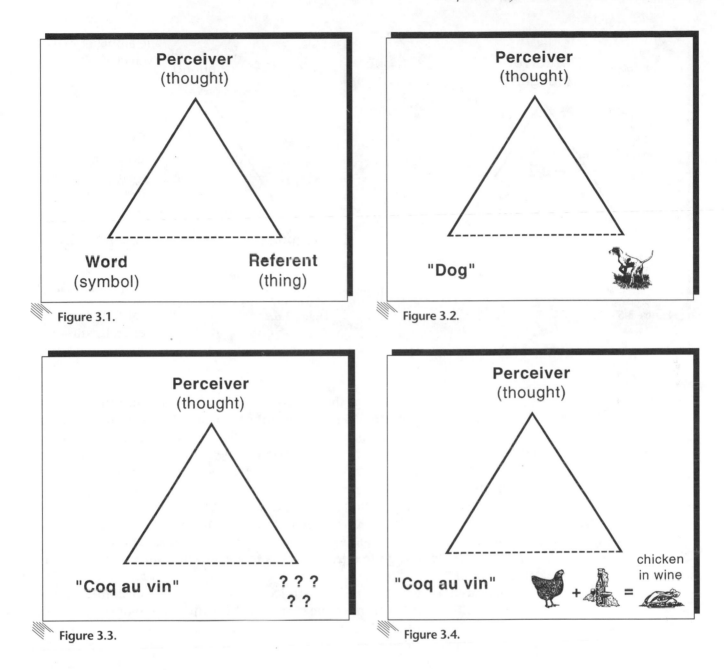

Figure 3.1.

Figure 3.2.

Figure 3.3.

Figure 3.4.

word that is unfamiliar or a word that is being used in an unfamiliar context, the process is even more complicated.

Let us presume a case in which the person hearing or seeing the word is a customer in a French restaurant and is trying to impress the person he is with. Let us further presume that the perceiver is a monolingual North American who speaks only English. He opens the menu and sees "coq au vin" is one of the items listed on the menu. Unable to make any connection between the sounds and a referent, the perceiver will have no meaning to attach to the sounds (Figure 3.3).

Afraid of what he might have to swallow if he does not swallow his pride, the customer asks the waiter for a definition of "coq au vin." The waiter supplies him with a definition: "coq au vin" is a chicken cooked in wine. The customer now has a referent for the item (Figure 3.4).

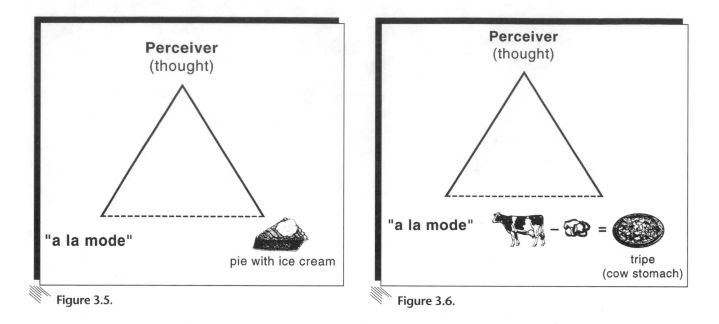

Figure 3.5.   Figure 3.6.

Another possibility is that the perceiver sees or hears enough similarities in the sounds that he attaches a meaning from his world of experience. Embarrassed at his problems in ordering an entree, our diner looks for something familiar for dessert. He sees "a la mode" on the menu. That, of course, means a dessert with ice cream on top, as in "apple pie a la mode." Everyone knows that (Figure 3.5).

The customer orders the dish, "tripes a la mode de Caen," to finish the meal. Unfortunately, the diner does not realize that while "a la mode" is a French term, it does not necessarily mean "with ice cream." The waiter's perception of the term is quite different. "A la mode" for him means "in the style or fashion of."

Instead of a piece of apple pie with ice cream on top, the customer's referent, the waiter places in front of the customer the waiter's referent (Figure 3.6), a steaming bowl of cow's stomach cooked in the style of Caen, a city in Normandy, France (Child 243).

Even then, once our perceiver learns that in this context "a la mode" designates a tripe dish, the process of meaning attribution is not over. The meanings of the word may still differ due to the experiences of the users. If one likes tripe as a dish, "tripes a la mode de Caen" will mean "tasty, delicious, a true delicacy." If one dislikes tripe, "tripes a la mode de Caen" will mean "yukky, repulsive, no way I'm going to eat that."

Meanings and Communication

As the meanings of words are not inherent in a combination of sounds nor in the combinations of markings on a page, communication is not a simple process. Rather than one person sending meanings to another, meanings are created between the two parties. The meanings will be dependent on the referents and experiences of the two parties. The process may result in a total lack of understanding between parties; it may result in full accord; or it may result in some stage in between.

To be effective as a communicator, one must be sensitive to the nature of language and the numerous possibilities for differing interpretations between senders and receivers. One must also be adaptive to ensure that senders and receivers are using the same set of meanings. Language is not so much a toolbox of words as it is an interactive process, wherein the perceptions of one person or party must join with the perceptions of another.

Nonverbal Communication

We are creatures who occupy space and live in time, and thus, it should be no surprise that we communicate by the manner in which we utilize these dimensions. Certainly language provides the basis for our communication, but we indicate through a number of different actions how those words are to be interpreted. In other cases, we manage to communicate without words at all. Nonverbal communication, simply put, is the "communication besides the spoken or written words" (Knapp 21; Mettaetal and Benjamin-Leiter 77). The number of ways that people communicate nonverbally shows us a fascinating combination of nature and culture.

> To be effective as a communicator, one must be sensitive to the nature of language and the numerous possibilities for differing Interpretations between senders and receivers.

Clothing and artifacts may carry a variety of messages about the wearer.

If the words say one message, and the sender's facial expression contradicts the verbal message, most will rely on the facial expression to interpret the true intent of the sender.

The impact of nonverbal communication on a communication situation is often crucial. For one thing, people trust nonverbal communication more than they trust verbal communication. If the words say one message, and the sender's facial expression contradicts the verbal message, most will rely on the facial expression to interpret the true intent of the sender. How socially attractive we are depends, to some degree, on how we communicate nonverbally. Persons showing positive nonverbal communication are judged more credible by those with whom they are speaking (Burgoon, "Nonverbal Behaviors . . ." 140). Nonverbal communication may also determine how much time one spends in jail. In one study, defendants showing moderate levels of anxiety were most likely to receive low credibility ratings and a high number of guilty votes. Defendants showing low levels of anxiety received the highest credibility ratings and the lowest number of guilty verdicts. High anxiety defendants were ranked in the middle (Pryor and Buchanan 96).

Types of Nonverbal Communication

Communicating with the Body

Our bodies provide a starting point for nonverbal communication. The way in which we occupy space may signal a number of reactions. Standards of beauty and attractiveness vary from place to place, and from time to time, so that the very shapes of our bodies may help or hinder us socially. Both anecdotal evidence and research indicate that the height of males influences how they are perceived in our society. No romantic western star is described as riding "short in the saddle." In presidential elections since 1900, the taller candidate has won with the exception of Jimmy Carter in 1976 (Knapp and Hall 112). Tall males are often given higher ratings than shorter males in a variety of situations (Elman; Lechelt; Lester and Sheehan). Moving beyond the shape of our bodies, how we employ our bodies is a major ingredient of our communication.

FACIAL EXPRESSIONS.   Facial expressions are one of the major ways in which we communicate nonverbally. The first way we communicate with facial expressions is to show our emotions. Before they speak words, babies reveal their feelings by facial expressions, and this process continues throughout life. While we combine facial expressions into a wide range of variations, we have a small number of basic expressions: surprise, fear, anger, disgust, happiness, and sadness (Knapp and Hall 272; Burgoon et al. 353). To these others add interest and distress-pain (Camras, et al. 80).

Beyond the primary function of communicating emotions, facial expressions also serve to indicate how verbal messages are to be interpreted. If someone answers a question with "Right!" and a smile, the presumption is that the answer is correct. If the response is "Right!" with a scowl, the presumption is that the speaker is being ironic and that the true message is exactly the opposite of the word used. Facial expressions may also take the place of words. A look of disgust or interest may signal disapproval as readily as words to that effect.

When a symbol was needed to warn children away from poisonous substances, the most effective approach was not to use words nor to use the old symbol for poison, a skull and cross bones. The most effective and direct way to communicate "Leave this alone!" was to create a cartoon face that immediately communicated disgust. "Mr. Yuk" communicates the same message even to sophisticated adults (Figure 3.7).

POSTURE AND GESTURES.   Besides the small movements of facial expressions, we communicate through the larger medium of our bodies by the use of posture and gestures. Posture is the way people hold their bodies. People indicate how nervous or at ease they are by the amount of rigidity in their bodies. Interest in a speaker is indicated by leaning forward or leaning away from the person.

Gestures are movements made by our extremities: our hands, arms, heads, and legs. Rather than something added to verbal communication, gestures appear to be inextricably linked with talk. One study brought pairs of students together to talk about movies. One set of pairs could see each other; the second set could not see each other. Both sets made the same kinds of gestures. As the authors state. "merely pronouncing words thus seems to give rise to some degree of body movement" (Rime and Schiaratura 239).

The meanings of many gestures are situational in that their meanings are created from their interaction with the communication situation and language. In a conversation, someone flings out an arm. The person could be indicating a direction or the person could be urging the conversational partner to leave. To interpret the gesture correctly, one would need to know the words accompanying it.

Other gestures, though, are independent of language and have taken on their own symbolic meanings. "Thumbs up" and "thumbs down" signal approval or disapproval. The hitchhiker's extended thumb is instantly recognized as a request for a ride.

Figure 3.7. Facial expressions can communicate powerfully even in an abstract form such as "Mr. Yuk," a poison warning symbol for children. Permission to reproduce "Mr. Yuk" given by Children's Hospital of Pittsburgh.

CLOTHING.   In addition to using our bodies as direct instruments of communication, we also drape or display things on our bodies which communicate messages of different kinds. The first use of coverings for the body was probably for protection, and that function still remains an important element of choice of clothing. In winter, we wear heavy coats, caps, gloves, and earmuffs. In summer, we resort to widebrimmed hats, sunglasses, and beach wraps. Certain professions such as welders, blast furnace attendants, and firefighters call for protective clothing as well.

Clothing also serves as a means of identification. Formal uniforms may designate a number of professions such as postal workers, flight attendants, pilots, ministers, nurses, and mechanics. Clothing also identifies people in more informal ways. A person's membership in a social group or social class may be indicated by dress. In one of life's many ironies, some groups of people who see themselves as independent often exhibit high standards of conformity in dress so that the "independents" can tell who is in the group and who is out. The American West created the cowboy as a symbol of the rugged individualist, but it is hard to recognize a person as a cowboy if he is not wearing jeans, a western hat, and boots. Similarly, some groups of motorcycle riders are recognizable because of their preference for boots, black clothing, leather jackets, chains, and their scorn of crash helmets.

ARTIFACTS. Additions to our clothing also signal other people about our roles and intentions. Some artifacts are evidently identifiers. Workers in large organizations often wear clip-on identification to show they belong on the premises and that they are not to be treated as clients, patients, or customers. Police officers wear or carry a badge to show that the bearer is authorized to behave in certain ways. Police officers also carry weapons and other equipment which serve as tools of the trade but also readily identify the wearer's purpose.

In a more subtle fashion, jewelry may tell people about a person's job, income, place identification, or how the person wishes to be perceived. A person wearing an ornate Navajo squash blossom necklace will create a different impression from a person wearing a single gold chain or a strand of pearls. A Mickey Mouse watch on an adult sends a message that the person is fun loving, perhaps even juvenile, while a Rolex may communicate money or ostentation.

Communicating with Space

DISTANCE AND COMMUNICATION. How we use the space we inhabit may also communicate. The distances maintained by people in different situations carry meanings as does the behavior initiated once people are within touching distance.

One specialist in nonverbal communication noted that Americans divide distance into four principle ranges, each of which signals a different relationship. The study was based on observations of middle-class, educated people primarily from the northeastern United States, but the conclusions still seem to apply in much of our culture. Public distance starts at twelve feet and moves further away. At this distance, people see each other's entire body. Relationships and communication are formal. Social distance is from four feet to twelve feet. This distance is used for business and more formal personal interactions. Personal distance ranges from eighteen inches to four feet. Here people maintain personal relationships which may range from close to cool. When people enter this range, they begin to approach each other on personal terms. Intimate distance is from zero to eighteen inches. Within this distance, we feel as though the other person is contacting us physically even though the person may not be touching us (Hall, *The Hidden Dimension* 116–25).

Within the intimate range, people experience the "fight or flight" response. They respond with hostility—fight—or move away—flight. A third option is to embrace, to hug, kiss, dance, etc. Intimate distance is so close that people have difficulty allowing people to exist within that space without relating to them.

TOUCH AND COMMUNICATION. Within personal space, touching behaviors come into play. Who touches whom and when and where may carry a variety of messages. Touch is obviously part of intimacy. As one observer puts the matter, "numerous studies . . . show that as the relationship between the individuals becomes more intimate, the level of nonverbal involvement increases" (Patterson, "A Functional Approach . . ." 477). Among the nonverbal behaviors that increase are intimate distance and the frequency and intimacy of touch.

Touch, though, can also signal power and social role. Typically, the more powerful engage in non-reciprocal touching behavior with those in lower positions. The boss may clap employees on the back as a greeting, but the employees risk affronting the boss if they use the same greeting. "Higher rank can

> The distances maintained by people in different situations carry meanings as does the behavior initiated once people are within touching distance.

provide a person with the power to touch, gaze, or stand close to a lower-rank person" (Patterson, "Social Influence . . ." 212). The assumed permission to invade the personal space of the subordinate may be charitable, as in the case of a physician and patient, or it may be aggressive, as in the case of a military drill instructor chewing out a recruit.

Communicating with Time

The temporal aspect of our lives comes into play in communication in several ways. Time is a construct that human beings have thrust upon the world. Seconds, minutes, months, seasons, and other divisions of time do not exist in nature any more than mathematics and philosophy exist in nature. Animals may have a sense of time but only in a rudimentary sense such as their migrating in a given season. They do not, however, check their watches or look at their calendars.

Different parts of the world use different calendars such as the Gregorian, Jewish, Muslim, Chinese, etc. Each gives time a different dimension or perspective. The reason that different peoples begin their new year at different times is due to the way their calendars calculate time. The Gregorian or western calendar is a solar calendar that divides the year according to the number of days. The Chinese calendar, and most other Asian calendars, is a lunar calendar that divides the year according to the cycles of the moon.

As the relationship between individuals becomes more intimate, the level of nonverbal communication increases.

Even when we use the same calendar and set our watches to the same standard (for most of the world, Greenwich mean time), we still react to time differently. North Americans tend to be very time conscious. American television, for example, is programmed, literally, to the second, and "dead air" is to be avoided at all costs. Programs start and conclude at exact hour and half hour divisions. Other countries broadcast with much less regard for precision. Programs may start at a variety of times other than the hour or half-hour. While a Norwegian program may start on the hour, it may only run forty minutes. In earlier times, the station simply pointed the camera at a fish tank and showed the fish swimming until time for the next program to begin. Now they run previews of their upcoming programs.

North Americans usually regard punctuality as a virtue. A person kept waiting in an office for fifteen minutes begins to fidget. A half-hour wait is considered long. Much longer, and the person may consider walking out. Latin American countries regard time much more leisurely. When told to arrive at eight, a person may come a half-hour before or after.

Recognition of how the other party regards time will make communication much easier. A long wait for one person does not necessarily signal disinterest on the part of the other person. A waiting period before a decision may mean a proposal is rejected or it may mean that the deciding parties are giving the matter full consideration. Social affairs may be regulated in different ways when it comes to time. Among many in the South and Southwest, "dinner at seven" means that one is expected to arrive at seven and the meal will be served as close to seven as possible. In the Northeast, "dinner at seven" may mean that one is expected to arrive no earlier than seven-thirty, have drinks and appetizers, and that the party may not sit down to dinner until nine or ten o'clock.

Paralinguistics

The form of nonverbal communication most closely linked to verbal communication is that of paralinguistics. Paralinguistics is the inflections and tonalities we give to words as we pronounce them. Among these vocal characteristics would be the pitch, rate, volume, and quality of the voice along with the use of pauses and accents, the product of articulation.

The importance of paralinguistics has been testified to in several interesting ways. In an interview, Margaret Thatcher, former prime minister of England, has talked about the value of having a translator sensitive to paralinguistics (Thatcher). In diplomatic discussions and negotiations, with the Russians, for example, it was important to her that the other parties received her messages in a form as close to the original as possible. Thus, she made sure she had a translator who not only translated the words but paid close attention to the rises and falls of pitch and the use of volume to highlight words. Then, when presenting the Russian version of her statement, he would attempt to reproduce the same emphasis she placed on the words. The result was that the Russian version came as close as possible to its English origin.

Closer to home, former president Richard Nixon became involved in the Watergate scandal which eventually forced his resignation. One of the key elements of that scandal was tape recordings he made of conversations in the presidential office. When they were called into evidence, a question arose in what form they should be presented. The United States Supreme Court ruled unanimously that "Richard Nixon's taped Oval Office conversations were better evidence of what transpired there than were typewritten transcripts of the same conversations" (Ellyson and Dovido 4).

Different languages and cultures employ paralinguistics in different ways. Japanese is characterized by being a mono-pitch language. One speaking Japanese correctly speaks always at the same pitch level with no rises or falls. Volume may increase or decrease as may the speaking rate, but the pitch remains constant. Another oriental language, Chinese, is quite different. Chinese employs at least four different pitch levels to distinguish the meaning of words: a high pitch, a low pitch, a rising pitch, and a descending pitch.

American English falls in between the two in the use of pitch. A rising inflection characterizes a word or phrase as a question or an indecisive statement. A falling pitch designates a command, decision, or affirmation. "You are going to take this class" spoken flatly is ambiguous. If the speaker places a rising inflection at the end of the sentence, it is heard as "You are going to take this class?" A falling inflection causes the sentence to be heard as an order.

The rate of utterance may indicate the nature of statements as well. Rapidly spoken phrases denote excitement, agitation, or fear. Slowly spoken phrases can signal a casual attitude or thoughtful consideration of a matter.

Loudness usually designates importance. Matters of personal concern often arouse one to show their importance by a rise in volume when speaking of them. On a small scale, the stressing of a word or phrase with added volume highlights that word or phrases and can decide the meaning of a sentence. Consider what emerges when different words are stressed in the same sentence:

⇒ "*I* will pay the bill tomorrow." (You will not have to pay it.)
⇒ "I *will* pay the bill tomorrow." (I promise to take care of the matter.)
⇒ "I will *pay* the bill tomorrow." (I am giving up trying to get out of paying it.)
⇒ "I will pay the *bill* tomorrow." (I am ignoring the credit card statement but not the bill.)
⇒ "I will pay the bill *tomorrow* ." (I will take immediate action, almost.)

The quality of the voice is determined by how the voice is resonated in the body. Different vocal qualities affect us in different ways. When exaggerated, vocal qualities call forth stereotyped characters. *The Wizard of Oz* movie typifies the cackling voices often associated with witches. Breathy voices designate sexiness in women. The old timer prospector speaks with a cracked and nasal voice.

The more subtle forms of quality also elicit responses. Social attractiveness, intelligence, and credibility can all be enhanced or diminished by the quality of one's voice.

Accents are combinations of the several characteristics of voice. Pitch, rate, quality, and articulation all combine to produce a distinctive manner of speaking. Like other aspects of nonverbal communication, accents may signal characteristics as social standing, roles, credibility, professions, and one's region.

Accents usually characterize the population of a region. As people learn to speak by imitation, they perpetuate the patterns of their families and area. When they contact people from a different region, the differences in speech then become apparent. Perhaps the most important thing to remember about accents is that everyone has one. "Accent-less" speech is simply that speech to which we are accustomed.

> Perhaps the most important thing to remember about accents is that everyone has one.

Is Nonverbal Communication the Result of Nature or Culture?

As we have seen, nonverbal communication is tied closely to our bodies, the nature of which each individual shares with all humanity. Because of this universal tie, we may wonder about the source of nonverbal communication, whether it is something that comes from human nature or if it is culturally bound. The short answer to the question is "yes."

Some portions of nonverbal communication are evident across cultures. Facial expressions are probably the most universal form of nonverbal communication. They are also the most persistent in that "emotional expression patterns for infants are similar to those described for adults. . . ." (Camras, et al. 100). One study compared the facial expressions of male university students in Tokyo and Berkeley, California. The results showed that the Japanese and Americans shared the same facial reactions to the same videotape (Ekman and O'Sullivan 176).

Other portions of nonverbal communication are more culturally bound. Even the facial expressions mentioned above came in for cultural control. The observers noted while the Japanese and Americans in the study shared facial reactions, they displayed those facial expressions differently when in the presence of an authority figure. The Japanese masked more of their feelings.

It has also been noted that congenitally blind people do not exhibit the same range of facial expressions as sighted people (Rinn 16). One explanation is that those blind from birth do not have the opportunity to observe and imitate the facial expressions of those around them.

Even though they seem a natural part of us, the elements of nonverbal communication are learned just as verbal communication is learned. Through a process of imitation and trial and error, people learn the norms for behavior and follow them.

Some of the learning may have such a long history that it seems an integral part of human nature. In southern Italy, the natives use a head toss for negation. Interestingly enough, the gesture is not common to the rest of Italy. Investigation reveals that the gesture is used only in that part of Italy settled by Greeks three thousand years ago. The lineage of the gesture is long but is still the result of cultural education (Bitti and Poggi 437).

In practice, the cultural background of nonverbal communication means that to be an effective communicator, one must be sensitive to differences of meaning and the norms of different cultures. In terms of space, for example, distances between people are not a constant from one place to another. Arab cultures, for example, stand much closer to each other than do Europeans or North Americans. Moving back may signal the other person that you are cold or aloof. Table sharing is common in European restaurants while North Americans feel invaded when a stranger sits at their table.

Nonverbal communication includes numerous elements of space and time, elements which are used in different ways by different peoples to communicate. Understanding the ways in which people utilize space, time, gestures, facial expressions, clothing and artifacts, and paralinguistics provides us with a sensitivity which can enhance our abilities to communicate.

> Even though they seem a natural part of us, the elements of nonverbal communication are learned just as verbal communication is learned.

Implications for Communication

This chapter has examined three major factors—culture, language, and nonverbal behaviors—that shape our practice of communication. Awareness of these three factors is a critical part of effective communication. We need to be aware of our own practices and their effects, and we need to be aware of the practices of the other party or parties with which we communicate.

One way of understanding communication is through the use of a *communication model,* a schematic representation of the communication process. Sketching a model helps us clarify the process. At the same time, we need to remember that "however we may choose to draw a diagram of human communication, . . . the process itself is more complicated than any picture or description of it which we are likely to put down" (Schram 24).

When we engage in communication, we bring to the communication situation a combination of elements. Among these elements would be our physical characteristics, our cultural training, our language training and skills, our nonverbal training and skills, our experience, our education, and other factors which contribute to our makeup. The other party or parties do the same (Figure 3.8).

Drawing on one's backgrounds, desires, interests, understandings, and abilities, one person creates a message to be sent. The message is then put into a symbol system which the sender hopes will convey to another what the first person is thinking or feeling. The symbol system may be words, nonverbal behaviors, print, electronic impulses, or some combination of elements. The process of creating the message is *encoding.*

The first person then transmits the message to another person via some *channel* of communication. A channel is the medium which carries the message. In interpersonal communication, the channel is usually the air which carries the sounds of the voice from one person to another (Figure 3.9). One could also see the various forms of nonverbal communication such as gestures and space as channels also. For other forms of communication, the channels could be broadcast signals, wires, or print media. The person receiving the message attempts to interpret it. The process of interpreting the message, making sense of it, is *decoding.*

Having decoded the message, the second person responds. As with the first person's message, the response will be shaped into some form of symbols. It is then the first person's task to make sense of the message. Thus, in communication, both parties play the roles of sender and receiver and engage in encoding and decoding. The work of encoding and decoding continues until the parties break apart (Figure 3.10).

Another concept informing our conception of communication is *feedback.* Feedback occurs in a system—mechanical, interpersonal, or otherwise—when a portion of the system's product is monitored and the results influence subsequent production. A simple example of a mechanical feedback system is the thermostat. The furnace system produces a product, heat. Part of that product, the air temperature around the thermostat, is monitored. Depending on the temperature of the air, the thermostat starts the furnace, lets it continue, or shuts it off.

In communication, the system consists of the senders and receivers who are linked together. The product of the system is the reactions they make, both intentional and unintentional. Feedback occurs when the communicators note the nature of their communication and react to it (Figure 3.11).

We can engage in feedback because, as one scholar has pointed out, "the message is, at some point in the process, separate from both the sender and the receiver" (Schram 26). This characteristic may be most obvious when we have mailed a letter that we wish we could recall and change (Schram 15). Like the letter, spoken words and nonverbal communication also have an existence separate from their creators and receivers.

Be it large or small, this distance between senders and messages, and receivers means that we can regard and judge our efforts at communication and the efforts of others. We can, in essence, step back and see how we are doing. Whether we have written a letter, produced a video, or spoken a phrase, we can look at it and decide how closely it came to being what we wanted. We can

Figure 3.8.

Figure 3.9.

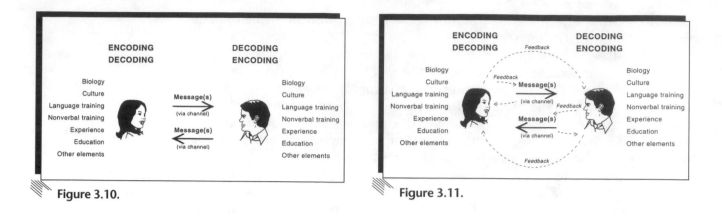

Figure 3.10.

Figure 3.11.

The more complicated the communication, the more complex will be the feedback process.

also note the reactions of the receiver and judge how closely our message comes to accomplishing our goals. Having seen the effect of our past communication, we can try to frame future communication to be as effective as possible.

For example, let us look at Lanie Wilson, a graduating senior, who is at the university placement center interviewing for her first major job. She wants a position in international business and to that end is interviewing with Narwell Incorporated, an international finance company.

After introductions, the interviewer asks her how much experience she has had travelling outside the United States. She responds that because of financial reasons, she has not been able to travel much at all and has not been abroad. The interviewer says, "uh-huh," frowns a little, looks down, and writes a note on the interview form.

She notes his response and quickly adds that while she has not travelled overseas, she has read widely about international business. She mentions also that she has studied German and Japanese and has conversational skills in both.

The interviewer looks up, smiles, and nods.

Wilson then elaborates on some of the major works on international business that she has read. By monitoring both her messages and their effect, she has directed the interview in a positive direction.

The more complicated the communication, the more complex will be the feedback process. In situations such as counseling, negotiations, and small groups, problems in feedback may have disastrous consequences while sensitive monitoring of feedback can be highly rewarding.

Conclusion

As communicators, we bring to each communication situation a number of factors. Our cultural backgrounds provide us with ways of seeing the world and ways of reacting to that world. Language allows us to deal with the world through the use of symbols while nonverbal communication may reinforce or, in some instances, replace, verbal communication.

Though communication often seems spontaneous, uninhibited, and easy, communication is not inevitable when we contact others. The assumptions people make about language and nonverbal aspects such as space, time, gestures, and clothing are not necessarily the same assumptions made by others, even others from our own background. To communicate well, people need to be aware of themselves as communicators and how they function. They need

also to be aware of how forces such as culture, language, and nonverbal training impinge on others. Self-knowledge and sensitivity are major ingredients in
effective communication.

Discussion Questions

1. How would you describe your own culture? What are some of its main
   features? What are some of its main beliefs?

2. Why may different sounds carry the same meanings in different
   languages?

3. Look at what you are wearing? Why are you wearing it? What do you
   think it communicates to others?

4. Why do we wear artifacts?

5. What is a comfortable distance for you when engaged in a conversation?
   Why is this distance comfortable? How do you think you would react if
   someone stood closer or farther away than your comfortable distance?

6. What kind of touching behaviors have you observed in your culture?

7. Why do North Americans see punctuality as important?

8. What are some examples of learned nonverbal behavior?

Sources and References

Bitti, Pio, Enrico Ricci, and Isabella Poggi. "Symbolic Nonverbal Behavior: Talking
    Through Gestures." *Fundamentals of Nonverbal Behavior*. Eds. Robert S. Feldman
    and Bernard Rime. Cambridge, England: Cambridge University Press, 1991.
    433–57.

Burgoon, Judee, William A. Donohue, and Mike Allen. "Nonverbal Behaviors,
    Persuasion, and Credibility." *Human Communication Research* 17 (1990): 140–69.

Burgoon, Judee, Douglas L. Kelley, Deborah A. Newton, and Maureen Keeley-Dyreson.
    "The Nature of Arousal and Nonverbal Indices." *Human Communication Research*
    16 (1989): 217–54.

Burgoon, Judee K. and Joseph B. Walther. "Nonverbal Expectancies and the Evaluative
    Consequences of Violations." *Human Communication Research* 17 (1990): 232–63.

Burke, Kenneth. *Language as Symbolic Action: Essays on Life, Literature, and Method*.
    Berkeley: University of California Press, 1966.

Camras, Linda A., Carol Malatesta, and Carroll E. Izard. "The Development of Facial
    Expressions in Infancy." *Fundamentals of Nonverbal Behavior*. Eds. Robert S.
    Feldman and Bernard Rime. Cambridge, England: Cambridge University Press,
    1991. 73–105.

Child, Julia and Simone Beck. *Mastering the Art of French Cooking*. Vol. 2. New York:
    Alfred A Knopf, 1970.

Circle of Life, The: Rituals from the Human Family Album. Ed. David Cohen. San
    Francisco: Harper, 1991.

Ekman, Paul and Maureen O'Sullivan. "Facial Expressions: Methods, Means, and Moues." *Fundamentals of Nonverbal Behavior*. Eds. Robert S. Feldman and Bernard Rime. Cambridge, England: Cambridge University Press, 1991. 163–99.

Ellyson, Steve L., and John F. Dovidio. "Power, Dominance, and Nonverbal Behavior: Basic Concepts and Issues." *Power, Dominance, and Nonverbal Behavior*. Eds. Steve L. Ellyson and John F. Dovidio. New York: Springer-Verlag, 1985. 1–28.

Elman, Donald. "Physical Characteristics and the Perception Masculine Traits." *Journal of Social Psychology* 103 (1977): 157–58.

Griffin, Em. *A First Look at Communication Theory*. 3rd ed. New York: McGraw-Hill, Inc., 1998.

Hall, Edward T. *The Hidden Dimension*. New York: Anchor-Doubleday, 1990.

———. *The Silent Language*. New York: Anchor-Doubleday, 1973.

Harper, Robert G. "Power, Dominance, and Nonverbal Behavior: An Overview." *Power, Dominance, and Nonverbal Behavior*. Eds. Steve L. Ellyson and John F. Dovidio. New York: Springer-Verlag, 1985: 29–48.

Hawking, Stephen. *A Brief History of Time: From the Big Bang to Black Holes*. New York: Bantam Books, 1990.

Henley, Mary M. and Sean Harmon. "The Nonverbal Semantics of Power and Gender: A Perceptual Study." *Power, Dominance, and Nonverbal Behavior*. Eds. Steve L. Ellyson and John F. Dovidio. New York: Springer-Verlag, 1985. 151–64.

Joseph, Nathan. *Uniforms and Nonuniforms: Communication through Clothing*. New York: Greenwood Press, 1986.

Knapp, Mark L. and Judith A. Hall. *Nonverbal Communication in Human Interaction*. 3rd ed. Fort Worth: Holt Rinehart and Winston, Inc., 1992.

Lane, Harlan. *The Wild Boy of Aveyron*. Cambridge, Massachusetts: Harvard University Press, 1976.

Lasswell, Harold D. "The Structure and Function of Communication in Society." *The Process and Effects of Mass Communication*. Eds. Wilbur Schram and Donald F. Roberts. Revised ed. Urbana, Illinois: University of Illinois Press, 1977. 84–99.

Lechelt, Eugene C. "Occupational Affiliation and Ratings of Physical Height and Personal Esteem." *Psychological Reports* 36 (1975): 943–46.

Lester, David and Donald Sheehan. "Attitudes of Supervisors Toward Short Police Officers." *Psychological Reports* 47 (1980): 462.

Lieberman, Devorah, Thomas G. Rigo, and Robert F. Campain. "Age-Related Differences in Nonverbal Decoding Ability." *Communication Quarterly* 36 (1988): 290–97.

Littlejohn, Stephen W. *Theories of Human Communication*. 5th ed. Belmont, California: Wadsworth Publishing Company, 1997.

Lonergan, Bernard L. *Insight: A Study of Human Understanding*. San Francisco: Harper and Row, Publishers, 1978.

Odgen, C. K. and I. A. Richards. *The Meaning of Meaning: A Study of the Influence of Language Upon Thought and of the Science of Symbolism*. New York: Harcourt Brace Jovanovich, n.d.

Patterson, Miles L. "A Functional Approach to Nonverbal Exchange." *Fundamentals of Nonverbal Behavior*. Eds. Robert S. Feldman and Bernard Rime. Cambridge, England: Cambridge University Press, 1991. 458–95.

———. "Social Influence and Nonverbal Exchange." *Power, Dominance, and Nonverbal Behavior*. Eds. Steve L. Ellyson and John F. Dovidio. New York: Springer-Verlag, 1985. 207–18.

Pryor, Bert and Raymond W. Buchanan. "The Effects of a Defendant's Demeanor on Juror Perceptions of Credibility and Guilt." *Journal of Communication* 34 (1984): 92–99.

Rime, Bernard and Lois Schiaratura. "Gesture and Speech." *Fundamentals of Nonverbal Behavior*. Eds. Robert S. Feldman and Bernard Rime. Cambridge, England: Cambridge University Press, 1991. 239–84.

Rinn, William E. "Neuropsychology of Facial Expression." *Fundamentals of Nonverbal Behavior*. Eds. Robert S. Feldman and Bernard Rime. Cambridge, England: Cambridge University Press, 1991. 3–30.

Sapir, Edward. *Culture, Language and Personality: Selected Essays*. Ed. David G. Mandelbaum. Berkeley: University of California Press, n.d.

Schram, Wilbur. "The Nature of Communication Between Humans." *The Process of Effects of Mass Communication.* Eds. Wilbur Schram and Donald F. Roberts. Revised Ed. Urbana, Illinois: University of Illinois Press, 1977. 3–54.

Thatcher, Margaret. Interview. *Book Talk.* C-Span. 9 December 1993.

Whitehurst, Teresa C. and Valerian J. Derlega. "Influence of Touch and Preferences for Control on Visual and Subjective Responses." *Power, Dominance, and Nonverbal Behavior.* Eds. Steve L. Ellyson and John F. Dovidio. New York: Springer-Verlag, 1985. 165–82.

_____ ⧚ Study Questions ⧚ _____

The Nature of Communication

1. What is culture?

   _____

   _____

2. How do people become aware of their cultures?

   _____

   _____

3. In language, what are the symbol systems used?

   _____

   _____

4. What is meant by, "Language is an arbitrarily chosen symbol system?"

   _____

   _____

5. Where do the meanings of words reside, in the words themselves or outside of the words? If outside, where is that?

   _____

   _____

6. How can you be an effective communicator despite the complexities involved in the communication process?

   _____

   _____

7. What is nonverbal communication?

   _____

   _____

8. How important is nonverbal communication in relation to verbal communication when trying to communicate with someone?

_____

_____

9. Facial expressions can convey at least two types of information. What are they?

1. _____

2. _____

10. In what way can meanings associated with gestures be situational?

_____

_____

11. What messages can clothing communicate?

_____

_____

12. In the communication sense, what are artifacts?

_____

_____

13. How can space be used to communicate a message?

_____

_____

14. What are the characteristics of how North Americans view time?

_____

_____

Is this the same way all other cultures view it?_____

If not, what are some differences?

_____

_____

15. What is paralinguistics?

_____

_____

16. Is nonverbal communication derived from human nature, or is it culturally bound? Explain your response.

_____

_____

17. What is a communication model?

_____

_____

18. What is encoding?

_____

_____

19. In reference to communication, what is a channel?

_____

_____

20. Describe decoding.

_____

_____

21. How does feedback work in communication?

_____

_____

Culture Analysis

Listed below are some items which are components of your culture, and consequently, you as a communicator. This information will not be collected, but it will serve as the basis for a class assignment on culture. Answer the questions. Then think how you might describe your own culture or how you might introduce a stranger to important aspects of your culture.

As with all assignments in this course, you will not be asked to reveal any information you are uncomfortable disclosing.

Family

➡ Do you live in an extended family, relatives nearby, or an isolated family?
➡ What is your parents' marital status? always married, separated or divorced, divorced and remarried, single parent, one or both parents deceased
➡ How many brothers and sisters do you have?
➡ Where in the birth order were you born? (only child, oldest, middle, youngest)
➡ Do you have half or step brothers and/or sisters?

Education

➡ How much formal education do your parents have?
➡ How much formal education do your grandparents have?
➡ What attitudes toward education does your family have? Your friends?
➡ Did you attend public or private secondary schools?
➡ How large was your high school?
➡ What was the atmosphere there?
➡ What percentage of your graduating class went on to college?

Home Setting

➡ What kind of area do you live in? (urban, suburban, town, village, rural)
➡ How stable is your neighborhood? (most residents have been there for years, some residents have been there for years, generally there is a large turnover in residents)
➡ How many times has your family moved since you've been born? How many different states have you lived in?
➡ Is your family's home in another country? If yes, where?
➡ Is your neighborhood dominated by one ethnic background? If yes, are you a part of the majority?
➡ What special observances does your home town celebrate? (Fourth of July parade, festival, traditional gathering, etc.)
➡ What kind of housing does your family have? (single family, duplex, multi-family) If your parents live in separate homes, do you live primarily in one, or do you spend significant time in each home?

Religion

➡ What is your religious background, if any?
➡ How strongly are you affiliated with your religious group?
➡ What are the major beliefs of your religious group?
➡ Are both your parents from the same religious upbringing? If not, how has this affected your religious choices?

Politics

➡ What is your party affiliation, if any?
➡ How would you classify yourself politically? (extreme right, conservative, moderate, liberal, extreme left, disinterested in politics)
➡ How did you develop your political beliefs?
➡ Have you taken an active part in campaigning for a law or candidate?

Business Life

➡ What working experience have you had?
➡ How much money are you contributing to your education?
➡ What are your parents' jobs?
➡ What are the most respected jobs in your community?
➡ What are the least respected jobs in your community?
➡ If you have decided on a major, what most influenced you in making that choice?

National Concerns

➡ Of what country are you a citizen?
➡ How would you describe the values of people in your part of this country?
➡ If you're a citizen of another country, how do its values differ from those in the United States?
➡ Have you traveled outside the U.S.? Where?
➡ Have you lived outside the U.S. for more than six months? Where?

Foods

➡ What would be a typical evening meal in your family?
➡ What are your favorite foods?
➡ If you wanted to introduce somebody from a different area to the foods of your area, what would you serve them?

Ethnic Heritage

➡ What is your ethnic background?
➡ How much contact with other ethnic groups or races have you had in your community?
➡ How much contact with other ethnic groups or races have you had in your school?

Language

➡ What is your first language?
➡ What is your second language?
➡ What is your third language?
➡ Do your family members normally communicate with each other in English? If not, what language do they use?
➡ Were your high school classes bilingual? What languages were used?

Ethics in Communication

KEY CONCEPTS

Nature of Ethics
Ethics as an Integral Part of Communication
Ethical Communication
   Respect for Audiences
   Consideration of Consequences
   Respect for Truth
   Using Information Properly
      Adequate Information
      Accurate Information
   Falsifying Information
      Plagiarism
   Respect for Others' Rights to Information

Communication is one of the most basic of human activities, a process by which we engage ourselves with others for understanding, for cooperation, and the accomplishment of a variety of goals. To exist as a human being is to interact with others, to influence others, and to be subject to their influence upon ourselves. We are, as one has observed, "a persuading and persuaded animal" (Johnstone, Henry 306). The interaction may be as complex as that of a family with a complicated web of relationships that extends over the lifespans of its members. The interaction may be as simple as a request for information from a stranger on the street whom we will never see again.

However complex or simple our interactions, we impinge on each other in multiple ways. It is a short jump from recognizing that we influence each other through communication to recognizing that communication is not a neutral activity. We do not simply influence each other; we influence each other in positive and negative ways, for good and for bad. Phrases from our daily rounds of communication indicate the kind of judgments we make about the worth and value of the communication: "She should never have told me that"; "He was very helpful"; "The government is engaged in another cover-up"; "She said what needed to be said"; "He's lying"; "She told it like it was."

When communicating, we do not simply choose words; we choose words for the effect they will have on our audiences, on ourselves, and ultimately, on society. Thus, when we communicate, we cannot escape ethical questions, questions which ask how helpful or harmful our actions are. An awareness of the ethical dimensions of communication provides us with a deeper understanding of ourselves and of our potential as human beings. Communicating ethically is important because it has the greatest positive impact for others and, ultimately, ourselves. This chapter examines the subject of communication and ethics by looking at the nature of ethics, how communication and ethics interlock, and at some guidelines for making ethical choices in communicating.

The Nature of Ethics

Ethics is the discussion of the judgments we make about the appropriateness, the right or wrong, of our actions and policies be those actions communicative, political, social, personal, or a mixture of areas. Ethics is the study of what, ultimately, is the best course of action: How should we behave to have the most positive effect upon society and to become the best individuals we can?

The question is certainly not a new one; the search for answers is both ancient and cross-cultural. With its text dating back to 2400 BC, the Egyptian *Book of the Dead* contains a kind of creed or standard of behavior which the virtuous were expected to recite to pass successfully from the world of the living to the realm of the dead. Among the statements, the virtuous are asked to affirm that "I have not oppressed the members of my family," "I have not defrauded the oppressed one of his property," and "I have not cut a cutting in a canal of running water," an important consideration in an arid land (Budge 360–71). In ancient India, in its religion and philosophy, "truthfulness means more than a moral obligation to avoid deceit. It is revered as one of the greatest of human accomplishments and the greatest service one person can render another" (Kirkwood 213).

Both the Jewish and Christian scriptures have clear indications of how one is to behave. The Ten Commandments (Exodus 20: 1–17) and the Sermon on the Mount (Matthew 5–7), for example, both contain guidelines for religion, marriage, treatment of others, honesty, and respect for the truth. The Confucian codes of China, dating from the sixth century, AD, detail how one should behave in a benevolent and virtuous way.

In his *Nicomachean Ethics,* circa 325 BC, Aristotle discusses what contributes to the creation of a good and just society. His view is that ethics is a kind of "practical philosophy," the application of good judgment when faced with decisions about courses of action. Through the use of our rationality, we seek a virtuous path, one that avoids the extremes of overreaction. For example, Aristotle views generosity as a virtue which consists of giving "to the right people, the right amount, at the right time . . . ." By practicing generosity, one avoids the vices of extravagance, spending too much on oneself, and stinginess, spending too little on others (1120a). By seeking the mean, one creates "happiness," a term which for Aristotle meant "living well," leading a rewarding and fulfilling life (Ostwald xxi).

The discussion of ethics has continued to be an area of discussion and research from its earliest beginnings until the present time. Even a quick search of listings in a university library will yield a lengthy list of materials ranging from a general discussion of ethics in society to discussion of ethics in specific fields such as medicine, education, and law.

Ethics as an Integral Part of Communication

In contemporary society, when we consider questions of ethics, we often turn immediately to the world of politics, not without reason. The administrations of presidencies in this past half century have all faced, and in some cases bungled, questions of truthfulness.

The most famous case of presidential truth or consequences was that of Richard Nixon. In 1972, during the election campaign, an attempt was made to burglarize the Democratic National Headquarters located in the Watergate Building. The Congressional hearings, judicial investigations, revelations, and public outcry stemming from that incident forced Nixon to become, on 8 August 1974, the first president to resign from office.

By its very nature, the democratic process creates decisions that are often difficult for its participants if they subscribe to a high ethical standard. How should a candidate behave in order to be elected? How does a voter choose between two candidates, neither one of whom is particularly desirable? How do elected officials balance the often conflicting needs and desires of their constituencies?

When we turn to non-political questions, we sometimes think that ethics is a matter of debating major issues such as euthanasia, war, or capital punishment (Williams 196). These are certainly significant matters, but the "major ethical issues" that most of us will face will be matters of how to behave in our daily lives and in our relationships with those with whom we have personal contact at home, at school, or at work.

Because it is relational, communication brings us face to face with questions that contain ethical judgments. We must decide what is the purpose or purposes of a relationship in which we find ourselves. We must decide how to behave. We must choose how to respond in that situation. Our responses will be based on how we regard the other party or parties and what the consequences of our actions will be. All of these are basic ethical questions in that they involve our deciding what is the "best" course of action.

> By its very nature, the democratic process creates decisions that are often difficult for its participants if they subscribe to a high ethical standard.

Discovering the ethical element in our communication does not mean that we go through a complete ethical inventory every time we engage in communication. Rather, we make basic assumptions about the nature of people and our responsibilities to them and then act on the basis of those assumptions.

It does not take long, however, before we find ourselves in situations in which we must attempt to satisfy conflicting demands. Then we come consciously face to face with the ethical issues in communication. How do you respond when a friend comes to you and asks, "How do you like this shirt?" and you think the shirt is hideous? How do you balance the conflict between sparing the person's feelings and saving the person from public embarrassment? What do you say or do?

A friend reveals to you that she has a six pack of beer hidden in her dormitory room, and you both know alcohol is prohibited by regulation on campus. Later, the resident counselor comes to you and asks if you know of anyone on the floor who has alcohol in her room. What would you say or do in response? How would you frame your communication with your friend and the counselor?

What if, in a more serious case, your friend insisted that she was not drunk and was perfectly capable of driving her car, but you could tell that she was completely intoxicated and a threat to herself and others on the road? How would you persuade her to stay off the road? Would it be ethical to lie to her to separate her from her car keys? If she proved unresponsive to your persuasion and drove off, would you call the police to alert them to a dangerous driver? If she were arrested for "driving while under the influence," how much of your role in the affair would you reveal? In what ways, if any, would your reactions differ if your friend were a "he" instead of a "she"? How would you respond if the person involved were a family member, a parent or grandparent?

In a more public setting, let us imagine that you are part of a committee presenting a proposal to your housing unit about parking facilities. Close to the time you are to present your proposal, you discover that a key piece of evidence is outdated and the latest information is damaging to your case. Do you simply present the evidence? Do you present the data with a qualifier about its timeliness? Do you leave it out entirely?

While the answers to these kinds of questions may be difficult, we have to make decisions and live by the consequences. The decision to communicate and the decisions made within the communication event carry with them ethical implications.

Ethical Communication

To make the best decisions in our communication, to communicate ethically, we must give thought to the manner in which we communicate. Formulating a list of rules to be applied in the different communication situations in which we find ourselves would be a futile endeavor. The situations are too vast and too varying. Rather, we would do better to suggest guidelines for ethical communication, considerations which should shape communicating practice.

Ethical Communicators Are Respectful of Their Audiences

Communication is a two way process. Communication implies a party other than ourselves and an attempt on our part to influence that person or party in some way. As one scholar has put the matter, "A *communicator,* with particular *motives,* attempts to achieve a specific *end* with a specific *audience* by employing (*intentionally or unintentionally*) communicative *means* or techniques to influence that audience" (Johanssen 16).

The nature of the influence we have on others will depend to a large extent on our attitudes towards our audiences. As several have observed, an ethical communicator is one who regards other persons as possessing inherent dignity and worth (Jaska and Pritchard 81; Nilsen 14). Human beings are to be regarded not as means to ends but rather as valued participants whose welfare is a significant and considered part of the interaction.

In terms of practice, this principle means that audience analysis is an important part of communication. We cannot respond appropriately if we are ignorant of the people with whom we communicate.

Respect for audiences includes respect for the ideas and feelings of the people with whom we interact. If people possess dignity and worth, then they need to be treated as such even when we may disagree with them strongly. One student was addressing an issue which some saw as racially charged. His response to those opposing his ideas was, "Get a life." His reaction demeaned not only those disagreeing with him but his own ideas as well.

> Respect for audiences includes respect for the ideas and feelings of the people with whom we interact.

Ethical Communicators Consider the Consequences of Their Communication

We do not communicate in vacuums. Our communication endeavors are never isolated one from the other. How we respond at school influences how we respond at home, and that in turn affects how we respond in our public lives. Having considered the natures of our audiences, we need to consider further the effect of our communication on them and upon ourselves.

Sam is chairing the planning committee for the Outing Club's spring break trip to Isle Royale. Committee members are all doing their work except for Larry who has missed several meetings and has not had his committee reports ready on time. Larry is slowing down the committee's progress and threatening the success of the trip. Sam has to talk to Larry about the problem and is frustrated enough to bawl him out about his poor work. Telling Larry off in loud and uncertain terms may make Sam feel better, but if Sam is an ethical communicator, he will consider the possible outcomes of his communication with Larry.

If Larry's work is late because he has been sick, an outburst may leave Larry resentful and even less willing to perform the necessary work. Relations will be strained more. The trip may be further endangered. Whatever the situ-

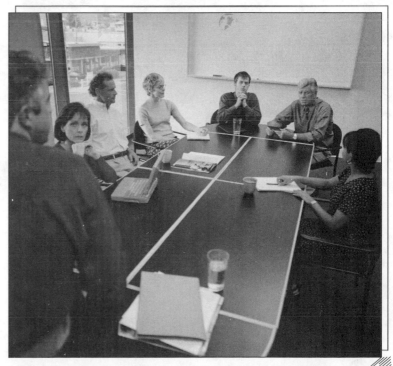

Audience analysis is an important part of communication.

ation, Sam's best choice will be an approach that encourages Larry to be a contributing member, reduces the possibility of conflict, and ensures the success of the projected trip rather than just venting his feelings.

Ethical Communicators Respect Truth

A great deal of the ethics of communication involves a respect for truth. Indeed, as one has put it, the assumption of truth undergirds the very concept of communication itself: "an inherent end of speech is the communication of belief" (Kupfer 118). If we cannot trust the other party, we cannot accurately judge how to respond. If we cannot accurately judge how to respond, then our communication becomes increasingly ineffective. If the lack of trust is pervasive enough, it is destructive finally to society. As one person has observed, "This is why some level of truthfulness has always been seen as essential to human society, no matter how deficient the observance of other moral principles" (Bok 18).

Let us say that an instructor receives a call from a student just before the student is scheduled to make a presentation in class. The student tells the instructor that he cannot make his presentation because he is sick. He says that he has a fever and has been up all night with nausea. His voice sounds hoarse and tired. The instructor is sympathetic and offers to let the student make up the presentation later. Two hours later, the instructor goes to lunch and across the restaurant, sees the same student. The student is active, lively, and in animated conversation with his friends. It is apparent that he is not the least bit sick.

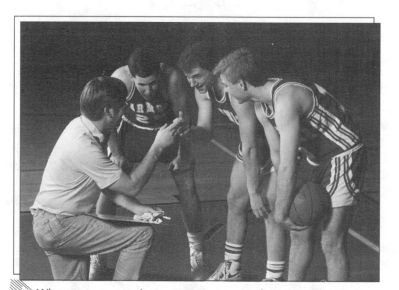

When we communicate, we expect people to react in some way to what we say and do.

The student has created trouble for himself, but he has also created trouble for other students. Once deceived, the instructor will be less likely in the future to accept reasons for missed work. Rather than accepting the word of the student, the instructor may demand proof of the illness and move the relationship toward a more legalistic level.

Instructors are not immune to disrespect for truth. An instructor assigns a five page paper due in two weeks and lists the penalties for turning in the paper later. You work hard and hand your paper in on the day it is due. After collecting the papers, the instructor says that he put the deadline and penalties on the assignment to get them in so he would have time to grade them, but he will not enforce any penalty if the work is late. Several people turn in their work the next week and receive the same grade as you. Given another week, you might have made your paper even better. You would probably feel that you have, to some degree, been cheated. The instructor not only gave different people different deadlines but deceived the class as to the true nature of the assignment. The instructor's credibility has been damaged so that you will probably be leery of anything the instructor says. In short, you will have increased difficulty making your judgments about the intent of what is said and what course of action you should follow.

Ethical Communicators Use Information Properly

ADEQUATE INFORMATION. As an ethical communicator, a respect for truth means being informed on a topic before posing as any kind of authority on the subject. Certain professions such as law, medicine, and education have formal standards of expertise and knowledge that must be met before one can be a practitioner. We would be appropriately appalled to discover that the physician who just treated us had never attended medical school.

The same principle applies in communication situations. If we are going to provide information to people, much less persuade them, we need to be well prepared for the occasion. To talk about. "How Students Can Handle Their Finances" with little or no background would be giving limited, if not false, information. To speak with any authenticity on the subject, we would need to look into such items as educational costs, credit card use, banks and credit unions, and work opportunities.

ACCURATE INFORMATION. In addition to securing information, we also need to consider the accuracy of the information and the accuracy with which we use it. When we communicate, we expect people to react in some way to what we say and do. When we use inaccurate information to influence others, we cause difficulty for them and for ourselves.

Accurate information is information that is timely, up to date, and applicable to the situation. In making a presentation on where to attend college, a speaker might quote a reference work that listed information about schools such as tuition, majors, and academic standing. If the reference book, though, were ten years old, the information would be of little use. Out of date information about other significant topics such as the environment, drug use, or crime rates would be just as useless.

Along with finding timely and adequate information, an ethical speaker will use quotations, facts, ideas, and figures accurately. Quotations will, for example, reflect the intent of the larger passage from which they are taken.

A *Consumer Reports* article evaluates commercial diet plans. Several of the statements made in the article could be used to persuade people of the merits of the plans. A psychologist specializing in eating disorders says, *"Weight Watchers* is the only place I ever send anyone" ("Losing Weight" 355). In another place, the article evaluates a well known program by saying, "People who tried *Optifast* lost 45 pounds on average . . ." ("Losing Weight" 357).

These quotations sound like endorsements of the plans until one sees their larger context. The psychologist is characterized as someone who "generally warns clients away from the very idea of dieting." The information on the success of the customers of *Optifast* adds that the customers "had gained back 15 pounds six months later." The article's conclusion? "Despite their sales pitches, there is no evidence that commercial weight-loss programs help most people achieve significant, permanent weight loss. If you want or need to lose weight, you would probably do well to try to reduce on your own, or through a free hospital-based program, before spending money on a commercial weight-loss center" ("Losing Weight" 357). Misquoting could give a very biased view of the information.

As an ethical communicator, a respect for truth means being informed on a topic before posing as any kind of authority on the subject.

Ethical Communicators Do Not Falsify Information

Worse than the distortion of information is falsifying information. Failing to find information useful to our goals, we make it up. Lena Guerrero, a person active in Texas politics, was appointed to an important state commission by the governor. Part of Guerrero's credentials were notations of her graduation from the University of Texas and membership in Phi Beta Kappa, a prestigious honorary society. As the featured speaker at a college graduation, she waxed sentimental about her own graduation, saying, "Now, I remember well my own commencement, and I think I can guess what you're feeling about now" (Burka 125). Investigative reporters discovered some important facts about her college years: Guerrero attended college but fell nineteen hours short of the required minimum. She had no college degree; she never graduated. Nor was she ever a member of Phi Beta Kappa. She had lied about the situation. Such invention of information is highly unethical.

Another way of falsifying information is through *plagiarism.* Plagiarism is a kind of theft, intellectual theft. We plagiarize when we use the words or ideas of another and fail to credit the source. Instead of attributing the material to its original creator, we pretend the words or ideas are our own. When writing, we acknowledge sources by the use of quotation marks and include a citation of the source. When speaking, we acknowledge sources by naming them in the context of the speech.

If one were speaking, for example, about the problem of dealing with aging pets, one could make the problem vivid for the audience by describing the behavior of an old beloved dog. The loyalty, affection, and trust of the dog and the owner's conflicting feelings could be poignantly pictured by a phrase such as "putting 'their kids' old dogs to sleep, friends that drool and quiver and stumble hobbling to our hands'." If ethical, the speaker, though, would give credit where credit is due by acknowledging the author: "As Walter McDonald aptly describes in his poem . . ." (McDonald 24).

The most blatant form of plagiarism is appropriating the entire work of another. This type of plagiarism occurs when, instead of composing their own speeches, students give speeches created by people other than themselves: their roommates, their friends, family members, or even professional writers. Besides constituting a lie about the true composer, such plagiarism subverts the educational process. We do not learn to communicate by using a stand-in any more than we learn to swim by having someone else take swimming lessons for us.

Ethical Communicators Respect the Rights of Others to Information

A respect for truth and an ethical consideration of others also means respecting the rights of others in regard to information and access to information. Collecting information is an integral part of the research process, but stealing information is theft, taking something that does not belong to us. Beyond the personal act of theft, stealing information is unethical because it prevents other people from securing information and unnecessarily makes their lives more difficult.

For example, a periodical article may be useful to our speech, but we should either take notes on the material or photocopy it rather than tearing it out of the magazine. Tearing out the article robs others of the opportunity to read it and creates added expense for the library which must replace it. That expense,

Plagiarism is a kind of theft, intellectual theft.

along with similar expenses, adds to the financial burden of the school and eventually, its students, including the person who tore out the article.

Conclusion

For the sake of our audiences, ourselves, and the people affected by our interactions we need to recognize the ethical component of our communication. Ethics is not just a matter of political or social policy but is a part of our personal policies as well, an integral part of our behaviors and our regard for others. Ethical communication will incorporate a respectful view of its audiences, a consideration of the consequences of the communication for all parties involved, and a respect for truth. Such a view is both a challenge and a reward.

Discussion Questions

1. Why does our communication have ethical implications?

2. How can communicators show respect for their audiences or co-communicators?

3. How does a respect for truth shape our communications? What happens in communication when we cannot believe the other party?

4. How would falsifying information affect communication?

5. How might communicators use information improperly?

6. What would you do if you were involved in the case described in this chapter about beer in the dormitory or a case where someone you know is drinking and driving? How would you choose to communicate?

7. What problems are created when people destroy information such as tearing out periodical articles or stealing books from the library?

Sources and References

Anderson, Kenneth E. "Communication Ethics: The Non-Participant's Role." *The Southern Speech Communication Journal* 44 (1984): 219–228.

Aristotle. *Nicomachean Ethics.* Trans. Martin Ostwald. Indianapolis: Bobbs-Merrill Company, Inc., 1962.

Arnett, Ronald C. "The Practical Philosophy of Communication Ethics and Free Speech as the Foundation for Speech Communication." *Communication Quarterly* 38 (1990): 208–17.

———. "The Status of Communication Ethics Scholarship in Speech Communication Journals from 1915 to 1985." *Central States Speech Journal* 38 (1987): 44–61.

Bok, Sissela. *Lying: Moral Choice in Public and Private Life.* New York: Vintage Books, 1989.

Bormann, Ernest G. "Ethical Standards for Interpersonal/Small Group Communication." *Communication* 6 (1981): 267–85.

Budge, E. A. Wallis. *The Book of the Dead: An English Translation of the Chapters, Hymns, etc., of the Theban Recension, with Introduction, Notes, etc.* 2nd ed. 1923. Surrey, England: Unwin Brothers Limited, 1977.

Burka, Paul. "Honesty is the Best Politics." *Texas Monthly* Nov. 1992: 122+.

Condon, John. "Values and Ethics in Communication Across Cultures: Some Notes on the North American Case." *Communication* 6 (1981): 255–65.

Confucius. *The Analects.* Trans. D. C. Lau. New York: Penguin Books, 1979.

Deetz, Stanley. "Reclaiming the Subject Matter as a Guide to Mutual Understanding: Effectiveness and Ethics in Interpersonal Interaction." *Communication Quarterly* 38 (1990): 226–43.

Garver, Eugene. "Essentially Contested Concepts: The Ethics and Tactics of Argument." *Philosophy and Rhetoric* 23 (1990): 251–70.

Grisez, Germain. "The Concept of Appropriateness: Ethical Consideration in Persuasive Argument." *The Journal of the American Forensic Association* 2 (1965): 53–58.

Hoff, Christina. "Moral Education in America." *The American Scholar* 53 (1984): 381–89.

Holy Bible.

Jaska, James A. and Michael S. Pritchard. *Communication Ethics: Methods of Analysis.* Belmont, California: Wadsworth Publishing Company, 1988.

Johannesen, Richard L. *Ethics in Human Communication.* 3rd ed. Prospect Heights, Illinois: Waveland Press, Inc., 1990.

Johnstone, Christopher Lyle. "Ethics, Wisdom, and the Mission of Contemporary Rhetoric: The Realization of Human Being." *The Central States Speech Journal* 32 (1981): 177–88.

Johnstone, Henry W., Jr. "Towards an Ethics of Rhetoric." *Communication* 6 (1981): 305–14.

Kirkland, William G. "Truthfulness as a Standard for Speech in Ancient India." *The Southern Communication Journal* 54 (1989): 213–34.

Kupfer, Joseph. "The Moral Presumption Against Lying." *Review of Metaphysics* 35 (1982): 103–26.

"Losing Weight: What Works. What Doesn't." *Consumer Reports* 58 (1993): 347–52.

McDonald, Walter. *After the Noise of Saigon.* Amherst, Massachusetts: The University of Massachusetts Press, 1988.

McGuire, Michael. "The Ethics of Rhetoric: The Morality of Knowledge." *The Southern Speech Communication Journal* 45 (1980): 133–48.

Nicotera, Anne Mayden and Donald P. Cushman. "Organizational Ethics: A Within-Organization View." *Journal of Applied Communication Research* 20 (1992): 437–62.

Nilsen, Thomas. *Ethics of Speech Communication.* 2nd ed. Indianapolis: Bobbs-Merrill Company, Inc., 1974.

Ostwald, Martin. Introduction. *Nicomachean Ethics.* By Aristotle. Indianapolis: Bobbs-Merrill Company, Inc., 1962. xi–xxiv.

Perelman, Chaim. "The Rhetorical Point of View in Ethics." Trans. D. Raymond Tourville. *Communication* 6 (1981): 315–20.

Rives, Stanley G. "Ethical Argumentation." *The Journal of the American Forensic Association* 1 (1964): 79–85.

Williams, Clifford. "Teaching Virtues and Vices." *Philosophy Today* 33 (1989): 195–203.

⚞ Study Questions ⚟

Ethics in Communication

1. What is ethics?

   _____

   _____

2. Why is communicating ethically important?

   _____

   _____

3. In what way do we incorporate ethics into communicating with others?

   _____

   _____

4. How is the statement, "Ethical communicators are respectful of their audiences," actually put into practice?

   _____

   _____

5. How does the communicator use information ethically?

   _____

   _____

6. What is plagiarism?

   _____

   _____

Communicating with Others One-to-One

KEY CONCEPTS

Interpersonal Communication
  Definition of Interpersonal
    Communication
  Number of People
    Dyadic
    Triadic
  Proximity
    Language in Interpersonal
      Communication
    Feedback in Interpersonal
      Communication
Interpersonal Communication Skills
  Listening
    Definition of Listening
    Listening for Ideas
      Concentrate on the Message
      Listen for Major Ideas
      Link New Knowledge with Old
        Knowledge
      Use Memory Devices
      Ask for Repetition
      Hear the Person Out
      Take Notes
    Listening for Feelings
Conversation
  Nature of Conversation
  Conversational Skills
    Initiating Conversation
      Purpose of Conversational
        Openers

Do Not Worry about Using
  Clichés
Options for Topics
Subject Matter
Maintaining Conversation
  Becoming More Knowledgeable
  Story Telling
  Respond Appropriately
  Reveal Appropriate Information
  Direct Conversation into New
    Areas
  Practice Question Linking
  Nonverbal Behavior to Maintain
    Conversations
Closing Conversations
  Recognize the Conversation
  Present a Pressing Claim
  Offer a Farewell
    Nonverbal Cues
Comforting
  Aim of Comforting
  Empathy
  Nonverbal Behavior in Comforting
  Three Goals of Comforting
    Acknowledge
    Elaborate
    Legitimize
  Showing We Are Available
  Avoid Arguments
  Reflection

Interpersonal Communication

Having discussed the nature of communication in general, we want now to look at the nature of communication in several different settings. The first of these is interpersonal communication which you may recall from its brief introduction in an earlier chapter.

What Is Interpersonal Communication?

Interpersonal communication is the sending and receiving of messages between two parties, usually in close visual and aural proximity which allows for immediate feedback and close attention to verbal and nonverbal cues.

Number of People

The concept of interpersonal communication involves several key ideas. The first is a small number of participants. Often, interpersonal communication is referred to as *dyadic* communication, a term from "dyo," the Greek word for two. The two parties involved in interpersonal communication may be two individuals such as two friends or a husband and wife. The two parties may involve more than two people, however. A couple talking to a real estate agent about a house, for example, would involve three people but two parties, the potential buyers and the agent. The number of parties may be enlarged to three—triadic communication—but when we move beyond three, the people involved begin to take on the characteristics of yet another communication configuration, the small group.

Proximity

Another important element in the creation of interpersonal communication is that the parties are in close proximity. Their communication is usually unmediated. Interpersonal communication, at its fullest, is characterized by being face-to-face communication: a teacher and student talk at the teacher's desk, a physician discusses a set of symptoms with a patient in an examining room, two friends talk over their day's classes across a table in the Student Union snack bar.

This small number of people involved and the close proximity affect the nature of the *language* used in interpersonal communication. In interpersonal communication we usually use language that is less formal than that of written discourse or public speaking (Tannen). We use more pauses, string together more phrases, and use a simpler vocabulary. We also adapt our language very specifically to our audiences. One moment, a person may be babbling nonsense to a child or a pet, and the next moment, the person is discussing the grocery bill with the spouse. Males talking to males will use a different kind of language than they will talking to females or mixed-gender groups, and females will employ a different kind of language depending on whether they are talking to another woman, a male, or a mixed-gender group (Pearson 174–209).

As interpersonal communication takes place between a small number of people who can easily see and hear each other, *feedback* has high importance. Details that may be meaningless in the larger context of a public speech may have great impact on interpersonal communication.

A person, for example, may be involved in what seems to be an engaging conversation. At one point, though, the conversational partner rolls her wrist a

As interpersonal communication takes place between a small number of people who can easily see and hear each other, *feedback* has high importance.

quarter turn and directs her glance downward for half a second. Instead of continuing to lean forward, the first speaker straightens up several inches. The partner picks up her books. The first speaker sits all the way back in his chair. The partner stands and they move into leave-taking phrases. Through a series of small movements and gestures, they have signalled each other that their need or desire to continue the conversation is ending.

Close proximity also means that physical contact is easily made and is often expected. Here a range of activities may be appropriate. Business interviews almost universally open with a handshake, a throwback to an earlier nonverbal gesture when men grasped each other's sword

Interpersonal communication, at its fullest, is characterized by face-to-face communication.

hand to signal that they came in peace. Children may want to be held while a parent comforts them. Latin Americans may give each other a "brazo," a hearty hug as a greeting or parting gesture.

The key elements of small numbers and close proximity with immediate feedback may be modified in some interpersonal situations. A phone conversation is a form of interpersonal communication, but while it involves a small number in close aural proximity, it eliminates all nonverbal cues with the exception of paralinguistics. When one moves to written form of communication—letters, e-mail, computer bulletin boards, notes on the refrigerator—one has eliminated both proximity and immediate feedback. These types of communication fall out of the category of interpersonal communication as it is discussed here.

Interpersonal Communication Skills

Listening

Definition of Listening

When we think of interpersonal communication, we most often think of what we need to do as senders rather than as receivers. Before we can respond appropriately to others, we need to judge the sender, the message, and our possible responses. To do that, we need to exercise good listening skills. Listening, as we define it, is *paying thoughtful attention to the verbal and nonverbal cues of others.*

Listening for Ideas

In listening for ideas, we are trying to gather facts or follow a line of logical thinking. Listening for ideas is the kind of listening that students do as part of the learning process, the kind of listening patients do when doctors explain ailments and medications, and the kind of listening customers do as a mechanic details what is wrong with the car. Here the main goal is the comprehension and retention of information.

One helpful way to retain information is to *link new knowledge with old knowledge.*

To aid the process and listen well, one can *concentrate on the message.* Distractions to good listening are many. We may be thinking of an upcoming vacation rather than attending to the professor's lecture. We may work in an environment with high noise levels. In crowded offices, the conversations around us may distract us. The best course of action in these cases is not to think of the distractions but rather to devote full attention to the message. Concentrating on eliminating the distractions will only create yet another distraction.

Another hindrance to good listening is when a person tries to take in an extended message word for word. Instead, the person should *listen for major ideas.* The major ideas are the foundations of messages. In attending to a lecture, one should pay attention to the main points. In listening to directions about how to reach a given destination, the turns and landmarks become the heart of the message. When the major points are not comprehended, the message will not make sense.

One helpful way to retain information is to *link new knowledge with old knowledge.* Sophisticated computers still use the original "qwerty" typewriter keyboard but add functions to it. If one can transfer the concept of "trump" from one card game to another, the learning time is shortened for the new game.

Tying ideas together can work in other ways as well. One can *use memory devices* to aid the retention of information. People tend to remember visual images more readily than words. Hence, one way to remember a word or concept is to connect the words with an image. The communication term, "feedback," could be recalled by, say, the picture of a small child pushing away his plate. The child would be giving his "feed back" and at the same time illustrating the verbal and nonverbal responses that allow a communicator to adjust future communication. Admittedly, the idea is obvious, even silly, but oftentimes the sillier or more bizarre the image, the easier it is to remember.

Some memory aids require the receiver to provide feedback to the sender. One simple act is to *ask for a repetition of an idea or ask for clarification.*

For accurate listening, one must also be careful not to be too hasty in responding. Often, it is a good idea to *hear the person out* before reacting. Pouncing on the information without hearing the complete message may reduce the amount of information conveyed and unnecessarily complicate the communication.

In talking with her financial aid counselor, Sandy Hargrave heard the counselor say that Hargraves's student loan might be reduced. Hargrave immediately began to object. After several interchanges, the counselor was finally able to follow up the original remark by telling Hargrave that other and better funding was now available.

A final aid to listening for ideas may sound simple, but *taking notes* provides the listener with a concrete collection of information that can be referred to for reference and memorization.

Listening for Feelings

Besides being attentive to facts, good listening is also attentive to feelings. Here comprehension of details is not so important as recognizing what the other person is going through. "My car won't start" may be a statement of fact, but it is also the kind of statement that will carry an emotional message as well. The feeling could be frustration if the intent is "So I missed my French exam, and

I'll have to go through the hassle of talking to the instructor and setting up another time." The statement could convey amusement if it means "I now have the excuse I wanted so I don't have to go to work." Other possibilities would include despondency ("Everything else is going wrong in my life, why not my car as well?") or contemplation ("Maybe I should think about buying a new car.").

To respond effectively, one must pay close attention not only to the words but also to the nonverbal cues. The rise, fall, and inflections of pitch may signal the speaker's feelings as may the volume and speed of the statement. Physical cues may also in-

To respond effectively, one must pay close attention not only to the words of the speaker but also to nonverbal cues.

dicate a person's state. A smile can contradict a seemingly serious statement. Eye blinking, hand movements, or fidgeting may signal the true emotional state of a person who claims, "I don't mind talking about this at all."

Verbal responses will, of course, also signal a person's state. Often though, a person may not come out with a direct statement of feeling such as "I am having a bad semester." Instead, the person may make an observation or indirect statement such as "I wish I could start this semester all over again." In some cases, the purported source of distress may have only the slightest connection with the true problem.

Sorting out the messages a person is sending may be a difficult task. A useful question to ask in these situations is "What would I be feeling if I were saying and doing these things?" (Bolton 57). This response allows people to begin with a known entity, themselves, and apply what they know to an unknown entity, the other person. Even if the first interpretation is not totally accurate, this approach may at least start someone in the right direction. After that, the person can adjust and work toward the most accurate interpretation.

Listening for facts and feelings provides us with a basis for interacting with other people. Good listening skills enhance communication in a variety of settings: in conversation, in comforting, and in conflict resolution.

Conversation

The Nature of Conversation

Conversation is the *informal exchange of opinions and information in which a major component of the process is the pleasure derived from the communication.* Conversation is, in some ways, communication for its own sake. Conversations may impart information or allow the parties to express their feelings, but the primary goal of conversation is the pleasurable exchange of talk, no matter what the topic. As such, conversation is a major ingredient of any number of relationships. One former F.B.I. agent even said that he used conversation as a way of encouraging confession or disclosure of information. In an investigative interview, he said, the first thing to do with the interviewee is to "get him talking about anything" (Wilt).

Listening for facts and feelings provides us with a basis for interacting with other people.

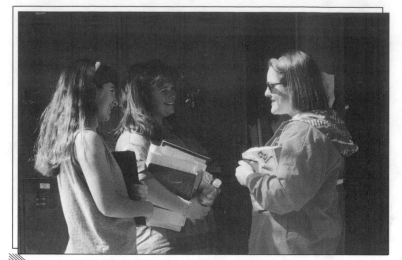

The primary goal of conversation is the pleasurable exchange of talk.

While at first glance, conversation seems to be only "making small talk," we discover on a closer examination that it is a form of communication that involves a number of subtleties. Opening and maintaining conversations demands that we find appropriate ways to approach other people and that together we find a pattern of talk that is mutually acceptable. Having opened the conversation, we must find ways to keep it going. Not only does this process demand attention to the responses of conversational partners, but it also demands our creativity as we phrase responses. Finally, we need to find ways to break off the conversation and part company.

Beyond the basics, our conversational style may indicate not only our thoughts and feelings but may also provide cues as to how our remarks are to be interpreted by our conversational partners.

> **Person A:** "I left my keys in the car."

How is Person B to respond to this remark? The response will depend on a number of contextual factors. A may be recounting a bad incident during the day. In this case, B's response would probably be along the lines of, "What did you do to get into your car?" On the other hand, A's hands may be full with packages and is making a request of B so that B's best response is, "I'll get them for you" (Jacobs and Jackson). Whether the statement is interpreted as a report or a request is determined by the context.

Another of the subtleties we must master is turn-taking, a kind of communicative dance that determines who will speak when and what will be the relationship between the conversational partners. How turn-taking is managed may determine who controls the direction of the conversation, how we are perceived in the conversation, and how topics will be treated (Lerner; Palmer; Drummond; Mandelbaum).

Through a series of different cues, we may also signal a conversational partner that our remarks are not to be interpreted at face value, but rather taken to be a form of verbal play (Glen and Knapp).

> **Person A:** "Did you remember that we are running together today at noon?"
> **Person B:** "I had forgotten. Thanks for jogging my memory."

When we engage in conversation, we involve ourselves in a process of communication that can be not only entertaining but also subtle. Conversation is a basic ingredient of relationships and mastering conversational skills is an important part of becoming a competent communicator.

Conversation is a basic ingredient of relationships and mastering conversational skills is an important part of becoming a competent communicator.

Conversational Skills

The basic conversational skills upon which the subtleties rest are the abilities to initiate, maintain, and close a conversation. How well we master these activities may have a major impact on our lives. One researcher has found, for example, that people with strong feelings of loneliness have difficulty engaging in conversation and "may be perceived as poor candidates for friendship" (Bell 231).

INITIATING CONVERSATION. Opening a conversation, getting the other person to talk, is not always easy. Most of us have been in some social situation in which we wanted desperately to say something but could find no words, or if words came, they were the wrong ones and only deepened the misery or heightened the tension. At other times, though, we may find ourselves in the midst of a pleasant conversation almost without realizing it. How "openers" are phrased can set the tone for what follows.

In opening conversations, it is often helpful to remember the purpose of the opener. It is not intended to convey important information, disclose significant feelings, nor to launch a person into a long term, rewarding relationship. The purpose of a conversational opener is (1) to recognize the other party and (2) to say something that will prompt an appropriate response.

As such, *we do not need to worry about using clichés*. The subject matter of a conversational opener is oftentimes of little importance (Adler 153). Some may refrain from attempting a conversation because they can think of nothing to say that is original or significant. The truth of the matter is that most conversational openers are trite and stereotypical. Realizing that frees us to begin from what is at hand rather than trying to find unique ways to approach each individual we meet.

It is also helpful to remember that in opening conversations, *we have three basic options for topics*. People typically open conversations with remarks about themselves, about the conversational partner, or about the situation (Carnes 70). For example,

Themselves
"Hi, my name is . . . I'm a political science major."
"You won't believe what my math TA did today . . ."
"Man, am I feeling good. I finally got my schedule worked out."

The Other Person
"Whatcha up to?"
"How did you do on the chemistry exam?"
"That's a nice jacket. Where did you get it?"

The Situation
"How about this weather we're having?"
"This stuff tastes pretty good."
"Gee, Toto, this sure doesn't look like Kansas."

The three can, of course, be combined into variations which include two or even all three possibilities as in "What do you think I should do about the English paper we have to write for Thursday?"

Another helpful triad to remember in phrasing conversational openers is the subject matter of the opener. *We can state a fact, give an opinion, or express a feeling* (Adler 154–55). People can phrase these in the form of a statement or the form of a question.

Themselves—facts:

"I'm from . . ." or "Where do you think I'm from?"

The other person—opinions

"I really like the color of your jacket."

The situation—feelings

"I feel lost in a class this size," or "How do you feel about being in a class this big?"

It may also be helpful in starting conversations to remember that failures do not necessarily mean that we are poor conversationalists. Some people are less responsive than others. Some may be unavailable to talk because of the press of other demands. If a conversational opener is unsuccessful, then we should try another approach or try another person. No matter how tempting the bait, not every cast catches a fish.

MAINTAINING CONVERSATION.   Shortly after conversation is initiated, the first major transition arrives. After we have recognized the presence of the other person and made an opening statement or two, we shift the talk to a topic or topics which will allow us to continue, or we break off the conversation and move to a conclusion. If we wish to prolong the conversation, we have a number of avenues available to us.

One useful practice for maintaining conversation occurs before we interact with others. *We become better conversationalists by becoming more knowledgeable and potentially more interesting.* We communicate from our experiences, both personal and vicarious, and if we limit our experiences, we limit our potential areas of discussion. Being informed is a major help to our conversational skills.

Knowledge can come from general reading or specific studies. Being informed about current events, be they international, national, or local, can easily provide material for talk. Staying informed on controversies and issues allows us to make intelligent responses and to ask good questions. We can also do background study for talking with specific people. Perhaps we have been invited to a dinner party and we know one of the guests is a nuclear engineer. Perhaps we will be asked to entertain a campus visitor from Indonesia. Perhaps we have a first date with someone we know is from a rural area and we are urbanites. A few minutes in the library reading encyclopedia or magazine articles about "Nuclear engineering," "Indonesia," or "Agriculture" will provide us with a source of comments and questions.

Another practice useful for maintaining conversations is *paying attention to the stories we hear.* One of our basic human impulses is to recount events in a way that engages the attention of others. Stories may be jokes, but they do not have to be. Some stories are sobering, others scary, and still others whimsical. People enjoy hearing a well-told story, even if it is only a minute or two in length. Honing our story-telling skills provides us with another element to add to our conversations.

Once conversation is engaged, it can be sustained by *making responses appropriate to what is being said.* When one person responds to another with a *non sequitur,* the conversation is likely to come to an abrupt halt.

> **Person A:**   What do you think we should do about our communication class small group project?"

> One of our basic human impulses is to recount events in a way that engages the attention of others.

Person B: "I have always hated lima beans."

or

Person A: "I am from Jakarta, the capital of Indonesia."

Person B: "How do you think the Cowboys will do in their game against the Giants?"

Besides listening for ideas and tying our responses to them, we need also to be sensitive to the feelings expressed by conversational partners. Conversations are far more likely to be successful when people show themselves sympathetic to what the other person is expressing.

Person A: "I just broke up with my boyfriend."

Person B: "Splitting up can really hurt."

or

Person A: "I sometimes find it hard to understand the English you speak here."

Person B: "That must make school doubly difficult."

One of the ingredients of conversation—and other relationships as well—is that of self disclosure. If the revelations are well timed, they can be an encouragement to deepening the relationship whether the relationship be a first meeting or a long-term relationship. We encourage conversational partners to communicate more freely when *we reveal appropriate information about ourselves.* By "appropriate information," we mean those personal facts which are in keeping with the level of the relationship. Obviously, we would not tell someone we are meeting for the first time the same kind of personal information we would reveal to our best friend.

Often, when one person reveals personal information, the other party will respond in kind. This kind of pattern is often observed in the early stages of conversations.

Person A: "I live in Owens Hall."

Person B: "I live in Earhart Hall."

or

Person A: "I did not realize how big this campus was until I started walking to all my classes."

Person B: "I think I have a quarter mile hike from my biology class to my PE class."

Another way a conversation can be maintained is *by directing it into new areas.* When we have reached the limits of a topic, we introduce a second, much in the same way we would open a conversation initially. If two people have been talking about sports and have said all they wish to say about the school's football team, they switch and begin talking about the basketball team. Having talked about the industry of a country, the topic could switch to urban life, agricultural practices, the educational system, or scenic places.

A useful technique for discovering new areas of conversation and to explore established areas is to *practice question linking.* In this procedure, one listens to what the conversational partner says, then "links" the response, in the form of a question, to information the conversational partner has revealed.

have become something of a cliché, the basic direction is still valid. In fact, if one cannot think of anything to say, the formula works well as a starter. As one's skills increase, the reflective statement will become more sophisticated, but the basic goal is still to recognize and describe the other's feelings. The point of reflecting is to help the other person "recognize and clarify the emotions which he feels" (Rogers 27).

Some examples of reflective responses are these:

Person A: "I don't know what I am going to do."
Person B: "You feel trapped with no outlet."
Person A: "This is awful."
Person B: "You really feel bad."
Person A: "I have to go home for my grandmother's funeral."
Person B: "It sounds like a bad time for you."

One problem to avoid with reflection is parroting rather than reflecting. Parroting is when, instead of rephrasing and clarifying a feeling, a person just says back what the partner said originally.

Person A: "I don't know what I'm going to do."
Person B: "You don't know what you are going to do."
Person A: "This is awful."
Person B: "Your situation is awful."

Dealing with someone in need of comfort may be uncomfortable at first. Wanting to do something but unsure of what to do, people may be motivated more by discomfort than charity. The above ideas will make comforting an easier process. The presence of another willing to listen is in itself a comfort. When that person can listen empathically and encouragingly, a great deal will be accomplished.

Conclusion

Interpersonal communication involves us with others on a personal level. Our verbal and nonverbal behavior, used in a variety of ways, create and sustain our relationships. Three of the major skills we use to foster relationships are listening, conversation, and comforting. Conversation is communication for the pleasure of exchanging views and feelings with others. Comforting is using communication to alleviate the problems of another.

Guidelines exist for all these activities, but practice is necessary to do them well. Sensitivity and judgment are needed to know when and how to use different styles of communication. Capable communicators are those who

\\\\ Conflict is an inevitable component of human relationships.

can respond with insight, empathy, and clarity. Communication offers challenges in even daily contacts, but when met, the challenges lead us to enriched and rewarding lives.

Discussion Questions ///

1. What situations can you think of that would be classified as interpersonal communication?

2. How would you think that language in an interpersonal situation would differ from language in a public setting? How would it differ from the language in a magazine or newspaper article? Why would the language of interpersonal communication be different from that of other modes of communication?

3. What kinds of actions contribute nonverbally in interpersonal communication?

4. What situations have you been in where listening for ideas was important?

5. How does listening for feelings differ from listening for ideas?

6. In what instances have you found it difficult to carry on a conversation?

7. What kind of person do you want to talk to when you are having problems? What makes you want to talk with this person?

Sources and References ///

Adler, R. A. *Confidence in Communication: A Guide to Assertive Social Skills*. New York: Holt, Rinehart and Winston, 1977.

Alberts, J. K. "Perceived Effectiveness of Couples' Conversational Complaints." *Communication Studies* 40 (1989): 280–92.

Beach, Wayne. "Forward: Sequential Organization of Conversational Activities." *Western Journal of Speech Communication* 53 (1989): 85–90.

Bell, Robert A. "Conversational Involvement and Loneliness." *Communication Monographs* 52 (1985): 218–35.

Berryman-Fink, Cynthia and Claire C. Brunner. "The Effects of Sex of Source and Target on Interpersonal Conflict Management Styles." *The Southern Speech Communication Journal* (1987): 38–48.

Bies, Robert J., Debra L. Shapiro, and Larry L. Cummings. "Causal Accounts and Managing Organizational Conflict: Is It Enough to Say It's Not My Fault?" *Communication Research* 15 (1988): 381–99.

Bulton, R. *People Skills*. Englewood Cliffs, New Jersey: Prentice-Hall, 1979.

Burleson, Brant R. "Comforting as Social Support: Relational Consequences of Supportive Behaviors." *Personal Relationship and Social Support*. Ed. Steve Ducks. London: Sage Publications, 1990.

———. "Comforting Communication." *Communication by Children and Adults: Social Cognitive and Strategic Processes.* Eds. Howard E. Sypher and James L. Applegate. Beverly Hills, California: Sage Publications, 1984.

———. "The Production of Comforting Messages: Social-Cognitive Foundations." *Journal of Language and Social Psychology* 4 (1985): 253–73.

———. "Social Cognition, Empathic Motivation, and Adults' Comforting Strategies." *Human Communication Research* 10 (1983): 295–304.

Burleson, Brant R. and Wendy Samter. "Consistencies in Theoretical and Naive Evaluations of Comforting Messages." *Communication Monographs* 52 (1985): 103–23.

———. "Individual Differences in the Perception of Comforting Messages: An Exploratory Investigation." *Central States Speech Journal* 36 (1985): 39–50.

Burrell, Nancy A., William A. Donohue, and Mike Allen. "Gender-Based Perceptual Biases in Mediation." *Communication Research* 15 (1988): 447–70.

Canary, Daniel J. and Brian H. Spitzberg. "Attribution Biases and Associations between Conflict Strategies and Competence Outcomes." *Communication Monographs* 57 (1990): 139–51.

Canary, Daniel J., Ellen M. Cunningham, and Michael J. Cody. "Goal Types, Gender, and Locus of Control in Managing Interpersonal Conflict." *Communication Research* 15 (1988): 426–46.

Courtright, John A., Frank E. Millar, L. Edna Rogers, and Dennis Bagarozzi. "Interaction Dynamics of Relational Negotiation: Reconciliation versus Termination of Distress Relationships." *Western Journal of Speech Communication* (1990): 429–53.

Donohue, William A., Mike Allen, and Nancy Burrell. "Mediator Communicative Competency." *Communication Monographs* 55 (1988): 104–19.

Drummond, Kent. "A Backward Glance at Interruptions." *Western Journal of Speech Communication* 53 (1989): 150–166.

Ewbank, H. L. "The Rhetoric of Conversation in America: 1776–1828." *The Southern Speech Communication Journal* 53 (1987): 49–64.

Fisher, Roger and William Ury. *Getting to Yes: Negotiating Without Giving In.* New York: Penguin Books, 1983.

Garner, Alan. *Conversationally Speaking.* New York: McGraw-Hill, 1981.

Glenn, Phillip J. "Initiating Shared Laughter in Multi-Party Conversations." *Western Journal of Speech Communication* 53 (1989): 127–49.

Glenn, Phillip J. and Mark L. Knapp. "The Interactive Framing of Play in Adult Conversations." *Communication Quarterly* 35 (1987): 48–66.

Hopper, Robert. "Speech in Telephone Openings: Emergent Interaction v. Routines." *Western Journal of Speech Communication* 53 (1989): 178–94.

Infante, Dominic A., Teresa Chandler, Jill E. Rudd, and Elizabeth A. Shannon. "Verbal Aggression in Violent and Nonviolent Marital Disputes." *Communication Quarterly* 38 (1990): 361–71.

Jacobs, Scott and Sally Jackson. "Strategy and Structure in Conversational Influence Attempts." *Communication Monographs* 50 (1983): 285–304.

Jones, Tricia S. "Phase Structures in Agreement and No-Agreement Mediation." *Communication Research* 15 (1988): 470–95.

Knapp, Mark L., Roderick P. Hart, Gustav W. Friedrich, and Gary Shulman. "The Rhetoric of Goodbye: Verbal and Nonverbal Correlates of Human Leave-Taking." *Communication Monographs* 60 (1973): 182–98.

Lerner, Gene H. "Notes on Overlap Management in Conversation: The Case of Delayed Completion." *Western Journal of Speech Communication* 53 (1989): 167–77.

Mandelbaum, Jenny. "Interpersonal Activities in Conversational Storytelling." *Western Journal of Speech Communication* 53 (1989): 114–27.

Maynard, Douglas M. "Perspective-Display Sequences in Conversation." *Western Journal of Speech Communication* 53 (1989): 91–114.

Millar, Frank E., L. Edna Rogers, and Janet Beavin Bavelas. "Identifying Patterns of Verbal Conflict in Interpersonal Dyads." *Western Journal of Speech Communication* 48 (1984): 231–46.

Palmer, Mark T. "Controlling Conversations: Turns, Topics and Interpersonal Control." *Communication Monographs* 56 (1989): 1–18.

Papa, Michael and Elizabeth J. Natalie. "Gender, Strategy Selection, and Discussion Satisfaction in Interpersonal Conflict." *Western Journal of Speech Communication* 53 (1989): 260–72.

Papa, Michael and Elliott A. Pood. "Coorientational Accuracy and Differentiation in the Management of Conflict." *Communication Research* 15 (1988): 400–425.

Patterson, C. H. *Theories of Counseling and Psychotherapy.* 4th ed. New York: Harper and Row, Publishers, 1986.

Pearson, Judy Cornelia. *Gender and Communication.* Dubuque, Iowa: William C. Brown, Publishers, 1985.

Putnam, Linda L. and Joseph Folger. "Communication, Conflict, and Dispute Resolution: The Study of Interaction and the Development of Conflict Theory." *Communication Research* 15 (1988): 349–59.

Rawlins, William K. *Friendship Matters: Communication, Dialectics, and the Life Course.* New York: Aldine de Gruyter, 1992.

———. "Openness as Problematic in Ongoing Friendships: Two Conversational Dilemmas." *Communication Monographs* 50 (1983): 1–13.

Rogers, Carl A. *Client-Centered Therapy: Its Current Practice, Implications, and Theory.* Boston: Houghton Mifflin Company. 1951.

Samter, Wendy and Brant R. Burleson. "Cognitive and Motivational Influences on Spontaneous Comforting Behavior." *Contemporary Perspectives on Interpersonal Communication.* Eds. S. Petronio, J. K. Alberts, M. L. Hect, and J. Buley. Madison, Wisconsin: Brown and Benchmark (1993): 297–316.

Samter, Wendy and Brant Burleson. "Evaluations of Communication Skills as Predictors of Peer Acceptance and a Group Living Situation." *Communication Studies* 41 (1990): 311–25.

Samter, Wendy, Brant R. Burleson, and Lori Basden Murphy. "Comforting Conversations: The Effects of Strategy Type on Evaluations of Messages and Message Producers." *The Southern Speech Communication Journal* 52 (1987): 263–84.

Sereno, Kenneth K., Melinda Welch, and David Braaten. "Interpersonal Conflict: Effects of Variations in Manner of Expressing Anger and Justification for Anger Upon Perceptions of Appropriateness, Competence, and Satisfaction." *Journal of Applied Communication Research* 15 (1987): 128–43.

Sillars, Alan L. "Attributions and Communication in Roommate Conflicts." *Communication Monographs* 47 (1980): 180–201.

Tannen, Deborah. "Spoken and Written Narrative in English and Greek." *Coherence in Spoken and Written Discourse.* Ed. Deborah Tannan. Norwood, New Jersey: Ablex Publishing Corp., 1984. 21–41.

Tutzauer, Frank and Michael E. Roloff. "Communication Processes Leading to Integrative Agreements: Three Paths of Joint Benefits." *Communication Research* 15 (1988): 360–80.

Waln, Virginia G. "Questions in Interpersonal Conflict: Participant and Observer Perceptions." *The Southern Speech Communication Journal* 49 (1984): 277–89.

Wilt, Frederick. Conversation with the author.

Witteman, Hal. "Interpersonal Problem Solving: Problem Conceptualization and Communication Use." *Communication Monographs* 55 (1988): 336–59.

※ Study Questions ※

Interpersonal Communication

1. How is interpersonal communication defined?

   _____

   _____

2. What is dyadic communication?

   _____

   _____

3. When communicators are in close proximity, what does that mean?

   _____

   _____

4. What is characteristic of the language used in interpersonal communication?

   _____

   _____

5. How important is the role of feedback in interpersonal communication versus in public speaking?

   _____

   _____

6. What is listening?

   _____

   _____

7. While listening for facts or ideas, it is advisable to practice good listening skills. List seven suggestions for good listening.

   1. _____

   2. _____

3. _____

4. _____

5. _____

6. _____

7. _____

8. How can you listen for feelings?

9. How is conversation distinguished from other types of communication?

10. What is the two-fold purpose of a conversational opener?

    1. _____

    2. _____

11. What are the three basic options for topics in conversational openings?

    1. _____

    2. _____

    3. _____

12. In what three ways can subject matter be treated in openings?

    1. _____

    2. _____

    3. _____

13. Seven suggestions are given for helping to maintain a conversation once it has been initiated. List those suggestions.

    1. _____

    2. _____

    3. _____

    4. _____

5. _____

6. _____

7. _____

14. What is question linking?

_____

_____

15. Suggest four different ways you can close a conversation.

1. _____

2. _____

3. _____

4. _____

16. What is comforting communication?

_____

17. What is empathy?

_____

18. How is comforting communication distinguished from conversation?

_____

_____

19. What is meant by elaborating?

_____

20. What is meant by legitimizing?

_____

21. What three things can you do to meet the goals of acknowledging, elaborating and legitimizing in comforting conversation?

1. _____

2. _____

3. _____

◈ Conversation Stoppers Exercise ◈

The conversational remarks below are followed by inappropriate responses: 1) tell what is wrong with the inappropriate response, and 2) phrase a better response.

1. "Tell me about yourself."
   "There's not much to tell."

2. "What happened at school today?"
   "Nothing much."

3. "I'm from _____."
   "I went through there once. It looked real run down."

4. "I just bought a Fiat."
   "Why did you buy a loser like that?"

5. "Boy, do I feel good. I got an *A* in my Shakespeare class."
   "Big deal."

6. "I have to get a good job this summer."
   "My family has enough money that I don't have to work."

7. "I think that's the best Chinese restaurant in town."
   "Chinese food—yuk!"

8. "What are you majoring in?"
   "High level nuclear physics. It's not something you could understand."

9. "Hot enough for you?"
   "No. I'm seriously thinking of moving to Death Valley."

10. "What did you think about last night's game?"
    "I don't go to the games. I think basketball is dumb."

11. "That was a great movie, wasn't it?"
    "If you say so."

12. "Pretty day, isn't it?"
    "It's supposed to rain this afternoon."

13. "Look at my engagement ring."
    "That's a small stone."

14. "I lost ten pounds."
    "You still look chunky."

15. "How do you like my new shoes?"
    "I don't think that style looks good on feet as large as yours."

⚞ People Search ⚟

Find someone in this class who meets one of the criteria. Write down the person's name. Then discover something you have in common with this person other than attending college and being in this class. You may not use the same person for more than one item. Find someone who

1. knows the capital of Venezuela:
   We have in common:

2. has blue eyes:
   We have in common:

3. knows how to ride a horse:
   We have in common:

4. is from Illinois:
   We have in common:

5. has sung in a choir:
   We have in common:

6. likes Mexican food:
   We have in common:

7. can juggle:
   We have in common:

8. was in a high school dance troupe:
   We have in common:

9. can't stand professional wrestling:
   We have in common:

10. traveled outside the U.S. this past year:
    We have in common:

11. can drive a tractor:
    We have in common:

12. knows the chemical formula for sulphuric acid:
    We have in common:

⟩⟩ Comforting Responses Exercise ⟨⟨

For each of these statements choose what you think would be the most comforting response. Tell why you think that response is the best. If none of the responses seem appropriate, write one of your own.

1. "I just got my grades. My GPA isn't high enough to get into the program I want."
   A. You need to study harder.
   B. Some people are smart enough for that field, and others aren't.
   C. How high a GPA do you need?
   D. That's tough to deal with.

2. "My car broke down in the middle of a busy intersection. Everyone was honking and shouting at me. I had to have the car towed to a shop. Then they told me it would cost eight hundred dollars to have it fixed."
   A. I kept telling you to have that funny noise checked.
   B. What did the shop say was wrong with it?
   C. You've really had a bad day.
   D. It could be worse.

3. "I feel so nervous about giving this speech."
   A. Getting up in front of a group can be intimidating.
   B. Just cool it. Chill out.
   C. Why do you think you're so nervous?
   D. Giving speeches is easy. I've never had any problems with them.

4. "I don't know how I'm going to get all this work done."
   A. You need to develop better time management skills.
   B. You sound as if you're really feeling the pressure.
   C. Why have you let yourself get so behind?
   D. Is there anything I can do to help you?

5. "I feel so stupid. The cashier shortchanged me and I just stood there and took it."
   A. It's only money.
   B. You have eyes. You have a brain. Count it yourself next time.
   C. I've done the same thing. I felt dumb, too.
   D. How much did you come up short?

6. "My folks just called and told me my dog died."
   A. Dogs' life expectancies are shorter than humans'. You just have to be prepared for these things.
   B. You feel as if you just lost an old friend?
   C. Dogs are dogs. You can always get another one.
   D. You haven't lived at home for three years. What's the big deal?

7. "_____ said something to me that really hurts my feelings."
   A. Just remember, "Sticks and stones may break my bones, but words can never hurt me."
   B. Call him up and tell him off.
   C. Really stabbed you, huh?
   D. What did he say?

8. "I let my group down in our presentation."
   A. The way you've been acting lately, I'm not surprised.
   B. You feel you failed them?
   C. From what you've told me, they're all idiots anyway. Don't worry about it.
   D. You never were much good at making presentations.

9. "You would never understand."
   A. Of course I would. I have taken a communication class.
   B. If you're going to be secretive, we're not going to get anywhere.
   C. Maybe I will, maybe I won't.
   D. Try me.

10. "My roommate is the most incredible slob. I can't stand living with her."
    A. Sounds as if you have a real mess to contend with.
    B. You're just compulsive.
    C. Use better judgment the next time you pick a roommate.
    D. You could solve the problem easily enough. Just clean up for both of you.

The Nature of Groups

6

KEY CONCEPTS

Defining Small Groups
  Number
  Access
  Common Goal
  Interaction
Small Group Purposes
  Social Groups
  Study Groups
  Therapy Groups
  Support Groups
  Problem Solving Groups
  Bargaining Groups
  Work Teams
  Membership and Roles
Forms of Small Groups
  Size
  Life Span
    Zero History Group
    Ad Hoc Group
    Ongoing Group
Groups' Two Inevitable Tasks
  Creating Relationships
  Accomplishing Tasks

Stages of Groups
  Orientation
  Sorting Out
   Norms
  Settle Down to Work
Groups Are Created by
    Communication
  More Than the Sum of Parts
  Group Climate
  Activities
    Inclusion and Exclusion
    Boundary Maintenance
    Decision Making
    Support
    Creating Identities
  Balancing Group Tensions
    Personal/Group Desires
    Internal/External Demands
    Individuality/Conformity
    Concentration/Relaxation

Amanda Phillips is a junior who lives in the Helen Magill White Cooperative House. A cooperative housing unit is a self-governing group that lives off campus. Members perform many of the tasks necessary to maintain the property and to provide services for the members.

Amanda has an early history class, so she gets up in time to eat breakfast. As she does most mornings, she sits with Susana, Emily, and Katrina. As they eat, they chat about classes, dates, their families, and other topics. After breakfast, they walk together to campus where they split up to go to different buildings.

After her history class, Amanda and four others in the class make arrangements to meet in the Undergraduate Library that evening to review their notes and help each other prepare for the upcoming exam.

During the lunch hour, she works as a server at the Student Union cafeteria.

Returning to the house, she does her assigned duty on the cleaning crew, vacuuming the downstairs. She also cleans the stairs that are not her duty, but she is substituting for Cheryl who will do the floors for her tomorrow. Later, the group will work on the special project it chose, cleaning the entryway carpeting.

After dinner, Amanda and the other members of their house's basketball team go the Student Gym to play an intramural game.

Later in the week, Amanda will attend a Bible study, make a group presentation in a computer engineering class, and meet with her co-travelers to plan their spring break trip to South Padre. She will also meet with her two roommates to find out who has been taking her soft drinks out of their refrigerator without telling her.

> The concept of a small group implies that *members all have access to each other.*

The Nature of Small Groups

Like Amanda, we find ourselves inescapably involved with groups and can look forward to continued group work throughout our lives. Fortunately, over the past several decades, information about small group communication has expanded widely. The result is that we have available a large amount of ideas and insights that can help us to function more effectively in the groups to which we belong. This chapter will describe what small groups are, the dynamics of small groups, and how small groups function.

Small Groups Are . . .

A small group can be defined by several parameters. The first and most obvious is number. What size must a group be to be a "small group"? Two people communicating are not a small group but are, rather, a *dyad*. Dyadic communication can create only one relationship: A-B. With three people, the situation becomes more complex as three people can create four times as many relationships as can two: A-B, A-C, B-C, A-B-C. Hence, we set the minimal number for a small group at three.

The upper limit is not so clear. The concept of a small group implies that *members all have access to each other.* As a group grows in size, access becomes more and more difficult to achieve. When a group reaches 12 to 15 members, it begins to fracture into sub-groups because it becomes too hard for members to link to everyone in the group. It has also been noted that the larger the group, the less members participate (Poole and Hirokawa 7).

"Small group communication" also implies that *group members are united by a common goal.* Amanda could go to the living room at the White House to read a magazine. Four other people could be in the room, reading, napping, or watching television. While the five people constitute an appropriate number for a small group, they would not be considered such because they are simply a collection of people. Each one is pursuing her own goal.

A common type of group is the study group.

It could be, though, that the television set is not functioning well. One comments on the situation. Another adds that the set is becoming worse and worse. All five join in the discussion. They resolve to see that the problem is solved. One volunteers to call to see how much it would cost to repair the set. Another offers to check on the prices of new sets. They agree to meet later and create a proposal to present at an upcoming house meeting.

The five now constitute a small group as they are more than people occupying the same space. They are now joined in purpose with each member contributing her efforts.

Finally, a small group implies *interaction.* If people do not communicate with each other, the group dies. If a group is to achieve its purpose, the members must engage in productive communication.

When we combine these characteristics, we create a definition of a small group: *A small group is a collection of people, usually three to 12, who attempt through communication to achieve a common goal.*

Groups Serve a Number of Purposes

Small groups are extremely adaptable, and we may find ourselves involved in a number of groups, each one existing for a different purpose.

Social Groups

People create *social groups* for the pleasure of enjoying each other's company. Rather than leaving meetings to chance, they plan times to be together and design activities to enhance their interaction. As Amanda and her friends share a table at breakfast, they become a social group. Other social groups would be meetings such as bridge foursomes, golf foursomes, clubs, and "game groups" or "theatre groups," people who attend events together.

Study Groups

Another type of group would be a *study* group. Many students find it helpful to meet with others in the same class to review notes, share ideas, review materi-

If a group is to achieve its purpose, the members must engage in productive communication.

als, and prepare for exams. Extracurricularly, students may join groups devoted to caving, riding horses, studying Indian philosophy, obtaining pilots' licenses, or gaming on the internet. Students in graduate school, medical school, and law school often use groups to master the large amounts of material they must cover. Outside of academics, people may join a group that meets to study and discuss religion, dog training, creative writing, car repair, radio-controlled airplanes, photography, or a wide range of other topics.

Therapy and Support Groups

The need for help gives rise to other types of groups. When faced with difficult situations, we may seek the company of others who have a similar problem. A *therapy group* is a group directed by a professional counselor who leads the group in discussing their situations. Therapy groups may form to address any number of needs: eating disorders, substance abuse, social anxiety, depression, relational problems, or grief.

Similar to a therapy group is a *support group*. Here people share their thoughts, feelings, and experiences but without the guidance of a professional therapist. The more experienced members of the group supply the leadership. These may help people to deal with problems similar to those encountered in therapy groups: alcoholism, an alcoholic parent, loss of a child, gambling, work-related stress, or dealing with diseases such as Alzheimer's, cystic fibrosis, or multiple sclerosis.

Problem Solving Groups

A very common type of small group is a *problem solving* group. Here the group addresses a significant difficulty with the goal of alleviating or eliminating it. The White House may discover that the circuit breakers in its electrical system are tripping at critical times and disrupting people's schedules. The maintenance committee investigates the situation, proposes a plan to upgrade electrical service, and presents it to the house for approval.

Bargaining Groups

Some groups grow predominantly out of work environments. A *bargaining group* comes into existence when contractual agreements are to be decided through discussion by two groups of opposing viewpoints. These could be teachers and the school board's negotiating team, labor and management, or competing divisions in the same company. They discuss their interpretations of the situation and propose courses of action. The bargaining process is a particularly interesting type of group activity as it begins with two groups and ends with one. For a successful conclusion to bargaining, the two opposing viewpoints must be blended into one viewpoint that both sides accept.

Work Teams

Work teams are increasingly a part of factories, maintenance facilities, and other corporate undertakings. These are essentially ongoing problem solving groups that accomplish a series of tasks cooperatively. Instead of work being a series of independent steps done by individuals, work becomes the concerted effort of a group that addresses the entire task. We will discuss work teams in more detail in a later chapter.

Memberships and Roles

Groups may be peopled in different ways. We can belong to each type of group and see a different set of people as each group meets. We may also belong to each type of group and see the same people at every meeting.

A family is perhaps the best example of the latter. At various times, it may configure itself as each kind of group:

> social group: taking a vacation, eating out, going to a movie or concert
> study group: learning how to use the new computer
> therapy group: family counseling, grief seminar
> support group: consoling each other
> problem-solving: where to go on vacation, how to finance college, buying
>   a new car
> bargaining: "We think we need our allowances raised."
> work team: raking leaves, cooking dinner, accomplishing household chores

Groups Exist in Different Forms

As groups exist for a variety of reasons, they will take different forms in response to their needs.

Size

Groups may vary in the number of members. If three people can accomplish a task well, it makes little sense to add more members to the group. On other occasions, a large group may be necessary to accumulate the amount of information necessary to make good decisions.

Life Span

Groups also exist for varying lengths of time. A *zero history group* is one that has just come into existence (Bormann and Bormann 98). All members are new to the group, and they must work through all the stages of group development to become a functioning body. They are "a diffuse and unfocused symbolic and social entity," that is, they do not yet share a common vision nor do they know the roles they will play in the group (Bormann in Hirokawa and Poole. *Decision Making* 104).

The shortest-lived group is probably an *ad hoc* (Latin for "to the thing") group. These are zero history groups formed to address a specific problem or situation. Once the prob-

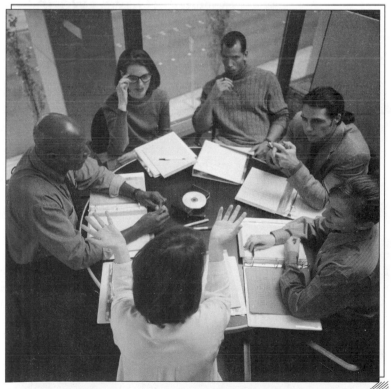

Group climate can be a strong indicator if whether a group will succeed or fail.

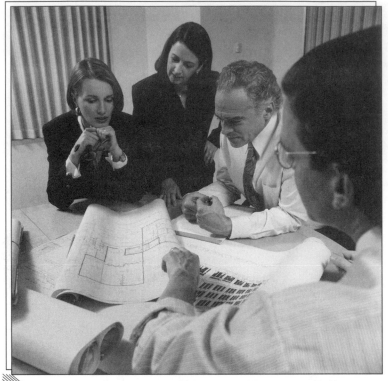

A problem-solving group will confront difficulties and discover effective ways to deal with them.

lem has been dealt with satisfactorily, the group disbands or reconstitutes itself as an ongoing group.

At the other end of the time spectrum are *ongoing groups* that address continuous needs and thus are groups with a past, present, and future. Often, these groups have been in existence far longer than the terms of their members. Group members come and go, but the group goes on.

An organization such as the White House Co-op has a full range of groups. Ongoing groups would be committees such as the finance committee, social activities committee, and maintenance, committees that have existed since the house was chartered.

Other committees are formed as necessary. If, for example, the cook at the White House left, the house would create an *ad hoc* committee to find her replacement. Once the new cook was hired, this group would no longer be needed, and it would disband.

Groups Have Two Inevitable Tasks

Whatever the history of a group or whatever the purpose of a group, groups have two tasks they must attend to if they are to be successful: creating relationships and accomplishing tasks.

Creating Relationships

It is obvious that social groups would be involved in creating relationships. After all, the enjoyment of other's company, enhancing relationships, is the fundamental reason these groups exist. On the other hand, relationships may seem a remote concern of a group such as an *ad hoc* problem-solving committee that meets only a few times and whose members have no professional or personal contacts outside the meetings. On the contrary, relationships are very important to the *ad hoc* committee, but its relationships will be different than those of a social group.

Even though its existence is brief, the *ad hoc* committee will need to become a network of positive relationships if it is to be successful. It will need to create leadership. It will need to create a way of doing business. It will need to create an atmosphere harmonious enough that group members will work together to accomplish its goals.

Accomplishing Tasks

Tasks are the jobs, the work that group must do to accomplish its goals. A problem-solving *ad hoc* group will be very strongly task oriented. Its primary goal is to find a solution to a difficult situation. It has neither the time nor the resources to work on building strong, ongoing relationships.

While good company is the goal of a social group, the members must also tend to a number of tasks that will support the group's friendly interaction. If the details are left unattended, the quality of the gatherings will subsequently suffer. Someone must tend to jobs such as coordinating meeting times, furnishing food, or buying tickets.

Groups Move (Back and Forth) between Stages

Whether a group is a zero history group or an ongoing group, it will work through various stages. A variety of terminologies have been used to describe these steps. For our purposes, we will discuss three stages: orientation, organization, and settling down to work.

Orientation

The first step is *orientation*. In travel, "orientation" means getting our bearings or figuring out where we are in relation to the points of a compass. In small groups, orientation means much the same thing in that the group has to discover a direction for itself.

In this stage, the relationship aspect of the group will be foremost. Finding themselves in a strange, unknown set of relationships, group members will try to sort out how they will behave in this particular group.

It is in this early stage that the group's first leader or leaders will emerge. The process of leadership selection is two fold. The group's first task is to select people unsuited to the job. Once the untalented or reluctant are removed from consideration, the group accepts the remaining person or goes through the throes of deciding between two or more contenders for leadership (Bormann and Bormann 100).

With established groups, orientation will not be as obvious as it is in the beginning stages of a zero history group, but it will still be a necessary function. The introduction of new members, the exit of old members, a change in purpose, the discovery of a new problem, even a change of meeting place may necessitate that group members adjust their relationships.

> In the process of sorting out, groups create *norms* for themselves, *written or unwritten guidelines for how they will behave and function within the group.*

Sorting Out

The second stage is *sorting out*. With the creation of at least a temporary set of relationships, the group turns its attention to how it will accomplish its business. In this phase, the group places primary importance on task. In the process of sorting out, groups create *norms* for themselves, *written or unwritten guidelines for how they will behave and function within the group.*

Groups are collections of individuals, yet they are more than the sum of their parts.

Zero history groups will probably have to devote more effort to the sorting out stage than will established groups. Still, established groups will have to go through sorting out periodically as relationships and tasks change. Decisions made earlier will not always fit the present situation.

Settle Down to Work

The next stage is *settle down to work*. Again, task aspects are foremost. The group has decided, for the most part, questions of who is to do what and how the work is to be done. Now the group attacks its assigned problem and marshals its forces to work toward a solution.

While we discuss these steps of group development in chronological order, in practice groups may work through them in different sequences. Some groups progress straightforwardly. Others move more in a circular fashion. After settling down to work and accomplishing its goal, a group may return to the orientation stage as it redirects itself toward its next assignment. Whatever the order, groups must meet the challenges of each stage if they are to succeed.

Groups Create, Sustain, and Mold Themselves through Communication

Out of the collection of individuals, the group has to create an entity that links all its members together.

A functioning small group is not static. It is brought into being as people communicate, and it sustains itself by ongoing communication. The nature of that communication gives each group its particular character. As one scholar has pointed out, a group's "shared history, constructed socially over time through language, arguments, stories, and symbols, represents a `deepstructure' that influences the 'surface structure' of a group's interactional patterns and decision making" (Frey in Poole and Hirokawa *Decision Making* 19).

Groups are More than the Sum of their Parts

At first glance, it would seem that the way to create an effective group is to bring together talented people. Assembling capable members is certainly an important step, but it is only the first step. Out of the collection of individuals, the group has to create an entity that links all its members together.

One of the best teams in the history of professional basketball—some would argue THE best—was the Chicago Bulls in the mid-nineties. Its roster included Michael Jordan, Scotty Pippin, and Dennis Rodman, all highly talented athletes but widely different in personality, temperament, and outlook. The other players added to the mix.

Had the players been sent to play as five individuals, they probably would have some success. What raised them to greatness was that, as the coach, Phil Jackson, put it, we created a "we" out of five "me's." The players realized that their goal of a championship was beyond their individual reaches and only through cooperation and mutual aid could they be successful. The combination of talent and successful group formation propelled them to championships (Jackson).

Groups Create a Group Climate

As group members interact with each other, they create a "climate" for the group. Just as "climate" indicates the nature of our geographic environment—cold, rainy, sunny, or cloudy with a thirty percent chance of precipitation—"climate" in the contexts of small groups will indicate the group's environment.

Some groups seem to be characterized by congeniality, mutual support, and creativity, and they are highly successful in achieving their goals. Other groups may create an atmosphere of tension and ill will. No leaders emerge. The more members attempt to communicate, the more angry and hateful they become.

The creation of group climate is not the work of one person nor is it a short-term activity. It is the product of members' total input to the group, even the person who says or does little.

Group climate is *pervasive* as it characterizes the group for a relatively *long period of time*. Two group members may become upset and argue loudly. The climate of the group is not determined by that one argument but by the inter-action that preceded it and the interaction which follows it. If the group's clime is one of distrust and antagonism, the argument will be another black cloud on the group's horizon. If the group constructively handles the conflict, the argu-ment can be a plus for the group.

Group climate is also pervasive in that the climate is perceived by more than one or two members. *Climate characterizes the group as a whole.* All mem-bers experience the tension, the cooperation, the distrust, or the mutual sup-port of the group.

Bringing these ideas together, we can define "group climate" as *"the rela-tively enduring quality of the group situation that (a) is experienced in common by group members, and (b) arises from and influences their interaction and behavior"* (Folger and Poole 84).

Groups Create Themselves through a Variety of Activities

In accomplishing their tasks, small groups display an interesting pattern of creation and self-regulation. For a group to function, its members must work out patterns of interaction acceptable to the group. Having worked out a pat-tern that allows them to interact, they are then able to change that pattern through the very interaction it allows. Thus, groups define themselves and, by their defining, open the way to changes in that definition (Putnam and Stohl 258; Poole, Seibold, and McPhee 84).

Inclusion and Exclusion

One of the first things a group will need to decide is *inclusion and exclusion,* who is to be admitted and who is not, who is to continue working with the group and who is to be expelled. In some groups, the process is done by appointment and membership is for a fixed term. An administrator, a nominating committee, or a legislative body may make the appointment. With other groups, the group members themselves decide who will be recruited or admitted. Here selection is done by such methods as self-selection, screening, and elections.

Amanda's cleaning committee came into existence by selection. She and the others volunteered for duty by signing up for a specific week on the clean-ing calendar.

Boundary Maintenance

Similarly, groups must also practice *boundary maintenance.* Groups must have some way of telling who is a member and who is not. If it is impossible to tell who is a member of a given group, then the group has no identity. If a group

For a group to function, its members must work out patterns of interaction acceptable to the group.

If it is impossible to tell who is a member of a given group, then the group has no identity.

does not define itself, create a sense of purpose for itself, and find a way to distinguish members from non-members, it will fade away rapidly.

Amanda's basketball team, for example, wears matching t-shirts in the colors of the house. The uniforms clearly mark the boundaries of the team as a small group. The "do something about the television" group nicknames itself the "Mass Com. Unit" and begins to form as a problem solving group.

Decision Making

Groups engage in *decision making*. Groups must confront a wide range of issues. Some of these might be procedural such as how best to arrange the meeting. Other decisions may concern what information is deemed acceptable and what is not. Other decisions may address what issues to take up, what stances to take, and whether or not to have refreshments and who is to supply them.

Support

To exist, groups must also *provide support* for their members. The support may come in a variety of ways. The accomplishments of the group may provide a sense of accomplishment for members. The social climate of the group—how positive or negative the group's relationships seem—may be a major factor in members' willingness to participate. Group members must provide each other with enough positive responses that members are willing to interact so that the group can accomplish its business.

When a player on the White House team misses a free throw, the others still applaud and cheer her on. When Amanda and Cheryl switch duties for a day on the cleaning committee, Amanda is supporting Cheryl by making her life a little easier.

Creating Identities

The *creation of identities* is also an important part of group formation. As groups come into existence, it is important that they create a sense of themselves as a group and that they create places for their members. Members establish identities for themselves based on their relationships to others in the group, the task of the group, and their relationships outside of the group.

Amanda's role on the basketball team is to play the guard position, a role that defines her area of activity and her role in both offense and defense. In her study group, she functions as the discussion leader who guides the group in its interchanges and its choice of topics. On the serving crew, she plays a subordinate role to the crew chief. Her group identity depends on which group she is in.

Groups Must Find Ways to Balance Group Tensions

Group relationships are obviously not the only relationships in the lives of group members. Groups exist within the context of members' other relationships. Groups often exist within the context of a larger organization. The various groups and committees in the White House Co-op function within the larger organization of the house with its constitution, by-laws, and traditions. Group members may be thus pulled in several directions by their loyalties to themselves, to others in their lives, to the group, and to the organization. To function well, groups must find effective means of dealing with the various tensions and different levels of commitment among individual members.

Personal Desires/Group Desires

One of the tensions may be between the *personal desires* of a group member and the *desires of the group*. A group member's actions will, to some extent, be determined by how compatible the members feel with the goals, norms, or directions of the group.

A group member's incompatibility with the sentiments of the group may even lead to the member pushing a *"hidden agenda."* A hidden agenda is *a plan for action pursued by one or more group members but is never openly acknowledged within the group.* Usually, the hidden agenda works against the goals of the group. The group's goal may be to "find the best person for the job" while a group member's hidden agenda may be "hire my friend."

Internal Demands/External Demands

Another pressure point for groups may come from the necessity of group members to balance the *internal demands* the group places on them with the *external demands* placed on them by relationships outside of the group.

What does Amanda do when the only time her computer science group can meet is at the same time she is scheduled to play an intramural basketball game?

Individuality/Conformity

Groups are collections of individuals who must subordinate to some extent their *individuality* to demands from the group for *conformity*. Again, a balance must be struck. If people assigned to a group strictly maintain their individuality, they will remain a collection of people arguing their separate viewpoints. On the other hand, if group members are too eager to agree with each other, the group process will be thwarted. If all agree with every suggestion, they will find themselves settling for untested and contradictory courses of action.

Concentration/Relaxation

Groups must also maintain a balance between *concentration* and *relaxation*. Studies of small groups have shown that group work is not a matter of unwavering attention to a goal with relaxation following the accomplishment of the goal (Poole, "*Decision Development . . .*" 222). Rather, groups move toward their goals by an oscillation between concentration and relaxation. They will give full attention to a phase of the task, such as defining a key term or settling a conflict, then they will release some of the tension by emotional expressions such as jokes and comments. Following that, they will then pick up another aspect of the task.

Conclusion

We form ourselves into groups to accomplish those things that would be difficult or impossible to accomplish on our own. In doing so, we play out two long term needs of people: the need for assistance and cooperation and the

> To function well, groups must find effective means of dealing with the various tensions and different levels of commitment among individual members.

need for socialization. Every small group will need to meet these needs, though in varying ways.

Small groups serve a number of purposes: therapy, socialization, study, problem solving, bargaining, and coordinated work. The size and life span of a group will depend on its purpose and membership.

Whether groups are at their beginning points as zero history groups or are long-term existing groups, they will be self-creating and self-sustaining. They will create the framework for their communication and with their communication alter that framework as they see necessary.

To exist, groups will need to accomplish the work of group development. Groups must work through orientation, sorting out, and settling down to work as they start up and continue their existence.

Groups will engage in a number of creative activities as they go about their business. Groups will solve problems, make decisions, maintain group boundaries, include some people and exclude others, and create identities for group members.

Groups will also need to find ways to balance the tensions and pressures they experience. These tensions arise from the divided loyalties group members may have. Some of these relationships are personal desires versus group desires, internal demands versus external demands, individuality versus conformity, and concentration versus relaxation.

Groups are a fascinating part of human communication. Knowing something of their nature and function will be an aid to us in the range of collective activities in which we find ourselves.

Discussion Questions

1. What kind of small groups have you participated in or have observed working?

2. How could a group's history or lack of a history affect its performance?

3. Why are task and relational work necessary for small groups to function?

4. How would task and relational roles function in, say, a study group? In a bargaining group? In a social group?

5. Why is it necessary for groups to practice boundary maintenance and find ways to include and exclude members?

6. Why do groups create identities for themselves and their members?

7. What are group norms? How can they function positively in a group? How can they function negatively in a group?

8. How could a hidden agenda affect group process?

Name _____ Section _____ Date _____

▰ Introduction to Small Group Communication ▰
Assignments

Not all decisions made in our society are the result of individual effort. Frequently it is a group of individuals who collectively reach a decision. Some groups are informal, with little structure and temporary in nature. Others are more formal and have on-going responsibilities.

This unit explains the small group presentation and written assignment which will help you understand the components of the small group process. You will also practice applying the skills necessary to:

1. Effectively communicate with others in a group
2. Be a contributor in a group
3. Enable your group to present an interesting, educational presentation

Suggested Topics for Small Group Presentation

The list below represents suggestions only. If your group thinks of an area of communication that could be presented to your class which isn't on the list, ask your instructor for approval before proceeding with research.

conversation
comforting communication
conflict in interpersonal relationships
communication in friendships
communication in families
cross-cultural communication
classroom communication
gender and communication
a field of communication: public communication, interpersonal communication, organizational communication, mass communication, issue management, performance studies
language and communication
conflict and negotiation
perception's role in communication
communication in organizations
symbolism in communication
visual communication
persuasion through communication (advertising)
mass communication shaping our world view
self concept and communication
censorship in the news
listening
feedback and communication
agenda setting function of media
freedom of speech
nonverbal communication

9. Why may groups members feel the pull of tensions such as individuality/ conformity or personal desires/group desires?

10. Why do groups go through stages of development?

11. What might happen if a group does not progress through the stages of development?

Sources and References ▰

A full bibliography of the small group material influencing this chapter can be found at the end of Chapter 7.

9. What is the second stage of group development? What happens at this stage?

_____

_____

10. What is the third stage of group development? What happens at this stage?

_____

_____

11. How are small groups "more than the sum of their parts"?

_____

_____

12. What is "group climate"?

_____

_____

13. Why is group climate an important concept?

_____

_____

14. What activities help groups establish themselves?

_____

_____

15. What kinds of tensions must small groups balance?

_____

_____

16. What happens to a small group if these tensions are not balanced?

_____

_____

Small Group Presentation Guidelines

Purpose

The small group assignment has a three-fold purpose:

1. Your group will experience working in a small group decision making process which will be good practice for future use in classroom projects as well as in business applications.
2. You will gain in-depth knowledge about one area of communication which will then be shared with the rest of the class to augment instructor presented material.
3. You will gain experience speaking in front of an audience.

Basic Requirements

Your group of 4 to 5 students will prepare and present a creative and informative presentation in which you explain in DEPTH an area of communication. The goal is to present information not already covered by the textbook and to expand the class's knowledge on your chosen topic. A suggested list of subject areas is shown on the previous page.

Each presentation must be a minimum of _____ minutes in length. Films, slides, etc. may take up no more than _____ minutes of your presentation time.

The group as a whole must develop and submit a typed outline of the presentation format at least _____ days prior to the presentation.

A list of a minimum of _____ sources must be included with the outline; _____ sources must be no more than 5 years old so that the class is presented with up-to-date information from your area.

Each group is expected to work as a unit outside of class in addition to the in-class periods set aside for that purpose.

A dress rehearsal is necessary for timing your presentation.

Evaluation sheets must be handed in by each individual prior to the presentation. Your group will be evaluated according to grading criteria style _____, p. _____.

During the presentation sources must be cited so the class is aware of where information was found.

Each member of the group is expected to participate in the actual presentation as equally as possible. In the event a member of the group is sick, etc., on presentation day and does not show up, other members are expected to cover the missing student's information since this is a GROUP presentation, not a collection of five individual presentations on one day. The group as a whole is responsible for the final product and individual members should be knowledgeable about the entire subject area.

A post-presentation analysis paper (see page ???) is required.

You will offer comments about the other presentations using the observation sheets on pages ???–???.

Additional instructor requirements:

Preparation Timetable

Our Group Topic Is _____ Due Date _____

A systematic approach to preparing your small group presentation is the best way to ensure success. Below is a suggested schedule for developing your presentation. The steps should be followed in chronological order with varying amounts of time possible between meetings. Keep a journal of what takes place at your meetings, who is the leader, what the atmosphere is, etc., in order to facilitate writing the post-presentation paper.

⟹ **Step 1** Exchange names and phone numbers with other group members to simplify arranging outside meetings. Compare schedules to find time blocks convenient for all participants. Begin gathering outside information. See bibliographies in this text for a start as well as traditional library sources including books, journals and abstracts. "Library Research in Communication," p. ??? of this workbook, should be helpful in guiding you to pertinent sources.

⟹ **Step 2** Narrow your topic. The suggested topics listed are broad, and must be narrowed to focus on more manageable areas of information for the time limit involved. For example, mass media communication might be narrowed to how television newscasts shape our perception of the world around us. As a group divide the topic for additional research. Meet again to review the information and monitor progress. FOLLOW THE PROBLEM SOLVING STEPS outlined in Chapter 8 of this textbook.

⟹ **Step 3** Develop an outline. After preliminary research has been conducted to get a general idea of what your area includes, meet to develop a tentative outline for the presentation. Don't fit the outline to the material found to date; decide on what you want, then go out and find the material necessary to fill in the gaps.

⟹ **Step 4** Prepare a format. Develop your presentation format as a group. Decide the most interesting way to present your material. Combine a straight-forward presentation of information with role playing, getting the class involved in exercises, questions and answers, discussion, etc. On presentation day talk through with the class the reason for the activities and exercises you've chosen. Don't assume the class will see the relationship between the exercise and the communication concept it illustrates. Work for a presentation which holds the audience's attention through a mixture of ways of presenting material. Use "skits" only when they really prove a point, not merely provide entertainment.

⟹ **Step 5** Evaluate the presentation. When you think the development of your presentation is finished, review "Basic Requirements," p. ??? and check off to make sure each requirement has been met. In addition, consider the following areas:

  ⟹ If AV equipment is needed, have arrangements been made to have it on hand? Read your text, Chapter 12, for help in using audio/visual aids.

  ⟹ Is the material being presented informative about an area of communication as well as interesting?

  ⟹ Does all the material support the central theme/topic? Are sources cited by participants to add credibility to the presentation? Is the information presented a supplement to text material, not a rephrasing of it?

  ⟹ Can the class follow the presentation just from hearing it? Is it organized? Is there an introduction of group members, an attention getting device in the opening, development of rapport with the audience, and a preview of the content of the presentation? Are there transitions, explanations, internal summaries? Is there a conclusion which summarizes the presentation and leaves the audience with a sense of completion?

  ⟹ Are unfamiliar terms defined?

  ⟹ Are enough supporting examples given to make the material meaningful?

  ⟹ Has the group practiced the whole presentation to check timing, physical set-up, etc.? This is best done in a classroom similar to the one in which the presentation will be delivered.

Notes:

Evaluation Rationale

All members of the group will receive the same grade since this presentation is a group effort. TURKEY CLAUSE: Occasionally an individual group member will choose, for whatever reasons, not to contribute to the group's efforts at developing a worthwhile presentation. The member may not do research in preparation for the project, miss the majority of out-of-class planning sessions, or withdraw during the work sessions. Each group should attempt to draw such an individual into the group process. Sometimes adjustments need to be made to accommodate work schedules, etc. If in spite of a good faith effort on the part of a group one of its members refuses to be an active participant, the group as a whole may choose to enact the turkey clause, in effect firing the person from the group. If such an action is regarded as necessary, the group must contact the instructor and document the wayward member's action. Upon approval of the instructor the turkey clause will be enacted. A student who is fired by the group will receive an *F* for the assignment.

⟨⟨ Written Assignment Small Group Process ⟨⟨

You are to analyze your group's interactions in light of the five areas listed below. Your analysis should reflect an understanding of the research and theory presented in the text through your use of appropriate **terminology** for small group processes. Failure to use such terminology will reduce your grade accordingly. Your paper should demonstrate an understanding of the group process. Be sure to give **specific examples** of events and behavior in the group to document the conclusions you draw in your analysis. A **journal** makes writing the paper easier—you will have the specific examples needed to support your claims. It is highly suggested that you take notes after each group meeting to facilitate writing your paper.

Explain what accounted for group strengths. What could have been done differently to minimize any weakness? The questions listed below should start you thinking about possible ways to approach each area to be analyzed.

The material included in your paper will be considered confidential.

THIS PAPER IS DUE _____.

Specific format instructions required by the instructor are:

➟ **Area 1** *What decision-making processes were used in your group?* How did your group use the problem-solving agenda given in your text? (Chapter 8) How were decisions reached by the group as you proceeded through the analysis? (majority rule, consensus, compromise) Were they successful? Why? If they were unsuccessful, how could they have been improved? How long did it take for your group to decide what it was that it wanted to do in front of the class? Was it too long? Why? What could have made it better? Were you satisfied with the topic that your group chose? Why or why not?

➟ **Area 2** *Describe the leadership process that functioned in your group.* Who REALLY was the leader of the group? Did the leader emerge? If yes, at what point? Why? Was the leader appointed or elected? What was the basis of electing that person? Did several leaders function? If so, how did this affect the group? If you felt your group was leaderless, what are some problems with leaderless groups? What style(s) of leadership was used in your group?

➟ **Area 3** *Identify and describe the various roles each member of your group, including you, played during your work sessions.* Give specific examples for each person's role(s) (positive and negative member's activities). Who did the most talking? Why do you think they did? Did this style continue throughout the group's development? If there was a change, was it a change for the better or worse in your opinion? Why? Did your position or role within the group change from meeting to meeting? How? Why? Were you respected (in terms of your role) within the group? Who did the least amount of talking? What steps were taken to get this person to open up more? Were the steps successful?

➟ **Area 4** *How did your group handle interpersonal and analytic conflict, if there was any?* Who was most instrumental in creating conflict? What impact did this conflict have on the group? What steps were taken to resolve the conflict? If no conflict existed, did your group suffer from "group think"? Why was there no conflict?

➟ **Area 5** *What kind of climate did your group establish?* What factors in the group process were responsible for the climate which developed? How did you feel about being a member of this group? Did your attitude change about your group from beginning to end? How did the environment in which your group functioned affect its success? Where did the meetings take place for your group? Did you feel comfortable meeting there? Could a better choice have been made? Was the time conducive to accomplishing your tasks?

Include a brief summary of your reactions to working in a small group situation.
Include the evaluation sheet with your paper.

⧫ Written Assignment Evaluation Sheet ⧫

The paper reflects a knowledge of research and theory from the text based on the use of proper terminology. (10 points)

The paper provides specific examples of events and behaviors to document conclusions. (10 points)

The paper sufficiently analyzes the decision making process employed. (15 points)

The paper sufficiently analyzes the leadership characteristics in the group. (15 points)

The paper sufficiently analyzes the roles (positive and negative group member activities) members played. (15 points)

The paper sufficiently analyzes the conflict in the group. (15 points)

The paper sufficiently analyzes the climate of the group. (15 points)

The paper is presented in a neat and technically well written manner. (5 points)

Sample Bibliographic Entries

Periodicals

An article in a journal with continuous pagination:

Ayres, Joe and Tim Hopf. "Coping With Writing Apprehension." *Journal of Applied Communication Research* 19 (1991): 186–96.

An article in a general publication:

Burka, Paul. "Honesty is the Best Politics." *Texas Monthly* Nov. 1992. 122+

Books

A book by a singular author:

Willard, Charles Arthur. *A Theory of Argumentation.* Tuscaloosa: Univ. of Alabama Press, 1989.

An edition of a book:

Cooper, Pamela J. *Speech Communication for the Classroom Teacher.* 3rd ed. Scottsdale, Arizona: Gorsuch Scarisbrick, 1988.

A book chapter:

Nelson, John S. "Political Foundations for the Rhetoric of Inquiry." *The Rhetorical Turn: Invention and Persuasion in the Conduct of Inquiry.* Ed. Herbert W. Simons. Chicago: Univ. of Chicago Press, 1990. 258–59.

A book with multiple authors:

Stewart, Charles J., Craig Allen Smith, and Robert E. Denton, Jr. *Persuasion and Social Movements.* 2nd ed. Prospect Heights, Illinois: Waveland Press, 1989.

Newspapers

Cullen, Kevin. "Canal Dig Yields Key Find." *Journal and Courier* [Lafayette, IN] 12 June 1997: B1.

Internet

Basic format:

Author's Last Name, First Name. [author's internet address, if available]. "Title of Work" or "title of line message." In "Title of Complete Work" or title of line/site as appropriate. [internet address]. Date, if available.

Martin, Ralph. [rmartin@recst.monst.edu]. "Where the Deer and the Antelope Play." In "Western Recreational Opportunities." [ec@monst.edu]. 13 June 1997.

An Interview

Doe, John. Professor of Animal Science, Purdue University. Personal interview, 13 May 1997.

⟩⟩⟩ Small Group Grading Criteria—Style A ⟨⟨⟨

For a C, the presentation meets the following criteria:

All members participate in the presentation
The topic relates to communication
Introduction introduces group members and previews the presentation
Presentation had required number of main points
Transitions are present
Conclusion summarizes main points
Speakers are understandable
Required number of references are used and cited
Presentation fits the time guidelines

For a B, the presentation meets the criteria for a C plus the following:

Involves interaction within the group
Uses references from highly credible sources, appropriate to the topic, and from recent publications
Employs supporting materials (visual aids, performances, illustrations) appropriate to the topic
Speakers do nothing that detracts from their presentations
Introduction captures the attention of the audience
Transitions link main points
Conclusion highlights implications of the material
Visual aids (posters, pictures, videotape, etc.) supplement the presentation rather than being the presentation

For an A, the presentation meets the criteria for a C and a B plus the following:

Presentation utilizes an interesting format
Presentation flows smoothly
Points strongly supported from credible sources
Supporting materials are neat, artistic, and clear
Program is interesting to the audience
Speakers are energetic
Presentation evidences maturity of thought
Program utilizes audience participation

For a D, one of the C criteria exhibits a major problem.
For an F, the presentation is not given, one of the C criteria is not done, or several areas exhibit major problems.

◥◣ Small Group Presentation Grading Criteria—Style B ◥◣

Organization 30%*

Introduction
> group members introduced
> attention getting opening employed
> rapport developed with the audience
> presentation previewed

Body
> main points obvious
> transitions used between main points
> easily followed

Conclusion
> main points summarized
> implications of material highlighted
> a feeling of completion developed

Content 40%*

> unified and related to group assignment
> supported with examples
> clearly presented
> interestingly developed
> appropriate vocabulary chosen
> jargon and unfamiliar terms defined
> expanded beyond the scope of text material
> sources credible
> sources cited

Delivery 30%*

> presented within the required time limits
> participation equally divided
> moved smoothly from one speaker to the next
> showed evidence of preparation for conducting exercises, role playing situations, activities, etc.
> visual aid used with confidence

(Individual Student Notes)
> rate appropriate
> eye contact frequent
> volume appropriate
> tone pleasing
> vocal variety exhibited
> absence of fillers

---

*suggested values only—may be changed by your instructor

enunciation/pronunciation correct
gestures meaningful
posture comfortable
communication with audience established

Comments:

⧚ Student Evaluation of Small Group Presentation ⧚

Constructive feedback should be

1. Solicited
2   Well timed
3. Descriptive of how you feel, not evaluative
4. Specific rather than general
5. Practical, related to something that can be controlled and changed

   In light of these guidelines, offer feedback about the small group presentation you have just watched. Focus on how interesting, informative and organized the presentation was to you. What was the strongest single aspect of the presentation? What one thing would you have done differently?

⧄ Student Evaluation of Small Group Presentation ⧄

Constructive feedback should be

1. Solicited
2. Well timed
3. Descriptive of how you feel, not evaluative
4. Specific rather than general
5. Practical, related to something that can be controlled and changed

    In light of these guidelines, offer feedback about the small group presentation you have just watched. Focus on how interesting, informative and organized the presentation was to you. What was the strongest single aspect of the presentation? What one thing would you have done differently?

___✎ Student Evaluation of Small Group Presentation ✎___

Constructive feedback should be

1. Solicited
2. Well timed
3. Descriptive of how you feel, not evaluative
4. Specific rather than general
5. Practical, related to something that can be controlled and changed

In light of these guidelines, offer feedback about the small group presentation you have just watched. Focus on how interesting, informative and organized the presentation was to you. What was the strongest single aspect of the presentation? What one thing would you have done differently?

_____ Student Evaluation of Small Group Presentation _____

Constructive feedback should be

1. Solicited
2. Well timed
3. Descriptive of how you feel, not evaluative
4. Specific rather than general
5. Practical, related to something that can be controlled and changed

In light of these guidelines, offer feedback about the small group presentation you have just watched. Focus on how interesting, informative and organized the presentation was to you. What was the strongest single aspect of the presentation? What one thing would you have done differently?

Working in Groups

7

KEY CONCEPTS

" **G**uys, I think we have a major problem."

Monday nights at the University mean house meetings for fraternities, sororities, and cooperative houses. Members collect in the largest room to review ongoing business and to introduce new business. Like the others, the Four Oaks Men's Cooperative collects in the living room to review ongoing activities and to introduce new business.

They have heard reports from the chairs of standing committees: social activities, service activities, intramural sports, house maintenance, and finance. When the president calls for new items for discussion, Ron Park stands up and states his perception that something is wrong. Ron is a junior in communication and has completed a number of courses in his major. He chose to live in a cooperative for financial reasons.

Ron elaborates on his ideas. "I think our parking situation is becoming worse and worse. It is harder and harder to find a place to park. I've talked to several of the older members, and they feel the same way. We need to do something."

When Ron sits down, another member reinforces Ron's ideas, "I think the parking situation may be hurting our membership. During rush, I met two or three guys who said they liked the house and the location, but they thought our parking lot was small. They thought they would have better luck finding a place for their cars at other houses."

"We always have a problem with the parking," one adds. "We've had a problem as long as I've been here, but we don't do anything about it."

"Maybe this is the time," Ron says.

"Give me a straw vote," the president says. "How many of you think we have a big enough problem to look into?"

"Let's just buy the house next door and turn the property into a lot," one suggests.

"That would cost too much," another answers.

"Hold it, hold it," the president says. "I want to see how many agree with Ron. How many of you would like to see the parking situation investigated?"

After a pause over half the hands go up.

"All right," the president says, "now we have the hard part. Who wants to be on a committee to look into parking?"

"I brought up the topic," Ron says, "I guess I ought to be on it."

"I think I can use this as part of a project in one of my civil engineering classes," one says. "Put me down."

"How about some of you new guys?" the president asks.

Another member volunteers. Once the committee is formed, the problem solving process begins.

Working in Groups

The parking committee at Four Oaks has been appointed. As a zero history, problem-solving group, it will work its way through the levels of group development. In some ways the committee is like a ship setting sail on unknown waters. They know the general direction in which they should go, but they do not know what they will find on their voyage nor what will be their final destination. Nor do they yet know how they will work together as a crew. This chapter will discuss the ways in which groups and group members can function to accomplish their tasks as well as the ways in which groups can hamper their own progress. As problem-solving groups are a form of group work that most of us engage in, our discussion will center on how to reach the optimum solution when addressing a problem.

Influences on the Quality of Group Work

The quality of a group's work will be determined by the interplay of several factors (Hirokawa, Erbert, and Hurst 270–71). The *informational resources* available to a group are a major influence as "the better informed members are about the problem they are required to solve . . . the better able they are to reach a high-quality decision."

The parking committee is very lucky. Located at a major university, they have available a large library and a host of experts on a variety of pertinent subjects. Consider how different their work would be if they were trying to solve their problem from an outlying area with little information.

The *quality of the group effort* is also an important aspect of group work. The more carefully group members check and recheck information, the more likely they are to make good decisions. Sloppily done group work usually leads to poor decisions and negative consequences.

A third aspect is the *quality of thinking* exhibited by group members, the ability to "arrive at warranted or appropriate" conclusions "from the decision-relevant information available to them." Materials and effort are useless without the intelligence to combine the two in successful patterns.

The fourth factor is the *decision logic* employed by group members. The best way of making decisions is done by "carefully considering the positive and negative qualities of all available choices, and then selecting the alternative that offers the most positive, and least negative, attributes." In short, by keeping their eyes on the ultimate goal, group members engage in better decision making than they do when distracted by secondary issues.

> The more carefully group members check and recheck information, the more likely they are to make good decisions.

Problem-Solving Procedures

The quality of decisions reached by groups is also dependent on the approach a group takes to reach a conclusion. Groups can take a variety of different paths as they move toward the goal of a solution.

Ineffective Problem Solving

Often, ineffective problem solving uses decision-making processes that fail to consider available information or that thwart the group process.

Autocratic decision making is one approach to problem-solving. Here a group leader decides which solution is best and then announces this decision

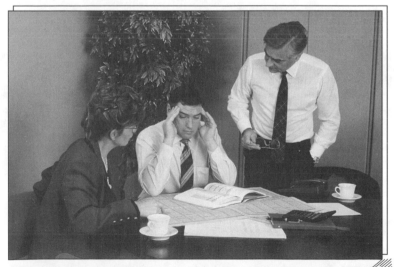

One weakness of small group work is that small group decisions often take more time than individual decisions.

to the group. In these situations, group members may have no options but to go along with the decision or to resign.

Minority decision making is similar to autocratic decisions, but here the decisions are made by a small number of group members (Jarboe 362).

Another inferior method of decision making is *rushing to judgment*. Here the group disregards or severely limits investigation and discussion and picks the first solution offered. Groups may make these decisions because of limited time or fatigue. Because the group fails to investigate a range of potentially better solutions, the group's selection often fails to remedy the problem situation.

Mob rule is probably the worst method of group decision making. It is a rush to judgment coupled with strong emotions. Caught up in its feelings and seeking a way to vent its anger, the group picks a solution that appears to offer a quick fix while providing an outlet for the anger. Usually, these decisions create more problems than they solve.

The Rational Model of Problem Solving

A better way to solve problems is for the group to adopt procedures that encourage investigation and definition of the problem, generation of possible solutions, and sound judgment in reaching decisions. In the early part of the twentieth century, John Dewey outlined such a method, and James H. McBurney and Kenneth G. Hance further refined the method in the thirties. The basic approach continues to be confirmed by small group research as a process that results in high quality decisions (Hirokawa, Erbert, and Hurst 271).

Define the Problem

The first task sounds simple enough, but it is not always utilized. The group should first *define the problem*. Discussing solutions and courses of action is pointless unless the group knows for what it is searching. Inherent in the articulation of the problem is a direction for the group to pursue and a limitation on the potential solutions it may create.

Sometimes the definition is easy to make. The Undergraduate Committee is told to pick "The Outstanding Senior"; the design committee is charged with the creation of a logo; or the entertainment committee has the responsibility to plan the spring banquet.

At other times, the task is not so easy. With the Four Oaks parking committee, its commission was very general, "look into the situation." The group's first task should be to ascertain how much of a problem exists and whether or not it is serious enough to merit the investment of a large amount of time and effort. If the situation is indeed a serious one, then they will need to define the problem in a way that focuses the group in its pursuit of a solution.

The expression of empathy in a group can aid understanding.

The group's definition will be something like "We need to find an acceptable way to provide sufficient parking space for members, visitors, and delivery vehicles."

Investigate the Problem

Once the group has articulated the problem to be solved, the next step is to *investigate the problem situation*. The goal in this stage is to find out as much as possible about the problem to be solved and what surrounds the problem. This information allows the group to work from knowledge rather than from ignorance. At this stage, a number of questions need to be asked and answered:

What is the origin of the problem?
Why did this problem develop?
    What circumstances led to the creation of this problem?
    What people led to the creation of this problem?
What perpetuates the problem?
What solutions have already been tried?
What resources do we have available to solve this problem?
    How much money do we have available?
    How much time do we have available?
    What people and talents are available?
To whom do we report our conclusions?
Who puts the solution into effect?

At this point in the problem-solving sequence, the group needs to be as open as possible. This research step should utilize as many types of information as necessary. Relevant information may be found in print sources, on electronic media, on the internet, and in people. Wherever the group needs to look, it should look.

Some of the sources a group might find helpful are:

Newspapers: local, other cities, national, foreign
Periodicals: general audience periodicals (*Redbook, Working Woman, More, Psychology Today, Time, Newsweek*), special audience magazines (*Motor Trend, Scientific American, Smithsonian, Outdoor Photography, Computer World*), academic journals (*Quarterly Journal of Speech, Management Quarterly, Metallurgy Journal*), trade publications (*Heating and Air Conditioning Bulletin, Auto Mechanics, Pipe Trades*)
Books
People resources: interviews, expert testimony
Electronic media: news reports, documentaries, special topic programs (*Western Civilization, Creativity, Hyperactivity and Medication*)
Internet: sites on institutions, corporations, libraries, products, and a vast assortment of others.

Information gathering is a task aided by small group work. Members can divide up the research, pool their resources, and accomplish the task much more quickly than could an individual.

The Four Oaks Co-op committee faces a daunting task of gathering information. They have to ascertain the ratio of cars to parking spaces controlled by the house. To make sure they are not responding to a situation unique to the present year, they gather this information for several years back. They also project their needs forward to meet future demands. As they may have to rent or purchase land, they calculate carefully how much money can be available to them. Since their problem is localized, they spend a considerable amount of time surveying the needs and desires of house members.

The committee needs to know where to obtain sound advice when they encounter questions beyond their experience. They talk with a Realtor about available property in the area and the cost of property. For advice about purchasing property, they contact an alumnus who is now a lawyer. They talk with members of the Alumni Board to discover their attitudes toward the problem.

They discover that at present members have eight more cars than the house has parking spaces. The house is in good financial condition, but they do not have large reserves of money. The Alumni Board is willing to entertain their ideas.

Set Criteria for a Solution

In this third step, *setting criteria for a solution,* the group creates and agrees on a set of "goals" for the solution. Formulating these criteria provides the group with an accepted basis for evaluating solutions and deciding among them. The final standard is not one group member's idiosyncratic preference for a given solution, but a set of criteria accepted by all group members.

Articulating criteria for a solution early in the group process saves time at the end of the process. The group does not have to review and revise its standards as it attempts to select the best solution available.

In its search, the Four Oaks Co-op committee weighs the information it has gathered in the research stage and on the basis of that information, sets its criteria.

The committee's criteria for a solution contains goals such as:

> The solution should provide parking space for members' cars.
> The solution should provide parking space for visitors' cars.
> The solution should provide parking space for delivery vehicles.
> The solution should provide parking space for the house's needs
>   in the future.
> The solution should make the house attractive to potential members.
> The parking space should be as close to the house as possible.
> The parking space should be within the financial means of the house.
> The solution should be in accord with local laws and ordinances.
> The solution should be acceptable to the Alumni Board.
> The solution should be acceptable to the University.
> The solution should be attractive visually.
> The solution should provide relief quickly.

Formulate Possible Solutions

With a solid base of knowledge from which to work and with consensus reached on the criteria for judging possible solutions, the group should next *formulate possible solutions.* Decisions will usually be better if groups debate the strengths and weaknesses of several possibilities rather than immediately settling on one solution.

> Decisions will usually be better if groups debate the strengths and weaknesses of several possibilities rather than immediately settling on one solution.

The Four Oaks Co-op committee *brainstorms* to generate solutions. They meet and toss out ideas regardless of how silly or impractical they are. Nobody says anything judgmental about the suggestions.

After the brainstorming session, they begin working their way through the list of suggested solutions. Some they discard quickly as they obviously run afoul of the criteria. One suggestion was to cut down the two oak trees in the back yard and pave the area to create more spaces. As the two large oak trees in the back are two of the "Four Oaks," half the source of the house's name, this possibility is quickly eliminated.

Other solutions will deserve more attention. In the end, they generate five possible plans of action:

1. Limit the number of members allowed to park in the lot with access based on seniority.
2. Create a rotating system of parking in the house parking lot so that every month eight of the members must find parking elsewhere.
3. Purchase the house next door and use it for expansion of parking.
4. Lease a lot three blocks away that is available for only one year.
5. Relocate the entire membership to a different piece of property with a larger house and sufficient space for parking.

Select the Best Alternative

Once a list of possible solutions is on the table for discussion, the group moves forward to *select the best solution*. The basis for the decision is the list of criteria generated earlier, and the final choice will be the solution that comes closest to fulfilling the criteria. Sometimes, one solution will emerge as clearly superior to the others. In other circumstances, the group may agonize over the relative merits of two solutions, each with strengths and weaknesses that balance the other.

In choosing a solution, the group must remember that "best" does not mean "perfect" and that "consensus" does not mean "total satisfaction." Most solutions will have both positive and negative aspects. In some situations, the key question will be which option offers the fewest negatives, and the group will be forced to decide between the better of two unattractive alternatives.

The Four Oaks committee gauges each of its possibilities according to its criteria. Here are some of their major considerations:

1. Limit the number of members allowed to park in the lot with access based on seniority.
   Pro: will control traffic in the parking lot at no cost, can be put into effect immediately
   Con: will discourage potential members, will make life inconvenient for those with less seniority
2. Create a rotating system of parking in the house parking lot so that every month eight of the members must find parking elsewhere.
   Pro: will control traffic in the parking lot at no cost, will evenly distribute the inconvenience, members can plan ahead for their months outside the lot
   Con: will make life difficult for everyone, may discourage potential members

> In choosing a solution, the group must remember that "best" does not mean "perfect" and that "consensus" does not mean "total satisfaction."

3. Purchase the house and lot next door and use it for expansion of parking.
   Pro: will readily supply extra space adjacent to present property, all members would have parking spaces
   Con: will require a large amount of money, will require maintenance or razing of the house
4. Lease a lot three blocks away that is available for only one year.
   Pro: will provide adequate parking for all members
   Con: will require significant expenditure, will still involve inconvenience, as parking is not adjacent to the house, will not provide a long-term solution
5. Relocate the entire membership to a different piece of property with a larger house and sufficient space for parking.
   Pro: will provide adequate parking for all members, will allow for a more commodious facility for members, will enhance recruiting for membership
   Con: will require a major fund-raising campaign to pay for the project, will require a great deal of time to find an adequate facility, will require disposing of present site

After several meetings, the committee decides that its best option is the second one, a rotating system where each month eight members will have to park off the house lot. At the same time, they also recommend that another committee be formed to investigate the possibility of moving to a different facility with a large building and more parking space.

While socializing may be a pleasant part of a problem solving group, too much socializing can distract the group from the task at hand.

Put the Chosen Solution into Effect

After selecting the best possible solution, the group needs to change its focus yet again and take up the task of *putting the chosen solution into effect*. In some cases, the group will report its findings to an administrative officer, a client, or another group such as a board of trustees or the city commissioners. In other cases, the group will itself be the unit enacting its decisions.

With a conclusion reached, the Four Oaks committee takes its decision to the house membership. It presents its work, its findings, and its conclusion, then asks for acceptance of the plan. After a long discussion, the house votes in favor of the committee's proposal.

The committee meets two days later, draws members' names from a box, and assigns every member with a car his "off the lot" month. They make and duplicate the schedule, distribute it to every member and place it on every bulletin board.

Decide What Happens to the Group

Once the solution is put into effect, the major work of the committee is done, but it still has one task left to accomplish: *decide what happens to the group once the solution is in effect.*

Many groups disband once their work is done. Commissioned to attend to a particular problem, an *ad hoc* committee has no reason for existence once the problem is solved. No more *hoc,* no more committee.

Other groups stay in touch with the problem and monitor how well the solution is working. The last possibility is that the group continues to function but leaves behind the problem just completed and takes up a new problem. This is the course of action followed by standing committees. Once an issue is decided, the committee moves on to another issue and after that, another issue, *ad infinitum.* For example, the social committee of the Four Oaks Cooperative is responsible for its Fall Formal Dance and after that the next event and the next.

The *ad hoc* parking committee has completed its major task, but with the support of the membership, the president asks the committee to monitor how well the solution works and to report to the house on the matter.

The committee listens to members' reactions and observations as the plan goes into effect, and it distributes a survey to determine satisfaction with the parking situation.

The group discovers that most are satisfied with the plan, but another problem has emerged. Some of those assigned to park off the house property are sneaking in to park when they are in a hurry or do not feel like hunting a spot elsewhere. The weekends are particularly troublesome because extra space is available when members leave campus from Friday to Sunday. Sometimes these people return to find their parking spaces occupied by those assigned off the lot. The off-lot parkers see little reason they should not be allowed to take advantage of the temporary availability of space.

The committee begins meeting again to address this problem.

The process by which groups arrive at decisions is a complex one, but by carefully working through the process, groups will achieve better results than they will attacking the problem indiscriminately. This is not to say that groups will always move through the above steps in a smooth progression. New discoveries may require a rethinking of the group's earlier accomplishments. Sometimes groups begin in the middle of the problem-solving sequence and sometimes, even at the end.

The most successful group work will need to meet the challenges of each of the steps of the problem-solving sequence, either in order or in a disjointed fashion. A smooth progression through the steps is ultimately more efficient than a haphazard approach.

Group Leadership

We noted earlier that one of the first steps in the formation of a zero history group is the selection of those who will not be considered for leadership positions. Then as orientation progresses, potential leaders come to the fore. Eventually, the group must find a leader or leaders. The alternative is lack of direction and a failure to organize.

When we consider leadership, often the first image that comes to mind is that of a strong-willed, forceful individual who drives the group toward its goal. This model of leadership can be an effective one, but it is far from being the only mode of leadership. Quiet and subtle leadership can be just as effective as more obvious forms. *The most effective group leader is one who is capable of using a number of leadership styles and adopts a style best suited to the needs of the group at any given moment.*

Three Traits of Leadership

Leadership is a difficult to quantify because it is a combination of a number of factors. We can—and will—give guidelines for effectively leading a group, but leadership is more than following a set of suggestions. Whether it be in a small group or in a large organization, the best leaders combine three qualities.

Good leadership carries with it the connotation of *vision,* an ability to see where the group should go and to make the vision clear to others. An effective leader is one who is "able to articulate visions of what the group can do and achieve" (Barge 317).

To accomplish that vision, a leader must provide *direction* for the group. A leader does not simply provide a goal, but a leader also helps the group focus its efforts on achieving that goal, whatever the goal may be: winning a game, securing funds, staging a dance, making a presentation, changing ineffective or harmful behavior, or succeeding on an exam.

To keep the group moving toward its goal, a leader must be able to balance the internal and external forces at work in a group. Thus, another important aspect of leadership is *mediation* (Barge 317–18). Obviously, a group leader will need to mediate between group members as they discuss ideas and engage in conflicts. The mediation, though, goes much further than in-group relationships. An effective leader must also mediate or balance information, group desires, time pressures, and demands external to the group. Leadership is "a type of social influence process" (Barge 304).

> A leader does not simply provide a goal, but a leader also helps the group focus its efforts on achieving that goal.

Leadership may also be supplied by more than one person in the group. If a person, in whatever capacity, provides direction for the group and integrates information and behavior with the group, that person is a leader. The person who leads discussions in a group plays an obvious leadership role. At the same time, the quiet person who supplies vital information to the group and links that information to the group's goals and needs is also a leader. Another who helps to maintain cordiality among members also performs a leadership task by smoothing interpersonal relations and helping to create a productive group climate. One might even go so far as to say that *"a leader is one who helps the group accomplish its purpose"* (Crable).

With these considerations in mind, let us look at how leadership can be accomplished in a small group.

Creation of Leaders

Oftentimes, the leader of a group is the person assigned to that post by rank, election, or authority. Military groups have officers; committees have chairs appointed by officials; a board elects one of its own as president. As one might guess, these types of leaders are generally known as *"appointed leaders."*

Appointment, though, is not the only way groups acquire leaders. Zero history, leaderless groups begin with no designated roles whatsoever, yet leaders arise in these groups as well. When leaders come to the fore from the body of the group, they are known as *"emergent leaders"* because they assume their roles as the group places more and more confidence in them.

Groups can function well with either type of leader. Groups have difficulties, however, when a conflict arises between the appointed leader and an emergent leader. The group has to deal with two potential visions, two directions, and two styles of mediation. Unless the group can find a way to resolve the conflict, it will be severely hindered from accomplishing its work.

Leadership Responsibilities

Group Leaders Should be Prepared

In accomplishing vision, direction, and mediation, leaders can take a number of steps to see their tasks and those of the group. One of these is very simple. Leaders not only need to do the appropriate share of homework and research as other group members, but group leaders must also devote time to thinking about the group and its work. Group leaders will need to assess how well the group is accomplishing its goal and then plan what approach is best for aiding or correcting the group's direction.

Group leaders will also make sure that the group has what it needs to accomplish its task. Group needs may be space, time, materials, or access to information.

Group Leaders Need to be Sensitive to Group Needs

One of the prime characteristics of effective group leadership is an awareness of what is transpiring in the group. If a person cannot determine the feelings and ideas of the group, it will be difficult to guide the group in appropriate directions. At some points, the best leadership is to remain quiet and let the group do its work. At other times, the leader may have to supply a series of provocative questions to encourage responses or may have to act as a referee in the midst of a heated argument.

Leaders will need to balance a number of factors. One factor is when to *encourage* and when to *discourage discussion*. The forthright may need to be silenced so that others can contribute. The shy and quiet may need to be nudged into contributing their expertise. In a large sense, the leader must also make sure that ideas have been sufficiently considered and agreements reached that reflect the true sentiments of the group.

Leaders must also help the group *balance the tensions between task activities and relational activities*. A social group that spends all its time planning will not be very enjoyable for its members. Neither will a problem-solving group if it spends all its time conversing and socializing.

A leader should also help the group *maintain its focus*. While digressions may help the group relieve tensions, a group leader needs to make sure that the group does not stray too far from its path.

Another important function of group leadership may be *motivating the group to perform its task*. One of the major reasons groups become discouraged is that members fail to see how the work at hand will benefit them. It is the duty of the group leader, then, to remind members of the positive aspects of their work. Benefits may come in different ways. Solving the problem at hand can be a major reward. Some benefits are easily measured: salary, bonuses, time off, or improved work conditions. Other benefits may be equally important but less obvious: pleasant group relations, personal satisfaction, a sense of respect, and accommodations of one's feelings.

Another important motivational fact is the *respect* that group members experience. When members feel that they are treated with integrity, they are more likely to invest themselves in the group process than when they are treated badly.

Group leadership is a talent that allows the leader to balance a number of factors in the group process. The same kind of balance is necessary when it comes to choosing a style of leadership.

Leadership Styles

Authoritarian

Leadership styles are characterized by the amount of direct control the leader exerts over the group. A structured, centralized style is the *authoritarian* style. Here the leader exercises tight control over the group's activities, often telling the group what will be done. Authoritarian group leaders decide on the course of action for the group and then make assignments for the members to carry out.

Authoritarian leadership is most appropriate when time is limited, group members are disoriented, members trust the leader, and when group leaders have the power to enforce decisions. Some roles that would call for authoritarian leadership would be those in military or quasi-military units, teachers of small children, tour guides, and crew chiefs.

Democratic

A second form of leadership is the *democratic* style. Here the leader consults with the group and after hearing its views, makes a decision. A democratic leader is not one who submits every issue to a vote of the group but rather is one who allows the group to express opinions about the problems to be solved. Final responsibility for the decision, however, rests with the leader.

A democratic style of leadership is most appropriate when members are involved with each other in their task, when membership is knowledgeable, when the leader is trusted, and when enough time exists to solicit opinions.

Consensus Seeking

A third style of leadership is *consensus seeking.* In this mode, the group leader is regarded more as "first among equals" than possessing more power or rank than the members. A consensus-seeking leader is one who functions as a discussion leader and mediator, and summarizer. The leader elicits opinions from the group, tries to help discover a common ground for the individual concerns of members, and then makes sure all understand to what they have agreed.

A consensus seeking style works best when members are informed, willing to interact, and flexible enough to make concessions in order to reach an agreement.

Laissez-faire

The last style of leadership is *laissez-faire.* Roughly translated, "laissez-faire" means "let the people do as they please" (Webster's *Seventh New Collegiate Dictionary,* 1967). Utilizing this style, the leader does little or nothing to influence the group's decisions or actions. The laissez-faire leader is one who sits back and let's happen what happens.

While this may seem a road to disaster, laissez-faire is often the best approach when group members are highly motivated, capable, and self-motivated. When all are doing what they are supposed to be doing, the best policy is to leave them alone to do their work.

Which Style Is Best?

Potential group leaders may ask, "which method should I use?" The answer is at once both simple and complex. The simple answer is "whichever style best fits your situation." The complex part is deciding which style or combination of styles that is.

When Ron is appointed temporary chair of the Four Oaks Co-op parking committee, he adopts a consensus seeking style as he sets up the first meeting of the group. He gathers the members and asks, "We need to set up a meeting. What times look good for you guys?"

At the first meeting, he is elected permanent chair of the committee.

A major motivational factor is the respect group members experience in the group process.

During the stage of investigating the problem, he notes that all members are doing well and need little guidance. He trusts them to gather the necessary information and does not interfere with their work, a laissez-faire approach to leadership.

In later discussions, he discovers that one member has overlooked an important area in his research. He utilizes an authoritarian style and directs that member to complete his research and to report within a specified time.

As the process draws closer to the end and the group is trying to select the best solution, Ron becomes a consensus seeker. He guides the discussion, offers his own opinions, and tries to help the group reach agreement.

Planning Meetings

In exercising leadership, proper planning of meetings can contribute greatly to efficient work within the group.

Set Meeting Times

Simple as it sounds, an important part of successful small group work is *setting meeting times* and making sure that all members have the information. It also helps to announce meetings far enough that members have time to prepare. The meeting time should allow for optimum attendance, preferably all members, and should be at a time when the group can do its best work.

Groups also work better in a series of short meetings rather than in one or two long marathon sessions. People find it difficult to pour their energies into meetings for prolonged periods of time.

Choose Appropriate Settings

The place where a group does its work is also a contributing factor to the group's success. The *setting* should be comfortable so that the environment does not interfere with the group's efforts. The setting should also provide the group with what it needs for its work such as privacy for discussion or space to spread out materials.

The Four Oaks Co-op parking committee tries first to meet in Ron's room but discovers it is too cramped. They next try the lounge, but the pool game and the television distract them. They end up going to the basement, which offers some quiet as well as large tables they can use for drinks and snacks, and to spread out their papers and materials.

Supply Materials

Besides a compatible setting, a group should also have the materials it needs to perform its work. Decision-making groups may need reports, statistics, and expert opinions. A decorating committee will need a sufficient supply of fabric, lights, and other materials. A group preparing a report may need audiovisual equipment. Steps should be taken to supply what is needed so the group's efforts will not be thwarted.

Create an Agenda

An *agenda* is a *schedule of what the group plans to accomplish in a meeting.* It is a guide for the group that helps the group pace itself and stay focused on its task. The agenda, written or oral, should tell what is to happen at the meeting or series of meetings, what is expected of group members, and what they should accomplish.

In planning a meeting, keep in mind the rate at which small groups function. A wise leader does not plan too much for a single meeting. It is better to overestimate the amount of time a task will take rather than face frustrating time pressures.

With the Four Oaks Co-op committee, the agenda for a one-hour meeting would look like this:

> It is better to overestimate the amount of time a task will take rather than face frustrating time pressures.

9:00–9:05	Settling in, getting drinks
9:05–9:10	Review of last meeting, preview of this meeting
9:10–9:25	Discussion of house membership parking survey form
9:25–9:45	Jim's report on parking situation at other cooperatives
9:45–9:55	Assignments and plans for next meeting
9:55–10:00	Final summary, dismissal

Members' Roles

We have discussed leadership at some length, but acknowledged leaders are only one part of the mix. The other, and equally important part, is the behavior of the group members.

Members Should Give their Time

Because small group work is often time consuming, members may need patience to work through issues faced by the group. Members should also contribute their time outside of meetings as well.

Members Should be Prepared

By parceling out work, a small group can accomplish more in a shorter time span than can an individual. Some activities member may do outside of meetings include gathering information through research or interviews, preparing documents, reading materials, writing reports, even supplying refreshments. If members arrive without having done necessary work beforehand, meetings will waste time and strain relationships.

Members Should Take Active Roles

Groups exist and function through the interaction of their members, and for people to make little attempt to contribute in meetings is to hamper the group's progress. While a good discussion leader will attempt to bring out the reluctant, a better approach is for members to put themselves forward.

Members Should be Constructive

Members' contributions should forward the group toward its goals. Despite disagreements, members should still strive to be respectful of those with differing opinions and be sensitive to their feelings and ideas. What one is tempted to say in the heat of a conflict and what one should say for the good of the group may be two different things. For the sake of the group, members should choose the latter. Another part of respect for others is allowing them to express themselves. Long-winded orations have little place in small groups.

Positive Group Member Activities

Group work can be a rewarding process or a time-consuming exercise in frustration. The difference between the two results is decided by the way in which group members play their roles. For a group to succeed it will need to accomplish a number of tasks. Who accomplishes the tasks is not as important as that the tasks be done. Sometimes the group leader displays the necessary skills. At other times, the tasks will be distributed evenly throughout the group. A person may possess only one of the following skills yet contribute an enormous amount to the group by the use of that talent (Based on Beene and Sheets).

Providing and Evaluating Information

The best decisions are informed decisions. If a group is to make the best possible decision, sufficient accurate information is a must. A group must also evaluate its information to decide what is valuable and acceptable. To reach a satisfactory solution, the Four Oaks Co-op parking committee gathers information on parking needs, property costs, legal restrictions, financing, insurance, and available property.

Creating Ideas

To act, a group must have some idea of its possible courses of action. The person who comes up with new ideas for solutions, criteria, and information sources helps the group to broaden its scope.

Elaborating Ideas

A group member may be creative with ideas and still not see all the possibilities inherent in those ideas. An elaborator is a person who takes an idea and expands it to show its possibilities, one who can envision the idea's potential.

In the parking committee one suggests taking a survey to determine the parking needs of the house's membership. Another elaborates by bringing in information from his recent class on research techniques. He talks about types of surveys, administering surveys, and in what ways they can be helpful.

Clarifying/Explaining

Clarification and explanation are necessary in groups because all members do not possess the same kind of knowledge, background, and abilities. Teaching is a part of small groups as members enlighten each other and provide a common base of information.

During one meeting of the parking committee, a member in computer engineering proposes making a computer model of neighborhood parking so the group can test the effect of variables on the situation. Some are unfamiliar with the construction and use of computer modeling, so the group stops for a mini-lesson on computer modeling.

Encouraging

Group members may have good ideas or suggestions but be reluctant to express them for a variety of reasons. The ideas may go unexpressed if someone does not provide motivation. Encouragement can come in many forms. It may be done through the creation of a positive group climate. It can be done by an individual who coaxes a person into talking. It can be accomplished by following a person's statement with positive reactions. Even if the idea is of marginal value, the member can still be praised or thanked for contributing.

Empathizing

While much of what transpires in a problem-solving situation is rational, emotions still play an important part. It is frustrating to feel that our ideas are not appreciated or to think that nobody understands our situation. Empathy from a group member shows concern and respect for an individual and contributes to positive relations in the group.

The Four Oaks Co-op committee holds open meetings to gather information from the membership. One member complains strongly that the parking situation interferes with his working schedule. A committee members points out that he also has to balance classes and work and shows that he knows the situation well. The disgruntled member leaves with added confidence that the committee will do its work well.

Mediating

Besides empathy, mediation is also necessary to smooth out conflicts and build respect. Not all group members will agree on all issues. Groups may even find themselves fracturing into two sides as members take opposing sides and refuse to budge. In these cases, a mediator is of immense help to the group.

A mediator will work back and forth between the opposing sides, trying to understand the positions, empathizing, and offering suggestions to resolve the impasse. By taking an active role and seeking solutions, the mediator allows the group to move forward in its work rather than come to a halt over a difference of opinion.

Relieving Tension

Tension relief is commonly needed when a group first forms or when new members arrive. People may be nervous about meeting strangers or feel awk-

A mediator will work back and forth between the opposing sides, trying to understand the positions, empathizing, and offering suggestions to resolve the impasse.

ward because they do not know the group's norms. Here tension can be relieved by someone who greets them in a friendly manner, introduces them to other members, finds them a place to sit, or supplies them with refreshments.

Tension relief is also useful to a group throughout its existence. We have already noted that groups work by alternating between concentration on the task and relaxation. Relieving tensions provides the group with a way of releasing its emotional involvement in the task and then returning to its work. Here the tension relief may be a joke, a story, or a short recess.

Testing Ideas

One of the most important jobs in a group is that of testing ideas. A person takes on the task of raising objections to an idea so the group can be sure that it has considered all the possibilities and ramifications of its ideas. These are the people who play the role of "negative other" or "devil's advocate.[1]" While staying in tune with the purpose of the group, they take stances against ideas and point out their flaws and shortcomings. They may even make counterproposals. The point is not to turn the group into a debating society but to make sure that the group has considered all the possible results of an idea or course of action.

Negative Group Member Activities

While group members who act positively can do much to advance the work of a group, conversely members can also seriously hamper the work of a group by their negative actions. The negative behaviors are detrimental because they divert the group from its purpose and prevent profitable relationships.

Withdrawing

One of the simplest methods of undermining a group is to refuse to participate in it. Whether disgruntled or designing, a person stops attending meetings, or if the person shows up, the person is unprepared to participate. Assigned tasks are unfinished or poorly done. Promised materials are incomplete. Others have to take on more work to make up for the withdrawer's failures.

The problem can sometimes be solved by the group dismissing the person, regrouping, and continuing its work. At other times, a confrontation is necessary to make the individual aware of the group's feeling and to deliver an ultimatum to the person.

Fighting

Disagreements and conflict are a normal part of group work. Fighting, though, is not a productive way of dealing with the disagreements. Group members engage in fighting when the point of their actions is not to help the group solve its problem but to score points in an argument. Instead of remaining focused on the group's work, fighters focus on themselves and the rewards they get from verbal combat with other group members.

Dominating

Groups should be a melding of members' viewpoints and contributions. When one member takes over the group and forces her will on the group, that person becomes a dominator. When members do not feel free to participate, they will feel frustrated. They will likely make few contributions or withdraw from the group.

Manipulating

Group members become manipulative when they work to accomplish their goals by bargains made with individuals outside of meetings. A manipulator may make threats, may promise benefits, or may cajole a reluctant member into agreement. Manipulation also occurs when group members attain their personal goals through unethical means such as providing incomplete or false information. These practices lower the quality of group decisions because they do not allow for open and informed decision making.

Excessive Socializing

One of the pleasures of group work is the relationship one enjoys with other group members. While socializing may be a pleasant part of a problem-solving group, too much socializing can distract the group from its task.

Group members control the direction of their group's development. Positive contributions such as supplying information and testing ideas will speed the group process. Negative activities such as withdrawing and dominating will hamper and perhaps destroy the group process.

> **Following the steps of rational problem solving will result in the best decisions.**

Conclusion

Small group communication is an interplay of many factors. A number of things will influence the quality of the work performed by the group. Problems may be solved in ineffective ways that create further difficulties or they can be addressed in more productive fashion. Following the steps of rational problem solving will result in the best decisions. Leadership style should be adapted to the group and the task at hand. By their positive and negative behaviors, group members aid or confound the problem solving process.

Notes

[1] "Devil's Advocate" is the popular name for the "promoter of the faith" in the Roman Catholic Church. In the procedures which decide whether or not to designate a person a saint, the promoter of the faith or "devil's advocate" raises objections and argues against the case for sainthood. ("Devil's Advocate." *New Catholic Encyclopedia.* 1967.)

Discussion Questions

1. How are informational resources, group effort, and quality of thinking linked?

2. What makes the ineffective methods of problem solving (rushing to judgment, etc.) ineffective?

3. What advantages are gained by using the rational model of problem solving?

4. How do vision, direction, and mediation combine in a good leader?

5. How can a group balance the tensions between an emergent leader and an appointed leader?

6. What determines which small group leadership model is appropriate in a given situation?

7. How does one create a helpful environment for successful group work?

8. How can members make positive contributions to their small groups?

9. Why are the negative group member activities harmful to a group's progress?

Sources and References ////

Andrews, Patricia Hayes. "Performance-Self-Esteem and Perception of Leadership Emergence: A comparative Study of Men and Women." *Western Journal of Speech Communication* 48 (1984): 1–13.

Barge, J. Kevin. "Leadership Skills and the Dialectics of Leadership in Group Decision Making. *Communication and Group Decision Making.* 2nd. ed. Eds. Randy Y. Hirokawa and Marshall Scott Poole. Thousand Oaks, California, 1996.

———. "Leadership as Medium: A Leaderless Group Discussion Model." *Communication Quarterly* 37 (1989): 237-49.

Benne, Kenneth D. and Paul Sheets. "Functional Role of Group Members." *Journal of Social Issues* 4 (Spring 12948): 41–49.

Billingsley, Julie M. "An Evaluation of the Functional Perspective in Small Group Communication." *Communication Yearbook 16.*

Boorman, Ernest. G. "Symbolic Convergence Theory and Communication in Group Decision Making." *Communication and Group Decision Making.* 2nd. ed. Eds. Randy Y. Hirokawa and Marshall Scott Poole. Thousand Oaks, California, 1996. 301–44.

Bormann, Ernest G. "Symbolic Convergence Theory and Communication in Group Decision Making." *Communication and Group Decisions-Making.* 2nd ed. Eds. Randy Y. Hirokawa and Marshall Scott Poole. Beverly Hills: Sage Publications, 1986. 219–36.

Bormann, Ernest G. and Nancy C. Bormann. *Effective Small Group Communication.* Edina, Minnesota: Burgess Publishing Company, 1988.

Broome, Benjamin J. and David B. Keever. "Next Generation Group Facilitation: Proposed Principles." *Management Quarterly* 3 (1989): 107–127.

Bunyi, Judith M. and Patricia Hayes Andrews. "Gender and Leadership Emergence: An Experimental Study." *The Southern Speech Communication Journal* 50 (1985):246–60.

Chilberg, Joseph C. "A Review of Group Process Designs for Facilitating Communication in Problem-Solving Groups." *Management Communication Quarterly* 3 (1989): 51–70.

Cline, Rebecca J. Welch. "Detecting Groupthink: Methods for Observing the Illusion of Unanimity." *Communication Quarterly* 38 (1990): 112–126.

Cragan, John F. and David W. Wright. "Small Group Communication Research of the 1980s: A Synthesis and a Critique." *Communication Studies* 41 (1990): 212–36.

Davis, James H., Lorne Hulbert and Wing Tung Au. "Procedural Influence in Group Decision Making: The Case of Straw Polls." *Communication and Group Decision Making*. 2nd. ed. Eds. Randy Y. Hirokawa and Marshall Scott Poole. Thousand Oaks, California, 1996. 55–80.

Dewey, John. *How We Think*. Boston: D. C. Heath and Co., Publishers, 1910.

Fairhurst, Gail T. and Teresa A. Chandler. "Social Structure in Leader-Member Interaction." *Communication Monographs* 56 (1989): 215–39.

Fisher, Bob and Bo Thomas. *Real Dream Teams*. Delray Beach, Florida: St. Lucie Press, 1996.

Folger, Joseph P. and Marshall Scott Poole. *Working Through Conflict: A Communication Perspective*. Glenview, Illinois: Scott, Foresman and Company, 1984.

Friedman, Paul G. "Upstream Facilitation: A Productive Approach to Problem-Solving Groups." *Management Communication Quarterly* 3 (1989): 33–50.

Gouran, Dennis S. "Inferential Errors, Interaction, and Group Decision-Making." *Communication and Group Decision-Making*. Eds. Randy Y. Hirokawa and Marshall Scott Poole. Beverly Hills: Sage Publications, 1986.

Gouran, Dennis S. and Randy Y. Hirokawa. "Counteractive Functions of Communication in Effective Group Decision-Making." Eds. Randy Y. Hirokawa and Marshall Scott Poole. *Communication and Group Decision-Making*. Beverly Hills: Sage Publications, 1986.

Graham, Elizabeth E. and Michael H. Papa, and Mary B. McPherson. "An Applied Text of the Functional Communication Perspective of Small Group Decision-Making." *The Southern Communication Journal* (1997): 269–79.

Hewes, Dean. "Small Group Communication May Not Influence Decision Making: An Amplification Of Socio-Egocentric Theory." *Communication and Group Decision Making*. 2nd. Ed. Eds. Randy Y. Hirokawa and Marshall Scott Poole. Thousand Oaks: California. Sage Publications, 1996. pp. 179–214.

———. "A Socio-Egocentric Model of Group Decision-Making." *Communication and Group Decision-Making*. Eds. Randy Y. Hirokawa and Marshall Scott Poole. Beverly Hills: Sage Publications, 1986. 265–91.

Hirokawa, Randy Y. and Dirk R. Scheerhorn. "Communication in Faulty Decision-Making." *Communication and Group Decision-Making*. Eds. Randy Y. Hirokawa and Marshall Scott Poole. Beverly Hills: Sage Publications, 1986. 63–80.

Hirowaka, Randy Y. and Dennis S. Gouran. "Facilitation of Group Communication: A Critique of Prior Research and an Agenda for Future Research." *Management Communication Quarterly* 3 (1989): 71–92.

Hirokawa, Randy Y., Larry Erbert, and Anthony Hurst. "Communication and Group Decision-Making Effectiveness." *Communication and Group Decision Making*. 2nd. ed. Eds. Randy Y. Hirokawa and Marshall Scott Poole. Thousand Oaks, California, 1996. 269–300.

Jackson, Phil, with Hugh Delenany. *Sacred Hoops: Spiritual Lessons On A Hardwood Warrior*. New York: Hyperion, 1995

Janis, Irving L. *Crucial Decisions: Leadership in Policymaking and Crisis Management*. New York: The Free Press, 1989.

———. *Groupthink: Psychological Studies of Policy Decisions and Fiascoes*. 2nd ed. Boston: Houghton Mifflin Company, 1982.

Jarboe, Susan. "Procedures for Enhancing Group Decision Making." *Communication and Group Decision Making*. 2nd. ed. Eds. Randy Y. Hirokawa and Marshall Scott Poole. Thousand Oaks, California, 1996. 345–83.

Keltner, john. "Facilitation: Catalyst for Group Problem Solving." *Management Communication Quarterly* 3 (1989): 8–32.

Ketchum, Lyman D. and Eric Trist. *All Teams Are Not Created Equal: How Employee Empowerment Really Works*. Newbury Park, California: 1992.

Manz, Charles C. and Henry P. Sims, Jr. *Business Without Bosses: How Self-Managing Teams Are Building High-Performing Companies*. New York: John Wiley and Sons: 1993.

Mayer, Michael. M., Kevin T. Sonoda, and William B. Gudukuns. "The Effect of Time Pressure and Type of Information on Decision Quality." *The Southern Communication Journal* (1997): 280–92.

McBurney, James H. and Kenneth G. Hance. *The Principles and Methods of Discussion*. New York: Harper and Brothers.

McLeod, Poppy Lauretta. "New Communication Technologies for Group Decision Making: Towards an Integrative Framework." *Communication and Group Decision Making*. 2nd. ed. Eds. Randy Y. Hirokawa and Marshall Scott Poole. Thousand Oaks, California, 1996.

Monroe, Crain, Mark G. Borzi, and Vincent S. DiSalvo. "Conflict Behaviors of Difficult Subordinates." *The Southern Communication Journal* 54 (1989): 311–29.

Nilson, Carolyn. *More Team Games for Trainers*. New York: McGraw-Hill, 1998.

Odenwald, Sylvia B. *Global Solutions for Teams: Moving From Collision to Collaboration*. Chicago: Irwin, 1996.

Poole, Marshall Scott. "Decision Development in Small Groups I: A Comparison of Two Models." *Communication Monographs* 48 (1981): 1–24.

———. "Decision Development in Small Groups II: A Study of Multiple Sequences in Decision Making." *Communication Monographs* 48 (1983): 206–32.

———. "Decision Development in Small Groups III: A Multiple Sequence Model of Group Decision Making." *Communication Monographs* 48 (1983): 321–41.

———. "Do We Have Any Theories of Group Communication." *Communication Quarterly* 41 (1990): 237–47.

Poole, Marshall Scott and Carolyn L. Baldwin. "Development Process in Group Decision Making." *Communication and Group Decision Making*. 2nd. ed. Eds. Randy Y. Hirokawa and Marshall Scott Poole. Thousand Oaks, California, 1996.

Poole, Marshall Scott and Joel A. Doelger. "Developmental Processes in Group Decision-Making." *Communication and Group Decision-Making*. Eds Randy Y. Hirokawa and Marshall Scott Poole. Beverly Hills: Sage Publications, 1986. 35–62.

Poole, Marshal Scott, David R. Deibold, and Robert D. McPhee. "A Structurational Approach to Theory-Building on Group Decision-Making Research." *Communication and Group Decision-Making*. Eds Randy Y. Hirokawa and Marshall Scott Poole. Beverly Hills: Sage Publications, 1986. 237–64.

———. "Group Decision-Making as a Structuration Process." *The Quarterly Journal of Speech* 71 (1985): 74–102.

Putnam, Linda L. and Tricia S. Jones. "The Role of Communication in Bargaining." *Human communcation Research* 8 (1982): 262–80.

Putnam, Linda L. and Cynthia Stohl. "Bona Fide Groups: A Reconceptualization of Groups in Context." *Communication Studies* 41 (1990): 248–65.

Putnam, Linda L. and Charmaine E. Wilson. "Communicative Strategies in Organizational Conflicts: Rehability and Validity of a Measurement Scale." *Communication Yearbook* 6. Ed. Michael Burgoon. Beverly Hills: Sage Publications, 1982. 629–52.

Scott, Craig R. and Jolie C. Fontenot. "Multiple Identifications during Team Meetings: A Comparison of Conventional and Computer-Supported Interactions." *Communication Reports* 12 (1999): 91–100.

Serafini, Denise M. and Judy C. Pearson. "Leadership Behavior and Sex Role Socialization: Two sides of the Coin." *The Southern Speech Communication Journal* 49 (1984): 396–405.

Sykes, Richard E. "Imagining What We Really Might Study If We Really Studied Small Groups from a Speech Perspective." *Communication Studies* 41 (1990): 200–11.

Smith, Christie McGruffie and Larry Powell. "The Use of Disparaging Humor by Group Leaders." *The Southern Speech Communication Journal* 53 (1988): 279–92.

Wall, Victor D. and Gloria J. Galanes. "The SYMLOG Dimensions and Small Group Conflict." *The Central States Speech Journal* 37 (1986): 61–78.

Wheeless, Lawrence and Lisa S. Reichel. " A Reinforcement Model of the Relationship of Supervisor's General Communication Styles and Conflict Management Styles to Task Attraction." *Communication Quarterly* 38 (1990): 372–87.

Zorn, Theodore E. and Lawrence B. Rosenfield. "Between a Rock and a Hard Place: Ethical Dilemmas in Problem-Solving Group Facilitation." *Management Communication Quarterly* 3 (1989): 93–106.

⫸ Study Questions ⫷

Working in Groups

1. What four things influence the quality of a group's work?

   _____

   _____

2. What are ineffective ways of problem solving?

   _____

   _____

3. What are the steps of the rational model of problem solving?

   _____

   _____

4. Why is it important in group problem solving to define the problem?

   _____

   _____

5. What is accomplished by setting criteria for a solution?

   _____

   _____

6. What are three traits of leadership?

   _____

   _____

7. In what ways should a group leader be prepared?

   _____

   _____

8. How can a group leader be sensitive to the needs of the group?

   _____

   _____

9. What is an authoritarian style of leadership?

_____

_____

10. What is a democratic style of leadership?

_____

_____

11. What is a consensus-seeking style of leadership?

_____

_____

12. What is a laissez-faire style of leadership?

_____

_____

13. Which style of leadership is best for a group?

_____

_____

14. What are recommended steps in planning a meeting?

_____

_____

15. What is an agenda?

_____

_____

16. What guidelines should group members follow to contribute to successful meetings?

_____

_____

17. What are the positive activities in which group members can engage?

_____

_____

18. Why is it important to have an "idea tester" in a small group?

_____

_____

19. What are the negative activities in which group members can engage?

_____

_____

20. When does "relieving tension" become "excessive socializing"?

_____

Decision Making Exercise

The "John J. Watson Outstanding Senior Award" was created by its namesake, a successful and wealthy alumnus of State University. Watson feels that his experiences at State U. prepared him well and led to his success in business. He wished to recognize present students who have done well at the school and has instituted this award which is given annually and carries a one thousand dollar prize. In addition, the winner's name is placed on a plaque in the Student Services Building.

You are a member of the selection committee charged with designating the outstanding senior, "that person who best exemplifies the qualities of academic success, leadership, service, achievement, and contribution to the school." Five finalists have been chosen. You and your colleagues are to choose the final winner.

John Porter—GPA 3.75/4.00; computer science major; State PC Club; research assistant in computer science; co-author, "Disk Changing Strategy for Elimination of Write-through," *ACM Transactions of Computer Systems*; volunteer tutor, Learning Center; works thirty-five hours a week at K-Mart to pay for schooling; intended profession: computer science professor.

Mary Jeffrey—GPA 3.8/4.0; electrical engineering major; business manager, *Debris* yearbook; vice-president, president, YYY sorority; president, Panhellenic; Student Union Junior Board; Student Union Senior Board; summer intern, IBM; intended profession: electrical engineer.

Susan Holland—GPA 4.0/4.0; physical education and recreational studies major; equestrian club; Special Olympics assistant; Director, student volunteers for Special Olympics; Student Body Vice-President; Young Republicans; Golden Key Honorary; modern dance troupe; intended profession: physical therapist.

William Huang—GPA 4.0/4.0; English major; team captain, School of Liberal Arts telethon; photography club; First Place Team, Midwest Mock Trial Competition; English Department literary awards: freshman, "Best Descriptive Essay," junior, "Best Analytic Essay," senior, "Best Poem"; student representative, University Board of Trustees; president, Young Democrats; intended profession: attorney.

Nancy Flores—GPA 3.9/4.0; creative arts major; campus director, Big Sisters program; docent, State Galleries; teacher, Super Saturday Arts Program; vice-president, Whittier Housing Cooperative; departmental recipient, three years, Delta Phi Delta scholarship; winner, Outstanding Senior in Creative Arts; president, two years, Fine Arts Club; winner, Sudler Commencement Prize for Outstanding Achievement in the Arts; summer intern, Indianapolis Museum of Contemporary Art; intended profession: art museum director.

Sample Group Outline I
"Group Roles and Group Leadership"

Introduction (Margaret)

    A. The purpose of our presentation is to describe and depict group roles and styles of leadership.

    B. Definition: "A group is two or more interacting persons who share common goals and who perceive themselves as a group" (Baron and Byrne, *Social Psychology*).

    C. Groups exhibit four different aspects.

        1. Group members play roles.

        2. Groups create status relationships among members.

        3. Groups create norms.

        4. Groups create cohesiveness.

I. Groups create three different kinds of roles (Baron and Greenburg, *Behavior in Organization*).

    A. Task-oriented roles help the group achieve its goals.

    B. Relational roles are concerned with relations within the group.

    C. Self-oriented roles hamper the group in its work.

        1. With self-oriented roles, group members place their own desires first.

        2. Blockers are resistant to taking part.

        3. Recognition seekers direct attention to themselves.

        4. Dominators assert their authority.

        5. Avoiders isolate themselves from the group.

Skit One: The scene is a kindergarten class. Matt, Dale, Mandi, and Keely play the parts of students in the class. Each group member is labeled with one of the self-oriented roles. Their task as a problem solving group is to assemble a puzzle. The "dominator" tries to make the others assemble the puzzle the way he thinks it should be done. The "avoider" refuses to take part. The "blocker" keeps interfering with the process. The "recognition seeker" wants everyone to pay attention to her.

II. A group leader is defined as "a person's ability to influence others to work toward achieving personal and organizational goals" (Megginson, Mosley, and Pietri, *Management: Concepts and Applications).* (Corinna)

III. Group leaders may be classified according to their styles. (Corinna)

    A. Leaders may be classified according to their approaches to people.

        1. Autocratic leaders make decisions unilaterally.

Skit Two: Margaret plays the role of the teacher. She steps into the classroom and assigns each student a part of the puzzle to assemble.

        2. Participative-democratic leaders involve all in the decision making process.

Skit Three: Margaret again plays the teacher. She asks the students which part of the puzzle each would like to assemble. She assigns tasks according to what each would most like to do.

B. Leaders may be classified according to their orientation towards the job.

    1. People-oriented leaders show concern for the welfare and feelings of group members.

Skit Four: Margaret talks with each student and learns what task each likes to do. She encourages them to work together and enjoy finishing the job. They appear to be having a good time.

    2. Product-oriented leaders focus on getting the job done.

Skit Five: Margaret directs the students to concentrate on finishing their work. She guides them individually and reminds them of a penalty if they are not finished.

IV. Which style of leadership is best depends on the nature of a given group. (Corinna)

A. Hersey and Blanchard's Life-Cycle Theory states that a group leader's style should be appropriate to the group situation (Megginson, Mosley, and Pietri, *Management: Concepts and Applications*).

B. The graph explains how factors interact.

    1. The x-axis indicates task behavior.

    2. The y-axis indicates relationship behavior.

    3. Maturity of the group plays a role.

    4. Choices for leadership can be indicated by which quadrant best describes the group.

        a. A group highly oriented to task and with good relationships should work best with a leader who uses a "selling or coaching" style.

        b. A group low in task orientation but with good relationships should work best with a leader who uses a "participating and supporting" style.

        c. A group highly oriented to task and low in relationships should work best with a leader who uses a "structuring and telling" style.

        d. A group low in task orientation and low in relationships should work best with a leader who uses a "delegating" style.

Conclusion: (Corinna)

We have attempted to demonstrate to you the types of roles found in small groups and the importance of leadership in small groups. We have simplified the setting and the task for our group, but you can readily see the effects of different leadership techniques on the self-oriented roles in the group. The key thing to remember is that no one form of leadership is best under all conditions and in all situations. The best style of leadership is the one that is best adapted to the roles and tasks of a given group.

Matt Boatman
Dale Brier
Margaret Farrell
Keely Fountain
Mandi Hepler
Corinna Mikesell

Bibliography ///

Bacon, Robert A. and Donna E. Byrne. *Social Psychology.* 6th ed. Boston: Allyn and Bacon, 1991.

Bacon, R. A. and Jerald Greenburg. *Behavior in Organizations.* 3rd ed. Boston: Allyn and Bacon, 1990.

Cartwright, Dorwin and Alvin Zander. *Group Dynamics: Research and Theory.* 3rd ed. New York: Harper and Row Publishers, 1968.

Cherrington, David J. *Management of Human Resources.* 3rd ed. Boston: Allyn and Bacon, 1991.

Dobson, James. *Love Must Be Tough.* New York: New York Press, 1989.

Farley J. E. *Sociology.* 2nd ed. Englewood Cliffs, New Jersey: Prentice-Hall, 1992.

Hare, Paul A. *Handbook of Small Group Research.* 2nd ed. New York: The Free Press, 1976.

McGoldensen, Robert. *The Encyclopedia of Human Behavior, Psychology, Psychiatry, and Mental Health.* New York: Doubleday and Company, 1970.

Megginson, Leon, Donald Mosley, and Paul Pietri, Jr. *Management: Concepts and Applications.* 4th ed. New York: Harper Collins, Publishers, 1992.

Muchinsky, P. M. *Psychology Applied to Work.* 3rd ed. Pacific Grove, California: Brooks/Cole Publishing Company, 1990.

Phillips, Gerald M. and Eugene Erickson. *Interpersonal Dynamics in the Small Group.* New York: Random House, 1990.

Schikendantz, Judith. *Understanding Children.* 3rd ed. New York: The New York Press, 1991.

Shaw, Marvin E. *Group Dynamics: The Psychology of Small Groups.* New York: McGraw-Hill, Inc., 1976.

Sher, Barbara and Anne Gottlieb. *Teamwork: Building Support Groups that Guarantee Success.* New York: Warner Bros., 1989.

Smith, Robert E., Jr. *Principles of Human Communication.* 3rd ed. Dubuque, Iowa: Kendall/Hunt Publishing Company, 1992.

Sample Group Outline II

Effective Communication in Job Interviewing

Introduction (Jo)

I.   The job interview is a topic with which we can all relate.

II. We invite you as an audience to interact with the presentation.

    A. Score the mock interviews.

    B. Decide which person is playing which role

III. I will talk with the interviewer (Ed) to ask about the type of questions he will ask.

IV. I talk to each of the interviewees.

    A. "How nervous are you?"

    B. "Remember that your ability to communicate effectively in a stressful situation is of critical importance" (Ryan and Cooper, *Those Who Can, Teach*).

V.   Each group member illustrates a different kind of interviewer.

    A. Scott—Mr. Unprepared

    B. Teresa—Ms. Shy

    C. Kristine—Ms. Ingratiator

    D. Mike—Mr. Slob

    E. Jamie—Mr. Perfect

VI. Positive communication is highly important in a successful interview. (Jamie)

    A. Positive nonverbal communication helps you as an interviewee (Dick Fox, "Learn to Sell Yourself in an Interview," *Agri-Marketing*).

    B. Answering questions in a clear, positive fashion is helpful (Kehoe Group, "Interviewing Success").

VII. Being too casual contributes to an ineffective interview. (Mike)

    A. Mr. Slob's clothing, t-shirt and jeans, were too informal for the interview.

    B. Mr. Slob's manner communicated disinterest in the position.

        1. He did not pay attention to the questions.

        2. "Good communication always is the essence of a successful interview" (Jennifer Laabs, "You Don't Say," *Personnel Journal*).

VIII. Do not dominate the interview. (Kristine)

    A. Quotation: "You will occasionally run into an interviewee who tries to dominate the interview" (Diane Arthur, *Interviewing . . . Orienting New Employees*).

    B. Be careful not to talk too much. That can lead to babbling.

    C. Let the interviewer ask questions of you.

    D. Nonverbal communication is important.

        1. Maintain appropriate distance.

        2. Don't dominate nonverbally.

    E. "There is a fine line between persistence and being a pain in the neck" (Lois Smith Brady, "Ambitious? Just Go For It," *Working Woman*).

IX Assertive communication is important to a successful interview. (Teresa)

    A. " . . . the recipient of nonverbal behavior is usually the superior" (Martin Remland, "The Effects of Nonverbal Involvement and Communication Apprehension . . . ,"*Communica-tion Quarterly*).

        1. Ms. Shy communicated her lack of confidence by a number of nonverbal cues.

            a. She sat a long distance from the interviewer.

            b. She avoided eye contact.

            c. She looked ill at ease.

        2. Others make assumptions about us based on our nonverbal cues.

    B. The question, "What salary do you expect?" was answered with a noncommittal response.

        1. "Job seekers asking for an equal to greater amount than their last position get hired within the first three months of looking" ("Asking for Less . . .," *HR Focus*).

        2. Employers regard "bargain rate" candidates as people easily lured away.

X. Good preparation is essential for a successful interview. (Scott)

    A. Mr. Unprepared was just that.

        1. He was unsure of himself.

        2. He did not know what to expect.

        3. He was ignorant of the company's product.

    B. The extent of your preparation can reflect your desire, maturity, and organizational skills.

    C. Plan ahead for the interview.

        1. Know yourself and your goals.

        2. Research commonly asked interview questions.

        3. Prepare concise and informative answers.

        4. Research the company.

            a. Learn the products and services.

            b. Learn the company structure.

            c. Review recent performance.

            d. Use your research as the basis for your own questions.

Conclusion (Jo)

    A. These interviews were changed to make points.

        1. They were shorter than real interviews.

        2. The characters were exaggerated.

    B. Our purpose was to highlight behaviors.

        1. We provided insight into interview questions.

        2. We showed how people should and should not respond.

    C. We showed the importance of verbal communication.

        1. Be assertive but not overbearing.

        2. Be prepared to answer tough questions.

        3. Be alert and attentive.

Teresa Hurrle
Kristina Kitts
Jamie Moore
Scott Nelson
Mike Sellers
Ed Weakley
Johanna White

Bibliography ////

Arthur, Diane. *Recruiting, Interviewing, Selecting, and Orienting New Employees.* New York: ANACOM, 1991.

"Asking for Less Often Means More Time to Find Jobs." *HR Focus* Jan. 1992: 16.

Brady, Lois Smith. "Ambitious? Just Go For It." *Working Woman* July 1991: 71–73.

Dettore, Albert A. "The Art of the Interview." *Small Business Reports* Feb. 1992: 11–15.

Fox, Dick. "Learn to Sell Yourself in an Interview." *Agri-Marketing* May 1992: 22–24.

Freeman, Robert D. "Back to the Basics of Interviewing." *HR Focus* Jan. 1992: 10.

184 *Principles of Human Communication*

Grossman, Jack. "How to Sell Yourself: A Guide for Interviewing Effectively." *Advanced Management Journal* 56 Spring 1991: 33–36.

Kacmar, Michelle. "Look Who's Talking." *HR Focus* Feb. 1993: 56–58.

Kehoe Group, The. "Interviewing Success." *Business Communication Activities.* 1988.

Kituse, Alicia. "Manager's Tool Kit." *Across the Board* Jan.-Feb. 1992: 62–63.

Laabs, Jennifer. "You Don't Say." *Personnel Journal* Sept. 1991: 125.

Remland, Martin S. "The Effects of Nonverbal Involvement and Communication Apprehension on State Anxiety, Interpersonal Attraction, and Speech Duration." *Communication Quarterly* 37 (1989): 170–83.

Ryan, Kevin, and James M. Cooper. *Those Who Can, Teach.* Boston: Houghton Mifflin Company, 1992.

Skopp, Jennifer. "Dress for Success Becoming More Casual in Today's Workplace." *HR Focus* Jan. 1992: 18.

Dealing with Difficult Group Situations

8

KEY CONCEPTS

Defining "Conflict"
Approaches to Conflict
  Avoidance
  Capitulation
  Coercion
  Fighting
  Separation
  Cooperative Conflict Resolution
    Negotiation
Minimizing Conflict
  Cultivate Good Group Climate
  Create Appropriate Norms
  Gauge the Conflict
Confronting Conflict
  Part of Solution and Problem
  Look to Behavior, Not Personality
    Talk to the Issue, Not the Person
  Describe How Issue Affects You
  See Other Person's Position
  Ask Questions Instead of Making Statements
  Allow for Feelings
  Declare a Break
  Vent Emotions
  Set Guidelines
  Separate Solution and Decision
  Compromise
Dealing With Difficult Group Members
  Recognize the Problem
  Look for Problem Areas and Sensitivities
  Hold the Group to Objective Standards
  Look for Common Ground
  Provide Members with a Safety Valve
Avoiding Groupthink
Vigilance in Problem Solving
  Decide How Important an Issue Is
  Do the Best You Can in the Circumstances

G roup work can be a rewarding experience, but it is not without its perils, as are any of our relationships. Even the best of friends and most loving of families have moments when they disagree, sometimes strongly. Groups also have to confront antagonistic situations.

Defining "Conflict"

Conflict is inevitable in human relations. The question is not how can we eliminate conflict, but rather how can we deal with conflict in the most positive way. Resolved conflict can strengthen and maintain a relationship while ongoing, unresolved conflict can weaken and possibly destroy the relationship.

Conflict occurs when the feelings, interests, or ways of behaving of one person interfere with the feelings, interests, or ways of behaving of another person. Another way of putting the matter is that we create conflict when we block each other from attaining our goals. The goal may be cooking dinner, winning a game, securing a promotion, or selecting our solution as the best approach to solving a problem. Whether in groups or interpersonal relationships, how we handle conflicts will determine how successful those relationships will be. As some have observed, "conflict is productive to the extent that it helps a group discover and examine its options as clearly as possible" (Wall and Galanes 63).

Approaches to Conflict

At the Four Oaks Cooperative, Tom and Jeff Walker are brothers who share a room. They have one car between them which their parents supplied and told them to share. One Friday afternoon, they discover that they both have dates that night, and that the dates will be on opposite sides of town about the same time. Each feels he has an equal right to the car for the evening.

We have a wide range of ways to react to conflict, some of them productive, others not. At one end of the spectrum is *avoidance.* Here the parties stay away from each other or rule some areas out of bounds for discussion. At a family holiday gathering, family members may stay off topics such as religion and politics which they know will be divisive. Instead, they look for points of mutual agreement. At other times, avoidance can lead to deteriorating relationships. One study of couples in therapy revealed that "avoidance, indirectness, and decreased involvement" characterized the behavior of couples unable or unwilling to maintain their marriages (Courtright et al. 429).

With this approach to solving conflicts, Tom would keep quiet as soon as he learned Jeff needed the car, not assert his own claims, and let Jeff take the car.

Capitulation is another approach to conflict that is similar to avoidance. Here one may state one's views, but then the person gives up the effort. Since little accommodation is given to the views and feelings of the capitulating party, the solution may cause resentment further along.

Here Tom would assert his claim, argue for it, but would eventually say something like "Okay. All right. Just take the car."

Often closely linked to capitulation is *coercion.* Here one party is forced into an undesirable course of action. Coercion involves the threat, real or implied, of harm that will come to a person if that person does not submit to the

> Whether in groups or interpersonal relationships, how we handle conflicts will determine how successful those relationships will be.

requests of the other party. As might be imagined, coercive resolutions to conflicts leave the coerced party feeling misused and resentful and hinder the creation of a satisfactory solution (Tutzauer 429).

If Tom used coercion, he might say, "If you don't give me the car, I'm not helping you with your calculus anymore. You can flunk on your own instead of passing with my help."

One of the most famous of coercive strategies to resolve conflict occurs in the book and movie, *The Godfather.* The Godfather, a Mafia crime boss named Vito Corleone, is having a disagreement with a bandleader who has a friend of Corleone's under contract.

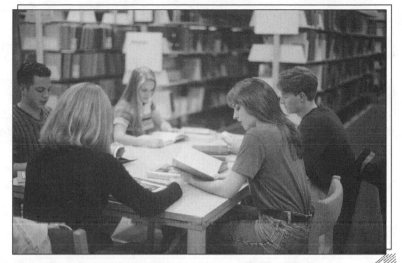

Research or investigating the problem is a major task for problem-solving groups.

Corleone wants the bandleader to sign a contract releasing the friend from the terms of the old contract. The bandleader refuses. Corleone than makes him "an offer you can't refuse." He takes out a pistol and tells the bandleader, "In one minute, either your signature or your brains are going to be on that contract." The bandleader signs (Puzo 42).

Another approach to conflicts is *fighting.* Here both parties may make their positions known, but instead of working toward a mutually acceptable goal, they maintain their positions without giving ground. They hammer at each other until one gives up or they separate.

On this Friday afternoon Four Oaks Co-op members hear shouting coming from Tom and Jeff Walker's room. Moving closer they hear, "I filled up the tank last time" followed by "Yeah? Well, I was the one who washed it last." The voices become louder and louder as each argues his point of view with little recognition of the other person. If the conflict continues to escalate, the verbal fight may become a physical fight.

Fighters may also try to accomplish their goals by sneak attacks as well as confrontation.

With the argument unsettled, Jeff goes to take a shower. While he is in the shower, Tom drives off with the car.

Sometimes, the best approach to handling a conflict is *separation.* Here the parties "agree to disagree." Realizing they cannot find a mutually satisfying solution to the difficulty, they part company.

Tired of fighting with his brother over the car, Tom moves out of the house and buys his own car.

By far the best approach to handling conflict is *cooperative conflict resolution.* Here the parties maintain contact and through *negotiation,* they explore the situation to discover a mutually satisfying solution to the problem. Negotiation is communication in which the parties confer with each other "so as to arrive at the settlement of some matter" (*Webster's Seventh New Collegiate Dictionary,* 1967). The "some matter" may be who gets the car Friday night or may be an international problem such as nuclear disarmament.

Sometimes, the solution involves *compromise* through which each party accomplishes some of its original goals while giving up others. At other times, negotiation can discover for both parties to accomplish their goals.

Tom and Jeff can perhaps solve the immediate problem by compromise: "Let's flip a coin and the winner gets the car." A more satisfactory approach would be "Let's see if we can borrow an extra car just for tonight." They might even be able to rearrange their schedules to accommodate both: "You take Beth and me to the party, go on to the movie with Sally, and after the movie you join us at the party."

A long range compromise would be, "I have first choice on weeks starting with even numbers, you have priority on weeks starting with odd numbers."

Minimizing Conflict

While conflict is inevitable in relationships, we can still do a number of things to smooth the way to accord. One way to handle conflict is to *cultivate the best possible group climate.* When group members respect each other and the group has a positive climate, members are less likely to create conflict and more likely to settle conflict productively than when a negative group climate exists.

As part of the climate, the group can *create norms that discourage unnecessary conflict.* Group members can decide how disagreements are to be stated, how conflicting parties are to address each other, and when mediation is to be introduced. With consensus reached on how conflict will be handled, the group can feel secure when conflict arises.

When group members *contribute positively,* conflict will be minimized. The fault finder's role is an easy one to assume, but constant negative reactions become in themselves an impetus to conflict. While groups need an idea tester or negative other, comments and ideas should be phrased in ways that attempt to help the group.

When conflict becomes open, group members have available a number of approaches and techniques to deal with the problem. One of the first things we need to do in conflict situations is to *gauge the importance of the conflict.* Conflicts range from small nuisances to major upheavals. Not all require strenuous effort or even recognition. Some of the seriousness of a conflict will be decided by the group and the norms it sets. In one group, gum chewing or snuff dipping may get on members' nerves so much that the matter becomes of concern to the whole group. In other groups, these practices would be accepted without question.

To gauge the importance of a conflict we can ask ourselves several questions. One of these is, *"How much does this conflict impair our ability to function as a group?"* If the matter is extraneous to the group's work, we should probably leave the matter alone.

Two candidates are running for the presidency of Four Oaks Cooperative. Kyle Murchinson backs one candidate while Jim Nakatana backs the other. Both Kyle and Jim, though, work together well on the social committee as their political differences are largely extraneous to the smooth operation of the social committee.

Another question is *"How much does this conflict interfere with my ability to function as a group member?"* If we find ourselves increasingly reluctant to participate because of the actions of another, we should probably address the conflict.

> Group members can decide how disagreements are to be stated, how conflicting parties are to address each other, and when mediation is to be introduced.

We can also ask, *"How long will I have to work under these conditions?"* We may find ourselves having to deal with an obnoxious person, but if we have only one meeting with a group and it lasts only an hour, we would do better to put up with the person instead of trying to eliminate the boor's grating habits.

Another important question is, *"Is the conflict whether or not I like this person?"* (Bormann and Bormann 152). Working relationships in groups do not necessarily mean warm, personal relationships between the members.

Confronting Conflict

Once conflict becomes significant, the way in which we address the situation can have positive or negative results for the group.

When we engage in conflict management, it is natural to think of ourselves as *part of the solution.* After all, we have some excellent ideas about what should be done. On the other hand, perhaps the hardest part of conflict management is also *to realize that we are part of the problem.* The tendency—indeed, the almost inevitable reaction—is to see the other party as the sole source of the problem and ourselves the more competent communicator in the situation (Sillars 191; Canary and Spitzbergh 146).

Another temptation is to frame the conflict in terms of the other person's personality or character flaws. Two roommates at Four Oaks are at odds because of their different ideas about how the room should be kept. Paul Jenkins is neat and orderly; Ed Williams is not.

Paul says, "You're the messiest person I have ever known. Your whole family is messy. And now I have to live with your mess. You are so inconsiderate that you can't even keep your stinking socks on your side of the room."

Ed counters with, "You're just compulsive. You have to be the most inflexible person I have ever known."

A more productive approach is to *look to the behavior, not to personality* (Donahue 10). Concentrating on the behavior we wish to see moves the conflict into a realm in which change is more easily accomplished. Finding a new personality is impossible. Picking up a sock and putting it into a laundry bag is easy to accomplish.

One important way one can look to the behavior is by *talking to the issue, not the person.* Instead of labelling the other person negatively, we talk about what we find bothersome in the situation. If a person objects to the statement of another, the response would focus on the statement, not the person who made it. To say, "How stupid can you be to make a statement like that?" is to put the other person on the defensive at a personal level. To say, instead, "I think the solution you suggest will cause other problems" is to focus discussion on the issue at hand. The second approach is the more productive of the two since it downplays personalities yet still addresses the difference of opinion.

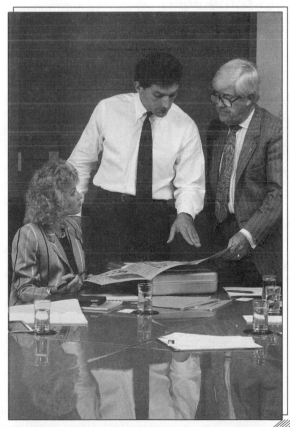

The best way to talk about conflict in a group is to speak to the issue, not to the person.

With this approach, Paul begins with, "I want to talk about how we keep the room. I don't like what we are doing."

Similarly, one can *describe how you see the issue affecting you* (Bolton 221–22; Adler 187–90, 219–27): "It makes me really angry when I have to clean up after you and when I find your stuff on my desk."

One of the more difficult tasks is to *see the other person's position in the contested manner* (Fisher and Ury 24; Bolton 200–24). Seeing the other person's position is not just a courtesy. People who can see the perspective of the other person are more efficient negotiators (Pappa and Pood 418).

In the case of Paul and Ed, both would have to work to see things through the other's eyes. Ed may have grown up in a home where neatness was not prized. Where things are is not important to him. He and his brothers shared space, and he thinks Paul is being picky to make such a big deal of whose space is whose. Ed thinks that keeping things in tidy stacks has no practical value and is organization for the sake of organization.

On the other hand, Paul may be an only child who is accustomed to controlling his own space. When Ed scatters his belongings around the room, Paul feels that his privacy is being invaded. He is highly organized because that is the way he functions best. He dislikes having to waste time finding items that should be readily at hand.

If they wish to share information about their perspectives, Ed and Paul would do well to *ask questions instead of making statements* (Tutzauer and Roloff 376). Instead of "Tell me why you can't pick up after yourself," Paul would do better to say, "Why do you leave your things all over the room?"

As conflicts give rise to strong emotions, it is also a good idea to *allow for feelings.*" Partners in conflict must find some way to control their own emotions and to deal with the outburst of the other. One good rule of thumb is "If it feels good, *don't* do it." To ignore caution and tell the other person off may be a great release, but it is also likely to be short-lived and counter-productive. Anger, typically, begets anger. A better approach to the situation is the old adage, "A soft answer turns away wrath."

> Partners in conflict must find some way to control their own emotions and to deal with the outburst of the other.

Ways can be found to handle emotions that appear likely to get out of hand. One way is simply to *declare a break.* After a pause, a walk around the block, or some refreshment, people may be better equipped for productive negotiation.

Another approach is for the angry person to *vent emotions outside of the conflict situation.* A third party who can be sympathetic and not become upset at what one says can be a big help (Bolton 24).

Feelings can be channeled when conflict partners *set guidelines for the conflict* (Fisher and Ury 31–32). Football players know that they will batter each other up and down the field, but they also know the limits of their battering. Clipping, grabbing facemasks, and other assaults are illegal and will result in punishments for the offender's team. Similarly, in conflict situations, people can establish what is acceptable behavior and what is not: "Shouting is all right, but we do not call each other names" or "We do not bring up problems until we have had dinner and a chance to unwind from the day."

In search for a solution, it may be helpful to *separate the solution from the decision* (Fisher and Ury 62–63). If one takes a stand, the other will likely take just as strong a stance. A more productive approach would be to put forth tentative solutions and discuss those. The approach is to say, "Here is one possibility; here is another; here is a third. Let's talk about them and see which one will work best for us."

cess is thwarted before a good solution is found. Rather than examining all possibilities, the group may discuss only one or two courses of action. In-group criticism of plans is discouraged and dissenters are ostracized. Little attempt is made to obtain relevant information. Outside criticism is regarded as the work of fools or scoundrels attempting to sabotage the group. Therefore, the group fails to consider carefully information and alternatives by employing effective decision making practices.

When groupthink prevails, the situation is similar to a preventable auto accident. Everyone in the car is pleased with how the trip is progressing and the good spirit in the car, but nobody pays attention to where they are going, and they drive happily over a cliff.

If a group seems closed to outside opinion and keeps internal criticism to a minimum, the group may be developing groupthink. If the group is congenial within itself and hostile to outsiders, again the group may be displaying groupthink. If the group seizes rapidly on a solution to a problem but has not investigated or discussed the problem fully, it is again showing signs of groupthink.

To avoid groupthink, the group should make provisions for full discussion of ideas and policies. Issues should be thoroughly researched. The group should discuss proposals from all sides. One member may even be designated the idea tester to see how well the group's proposals stand up against criticism. A climate of openness and honesty will also do much to prevent groupthink.

Vigilance in Problem Solving

The preceding chapters have outlined how groups can function best. If we lived in an ideal world, all small groups would approach problem solving with an open mind, sufficient time to effect the optimum solution, and would follow fully the guidelines provided here. As more than one person has observed, however, we do not live in an ideal world.

In the multitude of our activities—both professional and personal—we must confront problems, pressures, and limitations on our abilities to deal with them. A person may be appointed to a committee only to discover that the committee cannot find the time, resources, or people necessary for the committee to do its job fully. In addition, not all decisions merit the time and expense of group meetings. Finding a solution to the parking problem at Four Oaks Cooperative, for example, requires a committee, but the routine and small decisions—paying bills, purchasing office supplies, running the vacuum cleaner—do not.

Despite the limitations and discouragements we often find in our decision-making situations, we should still practice *vigilance in problem solving* (Janis, *Decisions*). In the hurly-burly of life, it is often impossible to carry out the step-by-step problem solving procedures that we have described. The fact that not all problems can be approached in a textbook manner does not mean, though, that the process should be abandoned if conditions are less than perfect. Instead, the process should be approximated as completely as possible as it allows for the best possible solutions, which bring the best consequences. "The quality of procedures used to arrive at a fundamental policy decision is one of the major determinants of a successful outcome" (Janis, *Decisions* 20.)

Practicing vigilant problem solving means that people follow two principles, both of which require awareness and sensitivity. The first is *deciding how impor-*

In the case of Paul and Ed, they have several options to explore. One could move out and trade places with someone else in the house. They could draw up a list of rules. Ed could be neater. Paul could be more flexible.

In searching for a way out of a conflict, people must be *prepared to compromise*. Each may need to give up some of his original goals or ideas. The starkest kind of compromise is a sales situation in which the dealer wants $X for a car, the customer is prepared to pay $Y, and the final price is $Z, halfway between $X and $Y. The "split the difference" approach is not, though, the only way to compromise. People can trade in a variety of things they find valuable: time, resources, space, and rewards. The best compromise is one that leaves all parties feeling as if they were successful in achieving their goals.

As Ed and Paul explore their conflict, they find that neither wants to move. Instead of both trying to meet the other's goals, they decide instead to create two separate spaces. They put a long strip of tape on the floor to divide the room in two. Paul agrees to say nothing about how Ed keeps his half. Ed agrees to keep his things on his side of the room.

A variety of approaches combining the above guidelines can ease the way to resolution of conflicts. In both interpersonal and group situations, we can find our way to accord by flexible and sensitive communication.

Dealing with Difficult Group Members

Because of the multiplicity of relationships in groups, groups may find themselves giving rise to conflicts which pit one or a minority of members against the rest of the group. These people may engage in some of the negative behaviors mentioned earlier such as fighting, withdrawing, or dominating. To be successful, groups must find ways to deal with these members.

Groups will need *to recognize the problem*. For a short time, it may be useful to overlook the problems caused by one member. The decision needs to be based on "What is best for the group?" If the problem becomes long-term and is hampering the work of the group, the members must deal actively with the situation.

One way to address the problem is simply to ask the person or persons why they are acting as they are. The offensive or obnoxious behavior may have its base in a larger problem and addressing the larger problem may make the person more cooperative.

In the Four Oaks Co-op parking committee, George is argumentative and uncooperative. Finally, Ron asks him what is the matter. It turns out that George and his girlfriend are having problems, and besides that, the transmission just went out on his car. After the group offers to help, he is more cooperative and the meeting moves forward.

In dealing with difficult people, group members should also *look for problem areas and sensitivities*. These are areas where group members are likely to take strong stands. Discussion in these areas may turn into what one calls "battles of the will." The only way it seems that a problem can be resolved is for one of the parties to capitulate to the other (Fisher and Ury 85).

If the problem areas are peripheral to the functioning of the group, conflict can be minimized by avoiding the topics. Another way around "battles of the will" is to *hold the group to objective standards in making decisions* (Fisher and Ury 84–86). As noted earlier, creating criteria for selecting a solution is a major part of group problem solving. Those criteria become the measuring

standard that determines the acceptability of all possible solutions. A gro
member may feel strongly about a pet solution, but if that solution does
meet the criteria, the group can reject it, not from personal whim but fro
reasoned standard.

Another way to deal with difficult people in small groups is to *look*
common ground between the person and the group. Here the group would try
find a way in which its desires and the desires of the troublesome group me
ber might be perceived as one.

On the parking committee, one member may object to changing the pres
situation because he does not want to park on the street where his car is m
likely to be damaged. The group could recognize his concerns and make saf
of the vehicles one of its criteria. The group could also remind the person
principle of the house, that they cooperate for the good of all.

Finally, a group may be able to deal with difficult members by finding w
to *provide members with a safety valve.* By "safety valve," we mean some way
which the member may express strong feelings or the group can recognize
person's views. Sometimes, all that may be necessary is to let people talk fre
about their views. At other times, a more formal outlet may be provided.
example, if all members do not concur in a decision, the dissenting memb
may submit a "minority report" along with the report of the committee.

Avoiding Groupthink

We have dealt at length with conflict and resolving conflicts in small gro
and stressed that unresolved conflicts may be detrimental to a group. One mi
think, then, that the ideal small group would be the one that exhibited
maximum amount of group harmony. That is not necessarily the case. T
much solidarity in a group can be as disastrous as too much discord. Whe
group becomes so unified and cohesive that it entertains no conflict, no
disagreements, the usual result is a bad decision. When a group develops
this manner, it is exhibiting "groupthink" which is defined as "a deteriorat
of mental efficiency, reality testing, and moral judgments that results from
group pressures" (Janis, *Groupthink* 9).

The term "groupthink" was coined by Irving L. Janis and is based on
examination of major foreign policy decisions both good and bad. The Kenne
administration, for example, made a disastrous decision to support the
planned and ill-fated Bay of Pigs invasion of Cuba. The invading forces w
poorly prepared. The landing site offered no "fall back" position. The invad
forces were easily defeated, and the project was a total fiasco. Later, thou
the same administration responded well to the Cuban Missile Crisis and gai
worldwide respect for its actions. In this incident, Kennedy and his advis
faced the threat of war with Russia and made decisions that averted arm
conflict and defused the situation. Janis' main question was, "How could in
ligent, well-meaning people make decisions so different in outcomes?"

The answer was that the good decisions arose from groups following
guidelines of openness and give-and-take we have discussed. The bad decisi
resulted from groups that put such a high premium on their unity that t
ignored information they did not like, failed to examine ideas critically, and
short, spelled the doom of their own plans. Groupthink is a kind of negat
consensus. The group agrees to agree so strongly that the problem solving p

tant an issue is* and how much attention it demands. Routine matters are
handled in routine ways. Ordering paperclips is probably an insignificant decision in most offices. Not all small decisions, though, are created equal. If a staff
member sees the paper clip order as usurping his authority or questioning his
abilities, then the issue involves more than simple judgment. Sensitivity to the
ramifications of decisions will lead to better analyses of problems and better
decisions about solutions.

The second main point of vigilant problem solving is that *we must do the
best we can in the circumstances* in which we find ourselves. The procedures of
people who make good decisions "involve working to the best of their limited
abilities, within the confines of available . . . resources, to exercise all the caution they can to avoid mistakes in the essential tasks of information search,
deliberation, and planning" (Janis, *Decisions* 29).

In short, vigilant problem solving is doing the best we can with what we
have. One may not have the time necessary to assemble all the available information on a problem. One response would be to say, "Since we cannot obtain
all the necessary information, we will not gather any." Though the group may
have to rely on brief summaries by knowledgeable people or may be able to
look at only a fraction of relevant material, the group should still gather as
much information as it can. Some information in the problem solving process
is better than none.

A group may have to deal with members whose personalities clash and
who have difficulty discussing what course of action to take. The group's leader
may be tempted to duck the issue and make the decision unilaterally. If the
leader were practicing vigilant problem solving, the leader would try to foster
as much creative discussion as possible even though the discussion might be
limited by the clashing personalities.

Vigilant problem solving is an approach to decision making that takes into
account the limitations we face as a part of life. Exercising vigilance in our
problem solving procedures—doing the best we can in our circumstances—will
help us find good solutions. While vigilant problem solving will not eliminate
all the pitfalls of making decisions, vigilance will ensure that the pitfalls are
kept to a minimum.

Conclusion

Human relations are not always a smooth road to agreement. We may find our
ways bumpy and rough, but knowledge and practice at negotiating difficult
territory will help us continue the journey with a minimum amount of discomfort. A knowledgeable approach to conflict can make our lives easier and
more productive than flailing away in hostility. Positive use of conflict can
help us avoid the destructive accord of groupthink. Finally, we need to do the
best we can in decision making even if our circumstances are far from ideal.

Discussion Questions ⁄⁄⁄

1. How do ineffective methods of conflict management (avoidance, capitulation, etc.) thwart the resolution of conflict?

2. In what circumstances, if any, would avoidance, capitulation, coercion, fighting, or separation be appropriate approaches to conflict management?

3. Why is looking to behavior in conflict management more promising than looking to personality?

4. What provides the basis for effective means of conflict management?

5. What makes a group member "difficult?"

6. How does a group avoid groupthink?

7. What kind of situations can you think of where you would need to practice vigilance in problem solving?

8. How does one foster vigilance in problem solving?

Sources and References ⁄⁄⁄

A full bibliography of the small group materials influencing this chapter can be found at the end of Chapter Seven.

≋ Study Questions ≋

Dealing with Difficult Group Situations

1. What is "conflict"?

_____

_____

2. What is "avoidance"? Provide an example.

_____

_____

3. What is "capitulation"? Provide an example.

_____

_____

4. What is "coercion"? Provide an example.

_____

_____

5. What is "fighting"? Provide an example.

_____

_____

6. What is "separation"? Provide an example

_____

_____

7. What is "cooperative conflict resolution"? Provide an example.

_____

_____

8. What are three things a group can do to minimize conflict?

_____

_____

9. What questions can group members ask to gauge the importance of a conflict?

_____

_____

10. In managing conflict, what is meant by "Look to the behavior, not to personality"?

_____

_____

11. How does one "talk to the issue, not the person" when managing conflict?

_____

_____

12. Why is it useful to see the other party's viewpoint when dealing with conflict?

_____

_____

13. How does one "allow for feelings" when dealing with conflict?

_____

_____

14. When is it necessary for a small group to address difficulties caused by an uncooperative member?

_____

_____

15. How can a group minimize "battles of the will" between members?

_____

_____

16. What is "groupthink"?

_____

_____

17. What are the characteristics of groupthink?

_____

_____

18. How can a group avoid groupthink?

_____

_____

19. What are the two main principles of "vigilance in problem solving"?

_____

_____

20. How does a group practice vigilance in problem solving?

_____

_____

﹏ Communication and Conflict Exercise ﹏

Following are descriptions of three situations, each viewed from two different perspectives. You will be assigned one case version to role play. In class discussion, describe the communication problem that is a source of the conflict. How do you think people involved would act? How could the conflict have been prevented? How can the conflict be resolved?

Conflict Roles I

Case 1   You are a twenty-two year old student, a senior living at home while you complete the student teaching requirement for your degree. As you leave in the morning, you tell your parents, "My cooperating teacher and I are going to a workshop after school." Following school you drive the seventy-five miles to the workshop, after which you and your cooperating teacher have a late dinner and drive back. You arrive home at about midnight.

Case 2   You have a dental appointment at 3:00 p.m. When you try to start your car, you discover that the battery is dead. You go back to your apartment building to seek your neighbor's help. You and your neighbor are good friends. You knock, but nobody answers. However, you discover that the door is unlocked. You remember that this is the hour that your neighbor jogs. You have borrowed your neighbor's car before, so you go in, take the car keys off the counter and borrow the car. You come back an hour later, your jaw full of novocaine and knock on your neighbor's door to return the keys.

Case 3   It is your night to cook. It is nearing the end of the month, so you and your roommate are short on cash. You have already planned what you are going to fix. You come home at the end of the day, tired and hungry, but ready to do your part. That is when you discover that you forgot to take the meat out of the freezer. Instead of a potential dinner, you have a frozen block of meat.

≋ Conflict Roles II ≋

Case 1   You are a middle-aged parent whose twenty-two year old son/daughter is living at home while completing student teaching requirements for an education degree. You expect your son/daughter home in time for dinner. Dinner comes and goes, no return. Early evening comes and goes, no son/daughter. You are becoming increasingly worried because he/she is very dependable and predictable. You call the cooperating teacher but get only an answering machine. You call the school principal where the student teaching takes place, but the principal cannot tell you anything. You are about to call the police at midnight when your son/daughter walks in the door.

Case 2   You have been in the apartment laundry center and are walking back to your apartment to leave for a job interview. You really want this position and don't want to be late. As you return you notice that your car is missing from the parking lot. You reach your apartment, find the door unlocked and your car keys missing from the counter. The time to leave for your interview comes and passes. You start to panic. You hear a knock on the door and open it to find your neighbor from across the hall standing there with your keys.

Case 3   It is not your night to cook. Your roommate is handling that chore tonight. As it is nearing the end of the month and you are short on cash, you are looking forward to eating at home. You arrive home at the usual hour, tired and hungry, but nothing is on the stove, nothing is on the table.

How to Create a Group Presentation

9

The nature and appearance of group presentations will vary widely depending on the occasion, the audience, and the presenters. In a college environment, student groups may be part of student government, campus organizations, classes, and housing units. They may form to petition grievances, promote programs, plan activities, persuade those charged with oversight, fulfill class assignments, entertain, and celebrate achievements. In the world beyond the campus, groups form for the same reasons: governance, problem solving, persuasion, project planning, and celebration.

The dynamics of group work have been detailed in earlier chapters. What follows here are guidelines, significant tasks that groups should accomplish as they move from initiation of a presentation to its completion.

Creating the Presentation

Ascertain the Purpose of the Presentation

As we have seen, groups exist for a number of reasons. Groups do best when they have a clear idea of the reason for their existence. At times, the group's assignment will be articulated for them very clearly in terms of audience, time, number of group members, and expectations: "Next week the board will need to see your proposal for financing the spring break trip to Isle Royale." At other times, the assignment will be vague, "Get together something for George's birthday."

It will be helpful to the group to articulate, even write down, its assignment or mission. This statement of overall purpose will serve as a guide and standard for decisions.

Know Your Resources/Constraints

The amounts of time, funding, personnel, equipment, and space available to a group will seldom be infinite. A complete knowledge of what is available to the group will help focus the group's efforts. Saving the rain forest, slowing global warming, and protecting endangered species are important environmental activities. If a campus environmental group, though, has only $157 available for its spring project, the group would do well to look for a smaller task.

Know Your Audience

"To whom are you speaking?" is an important question that underlies the success or failure of a presentation. We do not just speak, we speak to an individual or to a group. An awareness of the nature of the audience permits a group to adapt its message to the needs, desires, emotions, and knowledge of the audience. An informational presentation on recycling would differ considerably if the audience were a kindergarten class, a college class, a county council, or the board of a large corporation.

Create a Strategy

A presentation will undergo a number of changes and modifications as it evolves toward its final form. Nevertheless, it is useful to outline an approach to the assignment. A persuasive presentation will, for example, call for a problem and solution format. An informational presentation will require a clear progression of information.

A complete knowledge of what is available to the group will help focus the group's efforts.

Assign/Claim Responsibilities

Group members should have clear ideas about what is expected of them. In some situations, all group members will work at the same basic tasks. In other situations, duties may be very specific. A television news story, for example, is usually the result of reporters, camera operators, sound technicians, editors, directors, and prompter operators.

Whatever the situation, the group should be more productive when members know what they are to do. Among their duties would be activities such as research, creating visual aids, securing equipment, directing, writing, videotaping, and presenting.

Create a Structure

At this point, the group should have a good idea of what it wants to say. The first thing to do is to arrange the body of the presentation with its main points. Following that, the "signal" portions should be created. These are passages that tell the audience what is happening in the presentation and what can be expected next.

The introduction should capture the attention of the audience, demonstrate the credibility of the speaker(s), tie the message to the needs and desires of the audience, and provide an overview of what is to follow. These things help orient the audience to what it is about to hear. Transitions help the audience move from point to point. The conclusion provides a last opportunity to reinforce points and should emphasize the main point of the presentation. Techniques for accomplishing these goals can be found in the discussion of public speaking.

Prepare Materials

Along with creating the text for the presentation, the group also needs to prepare its supporting materials. These may be skits, videotapes, visual aids, and demonstrations. These should have reciprocal relationship with the text. They strengthen the text while the text provides the context that makes them significant.

Create a Timetable

Group members need to know when their portions of the presentation are due. The timetable for each stage will, of course, depend on the amount of time available for the entire project. Having a schedule allows group members to pace their work.

Rehearse

While a lot of work goes into creating the elements of a presentation, it is in rehearsal that the elements come together into a coherent whole. Rehearsals familiarize group members with their roles and their patterns of interaction. At the same time, rehearsal provides opportunities to revise and improve the presentation as members discover the strengths and weaknesses of the presentation.

It is best to rehearse in conditions that are as close as possible to the site of the finished presentation. The more familiar members are with the setting, the more comfortable they will be in the actual presentation.

Rehearsal should also be as close to the intended presentation as it can be. It is important for members to practice their parts of the presentation,

> Group members should have clear ideas about what is expected of them.

handle props, play their roles, and use the actual visual aids. Early rehearsals tend to be rough stages in the march toward the final effort. As problems are solved, rehearsals become smoother. Finally, a "full dress rehearsal" or several such rehearsals provide the polish and confidence that distinguish effective presentations.

For a high quality presentation, the group should "over-rehearse." All aspects should be in place, and the group members so versed in their roles that they feel capable of handling any problems that arise in presentation.

Along with polishing, the presentation should be timed and adjustments made so that it falls with the assigned times.

When the time comes to make the presentation to its intended audience, other considerations arise.

Making the Presentation

The presentation day can bring stress, but it also brings rewards. Some of the stress can be controlled by a combination of mental and physical exercises.

Dealing with Anxiety

A major deterrent to unnecessary anxiety is the knowledge that everything is in place and what has worked in rehearsal should work in the presentation. A checklist can be reassuring. Members can list the items necessary for their part of the presentation, then go down the list to make sure they have what they need on presentation day.

Members should dress appropriately for the occasion. Business presentations usually require suits, but other situations may be more casual. If in doubt, it is best to dress too formally than to dress too casually. It is easy to shed a jacket, remove a tie, and roll up one's sleeves than it is to find a suit on the spur of the moment.

In the waiting period before starting, one needs to tune oneself to the task. Talking about last night's date or the basketball scores immediately prior to presenting is likely to distract from the task at hand.

A good technique for preparing is for members to concentrate on the main points of their portions rather than trying to review the part word by word. Concentrating on the major points makes sure that the most important items will be presented even if the details are not perfect.

It also helps to anticipate what is a common reaction on presentation day, especially for the inexperienced. No matter how confident one may feel in rehearsal, stepping in front of an audience seems to reduce one's confidence level by half. While the experience may be unnerving, anticipating it can reduce its effect considerably. "Over-rehearsing" is the best protection against the sensation.

One can relieve tensions with physical remedies as well. Some people pace prior to going on. Others chew gum, knit, or squeeze a ball. One technique for tension relief is to tense the muscles, then relax. Deep breathing is a major aid to relaxation.

Controlled tension can be energizing.

Positive Aspects

Not all tension is bad, however. Controlled tension can be energizing. The elevated heart beat and the release of adrenaline give us a boost that makes us livelier. Channeled into the presentation, the energy can lift our work to a higher level than we have experienced in rehearsal and make our presentation even more impressive.

We also find it helpful to be flexible. The final presentation will probably not be a perfect imitation of the rehearsed version. We may find ourselves using words different from those we thought we were going to say. A slide may linger longer than we anticipated. The audience may laugh or applaud at unexpected times. These are not moments for panic. We simply adapt and move on.

After the presentation, one can relax for a moment, but some work remains to be done.

Post-Presentation

After the presentation is finished, the first thing we should do is to enjoy the relaxation and exhilaration that come from completing a demanding task. One of the rewards of finishing a project can be a sense of relief that we have successfully come to the end of the task.

Before we move on to other experiences, it is useful to do some final tasks. One is to clean up our mess. We need to gather up our supplies and materials and see to it that they are appropriately stored or discarded. For one thing, the action may increase our credibility by showing we are responsible people. For another thing, we can account for all we brought and not leave anything valuable behind.

Even if we are not to make the presentation again, it is helpful for the group to meet again to discuss the strengths and weaknesses of the presentation. As group presentations are so common, the recently completed presentation can provide us with help on our next project. We can adapt effective measures to other presentations and work to eliminate things that were ineffective.

If the group is to make the presentation again, the review process provides an opportunity to further refine and develop the presentation. Further rehearsals can incorporate the insights.

Conclusion

A group presentation presents challenges in all its stages: its creation, the actual presentation, and the post-presentation. The challenges can be met by following guidelines. While the guidelines do not guarantee a perfect presentation, ignoring them is a sure recipe for disaster.

Good luck with your group presentations.

_____ ≫ Study Questions ≪ _____

How to Create a Group Presentation

1. Why is it important for a group to ascertain the purpose of its presentation?

   _____

   _____

2. How will resources and constraints influence a presentation?

   _____

   _____

3. How will the audience of a presentation influence the creation of the presentation?

   _____

   _____

4. How does assigning/claiming responsibilities aid a group in creating a presentation?

   _____

   _____

5. What elements make up the structure of a presentation?

   _____

   _____

6. What kind of materials may a group have to prepare for its presentation?

   _____

   _____

7. How does a timetable aid in the creation of a presentation?

   _____

   _____

8. What should a group accomplish in its rehearsals?

   _____

   _____

9. How can group members reduce their anxiety levels when making a presentation?

_____

_____

10. What should group members do following their presentation?

_____

_____

Small Groups as Teams

KEY CONCEPTS

"Team" Defined
   Self-Directed Work Team
   Philosophy of Teams
Team-Oriented Organizations
   Egalitarian Atmosphere
   Shared Duties
   Inside to Outside Movement
   Long Life Spans for Groups
Team Characteristics
   Process
   Vision
   Part of a Larger Whole
   Leaders Have Multiple Skills

S mall groups are an integral part of our lives, and one of the reasons we rely on small groups is that we can adapt them to the changing conditions in which we find ourselves.

One relatively recent adaptation of small groups has occurred in the workplace where small groups have been created to take the place of traditional hierarchical structures. The usual name for these small groups is "teams," but "teams" is defined very specifically.

"Team" Definitions

In general, a "team" can be any collection of people working in concert. Eighteen people playing baseball constitute two teams. A string quartet can be labelled a team. A highly structured, tightly controlled, stratified work group can also be called a "team" even though its structure is diametrically opposed to the team concept.

Based on our earlier discussion of small groups, we would describe a "team" as an "ongoing, problem-solving, task-oriented small group, guided by emergent leaders." An understanding of teams can benefit us in several ways. A study of teams will inform our understanding of small groups in general. Knowledge of teams also prepares people for the work environments in which they may find themselves.

In many ways, a typical classroom small group assignment calls for people to turn their small group into a team. The group has a mission to prepare a report, to solve a problem, to design a piece of equipment, or to create a plan. All members receive the same reward, the grade. Leadership emerges from the group. Work assignments are made by discussion and consensus. Individual members perform a number of tasks: research, organization, creating visual aids, writing, and presenting. To accomplish its goals, the group must solve whatever relational problems arise in the course of its efforts.

When this approach to work expands to characterize an entire organization, we have an organization relying on Self-Directed Work Teams (SDWT). The team approach may be used in any number of settings in for-profit organizations such as businesses and factories and not-for-profit organizations such as health clinics and charitable enterprises.

> Underlying the team approach is a philosophy that puts high value on people's abilities to motivate themselves and to achieve.

Team Philosophy

Underlying the team approach is a philosophy that puts high value on people's abilities to motivate themselves and to achieve. To create an efficient work force, workers must be provided with an environment in which they can work freely to solve problems. People are trustworthy and will rise to challenges when supplied with the necessary resources and support.

Team Characteristics

Hierarchies

Team-oriented organizations differ from traditional organizations in several ways. One of the major differences is a flattening of hierarchy. Traditional organizations have a large number of layers as they go from first line workers to supervisors to managers and up the line all the way up to the president. Team-oriented organizations have as few layers as possible. Where a traditional organization may have ten layers of command; with a team orientation, the same organization may have only three layers.

Atmosphere

The egalitarian atmosphere fostered by the team approach creates the small number of hierarchical levels. The distinctions between different roles blur or disappear. Workers may all wear the same uniform, be they president or press operator. No one, except for the handicapped, has a reserved parking space. Managers from headquarters may be required to spend a week a year working at a production plant as a member of a work team. As managers tend to have fewer manual skills than workers, the managers may end up with the simpler jobs which are likely to be the hardest and dirtiest work. Instead of assigned leaders, teams rely on emergent leaders. The foreman or supervisor becomes a team member on a par with all other team members.

Shared Duties

Teams also replace specific task assignments with shared duties. On the work floor of an assembly plant, many jobs have to be done. The traditional approach is to assign one person to one job. Assembly, equipment maintenance, supply, supervision, and clean-up will be done by five different sets of workers, each acting in a limited scope.

In a car assembly line, engine installation personnel do nothing but put in engines. Headliner installers only install headliners. Wiring harness assemblers hook up wiring harnesses all day. Supervisors monitor work but are not allowed to do any hands-on work.

With a team orientation, the same people, now team members, can engage in any task in which they are competent. In some auto plants, the same small group assembles the entire car from start to finish. During the course of a week, each member may install engines, put in headliners, assemble wiring harnesses, and supervise a co-worker.

It may be that an activity demands a level of skill that not all team members have. Those capable of performing the work will do it and be rewarded with higher pay for their higher skills. Those lacking skills can go to training sessions to acquire skills that will allow them to contribute more to the team and to receive higher pay.

Movement

As the small group, team orientation takes hold, it creates a major change in the flow of responsibility and activities.

In a traditional, top-down organization, the movement is from outside the group to inside the group. The supply department is responsible for seeing that the assemblers have what they need. If assemblers run out of supplies, they wait until they are delivered. If a machine breaks down, the assemblers are idle while the maintenance people come in to fix the problem. If the foreman detects a relational problem, experts from human resources come in to try to resolve the issue.

With a team orientation, *the movement is from the inside to the outside.* The team is responsible for securing its own supplies. If a machine breaks down, the assemblers switch into their maintenance mode and fix the machine. The team makes work assignments rather than having a superior tell them what to do. If a team member is not contributing appropriately, it is up to the group to bring the person up to standards.

Life Spans

Another characteristic of teams is that *they usually have long life spans.* If they make valuable contributions to their larger organization, they will continue to be needed. The long life span creates a group dynamic different from, say, that of an *ad hoc* committee. Teams have to solve their problems in ways that guarantee the continuing life of the group.

Most of what has been said earlier about groups will apply to teams. For example, they will need to tend to both task and relational matters. They will need to find an effective method of decision making that is compatible with the style of the team. They will need to find ways of managing conflict. They will need to create capable leaders.

In a traditional, top-down organization, the movement is from outside the group to inside the group.

Teams Inform Group Work

In addition, teams call attention to group characteristics that may be overlooked in other settings. A look at these characteristics can enhance our understanding of effective small group work.

First of all, members must know that *team activity is a process* (Hartzler xv; Syer and Connolly 3). A team has a past, present, and future. Past actions and decisions create the team that exists at the present moment. Actions and decisions made now will affect the future nature of the team. A team is a constantly changing entity.

Similarly, the small groups in which students may find themselves are also processes. A small group charged with creating a class report will have a short lifespan, but the quality of the product will depend on the group process that leads to it.

Second, successful *teams possess a vision,* a strong sense of their ultimate purpose and goal (Gardenschwartz and Rowe; Fisher 97–98; McIntosh-Fletcher 23). In a manufacturing setting, the vision may be to create a product that is most satisfactory to customers. In an academic setting, it may be to design the best curriculum for a major.

A small group with a class assignment will need to have an idea of what it wishes to attain. Without a goal toward which it can aim, the group may find itself frustrated without a sense of direction. The goal may be meeting all the criteria needed to achieve an A on the presentation. In a Rube Goldberg Contest, the goal may be to design the most complex method possible to accomplish a simple task such as sharpening a pencil or opening a can of soda.

Third, *teams are part of a larger whole* (Sherriton and Stern 23–68; Syer and Connolly 11–14). It is obvious that a team is part of an organization that is larger than the team. A factory may have tens of teams, a business, hundreds. Less obvious is the fact that what happens in the larger organization affects what happens on the teams. A new product, a change in the market or economy, and personnel changes in a company or facility can create a new set of problems for teams to confront.

At first glance, it might seem that student groups are little affected by the larger organization. They are, nevertheless. Class assignments must be finished before the end of the semester. A university's registration processes determine class memberships. In living units, committees must answer to members in the unit as to plans, projects, and finances.

Team Leadership

Lastly, team leaders must have multiple skills beyond technical abilities. A successful leader will need vision to see the reasons and goals that animate the team. The leader must be an example. The leader should be a person who embodies the spirit of the group and whose behavior models the kind of action necessary for the team to accomplish its goals. The leader must also be a coach who guides, teaches, and encourages team members (Fisher 134–45).

In a university setting, small group leaders must do the same things. The chair of a housing unit's social committee must have a vision, an image of what a successful social season will be. The chair must contribute time and effort, be the kind of person people want in their groups. The chair must also guide the members as they carry out their responsibilities. Typically, leadership positions in an organization are held by upperclassmen, and for good reason. These are people who have learned what needs to be done and how to accomplish goals. If they are doing their jobs well, they are also training underclassmen, their potential successors.

> A successful leader will need vision to see the reasons and goals that animate the team.

Conclusion

Teams are a special kind of small group as they are ongoing, problem-solving, task oriented, and guided by emergent leaders. Instead of specializing in one skill, members practice a range of skills. Teams inform the study of small groups by highlighting four characteristics: groups are processes; groups need vision; groups are part of a larger whole; and leaders must display vision, exemplary behavior, and coaching skills.

Discussion Questions

1. What is the difference between a team and a collection of people?

2. What characteristics would people need to be good members of a self-directed work team?

3. How can the larger environment affect a team?

4. Under what conditions would a self-directed work team do well?

5. What conditions would make it difficult for a self-directed work team to succeed?

Sources and References

Fisher, Bob and Bo Thomas. *Real Dream Teams*. Delray Beach, Florida: St. Lucie Press, 1996.

Fisher, Kimball. *Leading Self-Directed Teams: A Guide to Developing New Team Leadership Skills*. New York: McGraw-Hill, 1993.

Gardenschwartz, Lee and Anita Rowe. *Diverse Teams at Work: Capitalizing on the Power of Diversity*. Chicago: Irwin, 1994.

Heerman, Barry. *Building Team Spirit: Activities for Inspiring and Energizing Teams*. New York: McGraw-Hill, 1997.

Ketchum, Lyman D. and Eric Tyrist. *All Teams Are Not Created Equal: How Employee Empowerment Really Works*. Newbury Park, California: Sage Publications, 1992.

McIntosh-Fletcher, Donna. *Teaming by Design: Real Teams for Real People*. Chicago: Irwin, 1996.

Manz, Charles C. and Henry P. Sims, Jr. *Business Without Bosses: How Self-Managing Teams Are Building High-Performing Companies*. New York: John Wiley and Sons, Inc., 1993.

Mohrman, Susan Albers, Susan G. Cohen, and Allan M. Mohrman, Jr. *Designing Team-Based Organizations: New Forms for Knowledge Work*. San Francisco: Jossey-Bass, 1995.

Odenwald, Sylvia B. *Global Solutions for Teams: Moving From Collision to Collaboration*. Chicago: Irwin, 1996.

Sherriton, Jacalyn and James L. Stern. *Corporate Culture: Removing the Hidden Barriers to Team Success*. New York: American Management Association, 1997.

Syer, John and Christopher Connolly. *How Teamwork Works: The Dynamics of Effective Team Development*. London: McGraw-Hill, 1996.

⧉ Study Questions ⧉

Small Groups as Teams

1. What is a "team" in the sense this chapter uses the term?

   _____

   _____

2. What does "SWDT" stand for?

   _____

   _____

3. What view of human nature underlies the team concept?

   _____

   _____

4. What is an "egalitarian" atmosphere?

   _____

   _____

5. How does a team orientation foster a "movement from the inside to the outside"?

   _____

   _____

6. How is team activity a process?

   _____

   _____

7. How does vision play a role in successful teams?

   _____

   _____

8. How are teams a part of a larger whole?

_____

_____

9. What kind of skills should a team leader possess?

_____

_____

Computer-Mediated Groups

11

KEY CONCEPTS

Advantages of Computer-Mediated Groups
   Communication Over Distance
   Instantaneous Transmission
   Asynchronous Communication
   Message Storage
   Bypassing Hierarchies
   "Sending" vs. "Sharing"
Disadvantages of Computer-Mediated Groups
   Lack of Nonverbal Signals
   Geographical Separation
   Speed
Techniques for Computer-Mediated Interaction
   Proximate Groups
   Distanced Groups
     Delhi Technique

Even a quick survey of the history of communication technology discovers an interesting phenomena: whatever the medium, it develops applications beyond its original purpose. As one observer has pointed out, we do not have "technologies operating autonomously on a passive organization or a society" (Shedletsky, 1). Our relationship with technology is one in which we engage in a two-way process with technology. As we adapt to media and accept the changes they make in our lives, we also shape and influence the media themselves, which then influence our lives, which then influence the media, and so on.

The alphabet and writing were developed about 3,800 years ago, primarily as a business tool. People needed to remember how many sheep or measures of grain they had bought or sold. From that beginning, its use spread to wills, histories, dramas, love letters, poetry, philosophy, and a host of other relationships.

The invention of the telegraph profoundly changed the nature of journalism. Originally, reporters covered events, but filing their stories was limited to the speed someone could travel. Consequently, news spread slowly. The invention of the telegraph allowed messages to be sent at great speed over long distances. Reporters could file their stories from the field. Occurring after the invention of the telegraph, the Civil War was covered much more closely than previous conflicts. News of the war could be disseminated far more widely and rapidly than ever before. Businesses supplying news via the telegraph became known as "wire services," a name that still applies today to the Associated Press and United Press International.

> With e-mail, bulletin boards, mailing lists, newsgroups, and chat rooms, the "neutral" source has created countless webs of relationships.

The same phenomena is easily seen in the relatively recent proliferation of computers and electronic communication technology. The internet began as a way to link military computers. Early analyses of electronic mail saw e-mail as a neutral medium that would be used for the transmission of information (Phillips 2; Olaniran 1). It is obvious now that the internet is anything but neutral. With e-mail, bulletin boards, mailing lists, newsgroups, and chat rooms, the "neutral" source has created countless webs of relationships. We do business, play games, research, and conduct romances electronically over great distances.

As we naturally form face-to-face small groups, electronic small groups or computer-mediated groups seem to have been an inevitable development. Many groups supplement their face-to-face communication with electronic means while other groups rely on electronic media as their prime mode of relating.

Computer-Mediated Groups: Pluses and Minuses

A Word as We Begin

This section of the text is difficult to write because of the broad range of backgrounds readers will bring to the discussion. Some will be unable to remember a time when a computer was not a part of their environment. They have grown up using computers for learning, recreation, and work, and are highly skilled in using and even creating programs. At the other extreme, some readers may have no background whatsoever with computers except to know that they exist.

Another difficulty is the speed at which change occurs in electronic communication. This section will be out of date quickly.

Still, I hope that this section serves as a useful introduction to those unfamiliar with computers and as a reminder of the basics for those who are highly advanced. Your reactions and feedback would be appreciated.

Advantages of Computer-Mediated Groups

Probably the most widely used form of computer-mediated communication is e-mail. Its overwhelming popularity appears to grow out of several characteristics, the combination of which makes it unique (Phillips, 3).

1. E-mail allows people to communicate over distances, great and small. For example, I regularly correspond with a friend in Zimbabwe, a site 5,000 miles away as easily as I correspond with the office next door to mine.
2. E-mail offers easy and almost instantaneous transmission. All we have to do is tap the "send" icon to speed the message on its way. Contrast this procedure with the numerous steps necessary to mail a letter such as addressing an envelope, sealing the envelope, affixing a stamp, finding a mailbox, and transporting the letter physically from one site to another.
3. E-mail is asynchronous communication. Senders and receivers do not need to be communicating at the same time. In contrast, a face-to-face conversation would be synchronous communication. Both parties would be engaging each other simultaneously. With e-mail, we can send a message at a time convenient for us, and the recipient can retrieve it when convenient, immediately or much later.
4. E-mail provides a storage for messages. We can save letters to a file and have copies readily available.
5. E-mail allows people to send messages that easily bypass the hierarchy or "chain of command." Provided that we can find the correct e-mail address, it is only a matter of typing a few letters or clicking to route a message to the boss' boss or all the way to the president or chairman of the board of a company.
6. E-mail does not "send" messages so much as it "shares" or "copies" messages. When we send a letter via the post office, the message is literally out of our hands unless we made a copy for ourselves. With e-mail, we retain the original in a file such as "sent." Thus the message remains with us as it reaches the extended recipients (Holman).

Of course, electronic media offer ways of connecting beyond e-mail. Bulletin boards collect messages for review. Chat rooms create synchronous—"real" time situations in which parties readily exchange messages. Mailing lists and newsgroups can provide postings to huge numbers of people. Groups may create web pages to publicize their endeavors and to report their findings. Adding dimensions to electronic communication, computer cameras coupled with microphones make computer-mediated groups seem almost like face-to-face groups.

Disadvantages of Computer-Mediated Groups

While computers extend the communication possibilities of groups, they also extend the possibilities of problems in communication. Awareness of the shortcomings of electronic communication can help us adapt better to the situations in which we find ourselves.

> Awareness of the shortcomings of electronic communication can help us adapt better to the situations in which we find ourselves.

One of the most obvious aspects of electronic communication is that we lose the richness that nonverbal communication brings to relationships. We may transmit verbal messages, but the messages carry no facial expressions nor dress nor decoration nor intonations nor distance nor touch.

The lack of nonverbal signals has lead to the creation of devices that give some flavor of what computer-mediated communication often lacks. People insert code words and abbreviations into messages to indicate their physical reactions. One responds to a joke, "lol," "laugh out loud." Writing in capital letters or "flaming" gives the idea of RAISED VOICES. For facial expressions, we sketch faces created from the keyboard and read at a 90 degree angle. These range from simple smiley faces :-) and frowny faces :-(to larger constructions such as Santa Claus *<{:O}) and waving bye d:-D-/-< (Tapscott 6). Combining "emotion" with "icon," the symbols are often labelled "emoticons."

Computer-mediated groups may be comprised of members who are widely separated from each other geographically. "Out of sight, out of mind" may apply. Members may feel more loyalty toward the colleagues they see daily than those whose only connection is a faceless text.

The speed of electronic communication can make it a nuisance. Because we can send a message instantly, we often presume that the response will be instant as well. "Why haven't you responded to my e-mail? I sent it ten minutes ago."

Cost is another factor as the communicating parties must rely on highly sophisticated equipment. The parties may also have to rely on technical experts to create the electronic environment that allows group members to interact. Hardware, software, air time, and technical support can become very costly.

Utilizing Computer Mediation for Small Groups

The Computer-Mediated Balancing Act

To make the best use of computer mediation, groups will need to strike a balance between the various elements of their situations. The first major element will be the people in the group. In a face-to-face group, the members' talents, personalities, and commitments will determine how successful the group is in accomplishing its purposes. In a computer-mediated group, the members' contributions will be further determined by their attitudes towards computers and their skill levels in using computers.

A second element will be the distance between members. When members are in relatively close proximity, electronic media can supplement face-to-face interactions. If they can readily meet face to face, members can even choose to avoid computer mediation totally. Members at great distances from each other may have no recourse but to use computer-mediation for all their transactions.

The third element is the equipment available to members. At a minimum, members need to have access to e-mail if they are to interact via electronic media. Beyond that basic requirement, groups can add other elements as equipment, time, and money allow. Chat rooms can provide synchronous exchanges, which can become electronic group meetings. Visual and verbal cues can be added to the meetings if the group has microphones, web cameras, and sufficient funding.

Techniques for Computer-Mediated Interaction

Depending on their circumstances, groups may use computer mediation in a number of ways.

Proximate Groups

By "proximate groups," we mean those groups whose members are close enough physically that they rely primarily on face-to-face interactions but also utilize computer mediation.

One of the most basic ways groups use computer-mediation is through *e-mail*. Messages can be sent from one member to another or from one member to the entire group or selected sub-groups. The asynchronous nature of e-mail makes it extremely useful for posting meeting times, sharing resources, and clarifying points. A further advantage of e-mail is that the message's information is already in text form and the receiver need not take notes. The message can simply be stored or printed out by clicking on an icon.

A *mailing list* or *listserv* is an extension of e-mail that functions as group mailing. Send a message to a mailing list, and your message goes to everyone on that mailing list. You also receive every message that others send to the list. Individual members can be reached by mailing to their private e-mail addresses.

Creating a *chat room* could be very handy for proximate groups if circumstances made meetings difficult. With a student group, one might live away from campus at a distance that made night meetings difficult. Others could have job responsibilities or child care responsibilities. A virtual meeting could bring the group together when it could not meet otherwise. A chat room would also be useful for last minute meetings when the group cannot coordinate a face-to-face meeting.

With a proximate group, the ratio of computer mediation to face-to-face will show a preponderance of face-to-face meetings. This ratio will allow most of the relationship building to take place in the face-to-face meetings. When communicating via computer mediation, members' images of each other will be based on actual observations as well as the textual cues of e-mail and postings.

Distanced Groups

"Distanced groups" are groups whose members are physically separated from each other and who use computer mediation as their primary method of interacting. Due to the physical separation, these groups will use computer mediation differently than will proximate groups.

Members in distanced groups will draw their images of each other primarily from looking at screens rather than looking at people. If the medium is strictly textual, it is possible that large conclusions will be drawn from small inferences.

The visual capabilities of computer-mediated communication may add to members' views of each other. Members can attach pictures of themselves to their messages. Utilizing web cameras and microphones, members can meet verbally and visually on the web and come close to face-to-face communication. Their communication will still be influenced by the media they are using. For example, conversations before and after the meeting will be limited if not nonexistent. Follow up discussions will be difficult. Members cannot meet socially before or after the meeting: no "having lunch," no "Let's get a cup of coffee."

As mentioned above, distanced groups also have to fight the "out of sight, out of mind" problem. Computer-mediated members can find each other interesting and their group project challenging. They cannot, though, act upon each other with the sense of urgency that can a colleague who is physically present. The press of immediate relationships may lead them to give lowered priority to the more impersonal relationships.

One solution to these problems is to plan face-to-face meetings to supplement the computer-mediated interactions. In business these meetings can be at professional conferences, at company sites, or conference centers. Computer-mediated student groups may find arranging face-to-face meetings difficult. Students will probably lack the financial backing a company or organization can offer. Nevertheless, relationships are strengthened by face-to-face contact in ways that are difficult or impossible via computer mediation. It is important that distanced group members utilize opportunities to meet and talk in person or even over the phone.

E-mail will continue to be an important medium for distanced groups. Given the low cost and speed of e-mail, the medium will probably be more important for distanced groups than it is for proximate groups. Distanced members cannot "just walk down the hall" to deliver a message. It is important the distanced members read and respond to their e-mail in a timely fashion.

Similarly, mailing lists can further enhance the communication of distanced members.

Bulletin boards or newsgroups can be used as home bases for the groups. These would provide a central location to which all would go to stay current on the group's activities.

Distanced groups may want to create webpages to communicate with the world at large. The webpages can provide summaries of results, plans for future action, links to related sites, links to group members, and opportunities for comments. Those interested in a group's project can check the group's web site to learn about the project or check the group's progress.

While group work will be advanced by e-mail, real-time exchanges provide the opportunity for groups to interact with quick give and take. A chat room, then, is a must for distanced groups. Members can approximate dyadic and group communication though, again, the interactions will be primarily textual.

The fullest approximation of face-to-face meetings are provided by what is, in essence, small scale video conferencing. Group members must have equipment and time. Web cameras and microphones allow group members to occupy the same "space" at the same time. Here members can see each other, though in diminished size. They can hear each other, though over speakers. They can interact but still have to adjust to "net lag," the pauses needed for one member's remarks to travel to other members at other terminals.

One special technique that may aid computer-mediated groups is the *Delphi technique* (Dalkey). The Delphi technique is a "way of having a meeting without really having one." Here a central coordinator elicits responses from members who work independently of each other. The coordinator summarizes the responses, sends the summary to group members, and elicits their reactions once again. The process continues until consensus is achieved.

For example, the Outing Clubs at four different universities in two states want to join forces for a major hike in the summer. The distance between the schools and the demands of their classes make face-to-face meetings very difficult. The group utilizes e-mail and a chat room, but they do not take care of all the group's communication needs. E-mail messages seem to go in circles while chat room exchanges and conference calls require that all four representatives be available at the same time.

The Delphi technique provides the group with another approach. The representative at University A is designated as the coordinator. She then sends the same message to her counterparts at other campuses: "Please send me your optimum dates and your group's top three preferences for a trail, and what your group thinks the trip should cost."

Each responds. The coordinator adds her ideas, then summarizes, poses another question, and sends out another mailing: "Here are the most popular dates and places. Please rank order these and send me the results. The cost preferences range from $X to $Y. What are your reactions to the potential cost?"

This process continues until the four groups reach a mutually acceptable solution on date, site, and cost. The Delphi technique can be used to address other problems as they arise. The same technique can also be used by proximate groups to save time. Instead of calling a meeting for every question that arises, members can deal with matters by utilizing the Delphi technique.

Conclusion

As other technologies have changed ways in which we think, act, and form relationships, computers also shape our patterns of communication and hence, our lives. Whether groups are proximate or distanced, computer mediation offers a medium which can enhance or hinder small group work. A knowledge of the potential of computer-mediated communication will help us best utilize this medium.

Discussion Questions ////

1. What can be gained by small groups when they use computer-mediated communication?

2. What can be lost by small groups when they use computer-mediated communication?

3. What considerations should guide small groups in their decisions of whether or not to use computer-mediated communication?

Sources and References ////

Althaus, Scott L. "Computer-Mediated Communication in the University Classroom: An Experiment with On-Line Discussions." *Communication Education* 46 (1997): 158–74.

Archee, Ray. "Using Computer Mediated Communication in an Educational Context: Educational Outcomes and Pedagogical Lessons of Computer Conferencing *Electronic Journal of Communication* 3 (1993).

> Computer-mediated members can find each other interesting and their group project challenging. They cannot, though, act upon each other with the sense of urgency that can a colleague who is physically present.

Braithwaite, Dawn O., Vincent R. Waldron, and Jerry Finn. "Communication of Social Support in Computer-Mediated Groups for People With Disabilities." *Health Communication* 11 (1999): 123–52.

Condon, Sherri and Claude G. Cech. "Discourse Management Strategies in Face-to-Face and Computer-Mediated Decision Making Interactions. *Electronic Journal of Communication* 6 (1996).

Coombs, Norman. "The Medium And The Message." *Electronic Journal of Communication* 3 (1993).

Curtis, Pavel. "Mudding: Social Phenomena in Text-Based Virtual Realities." *Culture of the Internet.* Ed. Sara Kiesler. Mahway, NJ: Lawrence Erlbaum, 1997. pp. 121–42.

Dalkey, Norman C. *Studies in the Quality of Life: Delphi and Decision Making.* With Daniel L. Ronrke, Ralph Lewis, and David Snyder. Lexington, MA: Lexington Books, 1972.

Day, Donald L. "Behavioral and Perceptual Responses to Constraint Management in Computer-Mediated Design Activities." *Electronic Journal of Communication* 3 (1993).

Hacker, Kenneth L. and Dennis L. Wignall. "Issues in Predicting User Acceptance of Computer-Mediated Communication (CMC) in Inter-University Classroom Discussion as an Alternative to Face-to-Face Interaction." *Communication Reports* 10 (1997): 107–14.

Herring, Susan C. "Gender and Democracy in Computer-Mediated Communication." *Electronic Journal of Communication* 3 (1993).

Hollingshead, Andrea B. "Information Suppression and Status Persistence in Group Decision Making: The Effects of Communication Media. *Human Communication Research* 23 (1996): 193–219.

Holman, Joanne. Comments to author. 6 April 2000.

Ko, Kwang-Kyu. "Structural Characteristics of Computer-Mediated Language: A Comparative Analysis of InterChange Discourse." *Electronic Journal of Communication* 6 (1996).

Loperfido, Allison M. "Electronic Mail as a Media Choice for Managers." *Electronic Journal of Communication* 3 (1993).

Miller, Keith, Susann LuperFoy, Esther Kim, and David Duff. "Dialogue Management for Computer-Mediated Spoken Bilingual Dialogue." *Electronic Journal of Communication* 6 (1996).

Ogan, Christine. "Listserver Communication During the Gulf War: What Kind of Medium is the Electronic Bulletin Board?" *Journal of Broadcasting and Electronic Media* 37 (1993): 177–96.

Olaniran, Bolanle A. "Individual Differences and Computer-Mediated Communication: The Role of Perception." *Electronic Journal of Communication* 3 (1993).

Pavlik, John V. *New Media Technology: Cultural and Commercial Perspectives.*

Phillips, Gerald and Gerald M. Santoro. "Teaching Group Discussion via Computer-Mediated Communication." *Communication Education* 38 (1989): 151–66./

Phillips, Steven R. and Eric M. Eisenberg. "Strategic Uses of Electronic Mail in Organizations." *Electronic Journal of Communication* 3 (1993).

Poole, Marshall Scott and Michael E. Holmes. "Decision Development in Computer-Assisted Group Decision Making." *Human Communication Research* 22 (1995): 90–127.

Poole, Marshall Scott, Michael Holmes, Richard Watson, and Gerardine DeSanctis. "Group Decision Support Systems and Group Communication: A Comparison of Decision Making in Computer-Supported and Nonsupported Groups." *Communication Research* 20 (1993): 176–213.

Rintel, E. Sean and Jeffery Pittam. "Strangers in a Strange Land: Interaction Management on Internet Relay Chat." *Human Communication Research* 23 (1995): 507–34.

Schuler, Douglas. *New Community Networks: Wired for Change* New York: ACM Press-Addison Wesley, 1996.

Shedletsky, Leonard J. "Computer-Mediated Communication Facilitate Seminar Participation and Active thinking: A Case Study." *Electronic Journal of Communication* 3 (1993).

Sproull, Lee and Samer Faraj. "Atheism, Sex, and Databases: The Net as a Social Technology." *Culture of the Internet.* Ed. Sara Kiesler. Mahway, NJ: Lawrence Earlbaum, 1997. pp. 35–51.

Tapscott, Don. *Growing Up Digital: The Rise of the Net Generation.* New York: McGraw-Hill: 1998.

Turkel, Sherry. "Constructions and Reconstructions of Self in Virtual Reality: Playing in the MUDS." *Culture of the Internet.* Ed. Sara Kiesler. Mahway, NJ: Lawrence Earlbaum, 1997. pp. 143–56.

Walther, Joseph B. "Group and Interpersonal Effects in International Computer-Mediated Collaboration." *Human Communication Research* 23 (1997): 342–69.

———. "Interpersonal Effects in Computer-Mediated Interaction: A Relational Perspective." *Communication Research* 19 (1992): 52–90.

Witmer, Diane. "Introduction to Computer-Mediated Communication: A Master Syllabus for Teaching Communication Technology." *Communication Education* 47 (1998): 162–73.

⫸ Study Questions ⫷

Computer-Mediated Groups

1. What are distinctive characteristics of e-mail?

   _____

   _____

2. What are the disadvantages of computer-mediated groups?

   _____

   _____

3. What elements contribute to the constitution of a computer-mediated group?

   _____

   _____

4. What is a "proximate group"?

   _____

   _____

5. What is a "distanced group"?

   _____

   _____

6. How may these two groups differ in their use of computer mediation?

   _____

   _____

7. What is the "Delphi technique"?

   _____

   _____

Creating a Presentation

12

KEY CONCEPTS

Public Speaking
  Definition
The Creative Process
  Freedom
  Beginning Early
Sizing Up the Situation
  The Speaker
  The Audience
    The Importance of the Audience
    Audience Analysis
  The Message
Composing a Speech
  Finding a Speech Topic
    When the Topic Finds the Speaker
    When the Speaker Has to Search
      Love/Hate Subjects
      Clustering
      Considering the Audience
Narrowing the Topic
  Shrinking the Subject Area
  Thesis Statements
    Topic
    Position
    Amplification
    Declarative Sentence
    Variations in Thesis Statements
Major Divisions
  Selecting Major Points
  Arranging Major Points
    Chronological Pattern
    Spatial Pattern
    Problem-Solution Pattern
    Structure-Function Pattern
    Topical Pattern

A t Macalester Industries, the Director of Human Services is presenting to the staff of the Human Services Office the recently issued Federal guidelines on hiring.

At the City Council meeting of a university town, citizens are walking to the microphone to voice their opinions about a new regulation limiting the number of unrelated people who may share a residence.

As the shift changes at St. Elizabeth Hospital, the floor nurse in the surgical ward reports on the conditions of the patients to the incoming shift.

At Stevenson Elementary School, the chair of the booster committee explains to the parent teacher organization how funds from the winter carnival will be spent.

At noon, in a room in the local cafeteria, the Lions Club meets and hears a report on its sponsorship of a summer softball league.

At the Forbes Group Home building, a facility for juvenile wards of the court, a contractor outlines for the board a plan to replace the windows in the building.

In the xxx fraternity, one of the members is explaining to the assembled group how they will undertake this year's service project, painting houses for several elderly people.

Public Speaking

All of the above have in common that they are participating in public speaking or as we shall call it, making a presentation. Though we often think of public speaking as the activity of professionals, such as politicians and ministers, public speaking is an activity that may engage us all. The skills to present material clearly to a group of people may be a requirement in a number of the roles we play: parent, citizen, organizational member, professional, coach, teacher, or club member. By *public speaking,* we mean simply that *a person addresses an audience of several or more people to accomplish some communication goal.* The communication goal may be one of many. Typical reasons for making presentations are to inform, to persuade, to entertain, to honor, or to mark an occasion. For reasons of time and length, our discussion of presentations will limit itself to informational and persuasive presentations.

Entering into the process of creating a speech can be intimidating.

The Creative Process

Making a presentation is not so much "giving a speech" as it is entering into a creative process that leads from the seeming disorder and chaos of its early stages to the ordered and crafted final product. As one has pointed out, the question in making a presentation is not whether or not we will be creative. "Creativity is a matter of degree," and thus the true question is, "How creative will we be?" (Kim 84).

Entering into the process of creating a presentation may be intimidating. Some of the trepidation people feel may be relieved by recognizing the nature of creativity, whether it is the creation of a presentation, a painting, a dance, a novel, a research project, or a way of solving problems. It also helps to realize that once past the trepidation, the creative process can also be exhilarating.

While the final product is expected to be orderly, planned, and neatly arranged, *the creation process itself tends to be sloppy, particularly in the early stages.* Occasionally, some genius conceives an idea and carries it through from first to last with little modification and little doubt, but these cases are extremely rare. Even when they occur, they are the result of long and regular practice. Brilliance and inspiration come to those who already know what they are doing, not to the totally unpracticed.

The creative process is characterized by false starts, mistakes, problems, revisions, changes, starting over, and trying out far more things that do not work than those that do. Even in biological terms, creation is characterized by excess and by far more failures than successes. Out of a brood of one hundred baby sea turtles, only about twenty will survive to adulthood. Of the thousands of seeds produced by a single tree, only a few will germinate.

The engineer looking for a solution to a building problem may investigate a number of possibilities before finding the one that works. A painter may make a number of sketches before putting brush to canvas. The stereotype of writers, including those writing communication texts, filling their wastebaskets with crumpled paper as they try to find the right words is not far from the truth, except in these days the writer uses "delete" instead of the wastebasket. The finished novels we buy have gone through a number of drafts before they reach the bookstore shelves.

The same pattern of repetition and refinement is at work in the process of composing presentations. We may create a list of thirty topics to find the one we want to talk about. We may have to look at a number of periodicals before locating the key articles for our speech. Certainly, we will need to rehearse the presentation many times before giving it, just as athletic teams practice plays over and over before using them in a game.

At times the creative process will be difficult and seem to drag along. At other times, the process will go so smoothly we may wonder from where all our wonderful ideas came. When one is working well, one has the impression that some outside source is assisting in the process. If we find things going smoothly, we should sit back and enjoy the ride, and it can be an exhilarating one. If things are not going smoothly, the important thing is to keep trying. Persistence is a major ingredient of creative accomplishment. Eventually, ideas will fall into place; the right wording will appear; the organization will become clear.

In the early stages of creating a presentation, *the key word is "freedom."* The time will come soon enough to be critical of the work, but the critical stage should be one of the later stages of work on the speech. In fact, we can create problems for ourselves if we become too critical too early and shut off the flow of ideas necessary to the work. In the early stages, we need to give our minds and imaginations free rein.

Another good guideline for creativity is to *begin the creative process early.* Creativity is both conscious and unconscious. We put some ideas together by actively thinking about them. Others come together when we are *not* actively thinking about them. Somehow, in the dark of our minds, connections are made, and when brought into the light, the new ideas make sense in ways we

> Brilliance and inspiration come to those who already know what they are doing, not to the totally unpracticed.

had not yet imagined. For the process to take place, we need to have time for ideas to germinate.

Generally, the earlier we discover a topic for a speech, the better the speech will be. Even if we cannot do a great deal with the topic for a while, just knowing the general subject will be helpful. One way to severely hamper the creative process is to put off working on a speech until the last minute, then in a whirlwind of energy and exasperation try to fashion a speech without sufficient time for development.

Sizing up the Situation

One of the first tasks of giving a presentation is to analyze our audience, our message, and ourselves. No one element of the triad constitutes the communication event, but through the interplay of the three, an environment is created and lived in. Change any one of the three elements, and the situation is altered. The wording of the presentation, for example, may be brilliant, but if spoken by a lifeless, mumbling speaker, the presentation will not live up to its potential.

The process of analyzing the three is not a matter of attending to each one in order. We are more likely to find ourselves jumping from one to another as an insight into the nature of the audience leads to a change of wording which leads us to seek more knowledge which leads us to reinterpret the audience, and so on. Working back and forth simply means that we are creating a well-rounded presentation.

The Speaker

The first part of the triad is relatively easy since, presuming we are the speakers, we should already be something of authorities on ourselves. In an earlier chapter, we discussed the various elements that contribute to our capabilities as communicators. We may still, though, make discoveries about ourselves as we work toward the speaking situation.

Some of the questions we want to ask ourselves as we analyze a speaking situation are:

➡ How much do I already know about the topic?
➡ Where can I find information about the topic?
➡ What information resources are available to me?
➡ What kinds of visual aids are available to me?
➡ How much time do I have to prepare?
➡ How do I feel about this presentation?
➡ What personal stake do I have in making this speech?
➡ What is my motivation for making this speech?
➡ What are my strengths as a speaker?
➡ What are my weak points as a speaker?
➡ What can I do to minimize my weaknesses?
➡ What can I learn from this experience?

As we answer these questions, we come to a better understanding of ourselves and our role in the speaking situation. The understanding will guide in the choices we make in creating our presentation.

The Audience

The better a speaker analyzes an audience, the more likely the speaker is to be effective. Presentations are, after all, situations in which human beings connect with other human beings. Knowing the nature of the people on the other side of the relational equation will help us react most appropriately.

In some cases, the job of audience analysis is fairly easy. Giving a classroom presentation, for example, usually involves students talking to people who are very much like themselves. Even if the ages are dissimilar, the audience will still have a number of traits in common. All are interested in a college level class. All are, or should be, concentrating on the goal of finishing the class in good order. All are at roughly the same level of ability. A classroom presentation also gives people the opportunity to observe the audience over a long period of time and adjust to its interests and abilities.

In other cases, insight, rapport, and empathy with the audience may be harder to achieve. We may be called upon to give a presentation to a civic group or club that we have never heard of before. Here we would have to analyze carefully the characteristics of the people to whom we would be speaking. A number of factors may determine the nature of the audience and guide the speaker in crafting the presentation. Some of the characteristics which should be examined are:

Figure 12.1. In analyzing your speaking situation, you need to consider yourself, your audience, and your message.

⮡ The age or ages of audience members
⮡ The gender of the audience
⮡ The educational level of the audience
⮡ The political beliefs of the audience
⮡ The religious beliefs of the audience
⮡ The values held by the audience
⮡ The reason the audience has assembled
⮡ The audience's knowledge of the speaker
⮡ The audience's knowledge of the topic
⮡ The social class(es) of the audience
⮡ The race(s) of the audience
⮡ The profession(s) of the audience
⮡ The expectations of the audience
⮡ The circumstances under which the audience is meeting
⮡ The place and time of the meeting

> The better a speaker analyzes an audience, the more likely the speaker is to be effective.

All these elements will shape the consciousness of an audience, the consciousness to which speakers must relate if they are to be effective. Knowledge of the audience allows speakers to shape their messages so that they will be the most effective with a given group. A variation in one or two of the audience's characteristics may be enough to change the speaking situation drastically. A farm co-op may have the same members attending two meetings yet be two very different audiences as when discussing drought relief and when gathering

Different audiences demand different approaches to communication.

for its annual banquet. The audience attending a national political convention—either Democratic or Republican—will be a different audience after the candidates are chosen than it was before.

Audience analysis is a combination of research and imagination. We will seldom be asked to speak to an audience about which we know absolutely nothing. Drawing upon what we know, we can begin to sketch an idea of what will be important in adapting to the audience and then complete the picture by study and integration of what we discover.

If, for example, someone were called upon to speak at the Westminster Retirement Village, one would know quickly that age would be an important factor. Most audience members will be in their sixties or older. If the speaker were not acquainted with people in this age bracket, the speaker would need to discover the characteristics of those over sixty. To find the information, the speaker could talk with someone well acquainted with the Village to determine the economic, political, social, and educational standings of the audience as well as other factors. The speaker could also read materials by or about retirees and interview people.

Without investigation, one might make some major errors in evaluating the audience. Some young people think that retirees spend their time wrapped in shawls and sitting in rocking chairs or doddering about while mumbling over pictures of their grandchildren. Many retirees are very active and involved with travel, the arts, politics, and numerous service activities.

> Audience analysis is a combination of research and imagination.

The Message

While we are discovering as much as possible about the audience, we should also be giving thought about what is to be said and how to say it. At this point, we are beginning to think rhetorically, giving thought how to best adapt ideas to the audience and the audience to the ideas. The working out of this task is the composition of the presentation.

Composing the Presentation

Finding a Topic

When the Topic Finds the Speaker

Interestingly enough, for a large amount of the public speaking we are called upon to do, the topic finds us rather than us finding the topic. That is, the circumstances dictate the topic of a presentation. We find ourselves in situations in which we rise to the occasion of addressing a topic.

The Director of Human Services at a manufacturing plant speaks about hiring guidelines because the company is under some compulsion to adhere to those guidelines and the Director is the person charged with the responsibility to see that the guidelines are followed.

At a city council meeting, citizens speak out because they feel the topic affects them and their living situation. They feel impelled to express themselves on the subject.

The student providing information about the service project and the parent in charge of the school's booster club do so because speaking is necessary to the successful completion of their tasks.

The speeches are also fueled by the desires of the audience. The employees of Macalester Industries find the topic of hiring guidelines necessary to their work. The city council has invited people to express opinions on the given topic. The members of the co-op house want to participate effectively in the service project and need the speaker's information to do so. Instead of expending creative energy trying to discover a topic, the speakers go directly to work on the topic thrust upon them. They begin to examine the topic, analyze the audience, and bring the two together.

When the Speaker Has to Search

In some instances, however, the topic of the presentation may be elusive, and our initial task will be to find a subject or topic that will fit speaker, audience, and occasion. One of the most intimidating of speaking assignments can be to "talk about whatever you want to talk about." When topic selection is the speaker's first step, some free ranging imaginative work may be helpful.

TALK ABOUT THINGS YOU LOVE. Presentations are usually best when the speaker and topic coincide. What is a sparkling presentation for one speaker may be dreary for the next. The difference is often due to the relationship between speaker and topic. One way to find a topic is to consider the things about which we feel strongly. Thus, what we find personally rewarding is a good source for speech topics.[1]

Let us say that someone has a pet, a cat. The person could talk about the history of cats, cats in literature, cat diseases, breeding cats, showing cats, cat diet, training cats, songs about cats, the psychology of cats and more. If a person had an interest in cartoons, the person could talk about famous cartoonists, the history of cartoons, political cartoons, comic strips, animated cartoons, styles of cartoons, drawing cartoons, the syndication of cartoons, and the printing of cartoons. Any area can yield a number of possible speech topics.

THINK ABOUT THINGS YOU HATE. Besides feeling good about things in our life, we probably also have some things that we abominate. These, too, can offer possibilities for a presentation.

A person may be bothered, for example, by people who drive around with their windows down and their stereos punching out music at high volume, a rude imposition on the unrequesting public. A subject like this could lead to a range of topics: the rise of car stereos, problems in designing car audio systems, how to select a car stereo system, damaging effects of loud noise, municipal noise ordinances, contemporary etiquette, even personal liberty versus public good.

Another person may strongly dislike professional wrestling. Here the subject would also yield some interesting speech topic: the history of professional wrestling, why is professional wrestling popular, the marketing of professional wrestling, the typical wrestling fan, recruitment of wrestlers, the training of wrestlers, and wrestling publications. One need not be a fan of a cultural phenomenon to explore it and its ramifications.

TRY CLUSTERING TO FIND A TOPIC.   Clustering is a technique originally designed to foster writing skills (Rico). An important part of understanding clustering is to realize the different functions performed by the two hemispheres of the brain. The left hemisphere operates in a sequential, rational, logical manner while the right hemisphere operates in a nonsequential, subjective, holistic fashion. The right hemisphere is primarily the source of concepts and creativity while the left hemisphere is primarily the source of order and critical analysis. Clustering works by giving the creative, noncritical portion of the brain free rein.

Clustering is similar to brainstorming in that the main principle is to bring out as many ideas as possible without critiquing them. Clustering differs from brainstorming in that it is a personal activity rather than a group activity and that ideas are recorded in a nonlinear fashion.

One begins clustering with a word or concept. We draw a circle around that. From that center, we radiate out other ideas inspired by the original word. We link each new idea to the original idea or to ideas growing out of the original. Gradually, we create a web of associations.

As one goes through this process, it is vitally important to avoid evaluating the ideas. The procedure should be one of simple creation, not creation and judgment. No idea is too wacky, too stupid, or too ridiculous not to be consid-

> Clustering is similar to brainstorming in that the main principle is to bring out as many ideas as possible without critiquing them.

RED BRICK

Figure 12.2a.

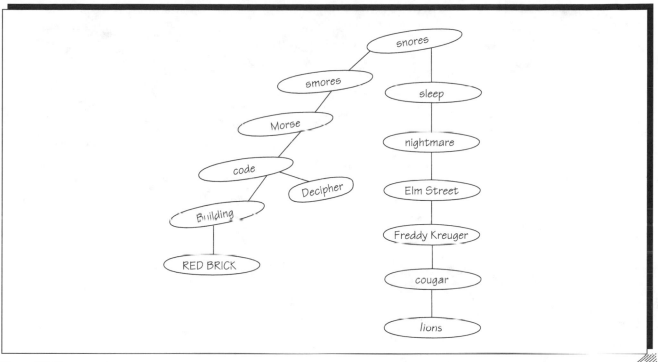

Figure12.2b.

ered. We simply go where our imaginations lead us. Following this process, even the simplest of words can lead to a wealth of topics.

Let us think of a familiar building, say, one made of red bricks, a humble enough building material but not one thought of as inspiring. To begin we put "red brick" in the middle of a sheet of paper.

The next step is to put down whatever concept pops into our head that is linked to "red brick." If we think of "red brick building," we would put "building" close to "red brick," circle "building" and draw a line linking it to "red brick." Each new idea that comes to us will be circled and linked to its appropriate neighbor. "Building" might make us think of "code" which could lead us to think of "Morse" which could lead to "smores" (a treat of marshmallows, chocolate, and graham crackers) which might make us think of "snores" which could lead to "sleep" which brings "nightmare" to mind which leads to "Elm Street" which makes us think of "Freddy Kreuger" which leads to "cougar" which we link to "lions" and so on and so on.

As we work along, we just let the words and connections come out. We should not try to force the associations. We let the links arise naturally. Some ideas will chain off the original direction; others will chain off into new directions. If we find ourselves stumped, we can ask, "what do I feel about this?" or "what strikes me here?"

After clustering for a while, we may begin to see ideas come together. We should resist the urge to stop and continue until something leaps out at us, until the light bulb comes on in our heads and inspiration strikes us. This kind of "aha!" experience is a strong indication that we have found a profitable

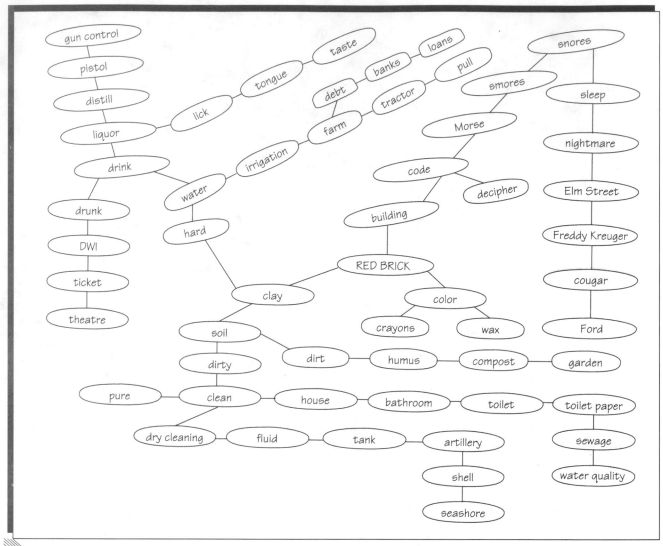

Figure 12.2c.

direction to pursue. We may need to begin the clustering process again with our "aha!" idea at the center. This will lead us to other considerations of the topic, but by this point we have already passed the stage of finding a topic and are working on narrowing the topic.

OTHER CONSIDERATIONS. Besides ourselves, we need also to look at other resources in the discovery process. One major consideration will, of course, be the audience. A good guideline for topic selection is to ask, "What will my audience find interesting?" Analyzing the intended audience can suggest topics and help narrow a general topic area.

A group of college bound, high school seniors would probably be interested in a topic such as "How to Select the Right College for You" while seniors in college would be more interested in "How to do Well in Job Interviews." Credit card usage is widespread, but that does not mean all talks about credit cards are well suited to all audiences. In college, a person might be interested in a topic such as "Tuition and Credit Cards." Someone working and travelling would find more interesting a talk on "Using Your Credit Card for Expense Accounts."

Research can also lead us to topics. The more informed we are, the greater our range of subjects and the possibilities for speeches. Reading widely gives us the scope necessary to find topics to fit various occasions and provides us with supporting information.

Narrowing the Topic: The Thesis Statement

Once we are over the hurdle of finding a topic, the next jump to be cleared is deciding what it is we want to say about that topic. If a topic has any breadth to it, we will not be able to say everything about it, even in a lengthy speech. Whether we want to talk about "pigs," "kitchen knives," "word processing," or "population control," we will need to concentrate on a small portion of the topic that can be covered in the allotted time.

Shrinking the Subject Area

One way to narrow a topic is to break it down into major areas or divisions. Then we pick the most interesting or relevant division as the subject of the speech. For example, the four topics above can be subdivided into the following areas:

Pigs: evolution of pigs, characteristics of pigs, breeds of pigs, raising pigs, marketing pigs, showing pigs

Kitchen Knives: types of kitchen knives, manufacture of kitchen knives, selecting kitchen knives, using kitchen knives, care of kitchen knives

Word Processing: history of word processing, word processing programs, learning word processing, economics of word processing, impact of word processing on office work, impact of word processing on writing styles

Population Control: world populations, populations of countries, rate of population growth, educational programs, sterilization programs, effect of population on food sources, effect of population on ecology, effect of population on economics, effect of population on politics

If the first efforts at dividing the topic into areas do not sufficiently narrow the topic, then a good course of action is to choose the most interesting division and subdivide it. For example, our original topic may have been "Pigs" of which one of the subdivisions was "Characteristics of Pigs." That subdivision can be divided even further: Characteristics of pigs: eating habits, temperament, likeable characteristics of pigs, unlikeable characteristics of pigs, reproductive systems of pigs, behavior of pigs, intelligence of pigs, etc.

Creating a Thesis Statement

We can further refine a topic by creating an appropriate thesis statement.[2] This statement will unite the elements of the speech in a sensible, coherent way. In fact, if we can compose a comprehensive thesis statement for a speech, a major portion of the compositional work has been accomplished.

The thesis statement should include three key elements. The first is, naturally enough, the *topic*. In addition to the topic, the thesis statement should also include the speaker's *position* on the subject. By "position," we mean a

> The more informed we are, the greater our range of subjects and the possibilities for speeches.

judgmental statement that indicates how the speaker views the topic. The view may be "good" or "bad," but it may also be phrased in words that indicate the topic's usefulness, effect, or characteristics. In most thesis statements, the topic will be the subject of the sentence and the position portion of the sentence will follow the verb "is" or "are."

Topic		*Position*
Pigs	are	likeable
Kitchen knives	are	good
Word processing	is	comfortable
World population growth	is	threatening

The last part of the thesis statement, the *amplification,* is the support or illustration the speaker offers to back up the judgment made in the first part of the sentence. In the amplification, we specify why the topic is what we say it is. We offer reasons for our viewpoint. We show why our announcement of the topic and our phrasing of our position is valid.

Finally, we should make sure our thesis statement meets a fourth criterion; it should be stated in a declarative sentence. "World population growth, a threat to environment and world economy" would not be an acceptable thesis statement as it contains no verb. Thus, it is not a full sentence. "Is world population growth a threat to the environment and economy?" is not an acceptable thesis statement either. It contains a subject and verb but is phrased as a question, an interrogative sentence, instead of making a statement.

Topic		*Position*	*Amplification*
Pigs	are	likeable	because they are clean, intelligent, and amusing.
Kitchen knives	are	good	when they fit the job, are made of proper steel, and are sharp.
Word processing	is	comfortable	to learn because it uses skills you know and is learned in stages.
World population growth	is	threatening	because of the pressures it exerts on the environment and the world economy.

Variations in Thesis Statements

While an effective thesis statement should contain the three elements of topic, position, and amplification, the three elements do not have to appear in the same order in every statement. One of the simplest variations is to place the position before the topic. The "kitchen knives" statement above could be rephrased and perhaps improved by changing it to "Good kitchen knives fit the job, are made of good steel, and are sharp." Here the position word "good" is used as an adjective describing "knife" rather than being placed after the verb. Whatever the word order, a thesis statement should still meet the four criteria: it should contain a topic, a position, amplification, and be a declarative sentence.

The Major Divisions of the Speech

Selecting Major Points

If we have done a good job of formulating a thesis statement, we already have a general outline of the presentation. The main points of the presentation will be what is included in the amplification part of the thesis statement. Each piece of amplification becomes a major point.

If we are using the "pigs" sentence as the basis for a presentation, the three main points become: (1) pigs are clean, (2) pigs are intelligent, and (3) pigs are amusing. Similarly, if the "population control" statement is the basis for a presentation, the presentation would have two main points: (1) population growth has a negative effect on the environment, and (2) population growth has a negative effect on the world economy.

Arranging the Major Points

Effective communication has organization to it, some pattern that makes sense to both the communicator and the audience. We use a number of organizing strategies in our communication, often without being aware of them. When we tell a joke, we know the punch line should come at the end of the joke. Somewhere in introductions, names need to be disclosed. When we tell stories, we put the parts of the story into an order that makes the story easier to tell. Similarly, we organize our speeches in patterns and have several available to us.

A student goes home for a weekend after the first month at the university and runs into an old friend who asks, "What's it like at ____ University?" The person starts to answer but stops, not quite sure where to begin. The manner in which the student finally frames the description of university life will influence the nature of the response.

The student could tell the story in a *chronological* pattern. Here the main points of the story would be arranged in a sequence based on time relationships. The story would be told in a manner which goes, "When I first arrived, I thought . . . Then after a week, I felt . . . Now, after a month, I think . . . ."

Another way the student could organize the story is in a *spatial* pattern, a pattern based on the geographic location of important aspects. Here, the story would move from place to place: "I enjoy living in the dorm . . . I go to classes in the Liberal Arts and Education Building . . . For recreation, I go to the student gym . . . ." Some of the organizing terms useful with a spatial pattern of organizing are "north, east, south, west," "up and down," and "inside and outside."

Still another approach is the *problem-solution* method of organization. The essentials of this pattern are first a difficulty and second a method of overcoming the difficulty. "The biggest problem I had was getting all my things into our small room . . . Then my roommate and I decided to build a loft."

Yet another way of organizing material is to use a *structure-function* pattern. With this pattern, one first describes an object then shows its application. Here the student's story might include, "One of the most important things you need on campus is your student identification card. This card is about the size of a credit card and . . . This cards allows you to do a lot of things . . . ."

If the main points do not fall easily into one of the major patterns, the student may relate the story with a *topical* pattern. Here the main points are simply arranged in a sensible or at least workable pattern. Often with a topical

> Effective communication has organization to it, some pattern that makes sense to both the communicator and the audience.

approach, one can change the order of the main points without damaging its sense: "The three things that impress me most about the university are the food, the dorms, and the high grading standards."

The above patterns of organization are the ones that recommend themselves for the organization of presentations. As speakers, we can adjust our thesis statements and the arrangements of our points so that we reach the best form for a speech. Some topics can be accommodated by only one approach while others lend themselves to all approaches. The "kitchen knives" speech could be organized in any of the five methods.

Chronological: "The first knife you should buy is . . . The second knife you should buy is. . . ."

Spatial: "When working at a cutting board . . . When working at the stove. . . ."

Problem-Solution: "For paring and peeling, use . . . For carving, use . . . For heavy chopping, use. . . ."

Structure-Function: "A well made kitchen knife is constructed of good steel with a properly shaped blade and a comfortable handle . . . These qualities allow you to use the knife in the most efficient way. . . ."

Topical: "My favorite kitchen knives are. . . ."

No one pattern of organization is superior to another. The question to be answered is: "Which pattern best fits this speaking situation?" The goal is to find a method of arranging the speech that makes the topic as clear as possible for the audience and allows the speaker to perform at optimum levels.

Conclusion

With the major points arranged in an appropriate fashion, a major portion of the presentation will be composed. At this stage, we will have moved through several important steps. We will have either been assigned a topic or discovered a topic that fits the speaker and audience. We will have analyzed the audience as completely as possible to effect an harmonious fit between it and the speaker's ideas. We will have composed a thesis statement that provides a foundation for the speech. What remains to be done is to consider the finer details of the presentation which will provide it with the polish needed to put it at its highest level.

Notes ◥◥◥

[1] For the "love/hate" idea, the author is indebted to Maureen Jungblut.

[2] The basic idea for this discussion was provided by Brenda Avadian, Speech Mapping Short Course, Central States Communication Association Convention, 14 April 1988, Schaumberg, Illinois.

Discussion Questions ///

1. What kinds of activities do we think of as creative?

2. How does creativity manifest itself in areas other than making presentations? In sports? In business? In relationships? In other forms of communication?

3. What does a speaker bring as a person to the speaking situation?

4. How do the variables between audiences (age, gender, education, professions, etc.) affect how a presentation is composed, delivered, or perceived?

5. Why would strong feelings (love/hate) about a topic be an asset to the speech composition process? How might such feelings be a detriment?

6. How could you narrow a topic (horses, university life, space travel, etc.) to a size appropriate for a five to seven minute presentation?

7. Why are the four characteristics of a thesis statement necessary for the statement to be effective?

8. Give an example of how a topic could be arranged in a chronological pattern.

9. Give an example of how a topic could be arranged in a spatial pattern.

10. Give an example of how a topic could be arranged in a problem-solution pattern.

11. Give an example of how a topic could be arranged in a structure-function pattern.

12. Give an example of how a topic could be arranged in a topical pattern.

Sources and References ///

Avadian, Brenda. Speech Mapping Short Course. Central States Communication Association Convention. 14 April 1988, Schaumberg, Illinois.

Jungblut, Maureen, Conversation with the author.

Kim, Steven H. *Essence of Creativity: A Guide to Tackling Difficult Problems*. New York: Oxford University Press, 1990.

Rico, Gabrielle Lusser. *Writing the Natural Way: Using Right-Brain Techniques to Release Your Expressive Powers*. Los Angeles: J. P. Tarcher, Inc., 1983.

⬚ Creating a Presentation ⬚

1. What is public speaking?

   _____

   _____

   _____

2. Name three guidelines for encouraging creativity in thinking.

   1. _____

   2. _____

   3. _____

3. Analysis is important prior to a presentation. What three things should a well prepared speaker analyze?

   1. _____

   2. _____

   3. _____

4. Why does it benefit speakers to choose topics about which they feel strongly?

   _____

   _____

   _____

5. What is clustering?

   _____

   _____

   _____

6. What three key elements should be included in a thesis statement?

1. _____

2. _____

3. _____

7. What grammatical form should the thesis sentence take?

_____

8. Which key element of the thesis statement contains the main points of a presentation?

_____

9. Explain each of the following patterns of organization:

chronological _____

_____

spatial _____

_____

problem-solution _____

_____

structure-function _____

_____

topical _____

_____

10. Give an example of a topic that could be arranged for each pattern of organization.

chronological _____

spatial _____

problem-solution _____

structure-function _____

topical _____

⚡ Narrowing a Topic Exercise ⚡

Subdivide each of the following topics into at least three areas. Compare your answers with other classmates to see the variety of ways a single topic can be divided.

1. The environment

   a.

   b.

   c.

2. Politics

   a.

   b.

   c.

3. Student rights

   a.

   b.

   c.

Choose one of your subdivisions from "the environment" and subdivide it further.

answer from above:

further subdivision:

1.

2.

3.

Discuss as a class the further narrowing of the topic.

Thesis Statement Development Exercise

Develop a completed thesis statement in the examples below by adding your amplification of the topic.

Topic	Position	Amplification
1. Aerobics	are beneficial	
2. Stress	is damaging	
3. Hobbies	are desirable	
4. Physics	is difficult	
5. Jazz	is enjoyable	

Provide a position and amplification for the topics below to form a completed thesis statement.

Topic	Position	Amplification
1. Dancing		
2. Computers		
3. Russia		
4. Football		
5. The President		

Write five thesis statements below on topics of your choice.

1.

2.

3.

4.

5.

⫸ Topic Organization Exercise ⫷

Identify which organizational pattern you would use for the following topics. Explain the reason for your selection. Possible organizational patterns: chronological, spatial, problem-solution, structure-function, topical.

Topic   **Organizational Pattern**

1. "Getting Through Chemistry 101"

2. "My Vacation at Padre Island"

3. "Why My Favorite Novel Is . . ."

4. "Changing Population Centers in the U.S."

5. "Using the Library"

6. "How to Prepare for an Exam"

7. "Overcoming Stagefright"

8. "Developing Good Study Habits"

9. "Interest Assessment Tests"

10. "The Fastest Way to Get to State U. from Chicago"

Introduction to Informative Speaking Assignments

While few of you will be professional public speakers, most of you will be called upon from time to time to speak before an audience, even while still a student. Sometimes the purpose of a speech is informative: explaining a project in a class; introducing a visiting alumnus to a housing unit; detailing a vacation for the travel club. Other times the purpose is persuasive: arguing against a tuition hike before the board of trustees; convincing the dorm committee to change visitation rules; recruiting donors for a campus blood drive.

After college there will be business presentations, community service activities, and opportunities to direct the forces that impact your daily living routine and will require good public speaking skills.

Suggested Topics for Informative Presentation

Choose a topic you are knowledgeable about or one which interests you enough to investigate. Below are suggestions to get you started. Your topic does not have to come from the list below but must be approved by your instructor.

what something is	fishing lures
how something works	thimbles
how something is done	puppeteering
how something is viewed	Special Olympics
unusual place I've visited	Toastmasters
hobby	square dancing
organization I belong to	clogging
special interest group	jewelry crafting
noteworthy person I've met	Cajun food
book worth reading	basket weaving
food's origin	photography
frightening experience	vegetarianism
embarrassing moment	anorexia
person worth imitating	training horses
favorite screen character	dolphin intelligence
least favorite job	teen alcoholism
favorite job	EMTs
Hall of Fame I'd most like to be elected to	administering CPR
place I'd like to visit	agribusiness
favorite author	food irradiation
history of a modern invention	the Shakers
course I've taken	bocci ball
animal husbandry	volunteering
tombstone rubbings	gourmet cooking
Civil War history	organized crime
restoring old cars	being a nerd
herb gardening	world dictator
reforestation	collective negotiations
rappelling	robotics
orienteering	enterprise networking
arrowheads	genetic engineering
spelunking	What is a cooper?
cricket	fountain pens
Halloween	book selling

television
rugby
Japan
oil painting
Indy 500 Motor Speedway
sky diving
trout fishing
violins
Middle East
coffee
waste disposal
bicycles
elephants
dictionaries

kayaking
race horses
great leaders
big brothers
micro computers
learning methods
philosophers
silver screen
theater
blacksmithing
herbal medicines
hang gliding
hot air ballooning

Speaking Options

As part of this course, you will make three presentations. Of these, two are informative while the third is persuasive. To meet this requirement, your instructor will select one or both of the following options. Each option allows you to choose, research, and present topics in a different way. Previous to selecting the topic for your first presentation, you will need to indicate your choice to your instructor. The two options are free choice or thematic. Both options include research as part of the preparation process. In addition to the typical library research, you may also use sources such as interviews, trade journals, and technical manuals, if they are appropriate.

⮕ Option 1—Free Choice
With this option, you have a free choice of topics. You may use whatever topic you choose as long as it meets the requirements of the assignment, informative or persuasive. The first two speeches will be informative speeches on *different* topics. The speech will include appropriate research as indicated by your instructor. Your instructor will specify the type and format of the persuasive presentation.

⮕ Option 2—Thematic
With this option, you will select a topic of concern or issue on the local, state, or national level (safety lighting at the university, legalized gambling, organ donation, health care, etc.). The more specific the issue, the more likely you will be able to address the issue significantly within the time limits of the class. "Pesticide Residue in Soil" is a more workable choice, for example, than "Saving the Environment." You will thoroughly research the topic. Your instructor will specify the number of sources needed. These sources should inform all three of your presentations. The first informative presentation will introduce your audience to the topic, its impact, and how it affects us. The second informative presentation will address a major area of the topic. The persuasive presentation will build on the two preceding presentations and persuade the audience to take some action relevant to the issue.

Good luck with your presentations!

⟩⟩⟩ Informative Presentation Assignment I ⟨⟨⟨

Informative Presentation

Purpose

The first speaking assignment has a three-fold purpose:

1. You will learn the techniques to successfully compose a presentation
2. You will learn how speaking style differs from written style
3. You will gain experience speaking in front of an audience

Basic Requirements

➮ You will develop and present to the class an original, informative presentation on a topic approved by your instructor.

➮ You should choose a topic you feel comfortable talking about, one which is of particular interest to you.

➮ Each presentation must be _____ minutes in length.

➮ _____ sources should be used in preparing the presentation.

➮ An outline of the presentation must be submitted (due date) _____ to the instructor.

➮ Presentations will be graded according to the criteria on p. _____, which must be handed in prior to the presentation.

➮ You will complete the observation sheets on pages 255–263 for designated fellow speakers.

➮ Additional instructor requirements:

Informative Presentation I Worksheet

Presentation Due Date _____

1. possible topics:

2. selected topic:

3. possible narrowed topic areas:

4. narrowed focus of presentation:

5. thesis statement:

6. main points:

   1.

   2.

   3.

7. support for main points: source:

   support for 1. a.

                   b.

   support for 2. a.

                   b.

   support for 3. a.

                   b.

8. transitions to connect main points:

   transition between 1 and 2:

   transition between 2 and 3:

9. possible attention getting devices to open the speech:

10. selected attention getting device:

11. conclusion that can be drawn from the presentation:

Notes:

⬚ Informative Presentation I Grading Criteria—Style B ⬚

Topic 10%*

➡ subject of presentation appropriate to audience, assignment
➡ topic appropriately narrowed to fit time guidelines

Organization 30%*

Introduction

➡ attention getting opening employed
➡ speaker credibility developed
➡ rapport developed with the audience
➡ presentation previewed
➡ thesis made clear

Body

➡ main points obvious
➡ transition used between main points
➡ easily followed

Conclusion

➡ implications of material highlighted
➡ a feeling of completion developed

Content 30%*

➡ significant material developed in presentation
➡ related to thesis
➡ supported with example
➡ clearly presented
➡ interestingly developed
➡ vocabulary appropriate
➡ jargon and unfamiliar terms defined
➡ sources credible
➡ sources cited
➡ visual aid(s) well constructed, enhanced presentation

Delivery 30%*

Physical

➡ eye contact frequent
➡ gestures meaningful
➡ posture comfortable
➡ notecards properly used
➡ sense of communication with audience established
➡ visual aid(s) used properly, with confidence

Vocal

➡ energetic
➡ rate appropriate
➡ volume appropriate
➡ tone pleasing
➡ vocal variety exhibited
➡ enunciation/pronunciation correct
➡ absence of fillers

Comments

*Suggested values only—may be changed by your instructor.

Providing Positive Feedback

Goal

To compliment a person on a positive aspect of that person's performance

Procedure

1. Attend carefully to the person's presentation.

2. Select some aspect of the performance that communicated well to you. Some aspects you might want to regard would be dress, posture, voice, visual aids, clarity of organization, humor, language, speaking style, or tone of the speech. Feel free to pick any other aspect that you wish.

3. Phrase your reaction using an "I" statement, for example, "I really liked your introduction. It caught my attention." The statement should tell what you like ("your introduction") and why you liked it ("It caught my attention.")

4. During the feedback session following the performance, make your statement to the performer. The performance goals are:

   ⮞ To attract the instructor's attention by raising your hand
   ⮞ To look at the person you are addressing
   ⮞ To tell the person what you like
   ⮞ To speak so the person can hear you

___◎ Student Evaluation of Informative Presentation I ◎___

In light of the guidelines for constructive feedback, offer observations about the presentation you have just watched.

What were the main points?

What new information did you hear?

What was the speaker's strength?

What one thing would you suggest the speaker work on to improve?

⟩⟩⟩ Student Evaluation of Informative Presentation I ⟨⟨⟨

In light of the guidelines for constructive feedback, offer observations about the presentation you have just watched.

What were the main points?

What new information did you hear?

What was the speaker's strength?

What one thing would you suggest the speaker work on to improve?

⟍⟍ Student Evaluation of Informative Presentation I ⟋⟋

In light of the guidelines for constructive feedback, offer observations about the presentation you have just watched.

What were the main points?

What new information did you hear?

What was the speaker's strength?

What one thing would you suggest the speaker work on to improve?

Oral Presentations

13

Tending to the Details

KEY CONCEPTS

S uccessful craftsmanship demands that we pay attention to the finer points of the process. The amount and type of spices give foods their distinctive tastes. What makes a house into someone's home is, among other things, the type of furniture and decorations that are added to the basic structure. To be at their best, presentations also require attention to details beyond creating the thesis and major points.

Introductions, Transitions, and Conclusions

Introductions

While the introduction is the first thing the audience hears, most speakers will probably find it easiest to compose an introduction if it is saved until the last steps of the composition process. The conclusion is also best left for the latter stages of composition. The reason for the seeming delay is simple: one cannot introduce a topic until one knows what one is going to say about it. Similarly, we cannot wrap up our main points until we know what those main points are and how we feel about them. The first step is to have the body of the speech in place, then go to work introducing it and concluding it.

Functions of an Introduction

The introduction should function as a warm-up and preparation for both the speaker and the audience. It allows the speaker to begin talking and ease into the major points. It allows the audience to tune in on the topic and prepare to process the speaker's remarks. Keep in mind that throughout the speech, the audience has a formidable job of processing information. It must attend to the speaker's ideas, understand them, and react to them, all on the basis of one hearing. If printed material is difficult, the reader can re-read the material any number of times until it is clear. A speaker's audience usually does not re-hear the speech. Hence, the more aid speakers give audiences to process the speech, the more likelihood that the speeches will be successful.

In some cases, such as presidential addresses, the text of the speech may be known in advance of the speech. In most cases, however, the audience will have little foreknowledge of what the speaker is to say. If the speaker were to start immediately with the first point of the presentation, the audience would have trouble keeping up with the speech.

The basic task of an introduction is to take the audience from where it is—usually ignorant of the speaker's ideas—to the point where it can attend to the topic and put the ideas into the proper perspective. The speaker needs to help the audience move intellectually and emotionally to this point.

Goals of an Introduction

How a speaker chooses to introduce the presentation will vary according to the audience, topic, and other factors in the situation. An informative presentation will be introduced in a different fashion than a persuasive one or a ceremonial speech. Whatever the presentation, the introduction should accomplish several goals.

GAIN ATTENTION. First of all, an introduction should *gain the attention* of the audience or strengthen its attention if it is already focused on the speaker. We want to create an interest in the topic and in ourselves as speakers, and a curi-

> The introduction should function as a warm-up and preparation for both the speaker and the audience.

osity for what will follow. Here we are answering an unspoken question of the audience, "*Should* we listen to you?" Of course, the steps a speaker takes to gain the audience's attention should fit with the topic and tenor of the presentation. As speakers, we have a number of ways in which we can gain the attention of the audience.

A speaker can make a *startling statement.* "Each of us is worth one hundred thousand dollars. That is the amount it is estimated it takes to raise a child from birth to age eighteen."

A *rhetorical question* can work well. A rhetorical question is one that is asked for the sake of making a point, not for the sake of receiving an answer. If one were speaking on the rising costs of a university education, one could begin with, "Do you want to pay another thousand dollars for your schooling next year?"

Humor serves as an attention-getter even though it is probably the most stereotypical way of beginning a speech. If one resorts to the familiar, "A funny thing happened to me on the way to speak today . . .," it will probably send the audience into a serious case of the ho-hums. On the other hand, wit, well applied, can work effectively.

Keep in mind that humor varies from one person to another and from one audience to another. What one audience finds hilariously funny may fall flat with a different group. For example, some may find the following story an amusing beginning for a speech on the perceptions of children; others may not find it amusing at all:

> A kindergarten teacher was working with her class one day when the principal entered the room. Instead of leaving teachers' paychecks in their mailboxes, it was his custom to hand them to the teachers personally. He gave the kindergarten teacher her paycheck and left.
>
> One of the children was curious as to what he had seen, so he asked the teacher, "Why did the principal give you an envelope?"
>
> The teacher explained that the principal liked to hand the teachers their paychecks and the envelope contained her pay for working.
>
> "Oh," the student responded, "where do you work?"

In using humor, we should keep in mind also that what is acceptable terminology to one group may be offensive to another. One theory of humor is that it is a way of expressing in socially acceptable ways that which would otherwise be unacceptable. Humor is a way of venting aggression, cynicism, obscenity, and skepticism (Freud 203–04). Thus, humor has a built-in potential for offending. Wise speakers are careful to use humor in ways that are in tune with the sensitivities of their audiences.

A *quotation* that capitalizes on the speaker's idea or reflects the theme of the speech can also provide a good beginning. For a speech on phobias, one could begin with Franklin Roosevelt's well-known remark, "We have nothing to fear but fear itself." For a speech on public service, John F. Kennedy's invitation would be fitting: "Ask not what your country can do for you, ask rather what you can do for your country."

Tell a story and tell it well, and the audience will probably respond positively. As part of an introduction, a story will have to be short, but an anecdote, serious or light, can set the mood for the speech. A speech about one's work experience could begin with a story: "My first day on the ranch, the

Keep in mind that humor varies from one person to another and from one audience to another.

foreman came to me and said they had just the right horse for me. As I had never been on a horse before, he thought I ought to have a horse that had never been ridden."

If one wears *special clothing,* one can be a walking advertisement for the speech. For a speech on judo, a student wore his judo *gi,* the uniform for that sport. Another student, talking about training procedures at McDonald's, wore her McDonald's uniform.

Another way is to *display an interesting object.* Wheeling in oxy-acetylene welding equipment for a speech on welding should gain the audience's attention as would bringing in a saddle, an assortment of knives, or a bunch of balloons.

A speaker may choose to *give a short demonstration.* Here one does a little bit of what one is going to talk about. A speech on juggling could begin with the speaker giving a short sample of his abilities.

SHOW RELEVANCE. If gaining the attention of the audience supplies an answer to the question, "*Should* we listen to you?", then the relevance portion of the introduction answers the question, "*Why* should we listen to you?" Here the speaker makes the presentation interesting by showing how the topic relates to the audience. A speaker can refer to the needs of the audience members, their backgrounds, their interests, or their wish for entertainment or knowledge.

At first glance, a speech about the Coast Guard would seem to have little relevance for an audience in the landlocked Midwest. One way the topic could be made relevant would be to link it to the feelings of the audience: "When we take a trip in our cars, it is reassuring to know that emergency aid is available should we need it. We know that the highway patrol, sheriffs' departments, ambulances, and wreckers are standing by. The same need for service and protection is felt by people at sea. That is where the Coast Guard comes in."

ESTABLISH CREDIBILITY. The introduction should tell why the speaker is worthy of the audience's attention. Here, the question to be answered is, "Why should we listen to *you?*" That is, the introduction should establish the speaker as a trustworthy source of information.

One way to establish credibility is to *show experience* with the topic. For example, one student began a speech on harness racing by pointing out that she had worked at a harness racing track for three summers.

One can establish credibility by *citing research.* Here the speaker demonstrates an above average knowledge of the topic. If one were speaking about crime rates, references to the sources examined could establish the speaker as a knowledgeable source of information: "In comparing the crime rate for our university and a similar school in an urban area, I examined the police reports of both universities for the past five years." Background research can also include people as well as print resources: "To find out about athletics and academics at our university, I talked with the athletic director, the basketball coach, the associate dean of students, and three varsity athletes."

Speakers can gain credibility if they *show longterm interest in the topic.* Here the experience is proof of the speaker's interest and genuine involvement. A presentation about horses could begin with, "I began showing horses when I was twelve, and I continue to participate even though I am a full-time student living on campus."

PROVIDE AN OVERVIEW. The introduction should also give the audience an idea of what to expect in the body of the presentation. The question to be answered in this portion of the introduction is, "What are we going to hear?" Providing the audience with an overview or preview gives it a framework to use while attending to the rest of the presentation. When the audience knows the topic and general ideas the speaker will deal with, it is easier for it to follow the specifics of the presentation. The simplest way to provide an overview is to use the thesis statement as part of the introduction. Having gained the audience's attention, shown ourselves to be credible sources, and demonstrated the relevance of our topics, we then tell the audience what it is about to hear.

Transitions

In addition to moving smoothly into the presentation and out of it, a speaker should also move smoothly between the main points. Stopping at the end of one main point and jumping to the next makes for a choppy speech. Without knowing the speaker has finished one point and is starting another, the audience may have trouble following what is being said.

One can effect transitions in several ways. The most primitive way is to *announce the finish of one point and the start of the next:* "That finishes my first point. Here is my second point." Even a primitive transition is usually better than none.

A more sophisticated approach to transitions is to compose a *mini-conclusion* to the first point and a *mini-introduction* to the second. Thus, a good transition is like a hand-off in a relay race. The momentum of the first runner is finishing while that of the second is beginning, yet for a moment, the two separate runners are linked together as they pass the baton.

To create a smooth transition, a speaker can compose two *parallel statements*. The first summarizes the first point while the second introduces the second point. If the topic were "word processing" or "child raising," the transitions might be phrased like this:

"Learning how to use a word processor involves basic skills that you already have (first point). For those skills that you do not have, your learning can take place in easy steps (second point)."

"Children can understand the limits of behavior when those limits are clear (first point). Since children cannot process complicated information, no matter how clear it is to adults, your guidelines should also be simple (second point)."

Another useful way to create transitions is to signal the audience with transition phrases. These are parallel constructions in which the first phrase or word indicates a summation of the first point and the second phrase or word indicates the next set of ideas. Some examples would be:

➔ "We have looked at . . . Let us now look at . . ."
➔ "So much for . . . But what about . . ."
➔ "Now that we understand . . . Let us examine . . ."
➔ "On the one hand . . . On the other hand . . ."
➔ "One of the most important ideas is . . . Another important idea is . . ."
➔ "We have examined . . . We will examine next . . ."
➔ "Now that we have seen . . . Let us turn to . . ."
➔ "As we have observed . . . Another important aspect is . . ."

> When the audience knows the topic and general ideas the speaker will deal with, it is easier for it to follow the specifics of the presentation.

By creating smooth transitions, we move ourselves and our audiences from point to point and make the speaking situation easier for both parties.

Transitions can also serve as a check on the effectiveness of main points and their arrangements. If a speaker is having difficulty linking the main points with transitions, the problem may not be with the transitions but with the main points. They may not be developed fully or they may be arranged in a confusing or ineffectual order.

Conclusions

In finishing a presentation, speakers need to make a smooth shift from motion to rest. Concluding is different from just stopping. When a speaker merely stops—abruptly quits speaking—the audience is left hanging without any sense of completion. When one concludes, one brings together the ideas of the speech, signals the audience the speech is ending, and eases out of the subject. A good conclusion reinforces the body of the presentation and leaves the audience with a feeling of completion and finality.

Several approaches are available for ending presentations smoothly. Interestingly enough, many of the techniques for concluding a presentation mirror the techniques for introducing one. A standard method of concluding is to *summarize the main points* and finish with a wrap-up sentence. If one were speaking on "pigs" and using the thesis statement we formulated in the previous chapter, the conclusion might sound like this: "Despite their reputation as being filthy, sloppy, and smelly, pigs are really likeable animals. They are clean; they are intelligent; and they are amusing. Instead of just being bacon on the hoof, they can be animals to like and to enjoy."

A *quotation* can provide the final touch. Here the speaker chooses a memorable statement that capitalizes on the ideas and moods of the speech. The quotation may be serious or humorous, but it should reinforce what has already been presented. The climax and conclusion of Martin Luther King, Jr.'s stirring "I Have a Dream" speech was a quotation from a spiritual: "Free at last! Free at last! Thank God Almighty, we are free at last!"

Another way to end a presentation is to finish with a touch of *humor*. To finish a presentation on early education, one might summarize the main points and conclude with, "Perhaps it was Sherlock Holmes who best summarizes my position. When Doctor Watson asked Holmes which part of a person's education was most important, Holmes replied, 'Elementary, my dear Watson'."

A *rhetorical question* can also serve to close a presentation. Such a question brings together the main points and asks the audience for a silent response that reinforces the theme of the presentation. In a presentation on "Use of Credit Cards," the speaker could end with a rhetorical question such as, "We have seen how students can incur a large amount of debt with cards, and we have seen how we can avoid that debt. All it takes is some planning and a little self-discipline. Are you going to let your financial life be controlled by a piece of plastic?"

For a more powerful ending, the final sentence can be a *powerful statement*. Here one ends with a vivid image, a declaration of intent, or a statement of strong conviction. The best known example in American oratory is probably Patrick Henry's conclusion to his speech urging independence for the American colonies: "I know not what course others may take, but as for me, give me liberty or give me death!"

Sometimes, one can conclude with a *story*. The tale or anecdote or fable should capture the theme of the presentation and provide a memorable illustration of the point or points the speaker wants to make. Often, a concluding story will illustrate the consequences if the audience uses or fails to use the information provided in the speech. A presentation about safety in the workplace could conclude with a story about someone who wore (or did not wear) appropriate safety garb. If the presentation were on, "Consulting Your Interests to Pick the Right Job," the speaker could conclude with a story such as this one:

> A friend of mine grew up on the seacoast. His father was a naval engineer, and my friend and his brothers spent a lot of time on the water. He really liked ships, but he thought he ought to try other possibilities. So one summer, he got a job on a dairy farm.
>
> One of his first jobs was to go to the pasture in the afternoon, open the gate, and start the cows back to the barn for milking. One day he went to the pasture, opened the gate, and all the cows started for the barn. All but one, that is.
>
> He urged the cow to go. She wouldn't. He tried chasing her. She still avoided the gate. All the time he was getting madder and madder. Still the cow would not cooperate.
>
> After a while, the farmer drove up in his truck, got out, and watched my friend chasing the cow. The farmer watched for a few minutes, then said, "It looks like you have a little problem."
>
> "They all went," my friend said, "except for this stupid cow!"
>
> "Well, son," the farmer said, "I think there's a reason for the problem."
>
> "What's that?" my friend asked.
>
> "That cow," the farmer said, "is a bull."
>
> That was when my friend decided that where he belonged was where his interests were already—on a ship.

The conclusion should incorporate what is needed to summarize and wrap-up. Conclusions should avoid including other elements. The conclusion is not the place to introduce a new main point. The conclusion should reinforce what the speaker has already said, not start in a new direction when the speaker has no time to develop the point.

Conclusions should avoid including other elements. The conclusion is not the place to introduce a new main point.

Language Choice

When we talk about composing a presentation, we are talking about how we use words to construct a message. The composition process is one of trying to find the right words and the right arrangements of words that will allow an audience to translate what we are saying so as to arrive at a viewpoint similar to ours. As language is the vehicle that will carry our intentions and meanings, choosing language is an important part of constructing a speech.

Language Should Fit the Topic—of RAMS and Ewes

To be effective as speakers, our language must *fit the topic* even to the pronunciation of words. To illustrate, let us look at two topics, one electronic, the other agricultural.

The language of the speech should fit the audience.

If a person were going to talk about personal computers, the person would need to be familiar with the terms used in describing personal computers and their components. Similarly, if a person were going to talk about sheep, the person would need to be at ease with the breeds of sheep, characteristics of sheep, and how to pronounce words associated with sheep. If the speaker pronounced "ewes" as if it were "eewees," anyone with a rudimentary knowledge of sheep would know immediately that the speaker had little acquaintance with the animals. If the speaker on computers referred to RAM (random access memory) as if it were an object—"This computer needs more power. I want to put more rams in it"—the audience would know the person had little experience with the chosen topic.

Language Should Fit the Audience

Besides fitting the speaker comfortably, the language should also *fit the audience.* People vary widely in their backgrounds, and thus the same topic may have to be expressed in different terms for different audiences. Explaining sheep to urban children would require different language than a speech on sheep raising for 4-H members, and still different language would be appropriate for the Wool Growers of America. Terminology for computers should differ when one is talking to a group of novices on "How to Get Started in Personal Computing" as opposed to talking to the local Mac Users Club or Hackers Anonymous.

Language Should Fit the Speaker

Another criterion that language should meet is that it should *fit the speaker.* Each of us has a different speaking style, and language use is an important part of that style. We want to pick words that fit us, but at the same time, we should be open to expanding our vocabularies. When using new terminology, we should become fluent enough that the new words and phrasing emerge naturally instead of sounding forced.

Language Should Fit the Mood

Language should also *fit the mood* of the presentation. Besides creating understanding, speakers also work to create emotional states in their audiences. Wording will differ from speech to speech depending on the emotional tone a speaker wishes to set. For a speech on "waterbeds," for example, the language would vary according to what the speaker wanted to say about the subject. If the person were speaking to the staff of a nursing home about the therapeutic value of waterbeds, the language should show that the speaker understands the serious work of running a nursing home and recognizes the importance of patient welfare. On the other hand, if the person were giving a humorous, after dinner speech about waterbeds, the speaker would point out the frivolous problems—leaks, squishes, seasickness, and weight—while making jokes and puns about the subject.

Lining up the Speech

In the process of composing a presentation, we reach a point fairly quickly when we feel the need to commit our ideas to writing. As we progress, the arrangements of points and subpoints becomes increasingly complex. Notes put ideas into visible form and allow us to alter what we want to say. Eventually, some form of notes accompany us to the lectern and serve as a guide while we speak. While notes are not an end in themselves, good notes are a valuable tool in the process of creating a speech

Outlining

In the early stages of composing a presentation, we may find ourselves jumping from one point to another, forward and backwards. That is fine for that stage of composition. The final outline, however, should arrange its items in the correct order for speaking.

Composition Notes

We can outline in a number of different ways—sentence, phrase, word—and we can vary the amount of details. The method we will describe involves sentence outlines which are later reduced to speaking notes. This approach allows us to develop the speech in detail and provides flexibility in the speaking situation.

To create an outline, we start with the thesis statement. So that it will be a constant reminder of what we are speaking about, we place it at the top of the outline. The next item is the introduction. Here we would do well to write it out in full to make sure it contains all the necessary ingredients: attention, relevance, credibility, and an overview.

Following the introduction comes the main point and below it, the supporting material and expansion of the point. The second (and third and fourth, etc.) point follows in like manner. It is also a good idea to write out the transition between the main points. The conclusion comes last, again written in full so we can be sure to include everything necessary (Figure 13.3).

In making an outline, we should make sure that points come in the proper order. Main points are the most important ideas. Under them, in descending order of importance, will be the various subdivisions. If a point is to be divided, it needs to be divided into two subpoints. Subdivisions are just that, divisions, and it is difficult to divide

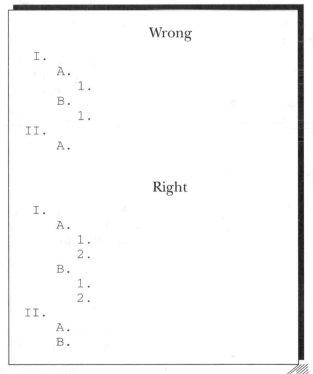

Figure 13.1.

```
Thesis Statement
Introduction:
   I. Main Point
      A. Subpoint
         1. sub-subpoint
         2. sub-subpoint
      B. Subpoint
         1. sub-subpoint
         2. sub-subpoint
  II. Main Point
      A. Subpoint
         1. sub-subpoint
         2. sub-subpoint
      B. Subpoint
         1. sub-subpoint
         2. sub-subpoint
 III. Main Point
      A. Subpoint
         1. sub-subpoint
         2. sub-subpoint
      B. Subpoint
         1. sub-subpoint
         2. sub-subpoint
Conclusion
```

Figure 13.2.

something into one part. Instead of a sequence of I-A-1-a, we need a sequence of I-A-1-2-B-1-2.

These sample outlines show how material can be arranged (Figures 13.1 and 13.2).

Speaking Notes

The closer we come to the speaking situation, the more the purpose of the outline changes from organizing the speech to serving as a memory aid for our remarks. When we move to actually giving the speech, we should be familiar enough with the material that we do not need to rely on a complete sentence outline. At this point, we can reduce the sentence to phrases or words and condense much of the outline. Speaking notes for our speech would look much like Figure 13.4.

Rehearsing the Presentation

The Nature of Rehearsal

Creating an outline goes a long way towards helping create a presentation, but if one stops with the words on paper, one still does not have a presentation. The *sine qua non* of a presentation is not putting words on paper but, rather, putting words into the air. Until a speaker gives the ideas voice, we do not have a presentation.

The creation of a presentation is not a matter of making an outline, then practicing that outline with no changes. The rehearsal period is as much a time for revisions and changes as any other. After trying to speak our ideas, we may even decide to scrap the entire effort and start over. If necessary, that is fine. What happens in rehearsal should inform the creation of a presentation as much as the research, the imaginative work, and the writing. If our rehearsal periods make us revise and rethink earlier work, we should not worry. That is just part of the process.

How to Rehearse

The appropriate way to rehearse a presentation is fairly simple: we need to rehearse aloud and in conditions as close to the speaking conditions as possible. Running over a presentation in our minds is helpful, but it does not begin to supply us with the knowledge that full rehearsal brings. We need to try out the actual behaviors—speech and movement—that we will perform when we speak. Only in this way can we have a true idea of what we will sound and look like to the audience and to ourselves.

Placing ourselves in the speaking environment can make the task of giving a presentation much easier to accomplish. The more familiar we are with the setting for a presentation, the more comfortable we will be. Rather than having to deal with the distraction of an unfamiliar situation, we can be at ease with

We need to try out the actual behaviors—speech and movement—that we will perform when we speak.

Thesis Statement: Dogs are good pets because of their social characteristics, their habits, and their hygiene.

Introduction: Some of them may have celebrity names. Some may have fancy names. Some may have plain names. The celebrity names are those like Lassie, Rin-Tin-Tin, and Benji. Fancy names often come with pedigrees, names like "Sir Wellington's Knight of King's Ridge." The plain names are Spot or Blackie or Old Blue or Squeaker. Whether the names be fancy or plain, dogs have been our friends and protectors for thousands of years, ever since some wolf, separated from its pack, attached itself to a human being. I have had dogs all my life. Most of you have probably had a dog as a pet. I have sometimes wondered why we have such close ties with dogs but not with other animals such as racoons, possums, and other wildlife that may live close to us but not with us. In looking at a number of books on pets, I have found several reasons why we have such long and close ties with the canine world. Dogs are good pets because of their social characteristics, their habits, and their hygiene.

I. Dogs are good pets because of their social characteristics.

    A. Dogs are descended from wolves, animals which have strong social instincts.

        1. Wolves are pack oriented.

            a. Wolves bond themselves to groups.

            b. Wolves enjoy associating with other wolves.

        2. Wolves are responsive to a pack leader.

            a. The "Alpha leader" is at the head of the wolf pack's hierarchy.

            b. The "Alpha leader" establishes his position by dominating the others.

    B. The dog's inherited characteristics make it a good pet.

        1. Instead of bonding with other animals, dogs bond with human beings.

        2. Dogs recognize their owners as "leaders of the pack."

            a. As our dogs' "Alpha leader," we can discipline them and control them.

            b. Recognizing us as their "Alpha leaders," dogs respond to our wishes.

Figure 13-3. Sample outline: "Why Dogs Make Good Pets"

3. "Unlike man's other favorite domesticate, the cat, a dog adjusts with difficulty . . . to an independent and wild existence and draws heavily on the mutual exchange of pack members and the guidance of a pack leader, or a human master, who is in fact a surrogate pack leader ("Dogs" *Encyclopedia Britannica:* Macropedia, 929)."

II. Dogs are good pets because of their habits.

  A. Dogs' schedules fit well with human schedules.

    1. Many animals such as racoons, flying squirrels, and skunks are nocturnal and keep their owners up at night.

    2. Dogs follow human sleeping patterns with ease.

  B. Dogs' natural behavior is not destructive to humans.

    1. Some animals' "playfulness" can be hazardous to your health.

      a. An adult racoon can rip your ear off or bite you to the bone.

      b. A "playful" cougar can disembowel you with one swipe.

    2. Dogs can learn easily how to behave with humans.

    3. Some animals tear up your house.

      a. Racoons, for example, will clear a closet shelf for their sleeping quarters.

      b. Dogs can learn to live and respect your property.

    4. Some animal's feeding habits make their life incompatible with humans.

      a. Some are such voracious eaters that you would spend most of your time providing them food.

        1. The common mole must eat constantly.

        2. The field mouse must eat its own weight in food every day.

      b. Some animals such as weasels and skunks, prosper on a diet of live animals such as mice.

      c. Dogs eating habits are easy.

        1. They eat at regular intervals.

        2. They eat food that is easy to obtain commercially.

⟋⟋ **Figure 13.3.** *continued*

III. Dogs are good pets because of their hygiene.

    A. A dog's smell is more compatible with humans than other animals.

        1. Woodchucks and possums, for example, smell bad.

        2. A dog's odor is easily remedied.

            a. Some breeds, such as poodles, have little odor.

            b. "Doggy odor" can be controlled by grooming and bathing.

    B. Dog's elimination habits make them compatible with humans.

        1. Nobody wants to live with urine and fecal matter.

        2. Wild animals are difficult to housebreak.

        3. Dogs are housebroken easily.

            a. Dogs do not like to foul their own quarters.

            b. Dogs respond well to training.

            c. Combining these two characteristics, it is easy for dogs to develop control of their elimination.

            d. Dogs can be trusted on valuable furniture and rugs.

Conclusion: We can see that we live with dogs for good reasons. Their characteristics match up well with our own, and dogs provide us companionship and loyalty at a minimum of effort to ourselves. When you go home at break and see Spot or Blackie or Old Blue, those friendly tail wags and warm welcomes are not accidental. They come from years of close association. You and your dog, My and I dogs, do well together because the dog's social characteristics, the dog's habits, and the dog's hygiene are so well suited to life with humans.

Bibliography

Coren, Stanley. *The Intelligence of Dogs*. New York: Bantam Books, 1995.

"Dogs." *Encyclopedia Britannica: Macropedia*. 1982.

Fox, Michael. *Superdog*. New York: Howell Book House-Macmillan Publishing Co., 1990.

Milani, Myrna M. *The Body Language and Emotion of Dogs: a Practical Guide to the Physical and Behavioral Displays Owners and Dogs Exchange and How to Use them to Create a Lasting Bond*. New York: William Morris-Quill, 1986.

Figure 13-3. *continued*

Monks of New Skeet. *The Art of Raising a Puppy.* Boston: Little, Brown and Company, 1991.

___. *How to Be Your Dog's Best Friend: A Training Manual for Dog Owners.* Boston-Toronto: Little, Brown and Company, 1978.

New Dog Encyclopedia. 1970.

Rood, Ronald. *May I Keep This Clam, Mother? It Followed Me Home: The Care and Feeding of Wild Pets.* New York: Simon and Schuster, 1973.

Villiard, Paul. *Wild Mammals as Pets.* Garden City, New York: Doubleday and Company, Inc., 1972.

Woodhouse, Barbara. *No Bad Dogs: The Woodhouse Way.* New York: Summit Books, 1982.

Figure 13.3. *continued*

the familiar. If we are to give the presentation in a classroom, we should try to find a time when the room is empty and rehearse the presentation in the actual room where we will deliver the speech. If the actual room is closed, we should try to find a similar place. If that does not work, we can at least use our imaginations to visualize what the room will be like.

If possible, we should also rehearse before a trial audience. The audience may be a roommate, a few friends, or family members. We should give the speech, then listen to their comments, particularly the ones we find ourselves affirming. Perhaps we are unsure about the effectiveness of our visual aids. If our roommate makes a comment that they are difficult to decipher, we have a good indication that the visual aids indeed need reworking. If our family says that they think our strongest point is our first one, we can adapt accordingly.

Speakers can also critique themselves. If as we rehearse we feel bothered by how a particular portion is going, chances are the audience will be bothered as well. We need then to rework and revise that portion until we are comfortable with it.

It helps, too, to keep in mind that each presentation we give is itself a rehearsal for the next one. Finishing a given presentation does not signal the end of one's speaking career. What we do in a given presentation, be it good or bad, will have some influence on subsequent presentations. After giving a presentation, we should give ourselves a little time to develop some objectivity about what happened, then assess how the experience went. Here we weigh the comments received and add them to our feelings. If some things went well, we polish the successes and use them at our next opportunity; if some things went badly, we work to eliminate the problems.

Speaking notes: "Why Dogs Make Good Pets"
Intro:
Celebrity names: Lassie, Rin-Tin-Tin, Benji
Fancy names: Sir Wellington's Knight of King's Ridge
Plain names: Spot, Blackie, Old Blue
Dogs are our friend and protectors
I have had dogs all my life.
Most of you have had dogs.
I have wondered why we have such close ties with dogs and not other animals.
I found several reasons for long and close ties with canine world.
Dogs are good pets because of their social characteristics, their habits, and their hygiene.

   I. Social characteristics
       A. descended from wolves—strong social instincts
          1. pack oriented—bond and enjoy association
          2. responsive to pack leader, "Alpha leader"
       B. inherited characteristics
          1. bond with humans
          2. recognize owners as "alpha leader"

Quotation: "Unlike man's other favorite domesticate, the cat. a dog adjusts with difficulty . . . to an independent and wild existence and draws heavily on the mutual exchange of pack members and the guidance of a pack leader, or a human master, who is in fact a surrogate pack leader ("Dogs," *Encyclopedia Britannica: Macropedia*, 929.

  II. Habits
       A. schedules fit well with humans'
          1. raccoons, flying squirrels, skunks nocturnal
          2. dogs follow human sleeping patterns
       B. natural behavior not destructive
          1. "playfulness" of some hazardous to your health—raccoons, cougars
          2. dogs learn to behave with humans
          3. some tear up your house—raccoons vs. dogs
          4. feeding habits
             a. voracious eaters
             b. live food for weasels and skunks
          5. dogs eating habits easy—regular times commercially available

III. Hygiene
       A. smell compatible with humans
          1. animals stink—woodchucks and possums
          2. dog's odor easily controlled—breeds, grooming
       B. elimination habits
          1. living with urine and fecal matter disgusting
          2. wild animals difficult to housebreak
          3. dogs easily housebroken
             a. don't foul own quarters
             b. respond to training
             c. combine the two for good results
             d. can trust trained dog in the house

Conclusion:
live with dogs for good reason
characteristics match ours
provide companionship and loyalty
when you go home and see Spot or Blackie, tail wags not accidental
result from years of close association
You and your dog, My and I dogs go well together because the dog's social characteristics, the dog's habits, and the dog's hygiene are so well suited to life with humans.

Figure 13-4. Sample speaking notes: "Why Dogs Make Good Pets"

A Word about Plagiarism

The composition process will take us far afield as we assemble ideas and put them into our speeches. Few of us are so well versed in a subject that we know all about it from our own resources and do not have to consult others. Research, either formal or informal, is often an integral part of preparing a presentation. The ideas of others add richness to our own. Borrowing ideas from others is perfectly legitimate—unless in doing so we commit plagiarism.

Plagiarism is a form of thievery. Instead of taking a person's money, car, or jewelry, we steal a person's words or ideas. Using ideas and wording from somebody else does not constitute plagiarism, but borrowing and not giving credit to our sources does. When we pass off borrowed ideas as our own, we commit plagiarism.

The most obvious kind of plagiarism is acquiring a presentation from somebody else and giving it as our own. A more subtle form is to copy a small portion of the presentation from another and not to acknowledge that source. For example, a person may be speaking on "gun control" and discover an article that says what he wants to say. The person uses ideas from the article and some of the wording but does not cite the source. That is plagiarism.

> To avoid plagiarism, we need to acknowledge the source of our ideas or borrowed wording.

To avoid plagiarism, we need to acknowledge the source of our ideas or borrowed wording. We can acknowledge these sources in several ways. One is in the introduction. Here we simply insert a sentence that tells where we found the material: "In my research I found an article by John Doe which, I think, goes to the heart of the matter." We can also cite sources in the body of the speech. As we introduce the idea, we tell where we found it: "An article in the April 1999 issue of *Public Policy* points out the shortcomings of the proposed gun control law."

If we borrow wording, we can indicate that as well. Here we mention the author, then follow that with the words we are borrowing: "As John Doe has said in the April 1999 issue of *Public Policy,* 'The constitution provides ammunition to both sides of the gun control controversy'."

Besides being ethical, avoiding plagiarism is relatively easy and is the mark of a good speaker.

Conclusion

In addition to developing a thesis statement and major points, creating a presentation demands attention to details. The introduction, conclusion, and transitions add important elements to the presentation. Appropriate language choices increase communication and understanding. Outlining gives form to the presentation while rehearsal provides a simulation of the actual speech. Material discovered in research needs to be included into the presentation with credit given to the sources.

Discussion Questions 〰

1. What are the goals of a good introduction? Why are they important?

2. How are introductions used in other forms of communication such as newscasts and stand-up comedy routines?

3. Why have transitions in a presentation?

4. What examples of conclusions can you think of that occur in communication situations other than presentations? How do these conclusions function in comparison with the conclusions in presentations?

5. How do language choices affect communication? How do language choices particularly affect public presentations?

6. What is the point of outlining a presentation?

7. What is the difference between plagiarism and research?

Sources and References 〰

Freud, Sigmund. *Humor and the Unconscious.*

⚡ Study Questions ⚡

Oral Presentations: Tending to the Details

1. What is the basic task of a presentation's introduction?

   _____

   _____

   _____

2. What four areas should be included in the introduction?

   1. _____

   2. _____

   3. _____

   4. _____

3. Give an example of three of the eight different ways to gain an audience's attention.

   1. _____

   2. _____

   3. _____

4. What question does the relevance portion of the introduction answer?

   _____

   _____

5. The answer to the question, "Why should we listen to *you*?" establishes what in the introduction?

   _____

6. How can a speaker demonstrate credibility?

   _____

   _____

7. Why is providing the audience an overview or preview important?

   _____

   _____

8. A smooth transition can be created in several ways. Describe four of them.

1. _____

2. _____

3. _____

4. _____

9. What purpose(s) does a transition serve in a presentation?

_____

_____

10. What should be included in a good conclusion?

_____

_____

11. What should be the effect of a good conclusion?

_____

_____

12. List six different ways to conclude a presentation.

1. _____ 4. _____

2. _____ 5. _____

3. _____ 6. _____

13. What should be avoided in a conclusion?

_____

_____

14. Several guidelines are given for choosing the language used in a presentation. What are those guidelines?

1. _____

2. _____

3. _____

4. _____

15. What should go at the top of the outline used for developing speaking notes?

_____

Why? _____

_____

16. Describe the process of converting an outline to speaking notes.

_____

_____

_____

17. How would you use a traditional outline format in a presentation?

_____

_____

18. What would be the ideal way to rehearse a presentation?

_____

_____

_____

19. What is plagiarism?

_____

_____

20. How can a charge of plagiarism be avoided?

_____

_____

21. If you use an article as the source of information for a presentation, but put it into your own words, do you still need to credit the source in your presentation to avoid plagiarism?

_____

Why? _____

Making an Announcement

Goal: To announce an event of interest to the class

1. Select an event. It can be a sports event, social event, meeting, day to be commemorated, lecture, play, movie, or anything else you think interesting.

2. Create a brief introduction that creatively captures our interest.

3. Organize the announcement making sure that you tell us:
    WHAT the event is
    WHEN the event will take place
    WHERE the event will take place
    WHO will be involved
    HOW one may attend the event

4. Create a brief conclusion that summarizes the event, urges us to attend, emphasizes what the event has to offer, or some other final statement.

5. Deliver the announcement. The performance goals are:
    To stand up
    To face the audience
    To introduce the announcement
    To make the announcement
    To conclude the announcement
    To speak so the audience can hear you
    To use only one note card
    To sit down

Adapted from: Auer, J. Jeffrey. "Creating an Extra `Real Life' Public Speaking Assignment." *The Speech Communication Teacher* V, iii (Spring 1991): 3. Used by permission of National Communication Association.

Announcement Speaking Notes

Introduction

If you have ever wanted a chance to travel back in time, you have an opportunity to do that this weekend.

Announcement

I.   The Feast of the Hunter's Moon: what it is

II. Features
    A. re-enactors
    B. musical groups
    C. craft workers
    D. foods
    E. costumes

III. Where—Fort Ouiatenon on South River Road

IV. When
    A. Saturday and Sunday, September 26 and 27
    B. 10:00 to 5:00

V.   How
    A. eight dollar admission
    B. take the shuttle bus from the amphitheater on N. River Road

VI. Why
    A. See how other people lived.
    B. Have fun.

Conclusion

So, if you want to experience life in a different time period, go to the Feast of the Hunter's Moon this weekend.

Sample Announcement

Introduction

If you have ever wanted a chance to travel back in time, you have that opportunity this weekend.

Announcement

The Feast of the Hunter's Moon is a restaging of the annual meeting of French traders and trappers and Indians during the eighteenth century (what). The event will feature re-enactors, musical groups, craft workers, and foods from the era (who). Those participating will be in authentic costumes.

The Feast will be held at Fort Ouiatenon on South River Road (where) this Saturday and Sunday, September 26 and 27, from 10:00 until 5:00 (when). Admission is eight dollars. The best way to get there is to take the shuttle bus from the amphitheater on N. River Road (how).

The Feast is an opportunity to see how people lived in a different historical period and to have fun seeing a variety of activities (why).

Conclusion

So, if you want to experience life in a different time period, go to the Feast of the Hunter's Moon this weekend at Fort Ouiatenon.

Brush with Greatness Speech

Goal

To tell an incident in your life when you encountered someone or something well known.

Procedures

1. Pick an incident in your life during which you had a "brush with greatness." This incident could be seeing or meeting a famous person, attending a well known event, or visiting a famous place.

2. Compose a story that tells about the incident. You will want to tell:
   WHAT happened
   WHERE it happened
   WHEN it happened
   HOW it happened
   WHO was involved
   what EFFECT it had on you.

3. Tell the story to your audience. The performance goals are:
   ⏺➤ To face your audience
   ⏺➤ To tell your story
   ⏺➤ To speak so your audience can hear you
   ⏺➤ To use positive nonverbal communication
   ⏺➤ To speak extemporaneously.

Adapted from: Raftis, Sean. "Brush With Greatness." *The Speech Communication Teacher* V, ii (Winter 1991): 5. Used by permission of National Communication Association.

Favorite Object Speech

Goal

To explain to your audience the importance an item has for you.

Procedures

1. Pick an object that is important or significant in your life in some way. The item could be, for example, a souvenir from a trip, a gift from someone close to you, an important tool, or something in which you have invested a large amount of time and effort.

    The object must meet two criteria. It must be in some form that you can bring it to class. (We will not go out to the parking lot to look at your car.) It may not be a live subject. (Leave Waldo the Wonder Guinea Pig at home.) You may, however, use a photograph or picture of objects not meeting these criteria.

2. Create an introduction to your presentation about the object.

3. Create a short (2–3 minute) presentation. At a minimum, you will need to tell your audience:
    WHAT the object is
    HOW you came to have it
    WHY it is important to you.

4. Create a conclusion to your presentation.

5. Deliver your presentation to your audience. The performance goals are:
    ➠ To face your audience
    ➠ To introduce your presentation
    ➠ To make your presentation
    ➠ To conclude your presentation
    ➠ To speak so your audience can hear you
    ➠ To use positive nonverbal communication
    ➠ To speak extemporaneously.

Adapted from: Gill, Mary. "Successful Self-Disclosure." *The Speech Communication Teacher* II, iii (Spring 1988): 7, 16. Used by permission of National Communication Association.

Favorite Outfit Speech

Goal

To explain to your audience the significance of your favorite outfit.

Procedure

1. Select an outfit that is indicative of how you like to dress. Wear something to class that "is you."

2. Create an introduction to your presentation.

3. Create a short (1$^1/_2$–3 minute) presentation about your outfit. At a minimum, you will need to tell your audience:
    WHAT the outfit is
    HOW you obtained it
    WHY you like to wear it
    WHAT you think it communicates to other people.

4. Create a conclusion to your presentation.

5. Deliver your presentation to your audience. The performance goals are:
    ➠ To face your audience
    ➠ To present your introduction
    ➠ To make your presentation
    ➠ To conclude your presentation
    ➠ To speak so your audience can hear you
    ➠ To use positive nonverbal communication
    ➠ To speak extemporaneously.

Adapted from Rollman, Stephen A. "Classroom Exercises for Teaching Nonverbal Communication." II, iii *The Speech Communication Teacher* (Spring 1988): 13. Used by permission of National Communication Association.

"Bragging" Speech

Goal

To tell something about yourself of which you are proud.

Procedures

1. Select three things which you have done which you feel good about having accomplished. These could be things such as scoring points in a game, reading a difficult book, achieving a particular grade, taking a trip, meeting a person, learning a skill, completing a craft project, or helping somebody in trouble.

2. Create an introduction to your presentation.

3. Create a short (2–3 minute) presentation telling about your accomplishments. At a minimum, you will need to tell your audience:
    WHAT you accomplished
    WHEN you accomplished it
    WHERE you accomplished it
    HOW you accomplished it
    WHY you accomplished it
    WHY you feel good about the event.

4. Create a conclusion to your presentation.

Recommend/Warn Speech

Goal

To recommend a positive course of action to your audience or to advise your audience as to an action to avoid.

Procedure

1. Select a positive or negative experience that you have had locally. The experience might be a delicious/awful meal in a restaurant, an exciting/boring movie or play, a helpful/hindering service, or a friendly/cold business.

2. Create an introduction to your presentation.

3. Create a short (1$\frac{1}{2}$–3 minute) speech in which you inform your audience of something it might want to try or want to avoid. At a minimum, you will need to tell your audience:
    WHAT the entity (business, play, etc.) is
    WHAT your experience with the entity has been
    whether you RECOMMEND or WARN about the entity
    WHY you take the stance you do.

4. Create a conclusion to your presentation.

5. Deliver your presentation to your audience. The performance goals are:
    ➥ to face your audience
    ➥ to introduce your presentation
    ➥ to make your presentation
    ➥ to conclude your presentation
    ➥ to speak so your audience can hear you
    ➥ to use positive nonverbal communication
    ➥ to speak extemporaneously.

Adapted from suggestions by Kathy Rowan, Purdue University.

Informational
Presentations

KEY CONCEPTS

Purpose of Informational Speaking
Principles of Effective Informational Presentations
  Clarity
  Repetition
  Relevance
  Significance
  Memorability
Skills for Informational Presentations
  Defining
    Defining by Authoritative Source
    Defining by Speaker's Definition
    Defining by Reference to Common Information
  Describing
  Storytelling
  Showing

Murry Kaplan, a retired bank executive, is walking his dog through his suburban neighborhood. A car pulls to the curb beside him. The driver rolls down the window and asks, "How do I get to Oak Street?"

In the meeting room at the corporate headquarters of Monroe Life Insurance, Becky Li, chief financial officer for the company, addresses the board of trustees about the company's standing. They are contemplating acquiring a Canadian insurance company and need to know their financial position.

On the production line at Linn Gear, the foreman, Sam Jackson, is reminding the shift of the new safety procedures to be adopted that day.

In the third grade classroom at Walton Elementary, Oskar Runeberg, is giving his students instructions about what to bring, what to wear, and how to behave on their field trip to the Children's Museum.

At the lunch meeting of the Rotary Club at the BLD Cafeteria, Sandra Spaak, an attorney, is telling the group about living wills.

In millions of conversations and talks, information passes between people. We inform each other and on the basis of that information, act. Organizations run poorly or well depending on how well they obtain, disseminate, and use information. In corporations, planning officers need sales and production figures. In unions, leaders need to know the problems and desires of the membership. In families, information is continually exchanged as members coordinate eating times, transportation, activities, and chores.

One common way of disseminating information is through presentations. These may be as short as five minutes, such as the presentation of material at the start of a work shift. They may be so elaborate that they are a series of presentations as people are taught a new procedure or learn about a new product. The audience may be as small as three or four people, such as, an office staff. The audience may number in the thousands and be linked by satellite transmission. Whether the message is simple or complex, the audience large or small, informational presentations are an important method of disseminating information.

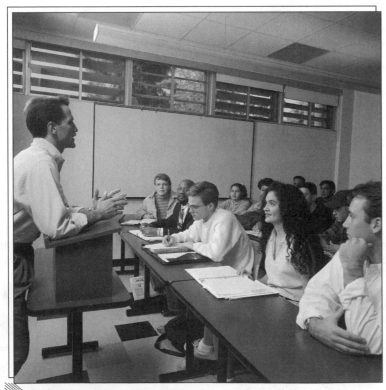

The aim of informational speaking is the communication of facts, figures, and ideas.

The Purpose of Informational Presentations

Informational presentations have as their aim the communication of facts, figures, procedures, and ideas. The *goal* of informational presentations is the *transmission of knowledge*. Informational speakers want to make their audiences aware of the existence of something about which they are unaware. The speakers want to move their audiences from ignorance to knowledge.

An informational speech is a "what is" speech as it aims at making an audience aware of what exists and how it exists.

Principles of Effective Informational Presentations

Whichever approach to a topic we take, we want to keep in mind the two major goals of a good informational presentation: (1) the information should be easy to understand, and (2) the information should be as easy as possible to retain. We can accomplish these goals by following the principles of clarity, repetition, relevance, significance, and memorability.

For clarity purposes, the speaker should use language the audience will readily understand.

Clarity

Just as it is hard to see through a dirty window, it is hard to understand a muddled presentation. A clear presentation is one which the audience finds easy to follow and understand. Attention to several details will increase the clarity of a presentation.

In making *language choices,* the speaker should choose words which the audience will readily understand. If unfamiliar words or concepts are used, they should be explained or defined. In some instances, one could appropriately say, "We should not obfuscate the issue" or "The quickest method of egress is the window" or "He is a superannuated faculty member." With other audiences, these sentences could be more confusing than enlightening. In those cases, the speaker might do better to say, "We should not confuse the issue," "The fastest way to exit is through the window," and "He is a faculty member who has been here a long time."

The *organization* of a presentation can aid the clarity of the presentation. Using the methods discussed in the previous chapter, a speaker could provide an introduction which would create a sense of expectation. Providing an overview with a thesis statement would give the audience an idea of how it is to respond. Further, the order of ideas can be helpful. The listener should be able to go from point to point smoothly. A speech on how to prepare an income tax return would probably be organized along these lines:

- Reading the Instructions
- Summarizing Your Records
- Filling out the Proper Forms
- Submitting Your Return
- How to Respond If You Are Audited

Informational speakers want to make their audiences aware of the existence of something about which they are unaware.

If the audience had to jump from point to point without seeing an apparent order, the speech would be more difficult to follow:

⬛➤ Submitting Your Return
⬛➤ Summarizing Your Records
⬛➤ How to Respond If You Are Audited
⬛➤ Filling out the Forms
⬛➤ Reading the Instructions

A speaker's *delivery* can contribute to the clarity of a presentation as well. If the speaker articulates poorly or has low volume, the audience will have difficulty following the speech. If the speaker's visual aids are hard to see or difficult to manage, the audience's attention will shift from the information to the problems with the visual aids. While we will discuss visual aids in the next chapter, let us acknowledge here their importance.

Repetition

A student, on a number of occasions in his college career, wondered why professors repeated class assignments so many times. The student would have the information about the requirements in his notebook, and he found the repetition of the assignment and its details monotonous, if not insulting. Then that student became a professor and discovered why his instructors repeated assignments. If he did not repeat the assignments, some students would not get the information.

Like cheap paint, a one time application of information will not cover the subject very well. To do well on exams, we have to look at class materials a number of times. To publicize an event well, we put posters on every available bulletin board, pass out fliers, run ads in the paper, and make announcements in classes. Similarly, in communicating information, speakers need to expose their audiences to information more than once.

The repetition of information should be integrated into the smooth flow of the presentation. A typical format provides a number of places where material may be repeated. The title of the presentation can provide the first view. The introduction gives the topic and main points. As they summarize material and point to the next main point, transitions are another opportunity to emphasize information. The main points, of course, elaborate on the information. As the presentation closes, the conclusion provides one last opportunity to reiterate important information.

Visual aids can also reinforce information. Two channels are better than one when it comes to making an impact with information. In addition to the speaker's words, the visual aids provide ways to illustrate, emphasize, and clarify points.

Visual images can help reinforce information.

Relevance

We pay attention to those subjects which affect us most closely. A talk on "Tuition Raises at the University of Moscow" would not be as interesting as a talk on tuition raises at our own university. "How to Thaw Water Pipes" is a good topic for an informational presentation, but the presentation will probably elicit more attention in January with sub-zero temperatures than it will in July.

People will understand information best when they see it as having importance for them. To be relevant, the presentation should address the needs, concerns, and interests of the audience. Careful audience analysis can indicate the direction a speaker should take in composing a presentation. The object is to make the topic one the audience sees as having an impact on their lives.

The speaker may show how the topic will be *useful* to the audience. Here the speaker demonstrates how the topic will make the lives of the audience members easier. For example, a speech on "How to Take Good Snapshots" informs people how they can save money and increase their enjoyment. They save money by not having to pay for bad pictures. Their enjoyment increases because their pictures come closer to capturing the mood they wished to preserve. A presentation on the university budget may promise to be a dry subject, but the topic becomes livelier when it is shown to have an impact on every student's pocketbook.

A speech topic may also be relevant because it appeals to people's *curiosity* and offers to satisfy that curiosity. Few of us will be astronauts, but many of may still wonder how the space shuttle gets into space and back again. An informational presentation can broaden our knowledge even if we are not directly connected with the subject.

The *language* of the presentation will have bearing on how relevant the speech appears to the audience. If the topic is addressed in clear and familiar terms, it is more likely to appear to be a part of the world of the audience. A speaker using an unfamiliar and difficult vocabulary may make the topic appear distant and removed.

> In making *language choices,* the speaker should choose words which the audience will readily understand.

Significance

Closely related to the relevance is the consideration of significance (Pearson and Nelson). As speakers, we should relate the information to our audiences, but we should also make sure the topic is one of significance to the audience.

Insignificant topics would be those considered by the audience as too simple or trivial or peripheral. An audience of college students, for example, would find relevant a topic that addressed the need to do well in school, provided them with a useful skill, and involved something they use daily. A presentation on "How To Sharpen a Pencil" would meet these three criteria. The topic, though, concerns a skill they all mastered a long time ago. In this context, a significant presentation would more likely be one on "How to Improve Memory Skills," "Creative Thinking," or "Avoiding Math Anxiety."

Memorability

If information can be put into some striking format, it is easier to remember than if it is presented flatly. Hence, the profusion of jingles, rhymes, and slogans that stick in our minds and serve as handy tools for retaining information. We could say, "Beginning with January, the longer months alternate with the shorter months until we reach August when the pattern reverses itself." Instead, we put the idea in rhyme which makes it catchier, "Thirty days hath September, April, June, and November."

Informational speakers need to look for ways to make the information vivid. As mentioned above, *catchy wording* can reinforce an idea. Students in water safety classes remember the proper sequence of rescue techniques by recalling "reach, throw, row, go." We can decide the proper direction to turn screws, nuts, and jar lids if we can remember the alliterative description, "Right is tight; left is loose." Port and starboard, directions on a ship, can be remembered when we associate the known with the unknown. "Port" has the same number of letters as "left." That leaves "starboard" to be "right."

Visual images can reinforce information. A speaker can say that using safety harnesses in cars is good protection in case of an accident. The point is more vividly made if we watch a slow motion film of unharnessed crash dummies breaking apart and flying through the windshield as a car hits a barrier in a crash test. The words of a speech on child abuse can make an audience aware of the problem, but the picture of one battered, innocent victim can be galvanizing.

Skills for Informational Speaking

The principles for good informational presentations can be accomplished in several ways. By developing skills in defining, describing, story telling, and demonstrating, we can aid our audiences in assimilating the information we present.

Defining

As we noted in our discussion of language, the meaning of words depends on the thoughts or perceptions of people, not on meanings inherent in the words themselves. The principle is one to keep in mind when composing informational presentations. If speakers presume that they and their audiences automatically share meanings, they may be in trouble. If audience members have one meaning for a word while the speaker has a second, misunderstanding rather than understanding may be the result.

A speaker was presenting information on negotiation between teachers' organizations and school boards. One of the points to which the speaker kept returning was that negotiations centered on two areas of disagreement, salaries and language. Neither term was defined. One audience member thought "negotiation about language" meant that the teachers were concerned about the language arts program (reading, literature, and writing) and wanted to negotiate changes in the teaching program. The speaker's meaning of the term was "contract language." By her definition, "negotiation about language" meant that the two parties negotiated about the terms of the contract such as class size, sick day policy, pay dates, and personal leave days. With the difference in understanding of the term "language," the speech was confusing to the audience member.

This kind of misunderstanding can be avoided if the speaker tells the audience the intended meaning of a word or concept. An audience may also be so unfamiliar with a word or concept that it has no meaning for it until the speaker provides one.

One way of defining is to refer to an *authoritative source*, as in "By 'meditation,' I have in mind the definition found in *Webster's New Collegiate Dictionary.* Or, "In the auto industry, 'captive import' means a car built by a foreign manufacturer but imported and marketed by an American company."

Speakers can also *supply their own definitions* of terms: "When I speak of 'house pets,' I am referring only to cats and dogs, those pets that may be given free run of the house."

A speaker can also define terms by *referring to information common to the audience.* Here the speaker utilizes the experience of the audience: "When I say 'long lines,' I am not thinking about five or six people in front of you. I'm talking about the lines we saw at registration that stretched from the bursar's windows, out of the building, and halfway up the mall."

Describing

Describing is using words to create images in the mind of an audience. Good description can help audience members to see how parts of a whole are linked together, to make audience members part of an experience, or to create empathy with the subject. Good description can make the abstract ideas of a presentation concrete for the audience.

One way to describe is by making a series of statements that *provide mental pictures* for the audience. If feasible, the mental pictures can be reinforced by the actual objects. In a presentation on making a salad, the speaker would describe the steps of the process: "To make a Caesar salad, the first thing you do is assemble the ingredients: Romaine lettuce, coddled eggs, lemons, garlic, anchovies, and oil. Next you take a large wooden bowl and coat the inside with oil. . . ."

Another way of describing is to *provide examples* of a concept or process. Here again, the speaker is trying to make an abstract idea concrete by providing specific instances that illustrate the main idea. For a presentation on dog training, the speaker might use examples to describe in this way: "Despite what the entertainment industry would like us to believe, dogs cannot reason at the levels displayed by Lassie, Rin-Tin-Tin, or Benji. Dogs see things in broad classifications. Your dog cannot tell the difference between the old shoe he may chew on and your new, hundred and twenty-five dollar high-tops which he may not chew on. Your dog cannot understand why it is all right to jump on the vinyl couch in the den but not all right to jump on the polished cotton couch in the living room."

A third method of description is by *contrast.* An idea or concept is made vivid by measuring it against another idea or concept. The comparison brings out the qualities of both items described. In discussing the ferocity of a blizzard, a speaker might describe the situation thusly: "A normal snow will mean freezing temperatures and some wind. A blizzard brings temperatures that threaten human life and gale force winds. In a blizzard, snow does not just fall. It blows, whips, whirls, stings, and drifts."

Analogies provide a fourth way of describing. Rather than telling what something is directly, we tell what it is like. An honor student could describe maintaining a scholastic record in terms that compare it to a difficult task: "High grades are great to have, but they are not without their drawbacks. Picture yourself trying to carry a cup filled to the brim with hot coffee as you walk across a pure white oriental rug. That's how I felt carrying a straight *A* average into the last semester of my senior year with a schedule that included two of my toughest courses."

> If speakers presume that they and their audiences automatically share meanings, they may be in trouble.

Storytelling

Stories have a strong impact on us. As children, we learn how to behave by listening to stories that show the consequences of good and bad actions. "The Little Engine that Could" makes a point about persistence. "Winnie the Pooh" tells us of the value of friendship. "Where the Wild Things Are" helps us come to grips with our chaotic urges. Fables and parables comment on life and religion. Some points are best made when they are illustrated by a story, rather than defined and discussed.

Stories can enliven our informational presentations by providing examples and applications of our points. Stories can be collected from newspapers and magazines. We can find stories in literature. We can use personal experiences as stories. We can pay attention to the stories that others tell us.

Good stories have form to them. They are not just a rambling collection of facts and events. To tell a story well, we need to know who the characters are, what they do, and how the events tie together. A well-told story establishes a sense of expectation in the audience as events move to a high point or climax, as in this story:

> When you are hooking up jumper cables to start a car, make sure that the cables are properly connected. The red ones go to the positive terminal. The black ones go to ground, some metal connection in the car. If you hook them up improperly, you can be in big trouble. I know. I did it one time.
>
> I was helping a friend start his car at night. The light was bad, and he hooked up the cables backward in his car. Instead of positive to positive, we were going negative to positive. When I tried to clamp the cable to the battery terminal, sparks flew in all directions. I heard loud popping sounds. I jerked back and banged my head on the hood of the car.
>
> We figured out the problem and managed to start his car. The next morning when I looked at my car, I found that we had melted two holes in my battery connector.
>
> Remember to hook up jumper cables positive to positive, red to red. Then clamp the black ones onto the frame or engine.

Showing

We learn many things by listening and reading, but some things are usually best learned by doing or watching someone else do them. Dancing, cooking, horseback riding, dog grooming, pool shooting, tightrope walking, and giving medical injections are skills that are usually learned by first watching someone else do them. In informational presentations, the speaker often becomes the "someone else" doing the activity, while the audience becomes the learning observer.

When speakers are showing or demonstrating, they become a kind of living visual aid. Besides speaking the words of their speeches, they carry out the actions they are describing. For a speech on golf, they demonstrate the proper grip and stance. For a speech on medical injections, they fill the syringe, eliminate the air, then inject it. Some of the best examples of the value of showing to communicate information are the televised cooking shows such as, "The French Chef" and "The Frugal Gourmet." In these presentations, the cooks mix, chop, blend, saute, and broil in time with their words. Then, finally, they show the finished product to cap the speech.

Adopting a "show and tell" approach to informational speaking places extra demands on speakers. They not only have to present information clearly,

Some points are best made when they are illustrated by a story, rather than defined and discussed.

they have to be able to talk while they are involved in an activity. Coordinating the words and actions requires extra practice and preparation. For example, a cooking show may prepare three or four versions of the featured dish to show what it looks like at various stages. The ready-to-cook dish is popped into the oven, and immediately thereafter, the cook pulls out the finished product. The payoff of the extra work is that the speech has added impact and interest for the audience.

Developing the skills of defining, describing, story telling, and showing will help a speaker develop a well-rounded approach. With these skills, a speaker should be well equipped to adapt to the demands of information and audience.

Conclusion

Informational presentations are "what is" speaking. Their aim is to help the audience to understand, to help it acquire knowledge. In approaching topics, speakers can frame their presentations in many ways. Principles of effective informational presentations include clarity, repetition, relevance, significance, and memorability. To reach one's potential as an informational speaker, one needs to develop skills in defining, describing, story telling, and showing. By combining these principles and skills, informational speaking can be effective, enlightening, and enjoyable.

Discussion Questions ///

1. What examples can you think of that involve the communication of information?

2. What is meant by "clarity" in informational presentations?

3. What examples can you think of where repetition plays a part in the communication of information?

4. What makes a topic relevant to an audience?

5. What makes the difference between an informational topic that is trivial and one that is significant for an audience?

6. In what ways can we make information memorable?

7. Select a word or concept. How can you define that word so that others understand your meaning?

8. Select an object or a process. How can you describe it so that your audience can understand it?

9. How do stories convey information?

10. Why is showing or demonstrating an effective means of communicating information?

Sources and References ⧹⧸

Pearson, Judy and Paul Edward Nelson. *Understanding and Sharing: An Introduction to Speech Communication.* 5th edition. Dubuque, Iowa: William C. Brown Publishers, 1994.

⧗ Study Questions ⧗

Informational Presentations

1. What is the aim of informational speaking?

   _____

2. What are the two major goals of informational presentations?

   1. _____

   2. _____

3. How can these goals be accomplished?

   _____

   _____

4. What is clarity in speech composition?

   _____

   _____

5. How can you increase the clarity of a presentation?

   _____

   _____

6. How should repetition be effectively used in a presentation?

   _____

   _____

7. What must a presentation incorporate in order to be considered relevant by the audience?

   _____

   _____

8. How can you make a presentation memorable?

   _____

   _____

9. In what way can a speaker's use of good descriptive language be helpful for audience members?

_____

_____

10. List four types of describing.

1. _____

2. _____

3. _____

4. _____

11. In what way can storytelling be beneficial when speaking?

_____

_____

12. How may showing or demonstrating be useful in conveying information?

_____

_____

Performance Considerations

15

A fter the presentation is composed, speakers still lack one thing. They have to take what they have created through imagination, research, and rehearsal and place it in public view. The speaker embodies the ideas and feelings, and creates the message in time and in the presence of its audience. That process creates an immediacy and impact missing from other forms of presentation. It also places an extra responsibility on speakers as they must make performance decisions in addition to the other decisions of composition. This chapter will present some guidelines to assist speakers in making effective choices.

Handling Speaking Notes

In extemporaneous speaking, most speakers rely on some kind of memory device such as notecards, a teleprompter, or cue cards. The choice of what to use will depend on one's speaking style and the circumstances in which one finds oneself. Whatever the format, good notes can inspire confidence and contribute considerably to the speech.

The basis for one's speaking notes is the outline prepared in the process of composing the presentation. The outline contains the introduction, main points, transitions, and conclusion. The speaking notes condense the outline into a form that is informative and easy to handle.

A typical method is to put the notes on 4x6 or 3x5 cards. Five cards should be sufficient for a three point presentation. The first card carries the introduction, the next three each carry a major point, and the last one carries the conclusion. The notes should be in outline form and contain only notes, not the entire speech. The function of notes is to jog the speaker's memory when needed, not to supply the speaker with a manuscript.

Good notes should be *highly legible*. The less time a speaker spends looking at notes, the more effective the speech will be. A speaker should be able to glance at the notes, pick up the next point, and smoothly incorporate it into the presentation. If the notes are jumbled or squeezed onto the cards in miniscule printing, the speaker may have a hard time finding the appropriate point in the confusion of entries.

It is also important to *rehearse with the actual speaking notes*. Using the same notes for rehearsal and speaking follows the principle of rehearsal we discussed earlier: a speaker should rehearse in conditions that are as close as possible to the conditions of the presentation.

Speakers need to work with their notes until they can move easily from one point to the next, one card to the next. Part of the rehearsal process is learning how to handle the notes so that they attract as little attention as possible. For example, when moving from one notecard to the next, it is a good policy for a speaker to maintain eye contact with the audience while changing the cards.

> The less time a speaker spends looking at notes, the more effective the speech will be.

Visual Aids

In earlier chapters, we have alluded to the importance visual aids can play in clarifying information and making points memorable. The words speakers compose and encapsulate in their notes can create a variety of images for their audiences. Words, though, are not always sufficient to create the fullest of understanding. Visual aids can provide additional emphasis, clarity, and interest to a speech.

Two basic principles stand out in the effective use of visual aids. First, good visual aids are *visual,* and second, good visual aids are *aids.* The concept is more than a tautology.

Visibility

If an audience cannot readily see or interpret the speaker's visual aids, then the speaker has created a visual hindrance instead of a visual aid. The audience is forced to choose between trying to listen to the speaker, and trying to decipher the small print or fuzzy pictures on the visual aids. Instead of the two media complementing each other, they are in conflict.

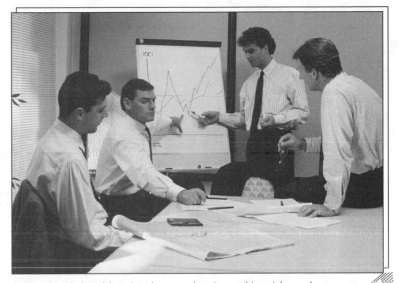

A visual aid should assist the speaker in making ideas clear.

The test for visual clarity is an easy one. We set up our visual aid. Then we step back from the visual aid as far as the last row of the audience. If we can still see *all* the details of the visual aid clearly, the visual aid is a good one. If we cannot see the details clearly and immediately, we need to revise the visual aid.

Here are the keys to high visibility.

Size

A visual aid may be a perfect illustration of the speaker's idea, but it will be ineffective if it is not large enough to be seen in detail. If one were making a speech on counted cross-stitch, beetles, or computer chips, the actual samples would be so tiny that few in the audience, if any, could see them. A photograph can provide a vivid illustration, but the standard photographic print is so small that details are lost at the distance of a few feet. The answer to the problem is to make the object larger and more visible by such devices as drawing diagrams and using photo enlargements.

Detail

A good visual aid will include only as much detail as can be easily seen and comprehended by the audience. It is also a good idea to include one idea or concept per visual aid. For example, an epidemiologist, someone who studies the spread and control of diseases, could be talking about the frequency of six different diseases in a state. Here the visual aids would probably be clearest if the speaker used a different visual aid for each disease. Trying to put all six on the same visual aid would result in considerable overlap. Sorting out the areas affected by each disease would be a difficult task for the audience.

Color

Some colors show up better than others at a distance. Contrary to popular opinion, red and yellow are not good colors for visual aids. At a distance, red and yellow lettering tends to fade out. Blues, greens, and browns will work better.

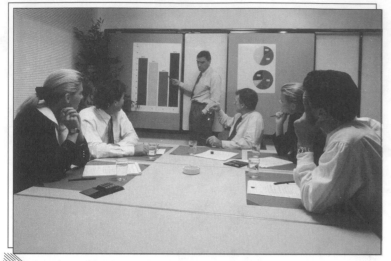

One key to high visibility of a visual aid is size.

Aiding the Speech

The "aids" in visual aids means that the visual elements in a presentation should assist the speaker in making ideas clear. The visual aids should support the speaker's points instead of becoming the primary channel of communication.

A presentation on animated cartoons, for example, could include film or video clips that illustrate the speaker's points about action, continuity, or the use of backgrounds. If, however, the clips were so long that the audience became caught up in the plot or antics of the characters, the visual portion of the speech would cease aiding the speaker's ideas and take on a life of its own.

Types of Visual Aids

Keeping in mind the guidelines for effective visual aids, speakers have available a wide range of materials to enhance their speeches.[1]

Actual Objects

The first approach to visual aids is to illustrate the presentation with the actual items about which one is speaking. This approach works well if the items are large enough to be seen and small enough to be handled easily. Speeches on geodes, track shoes, or violins, for instance, could easily be illustrated by the speakers displaying actual geodes, track shoes, or violins.

Models

While actual objects can provide a sense of authenticity to a speech, they are not always the best visual aids. The story is told at Purdue, a university with noted programs in agriculture, that an instructor heard some unusual sounds in the hallway just prior to class. Investigating, he found four students trying to herd a Holstein cow up the stairs and into the classroom. The cow was to have been the visual aid for one of the student's speech on dairy production. While indeed authentic, the novelty of the cow, not to mention the possibility of the cow's by-products, would be so distracting that the point of the speech would probably be lost. One hopes the instructor had the presence of mind to tell the students that their choice of a visual aid was udderly wrong.

When the actual object is too large, too small, or too impractical to function as an effective visual aid, a model can be used. A presentation on the harmful effects of music at high volume would probably need to show the workings of the middle and inner ear. Besides being difficult to obtain, these components of the body are so tiny that few could see them. One way to solve the problem would be to use a large model of the ear that would make the parts evident to the audience. A presentation on volcanoes, for example, could use a papier-mâché or fiberglass model to show how volcanoes are formed and how they behave.

When the actual object is too large, too small, or too impractical to function as an effective visual aid, a model can be used.

Pictures

Pictures are another way of handling items which are of difficult size or difficult to obtain. A poster, drawing, or enlarged photo of the item can be used instead. A speech on diamond cutting would want to show the differences between rough stones and finished stones. Using actual diamonds would be ineffective as the audience would not be able to see them. Much better would be large pictures of the rough stone, the planned cuts, and the finished product. At the other end of the scale, a speech on intercontinental ballistic missiles would also require pictures as visual aids.

Diagrams

Diagrams are akin to pictures, but diagrams are less realistic and more symbolic. Diagrams can be used to show spatial relationships and patterns not readily observable in actual objects or pictures. Diagrams can also exclude unnecessary details and can emphasize a portion of a system or object. A speech on an automobile air conditioning system could use a diagram that showed the components and their relationship. The diagram would be clearer than trying to point out the components in a picture of an engine compartment (Figure 15.3).

Charts and Graphs

Actual objects, pictures, and diagrams are ways to illustrate concrete objects. When speakers need to demonstrate relationships, particularly numerical relationships, they turn to graphs and charts.

The three main types of charts and graphs are pie charts, bar graphs, and axis or line graphs. The first, the *pie chart,* is so named because it indicates the quantity of an item by showing how big a "slice" it takes of the "pie," a circle representing one hundred percent of a population. One draws a circle, then indicates the proportions of its divisions, and labels them appropriately (Figure 15.4).

A *bar graph* uses different lengths of bars or columns which are measured against a scale. The side-by-side illustration makes it easy for the audience to compare the different elements against the scale and against each other. For comparing two makes of cars, the speaker could use several bar graphs to show the differences between the two in cost, performance, mileage, and wind resistance (Figure 15.1).

An *axis* or *line graph* shows the relationship between two related sets of numbers. The horizontal and vertical axes represent two variables that interact with each other. Typical sets of figures would be such things as age and income, income and health care protection, time and economic growth, city size and pollution levels, classroom space and school enrollments, and rehearsal time and speech success. With an axis or line graph, one can obtain specific information, such as school enrollment in a given year, and one can also see the progression of a situation or condition such as enrollment trends (Figure 15.2).

Displaying Visual Aids

Once the visual aids have been made, the speaker should work to make them an integral part of the presentation. Much of the success of visual aids depends on how well they are incorporated into the overall presentation. The format of

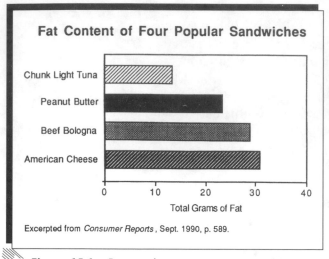

Figure 15.1. Bar graphs can compare quantities.

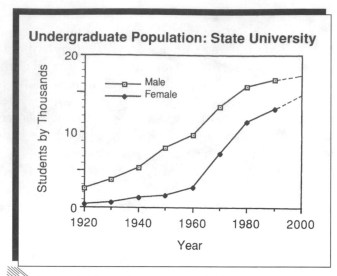

Figure 15.2. Axis or line graphs show the relationship between two factors such as time and growth.

Figure 15.3. Processes and systems may be illustrated with diagrams.

Figure 15.4. Pie charts show how quantities are divided.

visual aids will depend on such considerations as, the topic of the presentation, the speaker's abilities, the audience, and available equipment.

Handling Objects

If the speaker is using actual objects or models, the items should be readily available when they are needed. At the same time, they should not be so prominent that they call attention away from the speech. A good practice is for speakers to place the objects of models on a table to the side. The items should be arranged in the order in which they will be needed for the speech. When an object is needed to illustrate a point, the speaker picks up the item, uses it, then replaces it on the table when it is no longer needed. The process can be mastered by the speaker working with the objects during the rehearsal period.

One also needs to make sure that besides being at hand, the items are ready to use. For example, if the speaker needs to unscrew a jar lid while speaking, the lid should be loosened sufficiently before the speech. If the speaker wants to use a battery-powered device, the batteries should be fresh.

Posters

One of the most common methods of displaying pictures, graphs, and diagrams is to put them on posterboard. Particularly for classroom speeches, posterboard is an easy and economical approach. Lettering can be done with stencils, lettering kits, or templates.

During the speech, the posters should be displayed on a sturdy stand. When they are placed in the chalk tray, they usually do a nose dive onto the floor.

A standard principle of the use of visual aids is "Use it, then lose it." Visual aids need to be shown only while they are relevant to the point being made. Until it is needed, the first poster should be covered. When the speaker is finished with a poster, it should be removed or covered.

Flip Charts

Flip charts are large tablets that allow the speaker to place information on succeeding sheets. This format allows a speaker to remove quickly a display when it is no longer needed. One simply flips the sheet from the front of the tablet over the top and lets it hang down the back. The first display is out of sight and the next one is showing.

As with posters, the graphic work on a flip chart needs to be clearly and neatly done. The flip chart should be placed on a sturdy support. Speakers must practice with the flip chart so they can move easily from one display to the next.

> Visual aids need to be shown only while they are relevant to the point being made.

Transparencies

Many places will have an overhead projector available for speakers. These are valuable because the visual aid can be created on regular sized paper then enlarged to a much bigger format. Displays for an overhead projector are made on transparent sheets of plastic, either clear or tinted.

Speakers can create transparencies in three ways. One is the "draw while you talk" approach. While the speech is being delivered, the speaker sketches the visual aid directly onto the roll of transparency material stretched over the base of the projector. Special pens designed for overhead transparencies will need to be used.

The advantage of the approach is that it helps keep the attention of the audience. One drawback is that the speaker must be sufficiently artistic to create a clear and useful illustration while attending to several other matters at the same time. This approach also allows little margin for error. It the speaker makes a mistake in creating the visual aid, it is immediately apparent to all.

The second way to create transparencies is to draw the transparencies in advance. Here the speaker draws each display on a single sheet of transparency material.

The third way is to do the work on paper, then take the paper to a photocopy shop that can turn it into a transparency. Using a photocopy machine to create transparencies allows speakers to use a wide variety of materials from print sources: headlines, line drawings, cartoons, etc.

The proliferation of personal computers and programs such as PowerPoint have made creating visual aids an easy process for many. One creates a graph, chart, or picture using the computer, prints out the result, then has that made into a transparency.

Besides print materials, photographs can also be used as the basis for transparencies. Again, the work will need to be done by a photocopy shop, but many of them have the ability to convert snapshots into transparencies.

Like all visual aids, transparencies should be highly legible. A handy test for visibility is to put the transparency on the floor, then try to read it. If we cannot read it at that distance, our audience will have difficulty reading it when it is projected onto the screen.

To use transparencies as visual aids, they should be placed in the proper order. The projector should be turned off until it is needed. Before the speech, if possible, the speaker should check the overhead projector to make sure where the off-on switch is located and to ensure that the projector is properly focused.

When it is time for a transparency, the projector is turned on and the transparency slid onto the base of the projector. If while facing the audience, the speaker can read the transparency, it is on the projector properly. If the speaker needs to point out details of the display, these can be indicated on the transparency with a pencil, pen, or some other kind of small pointer. It is usually not a good idea to point out details on the image on the screen. The speaker has to stand in the glare of the projector and usually blocks some of the material.

If a second transparency is needed immediately following the first, the speaker simply removes the first one and brings on the next. If the next transparency is not needed immediately, the projector should be turned off so that the audience is not staring at a blinding, white screen. If turning the projector off and on is distracting, one could cover the base of the projector with some kind of opaque material such as a sheet of cardboard.

Transparencies can also be used in overlays to create a sense of the relationship between elements of an illustration. Instead of showing each item in succession, the items are added to each other until a composite picture is formed. For example, if one wanted to illustrate the main stages in constructing a tire, one could use three transparencies. The first would show the body of the tire. Laid atop that would be a second transparency showing the belts of the tire. The third transparency would show the tread. This technique can be used to show steps in a process, special locations or structural elements.

Slide Projectors

Slides offer the possibility of dramatic illustrations that may not be available otherwise. As photographs are primarily of things that truly exist, they can have a stronger impact than other media. The horror of a car wreck or the poignancy of a parent and child can be captured and communicated by a vivid photograph. The problem of using slides is that they require a room that is at least semi-dark if they are to show up. The darkness makes it difficult for speakers to see notes and for the audience to observe nonverbal behavior.

A remote control for the slide projector is a major help. Without one, the speaker has to speak from the back of the room. The slides should be in the proper order and right side up. Again, rehearsing with the slide projector will help eliminate any problems in the presentation.

Speakers using slide projectors should make sure they have a spare projector bulb on hand. Using a slide projector without a backup bulb is like taking a car trip without a spare tire. We run the risk of being stranded in the middle of the speech with no way to show our visual aids.

If the presentation has stretches in which no slides are being used, the speaker should insert a blank slide between sections of slides. Blanks are made by placing a piece of opaque material such as aluminum foil or thin cardboard into a slide frame. The empty slide frames are available at photography stores. Many projectors have a "blackout" feature that blocks the lens if no slide is provided.

Videotape

Videotape and video cassette players are seemingly ubiquitous now. Besides that, one finds them everywhere. Videotape can be a powerful way to reinforce or illustrate points whether the tapes are professionally prepared or homemade. Because of its power, videotape is best used sparingly. As it combines both sound and sight, it is a strong medium unto itself and will compete for attention with the speaker.

Speakers using videotape should have the tape cued to the starting point before they begin speaking. Speakers lose valuable time and may lose credibility as well if they have to fast forward and rewind the tape to hunt for the appropriate section. If a speaker is using parts of several tapes, the presentation will look more polished if the parts are edited onto one tape in the correct order. Using only one tape eliminates the distracting shuffle of loading and unloading a series of tapes.

Visual Aids and Speaker Credibility

We should keep in mind that visual aids communicate more than just the information they carry. If the visual aids are well done, easily seen, and smoothly integrated into the presentation, the speaker will be perceived as a person who has spent time preparing and hence as a person knowledgeable about the subject. Good visual aids will also likely increase the audience's willingness to attend to the speech. On the other hand, if the visual aids are sloppy, hard to see, and done in a slapdash manner, the speaker's credibility will suffer. The audience may well feel that if the speaker does not care enough about the occasion to spend time making good visual aids, then it does not care to listen to what the speaker has to say.

Visual Hindrances

While visual aids can enhance a speech, they can also detract from a speech. When the visual elements begin to call attention to themselves and away from the speech, we have created not a visual aid but a visual hindrance.

Pass Arounds

One major hindrance is "pass around" visuals. These are usually small items introduced with, "I'm going to pass around these (pictures, rocks, stamps, insects, etc.), and you can look at them while I speak."

This approach is problematic for several reasons. Audience members are more likely to be paying attention to what they have in their hands instead of

> If the visual aids are well done, easily seen, and smoothly integrated into the presentation, the speaker will be perceived as a person who has spent time preparing and hence as a person knowledgeable about the subject.

Good visual aids will likely increase the audiences' willingness to attend the speech.

what the speaker is saying. Interested listeners will be distracted by people passing the items. The speaker has little control over when the audience pays attention to the words of the speech and when it pays attention to the visual support. Also, only a fraction of the audience will be able to see an item at the appropriate time in the speech.

Unmanageable Items

Another hindrance is items that cannot be handled easily. If the visual aids do not fit smoothly into the speech, the speaker should probably look elsewhere for supporting materials. Some items may be too large and heavy such as a tractor tire or a tombstone. Some, such as an engine part, may be too dirty to use in the speaking situation. Other items may be too messy or too dangerous.

Unmanageable items also include animals. The patient, well-behaved animals seen on television are the result of long training periods by professional handlers. These animals are accustomed to performing in the welter of lights, cameras, and strangers. Unless one's dog is obedience trained, the animal may panic at the strange collection of smells and sounds he encounters. When cats are frightened, they climb. A presentation on the pleasures of cat ownership will be severely undermined if the speaker has to keep tearing the cat off her head.

Weakly supported items can imperil the best speech. One's posters may be beautiful, but if they keep falling to the floor, the effectiveness of the speech may fall with them.

Visual aids can be a major component in the success of a presentation. If well done, they can reinforce major points and add clarity to concepts. They can also add to the overall atmosphere of the presentation and increase or decrease audience attention. Thoughtful use of the various media distinguishes good speakers.

Vocal Communication

The speech composition and visual aids are important ingredients of a presentation. So, too is the way in which speakers use their voices to deliver their work. Knowledge of how one's voice works will aid in making better presentations.

Breathing for Performance

The process of voice begins not with sound but with breathing. Voices are created by the passage of air over the vocal folds, two membranes of skin located in the windpipe just behind the thyroid cartilage. The thyroid cartilage is in the front of the neck and is commonly known as the "Adam's apple." The group of muscles and cartilages making up the vocal mechanism is called the larynx. If we put tension on the vocal folds, the air passing over them will cause them to vibrate and produce sound, our voices. That basic sound is then given resonance and finally shaped by the articulators (tongue, teeth, and lips) to form words.

When we breathe for survival, as a baby does, breathing is an automatic process of moving air in and out of the lungs in orderly fashion. When we breathe for speech, the process is more complicated because we have to time inhalation, control exhalation, and guard against muscular tension. The basic idea is to bring air into the body as efficiently as possible, then control the exhalation for maximum efficiency.

To breathe for speech, we need to take in as much air as we can comfortably. With good breath support for the voice, we can talk with sufficient volume and for sufficient time. Quick, shallow breathing is not only uncomfortable, it decreases volume and creates a sense of choppiness in the delivery. Note that when we breathe for sustained vocalization, we inhale through our mouths instead of our noses. Breathing through the nose is simply too slow.

We want also to keep tension out of the neck area as it affects the voice production mechanism adversely. Breathing should be controlled from the shoulders down with the muscles of the chest and abdomen doing the major effort. If we are breathing properly, the rib cage and abdominal area will move noticeably, but the shoulders will move very little.

Characteristics of Voice

Proper breathing relaxes the speaker and makes the speech more intelligible to the audience. In addition to producing voice, we can do things vocally to make the communication clear and understandable. We can utilize the various characteristics of voice-paralinguistics to emphasize points, build emotions, and create moods.

Pitch

Pitch is the highness or lowness of our voices on a musical scale and is a function of how quickly our vocal folds vibrate. We need to speak at a pitch that is comfortable and efficient for us. The best pitch for a person is *optimum pitch* which is located about one-fourth to one-third from the bottom of the pitch range.

The goal in using pitch is to achieve a good basic pitch—optimum pitch—and then to be able to use rising and falling pitches to communicate. An upward inflection can connote questioning, a lack of finality, or indecisiveness. Constrastingly, a downward inflection can connote finality, decision, or command. "You are going to dinner" with a rising inflection will sound like a question; the same phrase with a downward inflection will sound more like a command. At a level pitch, the phrase will probably be interpreted as a statement of fact.

Loudness

As well as using varying pitches, we also use variations in loudness. The basic guideline is that speakers must speak loudly enough that the audience—all of the audience—can hear the message. To accomplish this, practice speaking to the back of the room.

If we imagine reaching those in back, we are more likely to use the right volume for the entire audience.

One of the most important vocal tools we can develop in the proper use of stress. *Stress is added volume to a word or phrase.* Stress functions as a kind of oral underlining in that we make a word or phrase stand out from its context. The difference can be heard between the flat statement "Now is the time for us to do something" and "*Now* is the time for us to do something." Stress can also offer different interpretations of the same words. Consider the difference between "*Now* is the time for us to do something" and "Now is the time for *us* to do something."

Time

As with pitch and loudness, a base level exists for time: speak at a rate at which the audience can comfortably comprehend the message. If we speak too rapidly, the audience will have difficulty keeping up with our ideas; too slowly, we will appear apathetic. A general guideline is that serious, tragic, and thoughtful material is delivered at a slower rate than light, comic, easy-to-understand material.

If we find ourselves speaking too rapidly, we can slow down easily. We just need to stretch out continuant sounds a little. For example, if we are racing through "Now is the time for us to do something," we can take longer to pronounce the vowels and "stretchable consonants." "Nnnnnnoooow iiiiissss theeee tiiiiiime . . ." will slow us sufficiently.

Quality

Quality is the overall effect of our voices and is the product of resonance. The voice is produced in the larynx, but overtones are added as the sounds move through our throats, mouths, and noses. Our vocal quality is the combination of our basic voice plus the overtones.

As quality is the most complex of the vocal characteristics, it is also the most difficult to correct and control. By listening to a recording of our voices, we can determine how pleasant or unpleasant they are for our listeners. If we find that our voice sounds grating or nasal, then we should work to eliminate those unpleasant characteristics. Experimenting with a trial and error process can help us obtain a more pleasant sound. If we have a large problem with vocal quality, we may need to seek the services of a speech clinician to correct the problem.

Physical Communication

Besides communicating with our voices, we also communicate physically. We occupy space, and how we handle ourselves in space can send messages to our audiences.

Good physical communication is not a matter of inserting appropriate gestures at the right times. Good physical communication is a combination of poise and movement that takes into consideration all aspects of a presentation.

Good physical communication begins in rehearsal, not at the moment when the speech begins. The better speakers know their material and the more they have rehearsed, the better prepared they will be in all aspects.

In the rehearsal period, speakers should have several goals. One is achieving a comfortable *stance* which will serve as the basis for gestures and movement. Speakers should avoid slouching, leaning on the podium, swaying,

> The general rule is that serious, tragic, and thoughtful material is delivered at a slower rate than light, comic, easy-to-understand material.

> As quality is the most complex of the vocal characteristics, it is also the most difficult to correct and control.

bouncing around, and other distracting actions. A good speaking stance is one that is comfortable, balanced, and relaxed. A good starting point is to stand with the feet about shoulder width apart and placed so that the ball of one foot lines up with the arch of the other. Standing in this position, we can easily gesture or move in any direction.

As to *gestures,* the best gestures are usually those that grow naturally out of the situation. Observing people in conversation, we can see them spontaneously punctuate their remarks with a number of different gestures. That same sense of spontaneity should characterize gestures made while speaking.

As our presentations progress through the rehearsal period, we may find ourselves making hand and arm movements to punctuate our points. Some may be made to indicate size or direction. Others may be made to emphasize a point. Still others may express our feelings. These should be allowed to develop. Generally, the better acquainted we are with the material of our speeches, the more likely we are to communicate effectively with gestures.

We need to keep in mind that the audiences of speeches are usually located beyond conversational distances. Gestures will thus need to be adapted to the larger setting. A general principle is to *make gestures above the waist* and broad enough so that the audience can see them.

We should also keep in mind that *clothing* communicates. Appropriate dress is, like other factors, determined by the speaking situation. An attorney would be out of place addressing a court while wearing jeans, boots, a flannel shirt, and a cap advertising a grain elevator. In another set of circumstances, talking to a group of farmers in the field, that dress might be most appropriate.

Discovering appropriate dress is part of the job of audience analysis. We can talk with someone acquainted with the audience and the audience's expectations to discover what would be best to wear. If unsure or unable to find that information, it is better to err on the side of formality rather than informality. If one arrives dressed in a suit only to find the audience in casual clothes, one can always remove the jacket, take off the tie or scarf, and roll up the sleeves. If one arrives in a sweatshirt and jeans to find the audience dressed in suits and dresses, one has little recourse but to brave out the situation as best one can.

Once arrived at the speaking situation, we should keep in mind that we begin to communicate before we ever open our mouths. We are "on" as soon as the audience focuses its attention on us, and we are not "off" until it turns its attention elsewhere. The audience receives messages from the way we dress, how prepared we appear to be, and how we approach the lectern. By plodding forward reluctantly, we tell them, "I really don't want to be here doing this." By being too nonchalant, we may communicate, "My material is really unimportant" or "You people are not worth talking to." The message we want our audiences to receive is, "I am prepared, and I want to talk to you about an interesting topic." We need to approach the front of the room in a manner that shows we are prepared and ready to speak. We can do this by having all our materials assembled and ready, and by moving forward in a confident manner.

Once at the podium or lectern, we need to take time to arrange our notes. When they are in place, we can take a relaxing deep breath and begin speaking.

When referring to notes, all we should do is drop our eyes to the cards, pick up the next idea, and continue speaking. The less time spent looking at notes, the better. When finished, we should not leave before our notes do. We

> We are "on" as soon as the audience focuses its attention on us, and we are not "off" until it turns its attention elsewhere.

319

can finish our last sentence, pause a moment to give impact to the conclusion, then gather our materials and move back to our place.

Flexibility

A well planned, well practiced presentation can provide us with reassurance and confidence when we face an audience. A well delivered presentation, though, is not necessarily one in which we do exactly and precisely everything we practiced in rehearsal. We need to be prepared for variations in the presentation even as we give it to an audience.

As one experienced speech teacher has pointed out, "Become reconciled to the fact that you will never give a talk exactly as you planned it" (Nadeau 83). In a well prepared presentation, the differences between the rehearsed version and the delivered version will not be major such as dropping a main point and composing another on the spot. The differences will more likely be in timing, wording, gestures, and other details.

Perhaps, in rehearsal we always used the same words to express the first main point. Then, in the actual talk we find a variation of these words coming out of our mouth. Changes like these are no cause for concern. To speak well extemporaneously, we must be flexible enough to accept variations and not be disturbed when changes pop up in the midst of delivery.

As speakers gain more confidence, they find that the variations can make the difference between a good speech and a great speech. If the presentation is already well composed, these moments of inspiration make it even better. We should welcome these moments, incorporate them into future presentations, and be ready for more pleasant surprises.

Communication Apprehension

Being called upon to perform may elicit feelings of nervousness as may times when we are called upon to act in unfamiliar ways. Playing in an athletic event, driving a car on ice, taking an exam, or asking someone for a date may all make us feel apprehensive. So, too, may the prospect of giving a speech.

Recognition

One of the first steps in dealing with feelings of trepidation before a presentation is to realize that we are not unique. Nervousness before speaking appears to be an almost universal phenomenon.

Sitting in class on a speaking day, we find our mouths are dry, our palms sweaty, our heartbeat is elevated, our breathing is becoming rapid, and we feel a strong urge to go to the bathroom. We have a gnawing fear that somehow we are going to make a fool of ourselves in public.

Everyone else in the room looks calm. The others scheduled to speak are reviewing their notes, even chatting with others. We know we are the only ones about to dissolve into a puddle of anxiety.

We are wrong.

If we talk to those other people, we will discover that they, too, have the same symptoms, the same feelings. They may have been looking at us and wondering how we could be so cool.

Another thing to consider is that what we are experiencing may not be so much fright as it is anticipation. Let us consider a time when we really wanted to do something: go skiing, have a date with X, acquire our driver's license, or attend a concert. In all likelihood, the same symptoms we associate with apprehension about speaking are the same symptoms we experienced before the big event, sweaty palms, elevated heart rate, etc. The only difference is that in one case, we label the symptoms "fright" and in the other we label them "anticipation" (Burleson). Much of our apprehension may lie in the way we define the situation.

Concentration

One approach that is not very useful in dealing with apprehension is to try to master our fears by overpowering them. Trying to discipline ourselves out of nervousness is an exercise in futility. By concentrating on the behaviors we want to eliminate, we usually make them worse. The better approach is to *concentrate on what we want to accomplish.* We will be in a better position if we direct our energies to the positive aspects of the situation rather than the negative ones. Instead of thinking about physical symptoms we are experiencing, we should think about the main points we want to make. Concentrating on those will channel our energies toward their proper goal, the delivery of the speech.

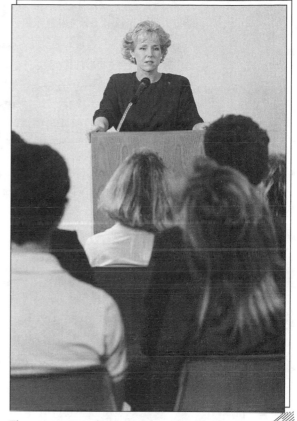

The more speeches you give, the more comfortable you will become.

Visualization

Another way to make the speaking experience easier is to visualize ourselves giving the presentation before we actually give it. Here we use our imaginations to walk ourselves through the speaking experience and see ourselves doing well in the process. We need to find a quiet time and a comfortable place. We close our eyes and relax. If the speech is to be given in a class, we begin by seeing ourselves sitting at the desk in the classroom.

We see that our notes are in good order. We see ourselves as confident and ready to speak. If that image makes us nervous, we stop with it. We keep the image in our minds until we feel comfortable seeing ourselves in the classroom. When we are at ease with that image, we move ahead. We see ourselves as our name is called. When we are comfortable with that step, we move on to the next. We see ourselves standing up and walking alertly to the front of the room. Again, if that image is problematic, we stop or retreat to an earlier, more comfortable image and work there until ready to advance.

We go through the entire presentation this way, all the way to the point where we move back to our seat hearing the applause of our audience.

> We will be in a better position if we direct our energies to the positive aspects of the situation rather than the negative ones.

Practice

The first few times we try any new enterprise, we probably feel awkward and uncomfortable. We have so many things to remember. The more we practice the activity, however, and the more we receive helpful criticism, the easier the activity becomes. If we want to become less nervous in speaking situations, we need to seek them out instead of avoiding them.

Preparation

Knowing that we have done all we can in preparation can be a major calming factor. If we have researched the topic, if we have composed the presentation in a clear manner, if we have rehearsed the presentation, then we can look back confidently on what we have done and know we can reproduce it for an audience.

Keeping these concepts and practices in mind will help us feel less anxious when facing speaking situations.

Conclusion

In preparing to speak, we need to deal with many factors. The mechanical aspects of the presentation need attention. Well done notes will aid in presenting the speech. Visual aids can be a great help to a speech. Creating effective visual aids involves following the principles of high visibility and using visual aids as support for ideas.

Proper use of the voice can provide ways to make speaking vivid and interesting. Good physical communication can underscore the message we want our audience to receive.

Anxiety may be a part of the speaking situation. Recognizing that such feelings are common can help alleviate them. We can further reduce anxiety by preparing well, using visualization, and concentrating on the idea of the presentation rather than on our feelings of inadequacy.

Finally, having assembled all the elements of the presentation, we must be ready for variations in its presentation. We need to accept the variations and use them to our advantage.

> Knowing that we have done all we can in preparation can be a major calming factor.

Notes ⋙

[1] This taxonomy of visual aids is from Ray E. Nadeau, *A Basic Rhetoric of Speech-Communication.* Reading, Massachusetts: Addison-Wesley Publishing Company, 1969. 103–12.

Discussion Questions ⋙

1. What kind of concepts can be clarified with the use of visual aids?

2. What is the difference between radio news which cannot provide visual images and television which can?

3. For what topics would a speaker use an actual object as a visual aid? A model? A picture? A diagram? A chart or graph?

4. How does a good speaking voice enhance communication in a presentation?

5. In what ways can physical communication enhance a speech?

6. In what ways can physical communication detract from a speech?

7. In what situations, other than making a presentation, have you been made to feel nervous or anxious? Why do you think you felt this way? What remedies did you find that helped?

8. What is the difference between fear and anticipation?

Sources and References ///

Avoiding Communication: Shyness, Reticence, and Communication Apprehension. Eds. John A. Daly, and James C. McCroskey. Beverly Hills: Sage Publications, 1984.

Burleson, Brant. "Remarks for Teaching Assistant Orientation." Purdue University, West Lafayette, Indiana. 29 August 1989.

Crannell, Kenneth. *Voice and Articulation.* 2nd ed. Belmont, California: Wadsworth Publishing Co., 1991.

Eisenson, Jon. *Voice and Diction: A Program for Improvement.* 5th ed. New York: Macmillan Publishing Company, 1985.

Glen, Ethel C., Phillip J. Glen, and Sandra H. Foreman. *Your Voice and Articulation.* 3rd ed. Englewood Cliffs, New Jersey: Prentice Hall, 1993.

Nadeau, Ray E. *A Basic Rhetoric of Speech-Communication.* Reading, Massachusetts: Addison-Wesley Publishing Company, 1969.

Richmond, Virginia and James C. McCroskey. *Communication Apprehension, Avoidance, and Effectiveness.* Scottsdale, Arizona: Gorsuch Scarisbrick, Publishers, 1989.

_____ ⋙ Study Questions ⋘ _____

Performance Considerations

1. For a three point presentation, how should notecards be arranged?

   _____

   _____

2. List two guidelines for effectively using notecards in a presentation.

   1. _____

   2. _____

3. How can you test for the clarity of a visual aid?

   _____

   _____

   _____

4. How much detail should be included in a visual aid?

   _____

   _____

5. What colors should you avoid in a visual aid?

   _____

   _____

   What colors are desirable in a visual aid?

   _____

   _____

6. When is it inadvisable to use actual objects as visual aids for a presentation?

   _____

   _____

7. How can models serve to augment a presentation?

_____

_____

8. What can graphs and charts represent that actual objects, models or pictures can't?

_____

_____

9. How long should visual aids such as posters be prominently displayed during a presentation?

_____

_____

10. Describe three ways to use transparencies as visual aids.

   1. _____

   2. _____

   3. _____

11. How can the use of visual aids increase a speaker's credibility?

_____

_____

12. When can visual aids become a hindrance?

_____

_____

13. Why is it undesirable to pass visual aids around during a presentation?

_____

_____

14. What is pitch?

_____

_____

15. What is optimum pitch?

_____

_____

16. Why is it advisable to vary the pitch and volume of your voice during a presentation?

_____

_____

17. How can you determine the proper volume to use for an audience?

_____

_____

18. What is stress in the context of the voice?

_____

_____

19. What is the most effective rate for speaking?

_____

_____

20. What is vocal quality?

_____

_____

21. What are the characteristics of good physical communication?

_____

_____

_____

22. Describe a good speaking stance.

_____

_____

_____

_____

23. What is the general principle for making gestures during a presentation?

_____

_____

24. How should you properly use notes during a presentation?

_____

_____

25. If you suffer from speech apprehension, what four steps can you take to overcome it?

1. _____

2. _____

3. _____

4. _____

≋ Public Speaking Assignment II ≋

Informative Presentation

Purpose

The second public speaking assignment has a three-fold purpose:

1. You will gain additional experience speaking before an audience;
2. You will refine your speaking skills by concentrating on improving areas pinpointed in the small group presentation and the first speaking assignment;
3. You will learn how to effectively choose and use a visual aid to enhance your presentation.

Basic Requirements

➠ You will develop and present to the class an original informative presentation on a topic approved by your instructor. See suggested topics pages 243–244.

➠ Each speech must be _____ minutes in length.

➠ _____ sources must be used in preparing the presentation.

➠ At least two visual aids are required.

➠ An outline of the presentation must be submitted by _____ .

➠ Presentations will be graded according to criteria on p. _____, which must be handed in prior to the presentation.

➠ You will complete the observation sheets on pages 337–345 for designated fellow speakers.

➠ Additional instructor requirements:

Informative Presentation II Worksheet

due date _____

1. possible topics:

2. selected topic:

3. possible narrowed topic areas:

4. narrowed focus of presentation:

5. thesis statement:

6. main points:

    1.

    2.

    3.

7. support for main points: source:

    support for 1. a.

                   b.

    support for 2. a.

                   b.

    support for 3. a.

                   b.

8. visual aid(s) to augment presentation (chart, graph, photo/drawing, three-dimensional object):

9. transitions to connect main points:

    transition between 1 & 2:

    transition between 2 & 3:

10. possible attention-getting devices to open the presentation:

11. selected attention-getting device:

12. conclusion that can be drawn from presentation:

Notes:

Informative Presentation II Grading Criteria—Style B

Topic 10%*

➥ subject of presentation appropriate to occasion/audience
➥ topic appropriately narrowed to fit time guidelines

Organization 30%*

Introduction

➥ attention-getting opening employed
➥ speaker credibility developed
➥ rapport developed with the audience
➥ main points previewed
➥ thesis made clear

Body

➥ main points obvious
➥ transitions used between main points
➥ easily followed

Conclusion

➥ implications of material highlighted
➥ a feeling of completion developed

Content 30%*

➥ significant material developed in presentation
➥ related to thesis
➥ supported with examples
➥ clearly presented
➥ interestingly developed
➥ vocabulary appropriate
➥ jargon and unfamiliar terms defined
➥ sources credible
➥ sources cited
➥ visual aid(s) enhanced speech

Delivery 30%*

Physical

⟹ eye contact frequent
⟹ gestures meaningful
⟹ posture comfortable
⟹ notecards properly used
⟹ sense of communication with audience established
⟹ visual aid(s) used properly, with confidence

Verbal

⟹ rate appropriate
⟹ volume appropriate
⟹ tone pleasing
⟹ vocal variety exhibited
⟹ enunciation/pronunciation correct
⟹ absence of fillers

Comments:

---

*Suggested values only—may be changed by your instructor

Student Evaluation of Informative Presentation II

In light of the guidelines for constructive feedback, offer observations about the presentation you have just watched.

What was the thesis of the presentation?

What were the main points?

What new information did you hear?

What was the speaker's strength?

What one thing would you suggest the speaker work on to improve?

____ ⑊ Student Evaluation of Informative Presentation II ⑊ ____

In light of the guidelines for constructive feedback, offer observations about the presentation you have just watched.

What was the thesis of the presentation?

What were the main points?

What new information did you hear?

What was the speaker's strength?

What one thing would you suggest the speaker work on to improve?

To Read, To Memorize, or To Speak

This is an exercise designed to make you aware of the effect of different styles of delivery.

On one sheet of paper write five steps which you think a person should follow to find a job. On the second and third sheets of paper write a paragraph about each step describing how someone might actually carry out that step. This information should be practical, common sense advice. No outside research is required for this assignment.

Bring the papers you have written to class where they will serve as the basis of the exercise.

_____

Adapted from: Gauland, Joan M. "To Read, To Memorize, or To Speak": *The Speech Communication Teacher* V, iii (Spring 1991): p. 11. Used by permission of National Communication Association.

Persuasive Presentations

Influencing Decisions

KEY CONCEPTS

Persuasion
  Six Features
    Influence
    Goal or Criterion
    Attempt to Reach the Goal
    Freedom of Choice
    Communication
    Change in Mental State
  Definition
Ethics of Persuasion
  Ourselves as Persuaders
  The Persuadee
How People Make Decisions
  Belief Systems
  Beliefs and Values
  Attitudes
  Belief Systems and Persuasion
    Importance of Beliefs
    Strength of Beliefs
    Ego Involvement
    Changing Belief Systems
    Individuality of Beliefs
    Consistency of Beliefs
  The Status Quo

The phone rings at the Crisis Center Hotline. The counselor picks it up and says, "Crisis Center Hotline. How may I help you?" The person on the phone says, "I feel so bad I want to kill myself."

It is Thursday before spring break. One student says to another, "Cut your four-thirty class tomorrow, and we can leave two hours earlier." "I don't know," the other replies. "The instructor is going to take attendance and give a quiz. I've missed a lot already, and my quiz scores aren't very good."

A person in her early twenties enters an automobile dealership. A sales representative approaches. "I'm graduating in May," the student says, "and I'm looking for a car."

At the state headquarters of the Teachers' Association, the legislative committee is meeting. "We need to send a strong signal to the legislature," one says.

On the grounds of the state capitol building, two groups are carrying signs and chanting. Television crews move from one group to another, taping the crowds and interviewing designated speakers, asking opinions of people entering and leaving the building and people passing on the street. One group chants, "Two, four, six, eight, you can't make us procreate!" The other group chants, "Abortion is murder!"

Human beings are not automatons. While we are to some degree programmed by our genetic heritage and our society, we still possess the ability to choose, to make decisions, and then live out our lives with the results of those decisions.

We do not make decisions in vacuums. We make them in the light of experience, information, emotions, and the counsel of others. When decisions are to be made, we influence each other in a variety of ways.

In the decision making process, we often see one solution as superior to others, but that opinion may not be shared by other people involved in the decision. Families split over a decision of where to go on vacation, Disney World or the Rockies. Businesses split on decisions of whether or not to bring out a new product and whether to expand, cut back, or maintain production levels. Schools split on decisions of what courses should constitute a required core, when courses should be offered, and who will teach them. In situations like these, people work to convince others of the rightness of their viewpoints. When people work to convince others to change their minds or their behavior, persuasion is at work.

> In the decision making process, we often see one solution as superior to others, but that opinion may not be shared by other people involved in the decision.

Persuasion

Persuasion is a complex phenomenon and thus difficult to define. One scholar has created a list of six features shared by most persuasive situations (O'Keefe 15–16).

Persuasion is an attempt to influence others. The aspect of influence is so inherent in the idea of persuasion that we think of persuasion as a *successful* attempt to influence. We may say, "I tried to persuade him, but I failed," but we would never say "I persuaded him but failed." Thus, when we are involved in persuasion, we are trying to affect or alter another person or party.

Persuasion involves a criterion or goal. With conversation, we join with others for the pleasure of communication. In informational speaking we attempt to create understanding. When we try to persuade someone, we have something in mind we would like to see that person do.

Persuasion implies an attempt to reach that goal. Not only do we have a goal in mind, we try to move the other party toward that goal. Persuasion implies effort.

Persuasion involves some measure of freedom and choice on the part of the persuadee. If someone knocks us unconscious and takes our wallet, that would most definitely not be persuasion. On the other hand, we may receive a call soliciting a donation for a group such as the Citizens' Action Coalition, the National Association for Historical Preservation, or the Fraternal Order of Police. The group wants our money, but we have the option of agreement or refusal.

Persuasion is achieved through communication. The use of communication is a direct outgrowth of the concept of free choice. Rather than resorting to physical coercion, we try to effect a change through interaction with the other person or party. Police departments, particularly large city police departments, may be called upon to deal with someone on a high building who is threatening to commit suicide. Specially trained units are dispatched to "persuade" the person not to jump. Part of their tactics involves communication, talking to the person to lower the sense of desperation. At some point in the proceedings, however, the team may simply physically overpower the person "have to jump him"—and drag him to safety (Dass and Gorman 105–07). When the team moves from talking to overpowering the person, persuasion is at an end and coercion has taken over.

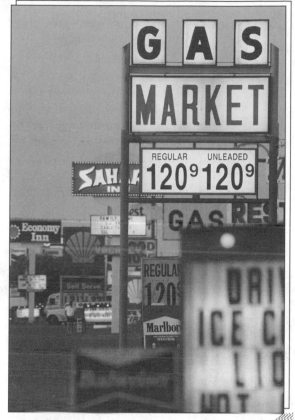

We are bombarded daily by persuasive messages.

Persuasion "involves a change in the mental state of the persuadee" (O'Keefe 116). Through persuasion, we attempt to change the way another person views the world or at least a small part of it. We may also change the way someone else behaves, but the change in behavior will need to be proceeded by a change of mind. We may wish a person to sign a petition asking for more safety lighting on campus, for the cessation of logging in a state forest, or the rezoning of a neighborhood. People will not sign the petition unless they see some good reason for doing so. If they do not want to sign the petition, we must find some way of changing the way they regard it. Without the change of mind, we will not achieve the desired behavior.

With these concepts in mind, we will offer a definition of persuasion that attempts to incorporate them: *Persuasion is the attempt through communication to change the way people think, act, or feel.*

Misconceptions of Persuasion

Despite its complexity and its universality, persuasion is still seen by some in a limited sense. Some, for example, think that persuasion is only involved with selling a product. While it is true that selling involves persuasion, sales are only a small area of persuasive activity.

While it is true that selling involves persuasion, sales are only a small area of persuasive activity.

Another mistaken concept is that persuasion is a formula or a set of steps one goes through to talk people into a course of action. As to persuasion being a handy-dandy procedure guaranteed to work on anyone, anywhere, the idea is sheer nonsense. Sales representatives often learn a pattern of exchanges, but those exchanges are by no means universal in their application. A procedure that works well in one setting may be a fiasco in another.

Some people, too, adhere to the "hypodermic needle" theory of persuasion "which suggests that the advocate 'injects' the audience with a persuasive message that makes them change their attitudes . . ." (Benoit 183). Like all communication, persuasion involves both parties as active participants in the event. Persuadees are involved parties in the persuasive process.

Ethics of Persuasion

As we have seen in an earlier chapter, ethics is the study of what is proper and improper, what is good and bad, and what standards of conduct we should meet. Ethics arise from the fact that we impinge on others and, as human beings, we can measure or evaluate our effects on others. The ethics of persuasion recognizes the interactive nature of communication. Through persuasion we may influence others in beneficial or nonbeneficial ways. While the ethics of persuasion can involve an extended discussion, we would like to make two points which should be considered before launching a persuasive effort.

Ourselves as Persuaders

The first consideration of ethical persuasion is to put our own ethical houses in order. We should realize that the final goal of any persuasive effort is to change the way someone else sees the world. When engaged in persuasion, we are attempting to alter another's life in some way, be that way large or small. Realizing this intrusion upon others, we should be convinced in our own minds that the course of action we are promoting is worthwhile. The product we are selling should live up to the claims made about it. The petition we are carrying should promote some course of action we see as having positive benefits.

The Persuadee

Secondly, we need to consider the effect of our persuasive efforts on the persuadee. We should be able to say, "I stand behind this as having good personal consequences for the individual whom it will affect" (Tead 46). What we want the other person to do should benefit the other person as much as possible. In sales, we would not persuade someone to buy a product that is faulty or ill-suited to the customer's needs. As a realtor, we would not knowingly sell a house with termite damage. As a termite exterminator, we would not urge a method of treatment that would endanger the resident's health or damage the building. As an attorney suing the exterminator, we would not persuade our client to accept a low settlement when a higher one is available, nor would we pursue a groundless case.

If we cannot affirm that the course of action we are advocating would have the highest positive effects for the person we are attempting to persuade, then we should refrain from the effort or recast our thinking.

When engaged in persuasion, we are attempting to alter another's life in some way, be that way large or small.

Having an ethical stance in persuasion does not mean, however, that everyone will agree with what we propose. People can ethically hold diametrically opposed positions.

Ethics in persuasion also applies to the content, arguments, and tactics we use in the persuasion process. An ethical persuader is not one who believes the end justifies the means. Falsifying data, for example, would violate standards of honesty as would withholding important information from the audience. Misrepresenting ourselves or our proposal would be unethical as would arguments based on racial prejudice. In persuasion, as in our other communication, we should act with integrity and respect for the other party.

How People Make Decisions

Belief Systems

In making decisions, people show their individuality. Each of us, as we grow, collects and assembles a group of ideas about who we are, what is our purpose in life, how we should treat other people, how society should arrange itself, what is good and bad, and numerous other such views. These beliefs are the result of our culture, our families, our societies, and our individual selves. By "*belief*," we mean "*the conviction that something—an object or an idea—exists or does not exist or that a set of conditions should or should not exist.*" The belief may be a simple assertion about the presence or absence of an object: "I believe I own a car." The belief may assert the existence of a concept and even the worth of that concept: "I believe I should drive safely for my sake and the sake of others."

The person who says, "I do not believe in anything" is self-deceiving. Without some structure of beliefs, one cannot live. We seek order in our lives and structure our views of the world in such a way that we can function as individuals and as members of society. Whether we are religious or agnostic; whether we are royalist, democratic, fascist, or communist; whether we are North Americans, Cambodians, or Nigerians; we create orders of beliefs and then base our conduct and decisions on those beliefs.

The most basic beliefs we have are, in essence, faith assumptions. We may assume the existence of God, the eternal nature of matter, the primacy of our own survival in the universe, the ultimacy of reason, or some other basis. On that basic assumption, we make other assumptions, and hold other beliefs about the nature of the world and our place in it. Depending on our most basic assumptions, we will view in different ways our relationships to family, work, income, and moral conduct. These views will, in turn, influence other decisions and actions.

Our actions and decisions, such as attending college, are based on our belief system.

353

Beliefs and Values

When *beliefs imply a strongly held judgment of worth,* we call that particular class of beliefs, "*values.*" Values are often central to our view of the world and influence our actions and our decisions in numerous ways.

People may hold the belief that "families are a major division of society." This viewpoint expresses a judgment about the existence or nonexistence of an entity. Going beyond this belief, people may hold convictions about the nature and worth of families. One person may hold the belief that "strong families are positive forces in the development of individuals and society." A second person may believe that "families are of minor importance." A third may hold that "families are the expression of a repressive capitalistic system." These latter three beliefs we would call "values."

None of us simply holds one belief or value. We have a number of these expressions of our convictions about the worth of people, races, genders, relationships, work, recreation, housing, religion, and other items. Grouped together, they form our "value system." This system is a collection of beliefs that are an important force in shaping our responses to our world and our communication because we base our decisions and actions on these values.

We can graphically represent a person's belief system with a pyramid. At the bottom of the pyramid, creating its base, are the basic beliefs we hold, beliefs which influence other, less important beliefs. As we ascend the pyramid, our beliefs become less and less important, yet more specific (Hart, Friedrich, and Brooks, 240–41).

A person might, for example, hold a very basic belief that the United States should be preserved and defended. Arising from that belief would be a secondary belief that American industry should be kept strong. From that view would come another view that the American automobile industry should be supported. From that belief would come the belief that one should not buy an imported car. The final result would be that the person buys an American-made car rather than an import. Another person, starting from the same basic belief, might decide to support a Japanese auto plant in the United States because it would provide jobs for Americans.

A person might have a very basic belief/value that "Good health is important." That assumption would lead to a more concrete belief that "Good diet is a major factor in achieving good health." In turn, that would lead to the assumption that some foods are to be avoided such as those high in fat, cholesterol, or sugar. The final belief would be, "I should have a salad and frozen yogurt for lunch instead of a hamburger and a hot fudge sundae."

> Values are often central to our view of the world and influence our actions and our decisions in numerous ways.

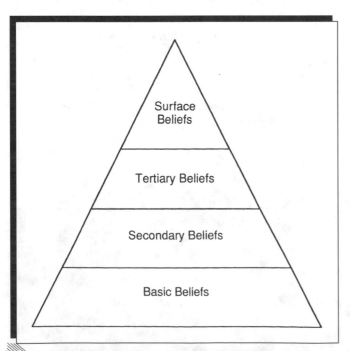

Figure 16.1. One way of viewing belief systems is to picture them as a pyramid with the most important beliefs at the bottom, the least important at the top.

Attitudes

Our belief systems give rise to our *attitudes,* our *general dispositions to act and react in certain ways.* If a person believes that American industry should be kept strong by avoiding foreign made products, then that person's attitude toward a Japanese car, Mexican roofing materials, or Argentinian beef would be a negative one. Even if the person did not know of a specific foreign made product, the attitude would lead the person to oppose it were it known.

Belief Systems and Persuasion

Belief systems are not static. Faced with a changing environment and a bombardment of daily decisions, we alter and adjust as necessary. A firm supporter of American industry might be talked into buying a Japanese or German car. A health-conscious person might decide to have a hot fudge sundae with all the trimmings. When approaching a persuasive situation, we need to keep in mind several of the subtleties of how we arrange our beliefs and decide our actions.

Importance of Beliefs

For one thing, it is usually the less important beliefs that are most open to change. People are more likely to change their minds when the change does not require a major restructuring of beliefs. A farmer may be convinced to switch from a "high till" method to a "low till" method of farming or even to a "no till" method. It would be far more difficult to convince the farmer to abandon farming, let the land go wild, and turn it into a nature preserve. In the first instance, the decision is over the means of tillage, not the elemental belief, "I want what is best for the farm." The second instance would demand a decision at a much deeper level, "How shall the land be used?"

Similarly, a health-conscious person could be persuaded to "just this once, just for fun" eat something ordinarily considered forbidden. The same person would be very resistant to persuasion that exercise programs should be abandoned, high fat diets should be followed, and the person should start smoking. A small variation in habits does not demand a change in the basic assumptions as does a major change.

Strength of Beliefs

The strength with which one holds beliefs is a factor in persuasion as well. How committed we are to beliefs will affect how open we are to persuasion on a matter. People are more willing to give up ideas that they hold lightly than ideas they hold tenaciously. People may label themselves "Democrat" or "Republican," thus announcing their belief in the political philosophy of a given party. The success of persuading people to do "cross-over voting"—voting for a member of the opposing party—will depend on how strongly a person holds to the belief, "I should support the Democratic/Republican ticket."

The strength of a belief depends on several factors. One of the most important is how strongly a given belief is linked to other beliefs, particularly basic beliefs (Hart, Friedrich, and Brooks 223–26). If a "minor" belief is linked to a "major" belief, it will be more difficult to persuade a person to give up the minor belief than it will if the minor belief is independent of any deeper belief or value. Conversely, it will also be easier to persuade someone to act on a minor belief if that belief is tied to a deeper belief or value than when the minor belief is held independent of a deeper belief or value.

Most people would say, "Yes," when asked, "Do you believe that we should help other people?" How much they are actually willing to help others will

> How committed we are to beliefs will affect how open we are to persuasion on a matter.

depend on how strongly that belief is linked to more basic beliefs. Let us say that someone is collecting for a charitable cause or relief fund. One person approached may have as a basic belief, "I need to make my life as comfortable as possible." Prying that person loose from money will be difficult because any contribution to others diminishes the person's potential for enjoyment. Another person approached may have as a basic belief, "God tells me to be charitable to others." Still another may believe deeply that, "I should alleviate suffering if I can." The last two are more likely to be convinced to give generously than is the first.

When two beliefs come into conflict, the one tied most deeply into a person's belief system will usually win out. We often say, "What people wear is unimportant. We should judge them by their character." Yet, if we look at any group of friends, particularly teenagers, we will probably find them all dressing in the same manner and dubious of someone who dresses differently. Here the belief that clothes are unimportant runs afoul of a deeper belief, perhaps unstated, that "I want to fit with my group."

Ego Involvement

Often what affects a person's openness to persuasion on an issue is the person's degree of ego involvement with the issue. The more a belief touches on what we feel is the essence of our nature, the more reluctant we are to give up that belief. Let us say that we have a person who is president of the XXX Fraternity, whose grandfather, father, and brothers were members of the XXX Fraternity, and whose best friends are in the XXX Fraternity. It would be difficult to persuade that person to the belief that "fraternities are useless and should be abandoned."

Changing Belief Systems

When a person changes deeply held beliefs, it causes a readjustment of the entire belief system, often in dramatic ways. "Conversion" aptly names the situation, for in a change of basic beliefs, a person's entire belief system is rearranged in accord with the new basic belief or beliefs. A person's belief system is changed or converted from one thing into another. The biblical story of St. Paul is a vivid example. After his conversion, instead of being a persecutor of Christians, he became a major force in the spread of Christianity. Malcolm X, the African-American leader, was, at one time, a petty thief, a pimp, and a convict. After his conversion to the Black Muslim Faith, he behaved in ways radically different from his earlier life.

Major changes do not need to be tied to religious conversion. Numerous stories exist of people who went into war as frivolous or callow youths and emerged with a serious and changed outlook on life. After surviving a life threatening illness, people often find their beliefs and values altered in large scale ways.

Belief systems can also be changed from the top down, but the process is gradual rather than dramatic. "*Erosion*" is the characterizing terms in this case. Small change follows small change until the small changes add up to a major change. A person may be dedicated to the belief, "I should exercise to stay healthy." The person regularly jogs, swims, or does aerobics. Then job pressures build up, and an exercise period or two are missed. A change in schedule makes it more difficult to find the time to exercise. A move puts the exercise

The more a belief touches on what we feel is the essence of our nature, the more reluctant we are to give up that belief.

facility farther away and harder to reach. A stretch of bad weather sets in. More and more exercise periods are missed until the person may have quit exercising all together and reached a new belief, "Exercise is not necessary for good health" or "Exercise is necessary, but I just don't have time."

Individuality of Beliefs

Another important consideration for persuasion grows out of the nature of belief systems; people will be persuaded on the basis of what *they* believe. The important aspect of a successful persuasion effort is not what the persuader thinks is important but rather what the *persuadee* thinks is important. People make decisions based on their belief systems, not upon the belief systems of others. One observer has put the matter this way: ". . . we do not change people through the things in them that we would wish to change, but through the things that they themselves wish to change" (O'Connor 441). If a persuasive effort does not speak to the beliefs of the persuadee, the effort is highly likely to fail.

If someone is carrying a petition through a neighborhood opposing a factory to be built nearby, the concerns of the various property owners should be addressed. To one person, property values may be the most important concern in the matter. To another, increased taxes may be the most important factor. To a third, the safety problems caused by increased traffic to the factory may be the chief objection. To succeed in persuading each person to sign the petition, the petition carrier must address the specific concerns of each.

Consistency of Beliefs

As people act and make decisions based upon their belief systems, they attempt to maintain a harmony of balance among the various ideas that they hold. We strive for consistency in our beliefs. We are uncomfortable when we feel our beliefs contradict each other and comfortable when our beliefs appear to be in agreement. We tend to act in accordance with our beliefs rather than in contradiction to them. When we act in contradiction to our beliefs, we usually feel some distress and begin to seek a balance between belief and action.

The consistency of beliefs and actions can be seen in very simple ways and very complex ways. People who think football is exciting watch games either in person or on television. People who do not find football interesting do not pay much attention to football games. On a more complex level, a number of beliefs and actions may cluster together. If one of our major beliefs is "Education is important," then we will spend time on school work, support educational institutions, and, eventually, encourage our children to study hard and do well in school. In addition, that belief may also influence what job we accept, where we live, what car we drive, the person whom we marry, and the kind of birthday presents we buy our grandchildren.

When we speak of "consistency," we must realize that the term is something of a misnomer. We are not necessarily totally balanced in our views. In fact, we may feel very comfortable holding views that are totally contradictory. The consistency comes not from the rational arrangement that we give our beliefs but rather from our ability to fit our view into a pattern comfortable to us. While we often see ourselves as rational beings acting out of a tightly organized system of beliefs and values, most of us are walking sets of contradictions. The limits of our consistency probably do not extend beyond three or four major views.

> The important aspect of a successful persuasion effort is not what the persuader thinks is important but rather what the *persuadee* thinks is important.

> When we act in contradiction to our beliefs, we usually feel some distress and begin to seek a balance between belief and action.

The "Letters to the Editor" page of a newspaper can provide us with numerous examples of our contradictory nature. One may praise free speech, then several lines later specify which groups should be barred from demonstrating on the courthouse grounds. Another may complain of high taxes and bad roads, never acknowledging that the shortage of tax funds may be a major contributing factor to the sorry shape of the roads.

One woman wrote a letter praising a national chain store for being closed on Easter Sunday. She told how pleased she was to go to church, then out to eat, then to drive by the closed store and think how nice it was that the store's employees did not have to work. Her conclusion was that people should not be required to work on Sundays. Several days later, another letter appeared in reaction. It asked why she was eating in a restaurant on Sunday if she thought people should not work on that day. The first writer saw "not working on Sunday" as including store workers but not including the cooks, waiters, and others in restaurants.

Contradictions may appear in a number of ways. A personal belief may contradict a political belief. People may be very charitable to people they know but oppose any kind of foreign aid, even famine relief. Even a strongly held view may not be probed to its furthest manifestation. People who oppose abortion on the basis of a belief in the sanctity of life may also argue in favor of capital punishment. On the other side of the question, people who support abortion may also argue against capital punishment, again on the basis of protecting the sanctity of life.

How truly consistent people are or how consistent they are from our point of view is of less interest in persuasion than in how consistent they feel themselves to be. If they are satisfied with their views of the world, they will be less open to persuasion than if they are dissatisfied with their views. Realizing what beliefs a person holds and how those beliefs fit together allows us to be effective in our persuasive efforts.

Change raises possibilities of discomfort.

The Status Quo: "If It Ain't Broke, Don't Fix It"

If people are comfortable with the *status quo, the way things are,* then they will see little reason to change. Once we reach a level of comfort and balance, we are disinclined to move (Festinger 1). Change raises possibilities of discomfort. If a business is profitable, why should it change its procedures? If a family's schedule is working well in balancing meals, games, and activities, why change it? If we are happy attending a given school, why would we want to transfer? If we feel that we can consume liquor and still drive safely, why not drink and drive?

We are likely to change beliefs when we feel discomfort in our situation. Unless we perceive some kind of problem with our world, we see no reason to change it. **Dissatisfaction,** not satisfaction, **leads to change.**

Sometimes, we discover our own reasons for needing a change and go looking for the solution to our problems. If we know that our car has a leaky radiator, a balky transmission, and burns lots of oil, we will start looking into other solutions for our transportation problems: repairs, a new car, a bicycle, or public transportation.

At other times, the perception of a problem comes from an outside source. We are satisfied with present conditions until someone points out enough bad features of the situation that we begin to question how truly satisfactory it is. Knowing a problem exists, we are then open to persuasion, to being convinced to change our way of thinking, action, or feeling so that we can alleviate the distress we feel.

We may be happy with our reliable car. Then, one day, a friend remarks that the squealing noise we hear when we stop means that the brakes are going bad. We check with three mechanics, all of whom say the same thing: bad brakes. The car, which seemed perfectly fine a short time ago, now seems a threat to our safety. Realizing that something must be done, we are quite open to being persuaded to spend a large sum of money to fix the brakes.

We may find our major in college very fulfilling and rewarding, and we look forward to spending our life in our chosen profession. The thought of changing majors is an idea we have never entertained. Then we discover that few jobs are available in our area and that the jobs pay poorly. Our chosen profession does not look as promising as it did at first. While we would not have been very open to persuasion earlier, we may now be a prime candidate. The solution may be to change majors, add a minor that looks promising, or become more aware of the intangible rewards of our chosen field. Whatever our decision, we will find our world altered in some way. From being satisfied, we have moved to dissatisfaction. After finding a solution, we are again satisfied but our situation has changed from its original character.

Dissatisfactions arise not only from *needs* but also from *desires*. Our car may be economical and run well, but it does not project the image we want. Our dissatisfaction with the car increases until we find ourselves at a car dealership purchasing a newer/sleeker/faster/richer looking model. We leave with a lighter heart and heavier debt. What impelled us to our choice of a new car was not the need for transportation as much as our personal desire for a different car.

Perceiving a difficulty motivates us to seek a way to remove the difficulty and to reestablish our sense of balance, to rearrange our network of beliefs and actions so that we can again feel comfortable. Persuasion is at work when someone, or even ourselves, tries to convince us that a problem exists in our world and then suggests a way to solve that problem. The problem may be personal, professional, social, or global. The changes sought may be our view of the matter, our attitudes, or our actions. As most of us are never totally satisfied with our lives, we are constantly open to persuasion on one topic or another.

> Dissatisfactions arise not only from *needs* but also from *desires.*

Conclusion

Persuasion is the attempt through communication to change the way people think, act, or feel. Good persuasion takes into account ethical considerations. Persuasion depends on what beliefs people hold and how they order those beliefs. Factors which may influence a persuasive effort are the import of a belief, the strength with which a person holds a belief, one's ego involvement with a belief, and how strongly a belief is tied to one's basic beliefs. In ordering their belief systems, people strive for what they perceive to be balance and harmony. Persuasion works when disharmony is introduced and a person seeks a way to re-establish a sense of balance and comfort. Realizing the nature of persuasion allows us to be more effective in our communication as both persuader and persuadee.

Discussion Questions

1. What examples can you give of persuasion as an attempt to change the way people think? Of the way people act? Of the way people feel?

2. Look at an issue of the campus newspaper. What persuasive efforts can you find in it?

3. In what situations in your own life have you wished that you could be more persuasive?

4. In what instances in your life have you been persuaded to do something you did not want to do or wished you had not? How did someone persuade you to act against your own wishes?

5. What, to you, constitutes an ethical approach to persuasion?

6. What examples can you give of people's actions that stem from their basic beliefs?

7. What examples can you give of people's secondary beliefs that stem from their basic beliefs?

8. "I should go to college" is a belief that leads to a great expenditure of time, money, and effort. What basic beliefs could prompt a person to make the decision to attend college?

9. What examples can you think of where people hold inconsistent views yet feel that their belief system is harmonious?

10. What examples can you give of the status quo as a factor in decision making?

Sources and References

Benoit, William L. "Argument and Credibility Appeals in Persuasion." *The Southern Communication Journal* 52 (1987): 181–97.

Brembeck, Winston L. and William S. Howell. *Persuasion: A Means of Social Influence.* 2nd ed. Englewood Cliffs, New Jersey: Prentice-Hall, Inc., 1976.

Dass, Ram and Paul Gorman. *How Can I Help?: Stories and Reflections on Service.* New York: Alfred A. Knopf, 1986.

Festinger, Leon. *A Theory of Cognitive Dissonance.* Stanford, California: Stanford University Press, 1957.

Hart, Roderick P., Gustav Friedrich, and William D. Brooks. *Public Communication.* New York: Harper and Row, Publishers, 1975.

Larson, Charles U. *Persuasion: Reception and Responsibility.* Belmont, California: Wadsworth, Inc., 1989.

Littlejohn, Stephen W. and David M. Jabusch. *Persuasive Transactions.* Glenview, Illinois: Scott, Foresman and Company, 1987.

Nadeau, Ray E. *A Basic Rhetoric of Speech-Communication.* Reading, Massachusetts: Addison-Wesley Publishing Company, 1969.

O'Connor, Frank. "Expectation of Life." *Collected Stories.* New York: Alfred A. Knopf, 1981. 431–43.

O'Keefe, Daniel J. *Persuasion: Theory and Research.* Newbury Park, California: Sage Publications, Inc., 1990.

Simons, Herbert W. *Persuasion: Understanding, Practice, and Analysis.* 2nd ed. New York: Random House, 1986.

Stewart, Charles J., Craig Smith, and Robert F. Denton, Jr. *Persuasion and Social Movements.* 2nd ed. Prospect Heights, Illinois: Waveland Press, 1989.

Tead, Ordway. *Administration: Its Purpose and Purpose.* New York: Harper, 1959.

_____ ≫ Study Questions ≪ _____

Persuasive Presentations: Influencing Decisions

1. What are the six features shared by most persuasive situations?

   1. _____   3. _____   5. _____

   2. _____   4. _____   6. _____

2. Define persuasion.

   _____

   _____

3. List three situations involving the use of persuasion other than selling a product.

   1. _____   2. _____   3. _____

4. Why is it a misconception that persuasion is a formula or set of steps one goes through to talk people into a course of action?

   _____

   _____

5. What is the hypodermic needle theory of persuasion?

   _____

   _____

   How valid is the theory?

   _____

   _____

6. What are the two main principles of the ethics of persuasion?

   _____

   _____

7. What two points, especially, should be considered before beginning a persuasive effort?

   1. _____   2. _____

8. What is a belief?

_____

_____

9. How are our belief systems developed?

_____

_____

10. What is a value?

_____

_____

11. What is a value system?

_____

_____

12. What is the relationship between beliefs and values?

_____

_____

13. What is an attitude?

_____

_____

14. Are belief systems static or permanent?

_____

Explain your response.

_____

_____

15. When trying to persuade someone, is it the more important belief or less important belief which is easier to change?

Why? _____

_____

16. What determines the strength of a person's belief?

_____

_____

17. When two beliefs come into conflict, which one will usually win out?

_____

_____

18. How does ego involvement interact with a person's openness to persuasion?

_____

_____

19. What happens when a person changes deeply held beliefs?

_____

_____

20. What is the difference when belief systems are changed from the top down (least important to most important) rather than from the bottom up?

_____

_____

21. How consistent is a person's belief system?

_____

_____

22. What is the primary factor that makes people susceptible to making a change?

_____

_____

≫ Speaking Assignment III ≪

Persuasive Presentation

Purpose

The presentational speaking assignment has a four-fold purpose:

1. You will gain further experience speaking before an audience;
2. You will continue to improve your public speaking skills;
3. You will learn how to construct a persuasive message;
4. You will learn how to adapt a persuasive message to a particular audience.

Basic Requirements

➡ You will develop and present to the class an original persuasive presentation on a topic approved by your instructor. Suggested topics are listed on pages 368–369.

➡ The persuasive presentation must show that a problem currently exists and present a proposal to reduce or eliminate that need.

➡ The persuasive presentation must concentrate on advocacy, persuasion and attitude change.

➡ Your instructor may require that the presentation be a presentational speech oriented toward a specific hypothetical audience and urging a course of action even though it will be delivered to your class. If no audience is assigned, you may select a hypothetical audience of your choice or speak to the real class population. In either case, identify which choice has been made and who your audience is.

➡ Whether the audience identity is hypothetical or real, the audience should be in a position to act upon the proposal.

➡ The assignment includes questions and answers with the audience about your proposal either during or after the presentation.

➡ Each speech must be _____ minutes in length.

➡ _____ sources must be used in preparing the speech.

➡ At least two visual aids are required.

➡ An outline of the presentation must be submitted by _____.

➡ Presentations will be graded according to criteria on p. _____, which must be handed in prior to the presentation.

➡ You will complete the observation sheets on pages 377–385 for designated fellow speakers.

➡ Additional instructor requirements:

Suggested Topics for Persuasive Presentation

You will be most effective in your persuasive presentation if you select a topic about which you have a genuine interest and have developed a position. Below are suggested areas to start you thinking. You will have to narrow the suggested topic to a manageable aspect appropriate to the time limits. You do not have to select from the list, but topics must be approved by your instructor.

Change a Lifestyle for Better Health

eating breakfast
energy through exercise
reducing stress
responsible alcohol use
alcohol and pregnancy
change in diet

Contribute to the Common Good of Society

donate blood
join the Peace Corps
organize a Community Watch program
vote
participate in community government
volunteer for a social agency
    tutor non-readers
    crisis center
    women's shelter
    Big Brothers/Big Sisters
    S.A.D.D.

Participate in an Activity for Enjoyment

join a special interest group
support an athletic team
visit an art gallery
visit a museum
travel to _____
buy tickets to University Convocations

Campaign Regarding an Environmental Issue

nuclear power—America's future hope, America's disaster in waiting
alternate energy sources
cross-state refuse dumping
recycling waste
whale hunting
animal rights vs. scientific experimentation
pet overpopulation
dolphin-safe tuna fishing

Address Student Concerns

sexual harassment
date rape
library resources
education funding
teaching assistants vs. professors in the classroom
dorm policies
student representation in university policy development
managing traffic on campus

Support/Reject and Issue of Public Policy

conscientious objector status
reactivation of the military draft
women participating in combat during wars
mandatory two-year service to the U.S.
gun regulation
computer information banks/privacy
defining pornography
euthanasia
ownership of the airwaves, the internet
defense spending
Strategic Arms Limitation
a national medical insurance plan
socialized medicine
prison reform
criminal rehabilitation programs
fighting the drug problem
legalizing all drugs
funding medical research for uncommon diseases
combating organized crime
addressing inner-city social problems
alternative educational systems
combating unemployment
censorship

〜 Persuasive Presentation Worksheet 〜

Due Date _____

1. possible topics:

2. selected topic:

3. possible narrowed topic areas:

4. narrowed focus of presentation:

5. thesis statement:

6. attention step:

7. development of need: support/evidence:

   1.

   2.

   3.

8. proposal details—how plan would work:

9. future implications if nothing is done to change problem:

   support:

10. How implementing proposal could solve problem:

    support:

11. steps audience should take to implement proposal:

12. visual aid ideas:

13. conclusion that can be drawn from speech:

Notes:

_____ ⟩⟩ Persuasive Presentation Grading Criteria—Style A ⟩⟩ _____

For a C, the presentation will meet these requirements:

Introduction previews main points of problem
Transitions are present
Presentation establishes need, has specific proposal, urges action
Main points are clear
Sequence of ideas is easy to follow
Conclusion reviews the need and solution
Physical communication does not distract (no swaying, bobbing, etc.)
Vocal communication is understandable
Presentation is free of disfluencies ("uh," "um," "you know," etc.)
Presentation maintains eye contact with audience 50% of the time
Presentation fulfills requirements of assignment (persuasive, appropriate number of visual aids,
     appropriate notes, etc.)
Presentation meets time limits
Visual aids are clear, neat, and legible

For a B, the presentation meets the requirements for a C plus the following:

Introduction has attention step, establishes credibility, shows relevance, and previews main points
Transitions link main points
Each major point is fully developed
Conclusion summarizes argument and calls for acceptance
(optional) Presentation uses five steps of the Monroe Motivated Sequence: attention, need, satisfaction,
     visualization, and action
Assertions supported with evidence
Sources cited
Speaker maintains eye contact with audience 75% of the time
Presentation is adapted to its audience
Physical communication emphasizes points of the presentation
Vocal communication is energetic and clear
Language is appropriate to topic and audience
Visual aids strongly support the main points
Visual aids are handled smoothly

For an A, the presentation meets the requirements for C and B plus the following:

Introduction shows creativity
Transitions show the flow of ideas
Arguments are logical and fitting
Presentation cites highly credible sources
Speaker is poised (in control of notes, visual aids, delivery)
Speaker maintains eye contact 90% of the time
Speaker develops rapport with audience.
(optional) Steps of the Monroe Motivated Sequence well developed

For a D, one of the areas for a C shows major problems.

For an F, the presentation is not given or several areas show major problems.

⧗ Student Evaluation of Persuasive Presentation ⧗

In light of the guidelines for constructive feedback, comment on the presentation you have just watched.

What was the thesis of the presentation?

What was the need outlined by the speaker?

How complete was the proposal?

Would you enact the recommendations of the speaker? Why or why not?

What was the speaker's strength?

What one thing would you suggest the speaker work on to improve?

_____ Student Evaluation of Persuasive Presentation _____

In light of the guidelines for constructive feedback, comment on the presentation you have just watched.

What was the thesis of the presentation?

What was the need outlined by the speaker?

How complete was the proposal?

Would you enact the recommendations of the speaker? Why or why not?

What was the speaker's strength?

What one thing would you suggest the speaker wo~~~~~~ ~~~~~ve?

Composing a Persuasive Presentation

KEY CONCEPTS

As we have seen, as long as we are satisfied with our situation, we see no need to change it. When we begin to sense that something is wrong, then we are open to possibilities for change. At the heart of the persuasive process is the interplay between a perceived difficulty and the search for relief from that difficulty.

The difficulty may be financial, moral, emotional, political, spiritual, or involve any facet of ourselves. The solution may be for us to act differently, think differently, or feel differently. We may change our habits; we may change our views; we may change our emotions.

Persuasion may be attempted in any manner of ways. Advertising bombards us daily with persuasive messages aimed at making us admire, then want, then buy. It is impossible to pick up a magazine or a newspaper, to turn on a radio or television set without subjecting ourselves to a host of persuasive efforts. Dealing with family and friends, we try to influence each other. In business institutions, persuasions goes on in dyads, in small groups, in bulletins, newsletters, and meetings.

Narrowing the field of persuasive communication to oral presentations still leaves us with an array of possibilities. We can make presentations to convince people to change either as a group or as individuals. We can try to persuade people to support an activity with their good will or with their arguments or with their money or with their labor.

Persuasion is effective only when the proposed changes match with the sensibilities of the audience.

Analyzing Your Audience

One of the most important aspects of persuasive speaking is audience analysis. A strong awareness of our audience should guide us throughout the composition process, because persuasion is effective only when the proposed changes match with the sensibilities of the audience. To be effective persuaders, we need to understand such audience characteristics as educational level, socio-economic level, age, family status, professions, gender, political affiliation, religious affiliation, and nationality. Most importantly, we need to know our audience in terms of its beliefs and values. If the course of action we advocate does not mesh with the values and beliefs of our prospective persuadees, our efforts will be for naught.

The analysis of beliefs and values needs to be as specific and detailed as possible. While an audience may agree on major concepts, minor areas may still show a divergence of viewpoints. A presentation made to a business, for example, would focus on the main concern of any business: what is in the best interest of the company? Yet, within that overarching concern, audience members may have other concerns. One person may demand that any course of action preserve the company's traditions. Another may want to encourage family relations within the company. Another may be sensitive to environmental issues. One may place a high value on innovation. One may rank quarterly returns as an important goal while another sees long term growth as the most important goal. The most acceptable course of action to this group would be the one that could come closest to addressing the concerns of all.

We also need to see what other factors such as timing, morale, and public knowledge may influence an audience.

One expert, a management consultant, was called in by a company whose plant was operating badly. The consultant's job was doubly hard in that another consultant had been working with the company for three years with little success. The first consultant's approach was to persuade the workers to better efforts with the threatening argument, "If this factory is not profitable, you will lose your jobs and the town will lose the factory."

As the second consultant drove into town, he noticed another factory that had closed. The people in the town, he decided, were not concerned whether businesses stayed open or not. He would have to find some other approach to the problem. After talking with people, he discovered that while they were unconcerned about the larger economic picture, they saw hard work as a matter of pride. He also noticed that they had little understanding of what they were trying to accomplish in the factory.

Analyzing and adapting to your audience is a critical part of persuasive speaking.

Instead of using "you will lose your job" as an approach, he used a different tack, one adapted to the audience's beliefs and values. His approach was, "To do a good job, you need to know what you are doing." A clarification of goals together with the workers' desire to show effort brought the factory back up to production as well as raising morale.

As persuasion is a matter of influencing the beliefs of an audience, the better acquainted a speaker is with those beliefs, the greater the chances of successful persuasion.

Composing a Persuasive Presentation

Composing a persuasive presentation is much like creating other presentations in that the process demands imagination and organization. Due to its nature, however, a persuasive presentation will demand particular patterns of organization.

Styles of Persuasive Presentations

Approaches to Persuasive Efforts

One of the first tasks in composing a persuasive presentation is to determine the goal of the persuasive effort. Do we wish the audience to change the way it thinks about an issue, the way it feels about an issue, or the way it acts? Or do we wish to touch on all the possibilities?

For example, a community may be involved in a controversy about a proposed dress code at the local high school. One question would be, "Is the proposed dress code legal?" Here, the main issue would be a critical one to be decided by reviewing laws and legal precedents. Persuaders for or against the code would seek to influence the way audiences considered the issue.

Another question might be, "Is the code fair?" The feelings of the audience would be of high importance here. Another issue would be, "Should we enact the dress code?" The main point of persuasion here would be some kind of action, a vote from the authoritative group to support, modify, or reject the proposed code.

Another important aspect of persuasive speeches is the way in which decisions will be made. In some cases, the persuadees make their decisions *individually;* in other cases the decisions are made by a group. In terms of the dress code issue, the student body may be urged to attend the school board meeting where the decision is to be made. In response, each student would make an individual decision whether or not to attend. When faced with the final decision, the school board would make a *collective* decision that would be binding on all members.

Presentational Speech—A Special Case

The presentational speech is a special type of persuasive presentation in that it involves a particular kind of decision making and seeks a particular outcome. *A presentational speech is a persuasive speech given to a decision making body urging a course of action.* Or, as another has put it, "presentational speaking is interactive advocacy of a specific proposal before a decision making group" (Vibbert).

The presentational speech has three important characteristics. The first is that it is *given to a decision making body.* The "body" can range in number from a small group of several people to an audience of hundreds. Examples of such "decision making bodies" would be school boards, county commissioners, city councils, grade appeals committees, families, church officers, club officers or administrative committees, councils, and a host of committees in business and society. All of these groups are charged with the oversight of activities or facilities and must make decisions about how best to carry out their responsibilities. The decisions they make are made by the members acting as a group and not as individuals. The responsibility for the consequences of the decision will be borne by all.

Another major characteristic of a presentational speech is that it urges a *course of action.* While ways of thinking and feeling may be influential in a presentational speech, the aim of the speech is to persuade the decision making body to do something. The speaker wants the audience to respond in a certain way, to adopt the action the speaker recommends. Whatever the speaker's goal, it will call for tangible results. The school board, for example, will be asked to accept or reject the dress code.

The final characteristic of a presentational speech is that it is *interactive.* In a presentational speech, the speaker does more than present a viewpoint and sit down. In a presentational speech, the audience may stop the speaker and ask for clarification of points or illustrations. When the speech is finished, the speaker may face questions that probe ideas advanced in the speech. A good speaker will be prepared for what may happen during the course of the presentation and after the presentation is given.

In a presentational speech, the audience may stop the speaker and ask for clarification of points or illustrations.

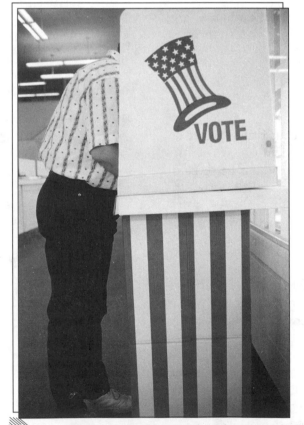

The aim of a persuasive speech is the persuade the decision making body to do something, such as voting a certain way.

The Persuasive Thesis Statement

The thesis statement of a persuasive speech should include the three main elements of any thesis statement: topic, position, and amplification. The persuasive thesis statement, however, will formulate these elements in a way that expresses a *strong sense of "ought" or "should."* While a thesis statement for an informative speech concentrates on making people aware of knowledge they do not have, the persuasive thesis statement concentrates on what the audience should do.

Let us say the topic is the recycling of newspapers, glass, and cans and that the audience is the town's, West Lafayette, city council. The thesis for an informative speech on the topic might be, "Recycling is a good way to dispose of trash because recycling is economical, easy, and protects the environment." Such a speech would describe recycling and its benefits. If the same topic were used in a persuasive speech, in addition to providing information, the speech would urge a course of action. A persuasive thesis statement might be, "The city of West Lafayette should initiate a recycling program because such a program is economical, easy to run, and beneficial to the environment." Here the thesis statement proposes that something be done: "initiate a recycling program." Further, the word, "should," implies a directive to action.

An even better thesis statement would be one that incorporates not only the course of action—the solution—but one that includes both the problem and the solution. *The problem-solution equation is at the heart of persuasion,* and a good persuasive thesis statement will include both major elements.

Reworking our thesis statement about recycling, we would add the problem to the statement: "To alleviate the problems of the present landfill program, the city of West Lafayette should initiate a recycling program." The statement contains the three elements of a topic sentence arranged to urge a course of action. The topic is "recycling program." The position is "should initiate." The amplification is "to alleviate the problems."

The elements of the basic thesis statement can be arranged in different ways and can be simple or elaborate. However the thesis statement is constructed, the main thrust should still express the existence of a problem and the possibility of a solution.

For example, the main points of the problem and solution could be included: "To alleviate the cost, difficulty, and environmental harm of the present landfill program, the city of West Lafayette should initiate a recycling program that is cheaper, easier to operate, and environmentally sound."

Variations in wording can also be used: "Because the present landfill program is costly, difficult to operate, and environmentally dangerous, the city of West Lafayette should initiate a recycling program which will be cheaper, simpler, and safer environmentally."

In some cases, the problems may be implied in the thesis statement rather than being expressed directly. Let us say that the Parking Committee at a major university is urging the conversion of a newly acquired piece of property into a parking lot for commuting students. The committee might put forth a statement such as, "The property bounded by North, Apple, South, and Walnut Streets should be made into a commuters' parking lot to make parking easier for commuting students." Here the problem is suggested by the fact that the new parking lot would make life easier for commuting students. The implication is that without the new parking lot, life will continue to be difficult for a certain group of students.

> The elements of the basic thesis statement can be arranged in different ways and can be simple or elaborate.

The best persuasive thesis statement would still incorporate all three elements: "The property bounded by North, Apple, South, and Walnut Streets should be made into a commuters' parking lot to alleviate the congestion and inconvenience in the present commuter parking lots and provide the commuting students with parking close to classrooms on the west side of campus." The sentence is longer, but it recognizes more clearly the situation being addressed. The topic is clear: "The property bounded by North, Apple, South, and Walnut Streets. . . ." The position is clear: "should be made into a commuters' parking lot. . . ." The amplification is clear: "to alleviate the congestion and inconvenience of the present commuter lots and provide commuting students with parking close to classrooms on the west side of campus."

Organizational Patterns

As one might suspect by now, one organizational pattern is the preferred one for persuasive speeches: the *problem-solution pattern*. Other patterns may be useful in certain parts of the speech. In describing the problem, one might use a chronological sequence to show how the problem developed. To explain how the solution works, one might use a structure and function pattern. A spatial pattern might be employed to show the impact of the problem in different neighborhoods or areas. The main pattern, though, should be what we have already stressed: show "that a problem is serious enough to require doing something about it" and then suggest "a plan to solve it" (Nadeau 181).

The Thesis Statement as an Organizational Tool

As we observed earlier, when we are making an informational presentation, a good technique is to place the thesis statement near the end of the introduction. Here the thesis statement provided an overview of the speech and cues the audience about what it can expect.

Using the entire persuasive thesis statement in the same way may not be such a good idea. The reason is simple: if we announce our solution before convincing the audience of the existence of a problem, we may needlessly antagonize the audience and hamper our efforts. After all, we give persuasive speeches because our audience does not yet accept our position. In our example of recycling, some council members may be dubious about the need or feasibility of a recycling program. Announcing at the start that we are promoting a recycling program may elicit a hostile reaction and strengthen their opposition. Introducing the solution after they have agreed that a problem exists will make our job easier.

Instead of inserting the thesis statement into the introduction, we will probably be more successful if we divide the thesis statement into two major parts. We use the "problem" part of the statement as the organizing concept for the first part of the speech and the "solution" portion as the organizing concept for the second part of the speech.

Adding the other necessary ingredients of a speech to the basic problem-solution framework, a simple outline of a persuasive speech would be:

➡ Introduction
➡ Problem
➡ Solution
➡ Conclusion

As we researched and developed the speech, the outline would expand to include appropriate headings under the main divisions:

Introduction
 I. Problem
   A. Source of the problem
   B. Nature of the problem
   C. Future effects of the problem
 II. Solution
   A. Description of the solution
   B. How the solution solves the problem
   C. Why the solution is the best course of action
Conclusion

The subheadings would not, of course, have to exactly match those above but would be chosen according to the dictates of the given subject.

The problem-solution patterns serves as a kind of action-reaction scheme. What we introduce in the first half is matched by what we introduce in the second half. *The problem and the ramifications that we outline in the first part need to be answered by the solution offered in the second part.*

With this format, the two halves tend to mirror or parallel each other. If we deal with "extent of the problem" in the first half, we will need to deal with "extent of the problem" in the second half and show how the problem would be contained. If we deal with "source of the problem" in the first half, we will need to show in the second half how the source can be stopped, slowed, or circumvented.

To return to our topic of recycling, an outline of the speech would look like this:

Thesis statement: "The city of West Lafayette should begin a recycling program to alleviate the economic, logistical, and environmental problems of the present landfill system."

Introduction: The recent announcement of the closing of the landfill by state authorities has made us all aware of the problem we face in disposing of our trash. Our task force has studied the problem for several months. We have done extensive research. We have consulted with the city engineer, the street department, the landfill operators, and environmental experts. We are convinced that our present system is inadequate and that a better course of action is available to us. Let us look first at our present situation.

 I. The current landfill program presents us with economic, logistical, and environmental problems.
   A. The current landfill program is expensive.
     1. Specialized equipment is needed to collect and compress garbage.
     2. Landfill rates are high.
       a. The cost per individual load is ____.
       b. The monthly cost of the landfill program to the city is ____.
     3. Our total cost of pickup and disposal is ____.
   B. Trash and garbage collection is difficult.
     1. Routes must be run twice weekly.
     2. Trucks must be driven a long way to the landfill.

C. The landfill program has negative environmental effects.
1. The landfill collects dangerous materials.
2. With the landfill close to capacity, more land will soon be needed.
3. The use of the landfill makes many items usable only once.
   a. New trees must be cut to provide more paper.
   b. New mining operations must be done to provide more metals.

II. A recycling program for newspapers, glass, and cans would be superior to the landfill program.
A. Recycling would be cheaper than the landfill program.
1. Recyclable materials are valuable and can be sold.
2. Recycling would require fewer trips to the landfill.
3. Recycling would require little specialized equipment.
4. Our total savings from instituting this program would be __.
B. A recycling program would be easier to run than the landfill program.
1. Recycling would cut garbage runs to once a week.
2. Recycling pickups are quicker than regular trash pickups.
3. Garbage trucks would be used less and last longer.
C. Instituting a recycling program would have a positive effect on the environment.
1. With less going to the landfill, less land will need to be devoted to trash disposal.
2. Recycling materials puts less strain on our resources.
   a. Fewer trees will be cut for paper.
   b. Less mining will be needed for steel and aluminum.

Conclusion: As we have seen, the present landfill program creates a number of problems for the city. A recycling program offers a method of disposing of trash and garbage that is cheaper, easier to run, and more protective of the environment than what we are doing now. For these reasons, we should initiate a recycling program as soon as possible.

REFINEMENTS IN THE PATTERN. Not every persuasion situation is such that all we need to do to be successful is to present the problem and then present the solution. Most major decisions in life are made by weighing the pros and cons, the positives and negatives of various options. In making our decisions, we try to strike a balance between all the factors that we see as important: our beliefs, our values, our attitudes, our needs, our desires, and our possibilities.

The final course of action is often one which has notable drawbacks but is still the one in which the advantages most outweigh the disadvantages. We may place a high value on saving money, but faced with the need for transportation, we buy a car and take on a large debt. We may value our close ties to our families but elect to attend college at some distance because the school offers the program we want, more financial aid, or what we consider the best education. Similarly, our persuadees must choose a course of action, and the choice is often made from several possibilities, each of which has advantages and disadvantages.

As few solutions are perfect, we may need to acknowledge the strengths and weaknesses of the course of action we are promoting. Failure to do so may indicate a limited understanding of the situation and undercut our per-

> Most major decisions in life are made by weighing the pros and cons, the positives and negatives of various options.

suasive effort and lower our credibility. In this case, we would acknowledge the shortcomings of our plan but also point out how the positive aspects of our plan outweigh the disadvantages. If we cannot find a solution with more advantages than disadvantages, then we need to rethink our approach to the problem.

Presenting both the pros and cons of a solution, that portion of the outline would look like this:

II. Description of the solution
    A. Disadvantages of the solution
    B. Advantages of the solution

Here we would have a "speech within a speech." Our major persuasive effort would be to show that our solution would relieve the problem. In this portion, we would try to persuade our audience that the positives of our solution so outweigh the negatives that our solution is worth accepting. We may also need to show how, compared with other possible solutions, our solution offers the best ratio of advantages to disadvantages.

A variation of the advantages-disadvantages approach is to present the most likely solutions and show the problems and advantages in each. Our preferred solution would need to show the greatest ratio of advantages over disadvantages.

An outline of this procedure would look like this:

II. Possible solutions
    A. Solution one
        1. Disadvantages
        2. Advantages
    B. Solution two
        1. Disadvantages
        2. Advantages
    C. Solution three
        1. Disadvantages
        2. Advantages
Conclusion: Solution ___ is the best for the following reasons.

THE MONROE MOTIVATED SEQUENCE.   Another variation on the problem-solution sequence was developed by Alan H. Monroe, a professor at Purdue University. Called the "Monroe Motivated Sequence," Monroe's approach leads an audience through a natural sequence of problem solving thought. For persuasive speaking, the Monroe Motivated Sequence moves through five steps as it progresses from introduction to conclusion (Monroe 186–214; Gronbeck, McKerrow, Ehninger, and Monroe 180–205).

The five steps of the Monroe Motivated Sequence are: *attention, need, satisfaction, visualization, and action.*

The *attention* step is the introduction to the speech. Like any other introduction, its aim is to move the audience from ignorance to awareness and to create an interest in the topic. The attention step should make the audience alert to what is about to be said. The attention step should be composed in such a way that the audience's response is, "I want to listen." Whether it is

Figure 17.1. Visualization is an important step in the Monroe Motivated Sequence and an aid to persuasion.

shocking or suave, the attention step should capture the audience's interest.

The *need* step is the presentation of the problem. Here the audience is made aware of a situation that is problematic and serious enough to require action. The speaker's aim in this portion of the speech is to help the audience realize, "Something needs to be done."

The *satisfaction* step is similar to the solution step we have discussed above. Having made the audience aware of a need or desire, the speaker furnishes a means of eliminating the need to satisfying the desire. The goal in this section of the speech is for the audience to feel, "This is the thing to do (believe, or feel) to satisfy the need."

The fourth step is the *visualization* step in which the speaker creates a word picture of what will happen if the proposed satisfaction is adopted or not adopted. The speaker calls on the audience to use its imagination to see the plan in operation and to experience its effects.

A speaker may take several approaches to composing the visualization step. One approach is to be positive and to show the benefits of the proposed plan. Here the speaker creates a picture of the good that would result from adopting the proposed satisfaction. A second approach is to use a negative view to show the detrimental effects of rejecting the proposed solution. The picture created here would be one of a bad situation continuing or becoming worse.

The two approaches can also be combined into a compare-and-contrast method which opposes the positives and negatives of courses of action. First, the negative consequences of ignoring the situation are vividly described. Then the good resulting from adoption of the solution is presented in striking images.

With the visualization step, the speaker wants the audience to respond with the feeling, "I can see myself enjoying the benefits of such an action."

The last step of the sequence is the *action* step. If no change occurs in the audience's ways of thinking, feeling, or acting, no persuasion has taken place. In the action step, the speaker asks the audience to do something specific, to take the final step of committing to change. The response the speaker seeks in this closing portion is, "I will do (believe, or feel) this." This step forms the conclusion of the speech.

Here are two brief examples of how topics can be organized according to the motivational sequence.

> In the action step, the speaker asks the audience to do something specific, to take the final step of committing to change.

Example I

Attention: Last year thousands of babies were killed in the United States.

Need: They were not killed by accident or illness. They were not even allowed to enter this world. They were sucked out of their mothers' wombs and ripped to pieces by abortion.

Satisfaction: House Bill 1234 will require a twenty-four hour waiting period after a woman contacts an abortion facility before the abortion can be performed.

Visualization: Instead of rushing capriciously into an abortion, women will be required to give thoughtful attention to the consequences of their actions. As they think about what they are considering, their minds will be changed, and lives will be saved.

Action: Write your legislators and ask them to support House Bill 1234.

Example II

Attention: This may look like a coat hanger, but it is really a murder weapon.

Need: Before Roe v. Wade legalized abortion, this and other gruesome methods were the only way out for pregnant women trapped by rape, poverty, or sexual abuse. Back alley abortions using crude instruments resulted in the agonizing deaths of thousands of women who, because of rape or incest, found themselves pregnant through no fault of their own. House Bill 1234 is another attempt to put abortion back into dirty corners by making a useless waiting period mandatory.

Satisfaction: House Bill 1234 needs to be defeated.

Visualization: Women are already responsible. A woman entering an abortion facility does not do so lightly. This bill would put a policeman at the door saying, "You do not know your own mind."

Action: Write your legislators and ask them to defeat House Bill 1234.

Evidence—Support for Points

A persuasive presentation is, by its nature, about possibilities and interpretations of situations. One person's problem is another person's solution. Many of the statements made in a persuasive speech are debatable. A speaker's claims to the truth of a fact or the pressing need for action may not, by themselves, be enough to change the mind of the audience. For persuasion to take place, the audience needs to see support for the speaker's claims and views.

The material that supports and reinforces the speaker's ideas is *evidence.* Broadly defined, evidence is "anything the audience will believe when presented" (Crable 174). In other words, evidence is matter offered to the audience in support of arguments and accepted by the audience as valid or truthful. We often think of evidence as "facts and figures," but evidence can also be subjective and even made up, as with a story offered to make a point. The primary consideration in choosing evidence is "what will be the most effective with a given audience?"

In matching evidence and audience, we have a wide range of materials from which to choose.

Facts

Facts may well constitute acceptable evidence. By "facts," we mean the specifics of a situation and its circumstances, the observations we make about the attributes of a given case. Most of us look to facts to give us a valid understanding of a situation. We ask, "What happened? What caused it? When and where was it done? How was it done?" A newspaper account of a traffic accident would, for example, be a compilation of facts about the incident. Many sources can supply us with factual evidence: newspapers, magazines, surveys, books, specialized publications, and eyewitness accounts, among others.

> We often think of evidence as "facts and figures," but evidence can also be subjective and even made up, as with a story offered to make a point.

Figures

Numerical evidence is a type of factual evidence. Instead of reasoning from the physical attributes of a situation, we use the mathematical relationships. These may be as simple as counting: "Last year Tippecanoe County recorded 'X' number of traffic accidents related to alcohol." The mathematical relationships may be complex and the result of complicated statistical calculations: "Given the current rate of property taxes, the limits set on taxing by law, the rate of inflation, and the projected birth rate for the next five years, we will need 'X' dollars for new school construction."

Testimonials and Expert Opinions

Testimonials and expert opinions are evidence offered by individuals. While the two are related, they vary in the amount and scope of experience people bring to a topic. Testimonials are based upon personal knowledge of an area while expert opinions are offered by people who, through extensive study or experience, are thoroughly versed in an area. Both types can be effective when used properly.

A neighborhood, for example, may have what it considers a dangerous intersection, one dangerous enough that members of the neighborhood want to persuade the city council to install a traffic light at the intersection. In making the presentation, both testimonials and expert opinion could be offered as evidence for the need for a traffic light.

Testimonials would include statements from parents who are worried about their children's safety and stories from drivers who have had accidents or near accidents at the intersection. Expert opinion would come from people such as a police officer from the town's traffic division or a civil engineer specializing in vehicular traffic. The police officer could cite the accident rate at the intersection and could offer judgments based on police records. The civil engineer could provide research data. This data could include statistics on the number of vehicles using the intersection as well as the physical features of the intersection, such as the width of the street, bordering shrubs, etc. The engineer could project the amount of traffic expected in the future at the intersection and provide evaluations of the situation based on study and professional practice.

Stories

Narrative or stories can offer powerful evidence to persuasive efforts. With stories, we can offer examples and illustrations of the points we wish to make. In persuasion, a well told story may make the point as nothing else will. If we are urging fire prevention in homes, statistics on the damage caused by fires may be persuasive. More persuasive may be the story of the parents forced to listen to the screams of their children trapped in a burning house because they did not teach the children how to escape a fire.

Emotions

While we think of ourselves as rational beings, we make numerous decisions based upon our feelings. In American society, for instance, it is considered crass to base the major decision of whom to marry upon rational grounds such as the potential spouse's projected health, financial success, and social standing. The decision is to be made by what we feel about the potential spouse. We

> In persuasion, a well told story may make the point as nothing else will.

purchase cars and clothing, to some extent, according to how the items make us feel. Warm clothing is a necessity in wintertime, but the decision of what to buy—a parka, a bomber jacket, a trench coat, or a fur coat—is based in part on whether or not we like the feel and look of the garment.

We are often persuaded by emotional evidence. Humane societies urge us to neuter our pets by showing us lovable puppies and kitties abandoned because pet owners contributed to pet overpopulation. Most restaurants do not appeal to our scientific knowledge of calories, vitamin and mineral content, and percentage of fat in their foods. Rather, they portray the restaurants as attractive places where we can enjoy the experience of satisfying our hunger and find engaging relationships.

Emotional evidence may take many forms. Indeed, any form of evidence may be couched in emotional terms. Facts and figures may be objective, but if the implications of the facts and figures are emotionally charged, the data and statistics become the subject of feelings as well.

Credibility

Properly chosen and used, evidence can bolster a persuasive effort and make it effective. Another important factor in the success or failure of a persuasive presentation is how the audience perceives the speaker: novice or expert, trustworthy or untrustworthy, organized or disorganized. The influence of the speaker on the success of a persuasive presentation has been discussed ever since the topic of persuasion arose. Twenty-three hundred years ago, Aristotle in his *Rhetoric* spoke of the persuasion that "depends on the personal character of the speaker" (1365b). Aristotle's term for this quality was "ethos." Modern rhetoric broadens the term to call it "credibility."

In a question of sickness or illness, we would more likely take the opinion of a physician over that of a lawyer. Both may be equally intelligent and ethical, but due to the fact that the physician has more experience in the area of medicine, we would be more likely to believe the physician's opinion. In a question of law, we would give the attorney higher credibility.

In a debate over whether or not to initiate a recycling program, whose analysis would we be most likely to believe: the owner of the county landfill, the owner of a recycling company, a professor of environmental science with no financial stake in the matter, or a person living next to the landfill? The answer to the question would depend on who we are and how we see the matter.

The person or party in a dispute most likely to be credible to us is the one who comes closest to our feelings and viewpoints. As college students, we would most likely believe the professor of environmental science because we have little stake in the business of trash disposal and because we place a high premium upon education. If the local landfill were owned by our family and we were dependent on it for our livelihood, we would probably give higher credibility to someone with direct experience in running a landfill. If we had a financial investment in a recycling company, we would be more likely to believe the owner of the recycling company. If our highest values concerned privacy and protection of private property, the testimony of the landfill's neighbor might receive our strongest support.

Kenneth Burke, a modern philosopher, has put the matter well: "You persuade a man only insofar as you can talk his language by speech, gesture, to-

The more we *identify* with our audience and the audience with us, the better our chances of successful persuasion.

Using language commonly used by the audience can demonstrate a commonality.

nality, order, image, attitude, idea, identifying your ways with his" (55). Credibility is not something we possess as speakers as much as it is something that is given or assigned to us by audiences. The closer we come to the concerns, sympathies, and manners of our audience, the greater the chances that we will be persuasive and the greater the chances that the audience will endow us with credibility. The more we *identify* with our audience and the audience with us, the better our chances of successful persuasion.

To achieve credibility, it is necessary to communicate in ways that place the audience and speaker on *common ground. Dress* is one way speakers can demonstrate commonality between themselves and their audiences. Consciously or unconsciously, groups develop ways of dressing that become almost uniforms for them.

By wearing the same clothing as the audience, a speaker can show an approval of the audience's taste and an identification with its lifestyle. Dress can also allow a speaker to fulfill the audience's expectations of what a person should look like in a given role. If, for example, a pharmacist were speaking to an audience, the expectations would be that the person would be knowledgeable about medications. In addition, because pharmacy involves health and careful dispensing of medication, the audience would also expect the person to be clean and neat and orderly. If the pharmacist showed up wearing old, dirty clothes, needing a haircut, and smelling bad, the audience would probably wonder if the right person had arrived to speak, much less grant the person high credibility.

Speaking style is another way of identifying with the audience. Using language commonly used by the audience can demonstrate a commonality. If the audience believes that an excited speaker is a committed speaker, then the speaker needs to be animated and lively. If an audience believes that an excited speaker is a superficial speaker, then the lower-keyed approach to the topic will be better.

The *kind of evidence deemed most acceptable* by an audience is also important in establishing common ground. Audiences deem speakers credible when speakers argue in ways acceptable to the audience. Some audiences place a high premium on numerical evidence, others on subjective evidence. Research viewed as authoritative by one group may be regarded as highly questionable by another. To be convincing, speakers need to find evidence that the audience will see as convincing.

An important question to ask in approaching a persuasive speech is, "What does the audience see as important?" Tying the presentation to *the concerns of an audience* can give added impact. Even if the speaker is arguing against a position held by the audience, the speaker can gain credibility by recognizing and empathizing with the views of the audience.

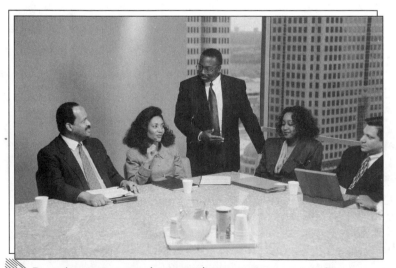

Dress is one way speakers can demonstrate commonality between themselves and the audiences.

A recycling program, on the surface, looks like a simple matter for residents. All they have to do is to put out the trash and garbage in a different way. Even that change, though, has ramifications for people, ramifications which would need to be addressed by a speaker arguing for such a program. The cost of city programs is paid by taxes which, in turn, are paid by homeowners. Sorting papers, bottles, and cans takes time. Habits would have to change. Space would need to be found for storing recyclables before they were put at the curb. While these are small issues, enough problems with these considerations could swing opinion against a program. To be convincing, a speaker would need to show that all these matters had been carefully considered.

To convince those unsupportive of the proposed program, a speaker would need to *show understanding and empathy for the objections.* Acknowledging the inconvenience and trouble would at least provide the speaker and the audience with a common level of understanding. The audience could feel that, despite the difference in views, the speaker is someone who knows how they feel.

If we find that we already share many of the characteristics of our audience, then we may create identification by reminding the audience of our similarities. As a college student speaking to other college students, it would be easy to find a number of similarities. If we were speaking to persuade a group of students to contribute to a scholarship fund, we could bring up the financial difficulties we have experienced, the opportunities we have, and our plans for the future.

If we do not share a great deal of common ground, we will need to search for ways to bridge the gap. As a college student speaking to a group of retirees, we would face an audience that differed widely from us in age, family status, professional status, economic status, social life, and outlook. Calling upon our experience, we could show empathy and understanding by talking about our grandparents or other relatives, family friends, or neighbors who are similar to our audience. If we have worked with retirees, we could mention that and the positive aspects of that experience. If we have little direct experience with retirees, we could allude to books and articles we have read on older citizens. The evidence we offer could show our understanding. Our stories and examples, for instance, would involve people the age of our audience.

In establishing common ground through identification, we need to use common sense and good judgment. One value in American society that seems universal is a dislike for hypocrites and phonies. While seeking common ground with our audience, we should not stray so far from our own personality and style that our concerns and behavior no longer appear to be genuine. Identification is regarded as positive by audiences, opportunism as negative.

Handling Interaction

A persuasive presentation, and particularly a presentational speech, may present us with a new challenge in public speaking—handling interaction. Even if we are not stopped in the course of a speech and asked to clarify a point, we may face questions and reactions after the formal part of the speech is over. Doing well in interaction demands knowledge, preparation, flexibility, and a speaking style different from the straightforward presentation of an informative speech.

Tying the presentation to *the concerns of an audience* can give added impact.

Even if we are not stopped in the course of a speech and asked to clarify a point, we may face questions and reactions after the formal part of the speech is over.

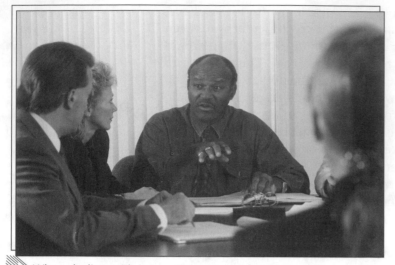

When dealing with interaction, we need to respect the questioner.

One goal of speaking in interaction is to *maintain poise.* The same kind of poise and control that is appreciated by an audience during a speech is appreciated in a question and answer session. While reacting to the audience, we want to continue to show ourselves as competent communicators. In some situations, a major part of maintaining poise may be staying cool. If respondents are angry or inflammatory, we should avoid the temptation to respond in kind. Persuasion is not a matter of out-shouting or out-arguing the other party but, rather, bringing the other person to see our point of view. Alienating people unnecessarily makes it difficult for them to find common ground with us.

Maintaining poise is easier to do when we have *prepared in advance* instead of regarding interaction as an off-the-cuff process. We can prepare for interaction by imagining what kinds of responses the audience is likely to have. We can then compose possible answers or at least establish the most effective ways of responding. Having someone listen to our presentation, then play the role of questioner can prepare us as well.

Being informed will also allow us to respond in our best fashion. For this, we will need to have information and evidence beyond what we have incorporated into our speech. The interaction may not call upon us to use all that we have assembled, but we are better off to have material that is unused than be forced to admit that we are ignorant about the respondent's question or point.

It is important to *watch the time* of our responses. Often, when we are prepared to speak on a topic, we can be caught up in enthusiasm for the subject and end up telling people far more than they ever wanted to hear. When responding to a question, it is best to make our answers brief, no more than a minute or two. If respondents want a fuller answer, they can always request more information.

A good way to phrase longer responses is to compose them as if they were mini-speeches. A sentence or two can provide the introduction. The body of the mini-speech is the answer, divided, if necessary, into points. A summary sentence or two provides a conclusion.

When dealing with interaction, we need to *respect the questioner.* Some respondents will demonstrate an understanding of our topic and an appreciation of our ideas. Others may ask questions so stupid we wonder if they even listened to what we had to say. When faced with an inappropriate, badly phrased, or ignorant comment, the best recourse is to respond to the best of our ability and politely as possible. As we are all fallible, the time may well come when we ask a stupid question, and when we do, we will appreciate being treated decently. Beyond that, we are more persuasive with considerate responses than with ridicule.

Conclusion

Persuasion is often the goal of presentations. To compose an effective persuasive effort, we need first to analyze our audience so that we may adapt our message as much as possible to its beliefs and values. In persuasion, we attempt to change the way our audience feels, thinks, or acts. With the presentational speech, we attempt to persuade a decision making body to act on a proposal. The basic organizational pattern for a persuasive presentation is the problem-solution pattern. First show that a problem is serious enough to require action, then show that our solution to the problem is the best remedy. The Monroe Motivated Sequence is an elaboration of this basic pattern and involves five steps: attention, need, satisfaction, visualization, and action. To handle interaction with our audience, we should be prepared to present additional information. Throughout the persuasive process, we should establish a sense of identification between our audience and our proposal.

Discussion Questions ⫻

1. What situations do you know that would require a presentational speech?

2. Select one of the examples raised by question one. What audience characteristics would be important to the success of the presentational speech?

3. Think of a topic you would use for an informational presentation. How would you reword the thesis statement for that speech to make it a persuasive thesis statement?

4. How is the problem-solution pattern used in advertising?

5. What advantages does the Monroe Motivated Sequence have over a simple problem-solution approach?

6. Why is evidence defined as "anything the audience will believe when presented"?

7. In what instance would facts be useful evidence?

8. In what instances would figures—numerical evidence—be effective?

9. In what situations would emotions be effective as evidence?

10. What situations would call for the use of testimonials and expert opinions as evidence?

11. In what instance would a story make good evidence?

12. Why is credibility important in persuasion?

13. How would you foster identification when speaking to a group of college students? Business people? School children? Residents of a retirement community?

Sources and References ◢

Aristotle. *The Rhetoric and Poetics of Aristotle.* Trans. W. Rhys Roberts and Ingram Bywater. New York: The Modern Library, 1954.

Burke, Kenneth. *A Rhetoric of Motives.* New York: Prentice-Hall, Inc., 1958.

Crable, Richard E. "Evidence, Warrants and Beliefs in Public Speaking." *Principles of Human Communication.* 2nd ed. Eds. Barry Brummett, Linda L. Putnam, and Richard E. Crable. Dubuque, Iowa: Kendall/Hunt Publishing Company, 1984. 174–80.

Gronbeck, Bruce E., Douglas H. Ehninger, Raymie E. McKerrow, Alan H. Monroe. *Principles and Types of Speech Communication.* 11th ed. Glenview, Illinois: Scott, Foresman/Little, Brown Higher Education, 1990.

Monroe, Alan H. *Principles and Types of Speech.* Rev. ed. New York: Scott, Foresman and Company, 1939.

Nadeau, Ray E. *A Basic Rhetoric of Speech-Communication.* Redding, Massachusetts: Addison-Wesley Publishing Company, 1969.

Vibbert, Stephen L. "Presentational Speaking as a Communication Skill." *Principles of Human Communication.* 2nd ed. Eds., Barry Brummett, Linda L. Putnam, and Richard E. Crable. Dubuque, Iowa: Kendall/Hunt Publishing Company, 1984. 238–42.

⚞ Study Questions ⚟

Composing a Persuasive Presentation

1. Why is audience analysis especially important before composing a persuasive message?

   _____

   _____

2. What is the most important thing to determine about an audience before trying to persuade it?

   _____

3. What is a presentational speech?

   _____

   _____

4. What is meant by the phrase, "A presentational speech is interactive?"

   _____

   _____

5. What is unique about the way in which a thesis statement is arranged for a persuasive speech?

   _____

   _____

6. Compose a thesis statement which could be used for a persuasive speech.

   _____

   _____

7. What organizational pattern is preferred for the persuasive speech?

   _____

   _____

8. In what way is the use of the thesis statement different in the persuasive effort than in the informative presentation?

   _____

   _____

Why is it used differently?

_____

_____

9. Describe the Monroe Motivated Sequence.

_____

_____

_____

10. What is the satisfaction step?

_____

How does it compare with the problem-solution format?

_____

11. What takes place in the visualization step?

_____

_____

12. Describe the different methods for presenting the visualization step.

A. _____

B. _____

C. _____

13. What forms the conclusion of the persuasive speech which uses the Motivated Sequence?

_____

14. Define evidence.

_____

15. List three types of material that may comprise evidence and give examples of them.

1. _____

2. _____

3. _____

16. What are some possible sources for facts to use in a persuasive effort?

_____

17. How do testimonials differ from expert opinion?

_____

_____

18. What part does credibility play in persuasive efforts?

_____

_____

19. What is Kenneth Burke's viewpoint regarding persuasion and identification?

_____

_____

20. How can a speaker foster a sense of identification with the audience?

_____

_____

21. How can a persuasive speaker successfully handle interaction with the audience?

_____

_____

____ Persuasive Thesis Statement Development Exercise ____

Provide amplification for the following statements to form a completed thesis statement.

	Topic	Position	Amplification
1.	Tuition	should be lowered	
2.	Vacations	should be extended	
3.	Working	can aid time management	
4.	Chocolate	is addictive	
5.	Writing well	takes practice	

Provide a position and amplification for the following topics.

	Topic	Position	Amplification
1.	Voting		
2.	Running		
3.	Alcoholism		
4.	Engineering		
5.	The economy		

Write five thesis statements below on persuasive topics of your choice.

1.

2.

3.

4.

5.

_____ ≈ Evidence Exercise I ≈ _____

Read the account, then determine if the statements following it are:

1. TRUE
2. POSSIBLY TRUE
3. NOT ABLE TO BE DETERMINED or
4. UNTRUE based on the evidence presented.

Be prepared to defend your answer by stating whether the evidence you used in making your evaluation was fact, figure, emotion, testimonial, expert opinion or a story.

Chris and Pat Clements are on trial for the murder of Joseph Brown, owner of a small manufacturing firm. Mrs. Brown found her husband's body in their garage with four cuts on his left hand and three bruises on the head, apparently inflicted by a blunt object. A baseball bat was found near the body. Fibers similar to those in a jacket worn by the victim were identified on Pat Clements' gloves. No fingerprints were found at the crime scene. Chris Clements was named by Mrs. Brown as responsible for her husband's death. The motive was Joseph Brown's refusal to void a contract that limited possible future income for Chris Clements. Pat Clements' help had been solicited by Chris, according to Mrs. Brown.

1. Chris and Pat Clements are related.

2. Pat Clements is on trial for the murder of Joseph Brown.

3. Chris Clements was responsible for the death of Joseph Brown.

4. Joseph Brown died as a result of blows to the head.

5. Joseph Brown was killed with a baseball bat.

6. Fiber samples indicated Pat Clements' involvement in the crime.

7. Chris Clements was angry with Joseph Brown because Brown would not void a contract.

8. Mrs. Brown cooperated in the murder investigation.

9. Joseph Brown was a successful businessman.

10. Mrs. Brown and Chris Clements were having an affair.

Evidence Exercise II

Which type of evidence—fact, figures, emotions, testimonials, expert opinion, or stories—would be advantageous to use in the following situations? If more than one type of evidence would be appropriate, list the strongest type first, followed by other types in descending order of importance.

1. petitioning the city council for a permit to hold a street dance at the beginning of school

2. asking a parent to borrow the car for a weekend

3. interviewing for an internship

4. requesting a grade change due to multiple correct answer choices on an exam question

5. convincing a police officer not to issue a ticket when you were driving eight miles per hour over the speed limit

6. seeking a full refund for an unsatisfactory product after using it for six months

7. asking someone out for a date

8. urging a client to buy your product

9. soliciting donations for the cancer society

10. running for student body president

Public Service Announcement

The class will be divided into groups. You and your group are to create a thirty second public service announcement. A public service announcement is a presentation offered by a television or radio station for the public good. Public service announcements are usually composed by not-for-profit organizations such as the Red Cross, United Way, American Heart Association, etc.

You may choose your own topic, but you must include in your announcement all the steps of the Monroe Motivated Sequence: attention, need, satisfaction, visualization, and action.

Some suggested topics are:

> donate blood
> buckle up
> contribute to . . .
> have your blood pressure checked
> neuter your pet
> recycle your trash
> don't litter
> register to vote
> don't drink and drive
> use the campus night escort service

After you have written your announcement, you will be asked to present it to the class. One person may read it or members of the group may play different roles in the presentation.

Persuasion and Reasoning

18

KEY CONCEPTS

Deductive Reasoning
  Patterns of Deductive Reasoning
  Syllogism
    Creating Syllogisms
      Major Premise
      Minor Premise
      Conclusion
      Enthymeme
    Weighing Syllogisms
Inductive Reasoning
  Patterns of Inductive Reasoning
  Arguments from Authority
    Creating Arguments from Authority
    Weighing Arguments from Authority
  Arguments from Statistics or Examples
    Creating Arguments from Statistics or
      Examples
    Weighing Arguments from Statistics or
      Examples
  Arguments from Signs
    Creating Arguments from Signs
    Weighing Arguments from Signs
  Arguments from Cause and Effect
    Creating Arguments from Cause and
      Effect
    Weighing Arguments from Cause and
      Effect
  Arguments from Analogy
    Creating Arguments from Analogy
    Weighing Arguments from Analogy
Fallacies in Arguments
  Fallacy
  Ad Hominem Arguments
  Ad Populum Arguments
  "Straw Man"/"Red Herring" Arguments
  False Dichotomy Arguments
  Begging the Question

In earlier chapters, we examined the nature of persuasion and the basic principles of constructing an effective persuasive presentation. As we have seen, when we attempt to persuade others, we set forth arguments and reasons for the acceptance of our viewpoints. When we use the term "argument" in persuasion, we do not mean "hostility" or "emotionally charged encounters." As one persuasion theorist has pointed out, the matter is more one of "winning belief" than winning quarrels (Simons 178). The object of reasoning in persuasion is not to score points but to bring the persuader and persuadee together in how they view a matter.

This chapter examines some of the ways available to us as we attempt to win belief and to reach accord with those with whom we disagree. Recognizing the techniques of persuasive strategies enhances our abilities as communicators and makes us better "consumers" of persuasion. When we know lines of reasoning, we become more effective in influencing others and better at evaluating the persuasive efforts presented to us.

We will examine lines of reasoning in three ways. First, we will look at some of the patterns of argumentation available to us in responding to situations. Second, we will look at ways we can evaluate ideas presented to us as receivers of communication. Finally, we will look at arguments whose weak points so often outweigh their strong point that they are labelled "fallacies."

Keep in mind that lines of argument are persuasive *strategies,* not persuasive *guarantees.* Lines of reasoning are approaches we can take in communicating with others. They are not magical formulae that will automatically render us successful. Neither are they fixed forms to be used in the same way with all audiences. Effective communicators adapt lines of reasoning from audience to audience and from situation to situation.

> Recognizing the techniques of persuasive strategies enhances our abilities as communicators and makes us better "consumers" of persuasion.

The Flow of Reasoning

Effective reasoning and argumentation tend to follow recognizable patterns. In making up our own minds, we usually follow one of two patterns. We begin with ideas we hold and apply them to new situations or we collect observations until their cumulative weight leads us to draw a conclusion that makes sense of the observations.

For example, in speculating about a grade for a class, one could begin with a major idea: "The syllabus says that students achieving 585 points or above will receive an *A*." One then applies that major idea to a specific situation: "My semester score is 593 points. I can expect an *A* in this class." We could also speculate on a grade from the other direction and start by compiling observations: "My quiz grades equal 83 points; my first exam equals 92 points; my second exam equals 87 points; my third exam equals 84 points; my term project equals 137 points. My total points to date are 483." Based on that collection of data, one could then reach some conclusion about the semester grade: "A perfect score, 100 points on the final exam, will still be two points short of an *A*."

The first method of reasoning is known as "deductive reasoning." The second is known as "inductive reasoning." As arguments become more complicated, the number of premises, evidence and conclusions increase, and the relationships between them become more intricate. The basic movements, however, remain the same.

Deductive Reasoning

Patterns of Deductive Reasoning

When we reason deductively, we begin with a certainty, or a very high degree of certainty, and end with a conclusion based on that certainty. We start with an accepted idea or principle, then apply that idea or principle to a specific case. The move is one from the principle to the particular, from idea to application, from the abstract to the concrete.

"Hondas are good cars," thinks a prospective buyer in the showroom, then turns to the sales representative and says, "I want that one."

"The vet said generic dog foods are not good for my pet, so I started buying a higher priced name brand."

Syllogisms

Creating Syllogisms

The best known type of deductive argument is the syllogism. The syllogism is a form of argument that has been discussed by rhetoricians and philosophers for more than two millennia. The classic syllogism contains three parts: a major premise, a minor premise, and a conclusion. The first we have already seen though not in its formal style:

> Major Premise: If students achieve 585 or more points in this course, they will receive an *A*.
> Minor Premise: I have 593 points.
> Conclusion: I will receive an *A*.

Syllogisms can be used to make judgments of value:

> Major Premise: Rembrandt was a great painter.
> Minor Premise: This painting is by Rembrandt.
> Conclusion: This is a great work of art.

Syllogisms can also argue which of two alternatives is the most likely to happen.

> Major Premise: For the university to meet its predicted financial needs, the legislature will have to appropriate more funds or we will have to raise tuition.
> Minor Premise: The legislature will not appropriate more funds.
> Conclusion: We will have to raise student tuition.

While syllogisms can be the subject of detailed discussion and analysis, the basic form is fairly simple. We first make a general statement about a classification or group. The statement should be one accepted or likely to be accepted by our audience. We then place an individual or small group within or without of that classification. Finally, we draw the logical conclusion (Nadeau 40).

If the pattern is not followed, the line of reasoning breaks down. If the minor premise does not fit as a subcategory of the major premise, whatever conclusion the speaker draws will be invalid. Changing the relationship of the major and minor premises changes the acceptability of the arguments.

Major Premise: Students who receive 585 points or more in this communication class will receive an *A*.
Minor Premise: I have 593 points in my biology class.
Conclusion: I will receive an *A* in this communication class.

Major Premise: Rembrandt was a great painter.
Minor Premise: This painting is by Sigmund Freud.
Conclusion: This is a great work of art.

A speaker will also be unsuccessful in using a syllogistic line of reasoning if the audience does not accept the major premise. If the speaker does not gain accord on the major premise, then the audience will be reluctant to grant accord on the minor premise and conclusion.

The syllogism is a widely used line of reasoning, but much of the time it is used in a shortened fashion. The elements are present, but one or two are left unstated, and it is up to the audience to fill in the blanks. Used in this form, it is often referred to as an "enthymeme," another major communication concept from Aristotle's *Rhetoric* (Book II, Chapter 22).

Enthymemes ask the audience to fill in the missing spaces. Rather than presenting a fully blown syllogism and letting the audience play a passive role in the persuasive interchange, the enthymeme calls upon the audience to play an active role. To follow the line or reasoning, the audience must make an effort to connect two thoughts. The involvement involves the audience in the reasoning process and gives the argument added impact.

In a grocery store, we might overhear, "Let's buy this cider. It's Purdue Cider."

In a class, someone might ask the instructor, "Isn't even a unit exam during 'dead week' against university regulations?"

The first example omits both the major premise and the conclusion. If we worked out the syllogistic line of reasoning, it would look like this:

Major Premise: Purdue Cider is excellent cider.
Minor Premise: This is Purdue Cider.
Conclusion: This is excellent cider.

On the basis of the conclusion, the persuader then urges action, buying the cider.

In the second, the major and minor premises are combined while the conclusion is left to the receiver's intuition. Reconstructed, the second enthymeme would look like this:

Major Premise: University regulations prohibit all exams during "dead week."
Minor Premise: What you are proposing is an exam.
Conclusion: You should not give us this test.

Weighing Syllogisms

When presented with syllogisms, we can evaluate them by checking them against their basic criteria. The first question we should ask is, "How readily do I accept the major premise?" If the major assumption is one we do not share, then we should reject the argument. If we accept the major premise, be it stated or unstated, then our next task is to judge the acceptability of the minor premise. Does the individual or subgroup fit logically in the larger classification of the major premise? If the fit is a good one, we can look forward to the conclusion. If the fit is a bad one, we should again be skeptical of the argument. Finally, we should judge how readily the conclusion follows from what precedes it. If the conclusion is in line with the major and minor premise, then we will, in all likelihood, accept the speaker's point. If the conclusion does not flow from the preceding statements, then we will reject or be dubious about the final point.

Inductive Reasoning

Patterns of Inductive Reasoning

Inductive reasoning is what one persuasion theorist calls "reasoning from evidence" (Simons 183). Here we begin with the specific and move to the general. We start by collecting observations, and when we have collected a sufficient number, we make a summary statement that makes sense out of what we have observed. For example, after collecting information on auto accidents at a given campus intersection, we could then make judgments about the relative safety of the intersection.

Note that while deductive arguments begin with certainty and end with a specific conclusion, inductive arguments begin with a number of specifics and end, not in certainty, but in probability. In essence, we make the best guess we can about what the evidence means. For example, after collecting and tabulating data about the intersection, we might discover that the intersection had four accidents for every five million vehicle crossings. Given that the average accident rate is one per five million crossings, we would conclude that the intersection is unusually dangerous (Fricker).

Inductive arguments may take numerous forms. We will examine several of the best known forms.

Arguments from Authority

Creating Arguments from Authority

We argue or reason inductively from authority when we examine respected sources and judge their collective opinions on a matter. Before buying a car, we may consult *Consumer Reports, Motor Trend, Road and Track,* and other automobile magazines to see what has been said about different brands and models. We talk to physicians about our health. We read guides to universities and colleges before making the choice of which school to attend.

For our arguments from authority to be persuasive, they must meet several criteria. The authorities must be respected by the audience; the authorities must be relevant to the case at hand; and the authorities must be in sufficient numbers.

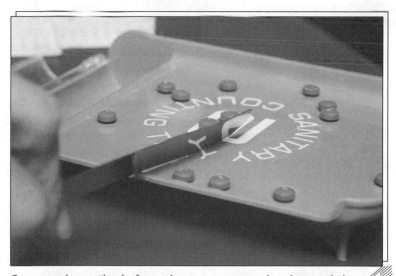

One popular method of creating an argument is using statistics from past experiments, such as the effectiveness of a specific drug.

Weighing Arguments from Authority

As the target of persuasive efforts, we should ask the same kinds of questions about arguments from authority that we ask when preparing the arguments. Do we respect the authorities? Are the authorities relevant? Are they in sufficient number to be convincing?

When deciding whether or not to attend a movie, we might look at what critics—authorities—have said about the film. Whom would you be most likely to believe: one negative report from the film critic, social editor, and press operator of the *Otaska News*, a weekly newspaper published in a town of 1,200 or five positive reports from the film critics in *The New York Times, Film Digest, At the Movies, Newsweek, and Sneak Previews?* While it is possible that the five positive sources from notable publications could be mistaken, most of us would tend to accept them more readily than the one negative response.

Arguments from Statistics or Examples

Creating Arguments from Statistics or Examples

When we argue from examples, we collect enough samples of a given action or condition that we can generalize about the nature of the occurrence or the situation. If a situation is dramatic enough, one example may make the point. Usually, though, several examples will be necessary to support the desired conclusion. When we collect a large number of examples and express our findings numerically, we argue from statistics.

Legal reasoning, for example, is often reasoning from examples (Levi 2; Golding 10). To decide what to do in a given case, people look at what was done in previous similar cases. If someone dies without leaving a formal will but instead a rough draft of a will is found, how legally binding is that rough draft? The answer will be found in earlier cases that addressed the same problem.

To discover the effectiveness of a new drug, the medicine is tested in a "double blind" experiment. People with a similar ailment are divided into groups. One group will be given the experimental drug. Another group will be given a placebo, something that looks like a drug but has no effect. A third group receives nothing, but its members are monitored as closely as those in the first two groups. The experiment is called a "double blind" because neither the person giving the drug nor the persons receiving the drug know who is receiving the drug and who is receiving the placebo. Experimenters collect numerous observations about the drug, quantify them, study them, and then draw conclusions about the drug's efficacy and applicability.

If we were arguing for better safety lighting in a given part of campus, one of the key points would be the problems created by the existing system. Here reasoning from examples or statistics would be very helpful. Central to the proposal for better lighting would be the number of accidents and assaults occurring in the area. To conclude that the area needed improved lighting, the persuader would need to collect enough examples to reach the conclusion, "This area is a problem sufficient to require action."

Weighing Arguments from Statistics or Examples

"How relevant are the examples?" is a question we should entertain when presented with arguments from examples. Cases of crimes committed in low

> If a situation is dramatic enough, one example may make the point.

light areas on other campuses will carry less weight than cases from the home campus.

"What is the scope of the evidence?" and "Do we have sufficient cases to draw an acceptable conclusion?" are questions that apply to both examples and statistics. One of the classic stories of advertising fraud is the aspirin company that advertised that "Three out of four doctors prefer our brand to all others." Investigation revealed that the company had, indeed, asked only four doctors for their opinions. For most of us to accept that argument, the number would have to be much higher and chosen from a true spectrum of doctors.

"How recent are the figures?" is another major question that must be asked of statistical evidence. One could report on the number of people listening to a given radio station, but unless the data are recent, they would be of little persuasive value to an advertiser.

"How fairly are the figures collected?" is another important question to which statistical data should be subjected. One does not obtain an accurate reflection of student drinking habits if the only people polled are those lined up outside bars on Friday nights. To obtain accurate statistics, those selected should be an accurate reflection of the larger group. Furthermore, everyone in the larger group must have an equal chance of being selected for the subject group.

Similarly, one needs to ask, "Who produced the figures?" If the source of the statistics is one whose livelihood or well being is tied to the figures, one should be wary of the evidence. One of the best known examples is the inflated figures produced by the United States armed forces in Vietnam. The Vietnam War was a controversial engagement and support in the United States was limited. To counter arguments against the war, the statistics of casualties, engagements, and losses were exaggerated to maintain the image that our forces were successful (Berman; Karnow; Sheehan). Even if figures are not distorted, they will have more impact coming from a disinterested source rather than one closely aligned with the product or idea.

Statistical evidence is dubious if it fails to use appropriate measures. One of the most common mistakes made in reporting statistics is to presume that the "average" or "mean" is a true reflection of the group being measured.

"The Ajax School Corporation continues to promote academic excellence by encouraging teacher-student interaction in small classes. The average classroom in the system now has twenty-two students."

If one class has thirty-five students and another has nine, their average size is twenty-two. The claim to academic excellence may be diminished if it turns out that many classes are as high as thirty students while a few very small classes pull the average into the low twenties.

To be an accurate reflection, the statistics would also need to include the *median,* the *mode,* and the *range.* The median is the point on the scale at which half the figures are above it and half below. The mode is the figure occurring most often. The range shows the highest point reached, the lowest, and the distribution of data between those two points.

Arguments from Signs

Creating Arguments from Signs

Reason from signs is a form of reasoning that is derived from indicators. In this method of reasoning, data are not important in themselves but are important

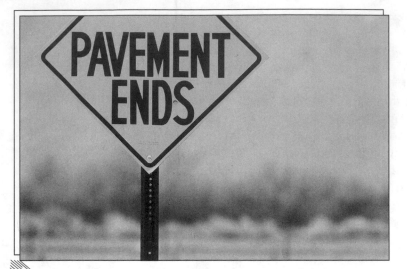

A sign does not cause the problem, but warns of the upcoming problem.

for what they point to or indicate. When arguing from signs, the data or pieces of information do not *cause* a condition or set of circumstances but instead *warn* us that the condition or set of circumstances is about to happen. In arguing from signs, a person introduces information, then shows towards what the information points. An argument based on signs uses the signs as a kind of predictor: "Since we see these signs, we can then expect. . . ."

If someone is driving on a trip, glances at the instrument panel and notices the gas gauge is nearing empty, the impact of that indication is clear. The driver needs to refuel soon or run the risk of being stranded. The low reading on the gas gauge is a sign of impending problems. It does not, though, cause the impending problem.

A typical argument from sign would be the forecasts for the national economy based on new housing starts and automobile sales. These two areas are considered valid indicators of the growth or shrinking or the economy. They are considered important indictors because they require large outlays of money and are the kind of purchases people make when they are affluent. Food purchases, for example, are less valid as indicators since food must be bought no matter what the economy.

Weighing Arguments from Signs

The validity of an argument from signs depends on the relationship between the sign and the conditions which it signals. If the two are closely correlated, the argument will be stronger than a line of reasoning in which the relationship is weak or non-existent.

If you were trying to ascertain the educational level of a person and you knew that person was a public school teacher, you could easily argue from sign to an acceptable conclusion. As a college degree is required of public school teachers, you could argue with a high degree of certainty that the person possesses a college diploma. The sign, "public school teacher," is linked very strongly with the conclusion, "possessing a college degree." You could not use the same sign to argue that the person was, say, an avid birdwatcher. No link exists between the two parts of that argument.

Arguments from Cause and Effect

Creating Arguments from Cause and Effect

Closely linked to reasoning from sign is reasoning from cause and effect. Again, we see a relationship between conditions and an effect. In an argument from sign, the pieces of evidence merely point to the existence of a condition. In an argument from cause and effect, the evidence shows what caused the condition. Reasoning from sign is arguing that something exists or will exist. Reasoning from cause and effect is arguing *why* something exists or will exist (Freely 153).

When using cause and effect reasoning, we can argue in two directions. We can argue from the causes or likely causes to say that the effect will take place, or we may argue from the effect and point to the reasons behind the condition. If one knows the cause, one argues from cause to the inferred effect. If one knows the effect, one argues from the effect back to the inferred cause (Freely 151). To be successful, both methods depend on the persuadee's acceptance of the described relationship. If our audience accepts the link between cause and effect, we can then argue for maintaining or changing the status quo by illustrating how current circumstances give rise to the particular set of causes and effects. Consider the following arguments:

Cause to effect: Tax revenues are down. University expenses are up. Inflation continues at five per cent per year. It is easy to see that a tuition increase is inevitable.

Effect to cause: Student tuition has been raised ten per cent. The reasons are clear: tax revenues are down, university expenses are up, and inflation continues at five per cent per year.

Weighing Arguments from Cause and Effect

The success of a cause and effect line of reasoning depends on the strength of the relationship between its two parts. Thus, in evaluating a cause and effect argument, the chief question to be asked is, "How valid is the link between the proposed cause and proposed effect?" Two conditions may exist in close relationship with each other, but that does not mean that one causes the other. For example, a positive correlation exists between the length of people's pants legs and their educational levels. To a point, the more education one has, the longer the person's inseam. The reason is simple. We grow over the span of our education. A high school graduate is considerably taller than a first grader and hence will have not only more education but longer legs as well.

In the 1992 presidential elections, some reasoned that Bush's successful military campaigns and skills in international diplomacy (cause) would lead to his re-election (effect). They did not. Following the election, Clinton's forces argued that his slate of new programs (effect) was prompted by his mandate from the people (cause). If one did not accept Clinton's forty-six percent of the popular vote as a mandate, then the argument was unacceptable.

In addition to judging the existence of a cause-effect relationship, one also needs to ask if other forces were at work in a given situation. What the persuader offers as the chief cause or causes may only be a small part of the larger picture. "What other causes might lead to the same effect?" is another important question that critical audience members should ask.

According to a survey of 123 models of 1988–1990 cars conducted by the Highway Loss Data Institute, the two models with the least injuries and collision damage were the Chevrolet Caprice and the Plymouth Grand Voyager ("How Safe . . . 16–18). The effect is clear. One might even use it to argue that the cars possessed superior designs or safety features or handling capabilities that lead to their impressive standings. The data could be used as selling points for prospective owners: buy one of these and be guaranteed a safer ride.

Upon closer inspection, it turns out that the cause had little to do with design. This model of Caprice did not have airbags, even as an option. Two

> The success of a cause and effect line of reasoning depends on the strength of the relationship between its two parts.

other factors were probably much more influential. One was weight. Both are large vehicles. In a collision, the larger the car, the less likely it is to be damaged, especially when it collides with a smaller vehicle. The second factor involves who buys and drives theses cars. Both the Caprice and Voyager are vehicles designed to carry a large number of people and are known as "family cars." The drivers and owners are people looking for practicality, not performance. They are likely to be conservative drivers, protective of their passengers. The safety record was as much a matter of driver caution as it was safety design.

Arguments from Analogy

Creating Arguments from Analogy

Another method of inductive argument is argument from analogy. An analogy is a comparison of two things that are similar in many ways. By understanding the first thing, we come to understand the second. The use of analogies is a common teaching technique. We can, for example, see the three parts of a speech as similar to an airplane flight. The introduction is like the takeoff; the body is like the trip; and the conclusion is like the landing. In a lesson on electricity, an instructor may explain the flow of electricity through a wire by comparing it to the flow of water through a pipe. The key terms in understanding the flow of electricity—volts, ohms, and amps—correspond to three easily understood terms about the flow of water: pressure, resistance, and amount.

> An analogy is a comparison of two things that are similar in many ways.

When we reason from analogy, we compare two things and on the basis of their similarities presume that their unknown characteristics will also be similar. A popular argument from analogy is the "If it walks like a duck . . ." argument. In attempting to classify a new fowl, we might observe that, "It walks like a duck; it swims like a duck; and it sounds like a duck." The conclusion would be that because the two birds share a significant number of characteristics, they must also share the same classification: the unknown fowl is a duck.

In a more sophisticated fashion, a legislator might argue: "The governor may call his plan an 'income adjustment,' but it is more than that. The adjustment will be paid by all wage earners in the state, just like a tax. The money will be collected by the Bureau of Revenue, just like a tax. The income will become state monies, just like a tax. The 'income adjustment' is nothing more than a new tax and should be treated as such."

One of our major social issues is the problem of health care. In the debate about the best approach to providing health care, we often hear an argument from analogy that compares the Canadian system of health care with the American system. The arguments run like this: "America and Canada face similar situations. Both are big, industrialized countries. Both have a large population, rising health care problems, democratic governments. They have about the same level of taxation. Canada has numerous problems with its universal care system of health care. Since the two countries are so alike, we know that the Canadian system would not work in the United States."

Weighing Arguments from Analogy

The major factor in the acceptability of an argument from analogy is how readily we, or our audiences, accept the similarities between the two things— objects, cases, situations—being compared. If we readily accept the similarities, then the final conclusion is likely to make sense. If we see significant dissimilarities, then we are likely to reject the argument. The key question is, "How genuine, complete, and significant are the similarities presented to us?"

If one were a gambler, one might be persuaded to put money on a horse in the Kentucky Derby if it could be shown that the animal had the same lineage, training, track record, and jockey as last year's winner. One would be far less likely to bet on a horse just because it was the same color as last year's winner and wore a saddle and bridle like last year's winner.

The argument against a Canadian-style health care plan is effective only if the audience accepts the two countries as being significantly similar. The argument will be rejected if the audience sees the countries as dissimilar in important ways.

If something "walks like a duck . . .," to some it may indeed be a duck. To others, it may be a new species of geese. The conclusion will depend on how well the persuader lines up the similarities.

From the preceding discussion, it should be clear how inductive reasoning leads from particulars to a general conclusion. One examines individual pieces of evidence and based on that collection of evidence reaches a conclusion that binds the separate piece of evidence into a coherent whole. Which method of reasoning is best—deductive or inductive—will depend upon the nature of the issue, the particulars of an audience, the type of evidence available, and the abilities of the speaker.

Fallacies in Arguments

A fallacy is a mistaken idea, an illogical projection from premise to conclusion. Simply put, a fallacious argument is one in which the premises and conclusions do not match up to make good sense. While they may have "the appearance of truth or reasonableness" (Freely 159), they do not stand up to close inspection. To some degree, we have already discussed fallacious arguments when we have pointed out where the above lines of reasoning can go astray and have urged close analysis of arguments offered in support of any proposition.

Beyond those examples, though, we have a group of arguments that stand as a class unto themselves due to their history of misuse. While they may be legitimately applied in some cases, more often than not they are the sign of slick appeals and shallow reasoning. Like the better lines of reasoning, they, too, have been in existence for centuries. Some are even dignified with Latin names while others have colorful names they have acquired over time.

The *ad hominem* ("to the man") argument is an attack upon a person rather than an attack upon an idea. If one cannot discredit a proposal, then one discredits the person making the proposal. If people can be convinced that the proposer is of dubious character, they may reject the proposal without evaluating it.

The *ad populum* ("to the people") argument is also sometimes called "getting on the bandwagon." The idea comes from earlier times when the circus would parade down the main street of a town. The bandwagon contained, of course, the band, a large group playing as loudly as possible. "Getting on the bandwagon" came to mean joining a large number of people making a lot of noise and a great display while moving toward some goal.

> Simply put, a fallacious argument is one in which the premises and conclusions do not match up to make good sense.

It is an "everybody is doing it" or "everybody wants it" argument. In pressing such an argument, several important ideas may be ignored or glossed over. First, how many people constitute "everybody"? Unless valid statistics can be produced to show a significant number in favor of a proposal, the argument should be rejected. Second, even if a large number favor a proposal, that does not mean the proposal has value. "Everybody" is not always correct.

The "straw man" or "red herring" argument is another line of reasoning designed to lead one away from the central issue of a discussion. Instead of contending with a strong opponent, one creates a figure of little substance or strength, a "straw man," and proceeds to pummel it. If a persuader cannot successfully attack a proposal, then the persuader diverts attention from it by attacking a proposal which is vulnerable. A "red herring" was a smelly fish dragged across a fugitive's trail to divert the pursuing hounds onto a false track.

The "false dichotomy" argument involves presenting an audience only two alternatives when, in reality, a variety of alternatives may be present. "It's us or rust" was the slogan of a national automobile rustproofing company. Despite its catchy rhyme, a car owner had more than the two choices. Other rustproofing companies could be used. The owner could sell the car before rust developed. The car could be stored in the winter and driven only after the salt trucks had quit running. The owner could even move to a warmer climate to avoid winter and salty streets.

"Begging the question" is a kind of circular argument whereby the premises prove the conclusion and the conclusion proves the premises. Begging the question is when one says, "It is what it is because it is what it is." Calvin Coolidge, president of the United States from 1923 to 1929, supposedly provided one of the classic begging the question arguments with a comment on the economy. He stated that "When a large number of people are out of work, you see a rise in unemployment."

Contemporary examples can be found in advertising, among other places. In touting the size of its van, Volkswagen proclaimed, "Eurovan is here! The World's Largest Van For Its Size" ("Selling It" 271). In other words, no other van of the same size is bigger. A box of Swanson Chicken Pot Pie advertises its contents as having "100% More Chicken than Swanson 7 oz. Pies" ("Selling It" 271). The box contains a fourteen ounce pot pie.

Conclusion

In discussing issues and arguing persuasively, we need to be aware of the lines of reasoning available for us to use. The two major methods of reasoning argue in different directions. Deductive reasoning moves from a general idea or principle to specific applications or illustrations. It can also be characterized by a movement from certainty or a high degree of certainty to a conclusion. Inductive reasoning moves from particulars to a general conclusion that combines the particulars into a coherent whole. Its movement is one that begins with evidence and ends with a conclusion based on probability. In addition to logical uses of arguments, fallacious arguments may have the appearance of reason but are severely flawed.

Besides recognizing lines of reasoning, effective argumentation also relies on our adaptation of reasoning to a given situation. Rather than being set patterns of organization, arguments must be adapted to the audience, speaker, topic, and other variables of each speaking situation.

Discussion Questions

1. In terms of reasoning and persuasion, what is an "argument"?

2. Cite an example of a syllogism. What are its major premise, minor premise, and conclusion?

3. Provide an example of an enthymeme. How does it function as a condensed version of a syllogism? What are its implied major premise, minor premise, and conclusion?

4. What is the difference between deductive and inductive reasoning?

5. Provide examples of the various types of inductive arguments (authority, statistics or examples, signs, cause and effect, analogy).

6. How do we judge the validity of the various inductive arguments?

7. Bring in an ad from a newspaper or magazine. What arguments does the ad make? How valid are the arguments in the ad?

8. What makes a fallacious argument unacceptable?

9. Cite an example of a fallacious argument. What makes the argument fallacious?

Sources and References

Aristotle. *Rhetoric*. Trans. W. Rhys Roberts. New York: The Modern Library, 1964.

Berman, Larry. *Lyndon Johnson's War*. New York: Norton, 1989.

Freely, Austin J. *Argumentation and Debate: Critical Thinking for Reasoned Decision Making*. 7th ed. Belmont, California: Wadsworth Publishing Company, 1990.

Fricker, John. Associate Professor of Civil Engineering, Purdue University. Personal interview. 9 June 1993.

Golding, Martin P. *Legal Reasoning*. New York: Alfred A. Knopf, 1984.

"How Safe is Your Car? What Insurance Data Say." *Consumers' Research Magazine*. Nov. 1991: 16–18.

Karnow, Stanley. *Vietnam: A History*. New York: Penguin Books, 1991.

Kirwan, C. A. *Logic and Argument*. New York: New York University Press, 1978.

Lee, Ronald and Karen King Lee. *Arguing Persuasively*. New York: Longman, Inc., 1989.

Levi, Edward H. *An Introduction to Legal Reasoning*. Chicago: University of Chicago Press, 1962.

Missimer, Connie A. *Good Arguments: An Introduction to Critical Thinking*. Englewood Cliffs, New Jersey: Prentice Hall, 1990.

Purtrill, Richard L. *Logic: Argumentation, Refutation, and Proof*. New York: Harper and Row, Publishers, 1979.

"Selling It." *Consumer Reports*. April 1993: 271.

Sheehan, Neil. *A Bright Shining Lie: John Paul Vann and America in Vietnam*. New York: Vintage Books, 1988.

Simons, Herbert W. *Persuasion: Understanding, Practice, and Analysis*. 2nd ed. New York: Random House, 1986.

Toulmin, Stephen, Richard Rieke, and Allan Janik. *An Introduction to Reasoning*. New York: Macmillan Publishing Company, Inc., 1979.

Verderber, Richard F. *Essentials of Persuasive Speaking: Theory and Contexts*. Belmont, California: Wadsworth Publishing Company, 1991.

Walton, Douglas N. *Informal Logic: A Handbook for Critical Argumentation*. Cambridge, England: Cambridge University Press, 1989.

Weddle, Perry. *Argument: A Critical Guide to Critical Thinking*. New York: McGraw-Hill, Inc., 1978.

Willard, Charles Arthur. *A Theory of Argumentation*. Tuscaloosa, Alabama: University of Alabama Press, 1989.

⟍⟍ Persuasion and Reasoning ⟍⟍

1. What is deductive reasoning?

   _____

   _____

2. How is a syllogism constructed?

   _____

   _____

3. What is an enthymeme?

   _____

   _____

4. How is the enthymeme used in persuasive speaking?

   _____

   _____

5. When presented with a syllogism, how can you evaluate it for validity?

   _____

   _____

6. What is inductive reasoning?

   _____

   _____

7. What criteria must be met by arguments from authority in order to be considered persuasive?

   _____

   _____

8. What five questions should you ask regarding examples or statistics before accepting them as valid evidence?

1. _____

2. _____

3. _____

4. _____

5. _____

9. How can you determine the validity of arguments from signs?

_____

_____

10. What measures the success of an argument based on cause and effect?

_____

_____

11. What is an analogy?

_____

_____

12. What is a fallacy?

_____

_____

13. What is the *ad hominem* ("to the man") argument?

_____

_____

14. What is the *ad populum* ("to the people") argument?

_____

_____

15. What is the "straw man" or "red herring" argument?

_____

_____

16. What is a false dichotomy?

_____

_____

17. What is "begging the question?"

_____

_____

Sample Exam Questions

1. Which of the following statements BEST illustrates what is meant by "process" in communication?
   A. Process means that communication is a set of standard procedures for accomplishing our goals.
   B. Process is the mixture of communicative styles.
   C. Process means that communication is ongoing and created by the communicating parties.
   D. Process is the forward movement of communication.
   E. Process is the handling of information by the receiving party in a communication transaction.

2. An important factor in persuasive speaking is how the speaker is perceived by the audience. Which term BEST identifies this factor?
   A. charisma
   B. credibility
   C. stature
   D. power
   E. poise

3. "Evidence" is BEST defined as:
   A. the facts and figures you present your audience.
   B. the course of action you want your audience to accept.
   C. the strength of your main ideas.
   D. the collection of visual aids you display to enhance your message.
   E. anything your audience will believe when presented with it.

4. Which statement BEST defines "climate" as it pertains to small groups?
   A. Group climate is the feelings that group members have toward each other.
   B. Group climate is the agenda created for the meeting, a predictable pattern akin to the weather.
   C. Group climate is the temperature and humidity of the group's meeting place which can positively or adversely affect the group.
   D. Group climate is the relatively enduring quality of the group situation that is experienced in common by group members and arises from and influences their interaction and behavior.
   E. Group climate is the positive atmosphere created by the group in its approach to problem solving that allows and encourages the growth of solutions and the proper judgment of solutions.

5. Gary B.'s small group was given the responsibility of selecting a site for an upcoming family reunion. The group came up with various possibilities and discussed them until everyone agreed on the best place for the reunion. Which statement BEST describes the methods of decision making used by the group?
   A. parliamentary procedure
   B. convivial
   C. leader made
   D. democratic
   E. consensus

6. To describe what it was like to attend the Indianapolis 500 with a half million in attendance, Sherry W. said, "It was as if you were one drop of water in the Mississippi River." Her method of describing is BEST labeled:
   A. description by analogy.
   B. description by providing examples.
   C. description by contrast.
   D. description by poetic language.
   E. description by formula.

7. Which statement BEST describes the first step a problem solving group should take when addressing a problem?
   A. Decide what happens to the group.
   B. Select the best alternative as a solution.
   C. Define the problem.
   D. Investigate the problem situation.
   E. Set criteria for a solution.

8. One method for finding a topic for a speech is to put down a word, then from that word, you create a web of associations. Which term BEST labels this method of finding a topic?
   A. brainstorming
   B. clustering
   C. self exploration
   D. free association
   E. Morgan's speech development technique

9. The three elements of a thesis statement are:
   A. the topic, the argument, the details.
   B. the subject, the ramifications, the solution.
   C. the topic, your position, amplification.
   D. the subject, the verb, the object.
   E. the introduction, the body, the conclusion.

10. Kathy S. is giving a speech on, "How to Raise Delicious Tomatoes." Her three main points are: "preparing the soil," "planting the tomatoes," and "caring for the tomato plants." Which statement BEST describes her method of speech organization?
    A. spatial
    B. structure-function
    C. topical
    D. chronological
    E. problem-solution

Answers for Sample Exam Questions

1. C
2. B
3. E
4. D
5. E
6. A
7. C
8. B
9. C
10. D

Appendix:
A Library Research Strategy for Communication

Scott Mandernack

Communication is a broad discipline, including research from the fields of psychology, sociology, anthropology, linguistics, medicine, technology and many others. Because of its interdisciplinary nature, library research in this field takes on added dimensions. As with any research, one must know how to identify and locate information sources, evaluate the information, and then synthesize it into a well-organized presentation. Knowing some basic concepts, procedures and resources will provide you with a good foundation on which to begin your research.

One single, universal process of conducting research cannot be prescribed for every topic or every individual. Research is dynamic and personal, with many factors contributing to each person's approach. However, understanding a basic **research strategy** —a process of identifying, locating, evaluating, and communicating information in an organized, logical fashion—will ensure that you have considered all of your options and efficiently found appropriate materials without neglecting important resources.

Getting Started

Having a good understanding of what you actually want to accomplish will determine the direction and ultimately the success of your research. Be sure you understand the requirements of your project and the timeframe you have to work in, and then set realistic expectations.

⟹ How long does your presentation have to be?
   The length of your paper or speech will determine to a large extent how much information you will need.

⟹ What will be the depth and scope of your research?
   Greater depth on a topic may require more resources and a greater diversity of materials.

⟹ Who is your audience?
   The assumptions you make about your audience may affect the level of materials you use, the amount of information, and the perspective you take.

➡ How much time do you have to complete your research?
Set your deadlines carefully. Consider the date that your project is due, and the amount of time that you have to work on it, and then create a manageable timetable for completing each step of your research. A general recommendation is to allow:
  ➡ 5% of the total project time for planning your project
  ➡ 5% for preliminary project selection
  ➡ 15% for topic formulation and focus
  ➡ 30% for gathering information
  ➡ 5% for preparing to compose
  ➡ 40% for composing and revising

Remember that you may need to revise your timetable as you more fully explore your topic and proceed with subsequent steps.

Be aware of the additional resources that are available to provide assistance. If you're a beginning researcher, get to know the library staff. They can be a valuable resource at any step of your research process. Also, get familiar with other campus resources, such as the campus computer labs, writing labs (perhaps also an online writing lab), learning resource centers, copy centers, etc.

Selecting and Refining a Topic

Finding the right topic for your research can sometimes be the most challenging part of the whole process. There are a few important, preliminary considerations to make before even beginning to look for your information:

➡ Consider your interest in the topic.
➡ Assess what you already know about the subject.
➡ Determine the perspective from which you will approach the topic.
➡ Articulate your specific interests and develop a focus.
➡ Determine the discipline(s) that will provide appropriate information.

If you are unclear about how to answer any of these questions, or if you feel you would like additional information about the subject area you have chosen, find some general background information to get an overview of the field of study. Understanding basic concepts, theories, etc., and putting the topic into an appropriate context may give some direction to your treatment of the subject.

Encyclopedias, dictionaries, and handbooks can be very useful sources for finding general information. They provide basic, introductory information on a topic and offer a broad perspective, summarizing major developments in the field, identifying key researchers or other notable individuals, or leading you to important works about the subject. As you read through some introductory essays, keep in mind how the various elements of the topic relate to each other. Are there approaches to the topic that you haven't considered? What discipline(s) are most likely to write about these perspectives? Remember, when using general information sources, you may need to look under broader subjects than the particular topic you have chosen. Your specific topic may be discussed within the context of a related subject. Use the indexes in these sources whenever possible.

While learning about a new subject area, you may come across unfamiliar words or terms, or familiar words used in an unfamiliar context. Dictionaries and encyclopedias—which may be either general or specialized for a specific field or discipline—may offer some clarification. It will be important that you understand how the terms relate to one another. Is one term synonymous with another? Do they convey slightly different meanings? Is one term more specific? Understanding how the concepts within the subject area—and therefore, the terms that are used—relate to one another is directly related to how you will go about searching for your information. With the increasing availability of networked databases and systems, with their enhanced search capabilities, your mastery of these electronic sources will depend largely on how well you understand your topic and enter the relevant terms.

Usually located in the Reference section of the library, general information sources are arranged so you can find quickly the information you need. A few examples of encyclopedias, dictionaries, and handbooks related to communication are:

➡ *Censorship: A World Encyclopedia*
➡ *Data & Telecommunications Dictionary*
➡ *Encyclopedia of Psychology*
➡ *Encyclopedia of Television*
➡ *Handbook of Organizational Behavior*
➡ *International Encyclopedia of Communications*
➡ *International Encyclopedia of Educational Technology*
➡ *Language and Communication: A Cross-Cultural Encyclopedia*
➡ *Oxford English Dictionary*

Other general survey sources may be identified by using the library catalog. By looking under the subject heading for the broad discipline that matches your topic, and then looking further for the standard subheading "Dictionaries," you may locate specialized dictionaries as well as encyclopedias and handbooks in that particular field. For example, searching under the subject heading "communication—dictionaries" in a library catalog will help you find encyclopedias, handbooks and dictionaries in the broad field of communication.

In online catalogs, additional search techniques may be used to identify general sources. Many computerized catalogs allow searching on key words in the bibliographic record. Conducting a keyword search will often result in more entries because the terms may appear in any part of the record rather than as subject headings only. For example, the keyword search "psychology AND dictionaries" will identify any record in the database in which these two words appear. You will find many of the encyclopedias and handbooks in the broad field of psychology with this type of search, but you may also find sources on specific branches of psychology, such as social psychology, experimental psychology, or pathological psychology.

Once you have a basic understanding of the subject area, you can determine the scope of your topic and consider focusing on particular aspects. The information you found from the general sources will help you to determine what approach is of most interest to you. It is important to understand the many avenues of inquiry that are possible and to make conscious decisions about which one(s) you will choose. Whenever possible, try to relate your topic to your own interests or experiences. Personalizing the topic will make the research more meaningful and relevant. You may wish to consider limiting your topic by such factors as:

➧ geographic region (i.e. country, state, city)
➧ time period (i.e. prehistory, 18th century, 1991, 2000)
➧ population group (i.e. students, accountants, women, minorities)
➧ other considerations (i.e. cross-disciplinary perspectives, etc.).

One method of articulating your topic ideas is to develop a concept map. Concept mapping is a method that can be used to describe, in graphic form, the relationships between issues and aspects of a topic area. Begin by placing the main idea in a central circle. As issues and aspects are identified, relate them to the main idea with a connecting line. You may generate several levels of relationships, as appropriate, to depict sub-aspects and issues.

For example:

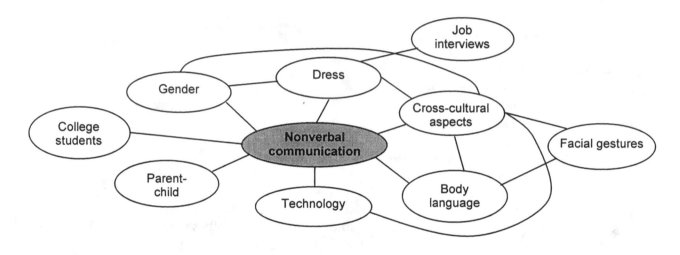

The resulting diagram will illustrate the diversity of perspectives regarding your topic and help you consider possible approaches you may take. Refining your topic into a well formulated research question will provide you with a theme or direction for your research. A well-defined focus will help to unify disparate elements, eliminate nonproductive efforts, and save you a great deal of time.

Searching for In-Depth Information

Once you have formulated your research question, you are ready to begin looking for in-depth information, which is more comprehensive and will provide additional detail. Depending on the nature of your topic, you will need to determine the time frame of materials which will be relevant to your research.

Retrospective information is that which is written after an event or idea occurs. Because a period of time has elapsed between the event and publication, this information often includes historical analysis or evaluation of the topic. This type of information is typically found in books or pamphlets. Many encyclopedia articles will include bibliographies of key works on the subject, which may provide you with some good sources to start with. To locate additional books, however, you must use the library's catalog.

Library catalogs provide access to the collections of a particular library or libraries. Items may be searched by author, title, subject, and often, by additional options, such as key words in the record or call numbers. Specific search methods (i.e. search commands in computerized catalogs, etc.) may vary from one catalog to another. However, understanding some general fundamentals will provide you with a good foundation in using any library catalog.

Most library catalogs utilize a controlled vocabulary for organizing records by subject. A controlled vocabulary is a pre-determined list of terms used when assigning subject headings to each item in the catalog. In many college and university libraries, the Library of Congress subject headings are used. The listing of Library of Congress subject headings (LCSH) provides you with the exact format of the subject headings that will be used in the catalog. In addition, it may also indicate narrower, broader, or related terms.

Using the *Library of Congress Subject Headings:*

a.   Identify term(s) relevant to your selected topic.

b.   Look up your term(s) in LCSH.

c.   Terms in bold-faced print are acceptable subject headings to use in the catalog. If the library has materials on this topic, they will be listed under this heading.

d.   If LCSH indicates that you should USE another term, turn to that heading.

e.   Having located an accepted subject heading, LCSH may provide related terms. These related terms will be preceded by **UF, BT, RT,** or **NT**.

  UF denotes a subject heading *not* used in the catalog.

  BT refers to "broader terms." You may wish to look under this heading, particularly if you looked in the catalog under the bold-faced heading and no items were listed.

  RT refers to "related terms." LCSH is telling you that this term is related to your topic and you may wish to also look under this accepted heading.

  NT refers to "narrower terms." You may wish to use this heading, particularly if you looked in the catalog under the bold-faced heading and many items were listed.

Sample entry from LCSH:

Apprehension
 USE Perception
	Perception
	 UF Apprehension
	     BT Intellect
	       Thought and thinking
	     RT Intuition (Psychology)
	     NT Intersensory effects
	       Subliminal perception

Online catalogs provide additional methods to search for information about a topic other than the subject heading approach. The ability to search free-text (which is to say, by any key word in the bibliographic record) offers tremendous capabilities and flexibility. A major concept to understand in online searching is that of Boolean logic, which is a method of combining terms in specified ways within each record. Boolean logic utilizes operators which instruct the system how to process the resulting combination. The major operators recognized by most online systems are:

AND—narrows a search; requires that *each* term be present in the same record, regardless of their order. Use to find records with several distinct concepts. For example: *perception AND children*

OR— broadens a search; requires that either term, or both, be present in the same record. Use to group similar or related concepts. For example: *perception OR intuition*

NOT— narrows a search; requires that the first term be present, but not the second. Use to exclude records with the specified concept. For example: *perception NOT subliminal*

Since the search terms may appear anywhere in the bibliographic record (as an author, a word in the title, a word in a subject heading, etc.) and in any context, these searches must be constructed carefully. A clear understanding of the topic and the terminology is critical to effectively utilize the capabilities of these operations.

After locating appropriate records in the catalog, be sure to copy all relevant information about each item. All bibliographic information is included—author, title, publisher, date and place of publication—and specific location information, to help you locate the item on the shelf. Many catalog records also provide additional information, such as a physical description of the item (number of pages, inclusion of illustrations and bibliographies, etc.) and notes, outlining the contents of the work.

A typical bibliographic citation for a book appears below:

> Jandt, Fred Edmund. (1998). <u>Intercultural communication: an introduction</u>. Thousand Oaks, Calif.: Sage Publications.

You can use information in a catalog record to evaluate an item's potential usefulness to your research even before you find it on the shelf. The *publication date* is an important indicator of the appropriateness of information about issues which may have radically changed in recent years. The *publisher* may provide an indication of the authority or perspective of the work: scholarly or university presses tend to treat a topic very differently than a popular publisher. The presence of *bibliographies* and *indexes* can be a useful evaluation tool: bibliographies will help in locating additional information, and often, a bibliography and index indicate a more scholarly approach. The *notes* field may specify the contents of anthologies or collections of essays, stories, or other works. Careful review of catalog records can give you a great deal of information and make your research easier and more efficient.

With the materials you have gathered from your use of the catalog, you may find that you have a good overview or historical perspective on the topic, but you may be lacking in the recent research, developments, or opinions.

Books, by their very nature, cannot report on the most current developments. They generally have a broader scope and therefore they take more time to write; additionally, the publication process itself may take considerable time. So, for reports of what may have happened last month, for example, you will need to use some other sources.

Contemporary information—that which is representative of the time in which it was written—is typically found in such publications as newspapers, journals, magazines, or web sites. Collectively, the print publications may be referred to as "periodical literature" or simply "periodicals." These publications vary widely in purpose, content, authority, and reliability.

To help eliminate confusion about the appropriateness of different types of periodicals for your research, some basic criteria have been established to help you determine the purpose and/or level of scholarship of magazines and journals. The nature of your topic will determine, to some extent, the most suitable type of publication.

Criteria / Type of Publication	Scholarly Journals	Substantial News/ General Interest	Popular	Sensational
Format	Generally have grave, serious formats.	Attractive in appearance.	Generally slick and glossy with an attractive format.	Often produced in a cheap, newspaper format.
Graphics	Contain graphs and charts, but seldom glossy pages or pictures.	Include photographs, illustrations and graphics to enhance the publication.	Contain photographs, illustrations, and drawings to enhance their image.	Contain melodramatic photographs.
Sources	Cite sources with footnotes and bibliographies.	Occasionally cite sources, but this is the exception.	Rarely cite sources, which may be obscure.	Rarely cite sources of information.
Authors	Written by and for scholars or researchers in the specialty.	Written for an educated, general audience by the magazine's staff, a scholar, or free-lance writers.	Written by the publication's staff or free-lance writers for a broad based audience.	Contain articles written by free lance writers or the publication's staff for an impressionable readership.
Language	Use terminology, jargon and language of the discipline. Reader is assumed to have a similar scholarly background.	Use language appropriate for an educated readership. Do not emphasize a specialty but assume a basic level of intelligence.	Use simple language to meet a minimal education level. Articles are kept short, with little depth.	Contain language that is simple and easy to read and understand. An inflammatory, sensational style is often used.
Purpose	Inform, report or make available original research or experimentation to the rest of the scholarly world.	Provide general information to a wide, interested audience.	Designed to entertain or persuade. A hidden (or not so hidden) agenda is to sell products or services.	Arouse curiosity and interest by stretching and twisting the truth. Outrageous, startling headlines are used to pique curiosity and gain readership.
Publishers	Generally published by a professional organization.	Generally published by commercial enterprises for profit.	Published for profit.	Published for profit.
Advertising	Contain selective advertising.	Carry advertising.	Contain extensive advertising.	Advertising is as melodramatic as the stories.
Examples	*American Ethnologist* *Journal of Communication* *Journal of Politics*	*Forbes* *Psychology Today* *Scientific American* *Time*	*Glamour* *People Weekly* *Reader's Digest* *Sports Illustrated*	*Globe* *National Enquirer* *Star* *Sun*

Indexes and abstracts will help you to identify appropriate sources of information from periodicals. (An abstract provides a citation and a summary of the article; an index provides only the citation information, with no summaries). Each index or abstract covers a select group of periodical titles, which may be determined by the general subject(s) or disciplines covered, or by the type of material. Indexes and abstracts are available in book form, in CD-ROM, and on the internet. As with library catalogs, the actual mechanics of using different indexes may vary from one source or system to another. However, understanding the general function of indexes, and realizing that different indexes serve different purposes, will provide you with enough information to use them effectively in your research. A selected list of indexes and abstracts appears below:

➠ *Business Periodicals Index (Wilson Business Abstracts,* online*).* Indexes several hundred international business periodicals, covering the broad areas of management and economics, including organizational behavior and communication, telecommunications industry, and more.

➠ *Communication Abstracts (ComAbstracts,* online*).* Contains abstracts of articles published in the primary professional literature (approximately fifty journals) of the communication field.

➠ *Film Literature Index.* A subject and author index to the international film and television/video literature appearing in over 300 periodicals, including both established film journals and specialized publications.

➠ *New York Times Index.* Indexes and abstracts news articles, editorials, and special features published in the *New York Times.* Entries are classified under subject, geographic, organization and personal name headings, and arranged chronologically under them.

➠ *NewsBank* . Provides access to selected full-text articles from over 500 U.S. and Canadian newspapers, news sources, and newswires. Contains comprehensive coverage of current issues and events, as well as biographies and reviews of films, theater, dance, music performances, and television programs.

➠ *ProQuest Research Library.* A general database of magazine, journal, and newspaper articles from over 2300 publications in a wide variety of subject areas. Searches may be limited to only peer reviewed titles or only newspapers. Many articles are available in full-text, full image format.

➠ *PsycInfo.* Covers the professional and academic literature in psychology and related disciplines including education, linguistics, medicine, psychiatry, sociology, and other areas. Coverage is worldwide, and includes references and abstracts to over 1300 journals and dissertations.

➠ *Social Sciences Index (Social Sciences Abstracts,* online*).* Indexes over 400 English-language journals in the fields of anthropology, economics, geography, international relations, political science, psychology, sociology, and related subjects.

Selecting the appropriate indexes for your research will be determined largely by your approach to the topic. Some topics may require articles from scholarly journals, whereas others may rely more on popular magazines or newspapers. Other topics may be considered from various disciplinary perspectives. Still others may take you into literature written last week or last month, whereas others may require that you find materials written ten, twenty or fifty years ago. Consider the following factors in selecting the indexes and abstracts that will be most relevant to your topic:

➠ **Subject relevancy**— Only with a thorough understanding of the topic can you decide what disciplines are most appropriate for reporting on the research in the specified subject area.

➠ **Time period covered by source**— Be certain that the index or abstract you select covers materials for the appropriate time period for your topic. Many of the computerized databases have been developed only in recent years and may be limited to more recent materials.

➠ **Level of material**— Some indexes, such as *Reader's Guide to Periodical Literature*, focus largely on the popular magazines while others lead to scholarly and technical papers, conference proceedings, manuscript collections, and the like. Your knowledge of the topic will determine what level of materials is most suitable.

➠ **Type of material**— The nature of your topic will be key to determining the type of material you use in your research. For some topics, magazine and newspaper accounts may suffice; others may require more in-depth analysis, leading to more scholarly research in the field. Some topics may be more appropriately covered in books, which provide a broader, more comprehensive overview of the subject area.

➠ **Breadth of coverage**— Each index and abstract determines its own collection of materials to be included. Some features to look for include: comprehensiveness of indexing (i.e. does it index *every* article in each of the magazines, journals, or newspapers it includes, or is it selective?); inclusion of international materials; inclusion of materials written in other languages.

Indexes and abstracts will provide references to articles on your selected topic. Those in the print format are usually arranged alphabetically by subject, though some also list authors and titles. The electronic databases often provide many of the same search features and functions as the online catalogs, providing access to articles by author, title, subject headings, the name of the magazine or journal, date, or any keyword in the record. Oftentimes, the electronic sources provide abstracts, which may also be searchable.

Each entry in an index or abstract is referred to as a "citation." The elements of a citation include: the author(s) of the article; the title of the article; the name of the periodical; the volume number, and sometimes the specific issue number; the pages on which the article appears; and the date of the issue. Be sure to copy all relevant information from the index so that you have complete information when you compile your list of references. The following example illustrates a typical bibliographic citation for a journal article:

> Peiser, Wolfram, and Peter, Jochen. (2000). "Third-person perception of television-viewing behavior." <u>Journal of Communication</u> 50 (1): 25-45.

A number of different styles for citing articles are employed throughout the literature. These various styles have been established to best serve the needs of researchers and of scholarly publication in particular fields of study. The standard styles used include the MLA (Modern Language Association) style and the APA (American Psychological Association) style, among others. Be sure to use the style appropriate for your research. Manuals explaining each style are available.

Web sites, which may be identified by using either a web directory or a web search engine, are another valuable source of information. A directory lists web sites that are pre-selected by individuals and arranged into categories or topical areas. There are many directories available on the web, some developed by libraries, some by organizations, others by internet service providers, or by commercial entities. The scope and size of directories vary widely, so choosing the right directory for your topic requires careful consideration. Some directories that have been well-rated include Open Directory Project (http://www.dmoz.org) or Yahoo! (http://www.yahoo.com).

Web search engines function in much the same manner as electronic indexes or library catalogs. However, since web sites are not organized into standardized fields (i.e. author, title, subject headings, publisher) as records in indexes or catalogs are, web search engines often use programs (called robots or crawlers) to crawl about the web indexing sites, usually looking at URLs, the headings of documents, or text in the documents. The results are generally sorted in some fashion, either by a relevancy algorithm, by date, or alphabetically.

Since there are millions of registered web sites, no single search engine or directory will be complete. Each has its own methods of selecting and indexing sites, so choose carefully. Some web sites that rate many of the available search engines include: *Search Engine Watch* (http://searchenginewatch.com), developed by Danny Sullivan; and *Search Engine Showdown* (http://www.notess.com/search/), developed by Greg Notess. A good rule of thumb is to try your search in several different directories or search engines, and then select the sites that are most appropriate.

Evaluating Information

Critical evaluation of the information that you find is an essential component of the research process. The fact that something appears in print or is on the web does not make it true or "correct." It is your responsibility as a researcher to think critically about the information and determine its quality, authority, perspective, and balance so you select the information that best supports your research.

Evaluation of your sources should consider the information itself as it is presented, but also, the publication in which it appears, which may lend evidence as to its quality and perspective. Particular consideration must be given to evaluating web sites. Since the nature of the web is to be a very open, unfiltered environment, there is little control over much of what is posted. Virtually anyone can create a web site on any topic, whether they have training, education, or experience in the subject field or not.

Whether you are reviewing a book, a journal article, a newspaper article, or a web site, keep in mind these general criteria in determining which sources are most appropriate for you:

Date of Publication or Creation   —How important is currency to your topic? Is the very latest information critical, or is the nature of your topic stable enough to use older sources? The subject discipline you're working in may, to some extent, determine the importance of the currency of the information. For example, technological developments may change very quickly, requiring very current information, but information about historical issues which may have been written many years ago may still be relevant and useful.

Reliability/Credibility   —Are the facts accurate? Do they support the thesis? Can you rely on this information? These are some of the questions researchers must ask to determine reliability of information. While experts in a subject area may easily judge a work's reliability, it is usually more difficult for the novice researcher. One way to determine reliability is to compare the work with other writings on the topic. If a source includes a bibliography or references to other works, or links to other web sites, follow up on some of these and compare what is presented among all the sources. If you detect conflicting information, you should question why there is a discrepancy. It may be that the source in disagreement is in fact the "correct" one, or it may be presenting new information, or offering a different perspective.

If you aren't sure about the reliability of some information, check some outside sources as well. Book reviews can be a source of information to determine reliability. Often written by other experts in the field, they may provide insight on the information presented and they often relate it to other works on the topic. Book review indexes, such as *Book Review Digest* and *Book Review Index,* may help to identify reviews of many published books. Some web search engines or directories have developed rating systems for web sites, which you may use as a guide to determine reliability as well. However, these ratings may consider site design or general appeal as much as the content, so take this into consideration.

Credibility refers to the authority and/or qualifications of the writer who makes the claims or presents the information in the work. Does the author have the appropriate training, education, or expertise? Are the "authorities" cited by the author qualified to make the claims they are making? Ascertaining the credentials of the author or experts named will help to determine the credibility of the work.

Some sources provide brief biographical information about the authors or creators of the publication or site. While this may give you some indication of the author's credentials, it's not always sufficient. A number of reference works can help identify additional biographical information for authors and other individuals: *Biography and Genealogy Master Index* serves as an index to hundreds of sources which provide biographical information on people from all nationalities, occupations, and time periods; *Current Biography* compiles short articles on individuals of current interest or popularity, from all occupations and of various nationalities; *Contemporary Authors* includes brief entries on writers in fiction, nonfiction, poetry, journalism, television, and other fields; and, *Biography Index* is a guide to biographical material appearing in selected periodicals and books.

Perspective —How an author's cultural or experiential background affects the approach he or she has taken may profoundly affect the viewpoints that are expressed or the conclusions reached. It may also determine what information has been included or excluded. Some of the background information found when looking into an author's credibility may help in determining one's perspective, as well. Consider the following:

➠ Affiliation of the author(s)—the person's political, professional, social, or economic affiliations may determine the views expressed.

➠ Place of publication—where a publication originates from may serve as a clue to its perspective. For example, information presented in one country may vary greatly from the information presented in another.

➠ Date of publication—perspectives often change over time; you must try to understand why people write what they do in the context of the times in which they live.

Another indication of perspective for web sites may be the *domain,* which is represented by the last 3-digit segment of the "root" URL Web sites are generated within one of several domains:

➠ **.edu** indicates the page is generated at or by an educational institution
➠ **.com** indicates it is generated by a commercial entity
➠ **.org** means it is sponsored or created by an organization
➠ **.gov** denotes a government agency

There are additional domains, but these are the most common. Much of the information on the web is business-related or commercial: companies may be marketing or otherwise trying to convince consumers of the value of their products or services. Similarly, much of the information on the web is personal: personal web pages, e-mail messages, newsgroup postings, and the like may be retrieved in your search results. These sources are not necessarily invalid for your research, however great caution must be used when basing your own analysis on the evidence they present.

Level of Information —Who is the intended audience for the source or site you are using: the general public? the educated layperson? professionals? practitioners? scholars? Is it written at a level that makes sense to you and to your knowledge and understanding of the topic? Consider the vocabulary used. Does the source include a bibliography or links to related sites, providing additional sources to consult?

Scope of Coverage/Depth/Breadth —Is the source comprehensive for the field of study, presenting multiple viewpoints and issues? Is it specialized, focusing on only certain aspects of the topic? Is it narrowly defined, offering limited views or perspectives? Is it ethnocentric? Does it provide enough evidence to support its claims or position?

Quality of Publication —Do you know anything about the publisher of the source? Is it published, sponsored, or endorsed by a professional association, organization, or society? Is the information accurate? How does it compare with other information on the topic?

Ease of Use —Does the source contain a table of contents and/or an index to facilitate use and find the specific information you need? Does it include a bibliography?

Special Features —Does the source contain graphs, tables, charts, maps, or other special features that add to its usefulness?

After evaluating each of your sources, you may find that you wish to eliminate some of them as inappropriate and find references to other materials that will better support your research. In some cases, you may find that there is not enough evidence available to support the specific view which you had proposed. You may need to go back and identify additional sources or perhaps even refine or modify your topic once again. Wherever it leads you, the objective of your research is to develop a well-formulated analysis of your topic, which can be adequately supported, and to present it in an organized fashion.

Conclusion

The basic research strategy presented here is intended to provide a framework for finding information in any subject area, for any information need. Whether you are writing a comprehensive research paper, conducting a five minute speech, or simply wanting to know about a favorite personality, applying this model will guide you through the steps of gathering the necessary information. At whatever stage of the process, or whatever source you are looking at, making informed decisions to evaluate the usefulness and appropriateness of any information is critical.

As a researcher, you must recognize that information itself does not constitute knowledge. Knowledge refers to an understanding or awareness gained through study or research. In order to effectively engage in that research, you must become "information literate," understanding how to effectively identify, locate, evaluate and communicate information.